DANIEL

God's Word for the *for the* Biblically-Inept™ SERIES

Daymond R. Duck

CARTOONS BY
Reverend Fun
(Dennis "Max" Hengeveld)
Dennis is a graphic designer
for Gospel Films and the
author of *Has Anybody Seen
My Locust?* His cartoons can
be seen worldwide at
www.gospelcom.net/rev-fun/
and monthly in *Charisma*
magazine.

STARBURST PUBLISHERS™

P. O. Box 4123, Lancaster, Pennsylvania 17604

Daymond R. Duck is the best-selling author of *On the Brink—Easy-to-Under-stand End-Time Bible Prophecy*. He is also a contributing author to *Forewarning—The Approaching Battle Between Good and Evil*. Duck has been interviewed on numerous Christian radio programs aired by some of the foremost prophetic ministries in the world. Duck speaks at prophecy conferences and preaches at revivals. He lives in Dyer, Tennessee with his wife Rachel, a registered nurse.

In loving memory of my parents, Herbert N. and Gracie M. Duck, whose many sacrifices and hard work paid off in my life.

To schedule Author appearances write: Author Appearances, Starburst Promotions, P.O. Box 4123 Lancaster, Pennsylvania 17604 or call (717) 293-0939

Website: www.starburstpublishers.com

CREDITS:
Cover design by David Marty Design
Text design and composition by John Reinhardt Book Design
Illustrations by Melissa A. Burkhart
Cartoons by Dennis "Max" Hengeveld

GOD'S WORD FOR THE BIBLICALLY-INEPT™

First Printing, August 1998

ISBN: 0-914984-48-9
Library of Congress Catalog Number 97-80894
Printed in the United States of America

READ THIS PAGE BEFORE YOU READ THIS BOOK . . .

Welcome to the *God's Word for the Biblically-Inept*™ series. If you find reading the Bible overwhelming, baffling, and frustrating, then this Revolutionary Commentary™ is for you!

Each page of the series is organized for easy reading with icons, sidebars and bullets to make the Bible's message easy to understand. *God's Word for the Biblically-Inept*™ series includes opinions and insights from Bible experts of all kinds, so you get various opinions on Bible teachings—not just one!

There are more *God's Word for the Biblically-Inept*™ titles on the way. The following is a partial list of upcoming books. We have assigned each title an abbreviated **title code**. This code along with page numbers is incorporated in the text **throughout the series**, allowing easy reference from one title to another.

Daniel—God's Word for the Biblically-Inept™   TITLE CODE: GWDN
Daymond R. Duck

> **Daniel—God's Word for the Biblically-Inept**™ is the second in this Revolutionary Commentary™ series designed to make understanding and learning the Bible easy and fun. Includes every verse of the Book of Daniel, icons, sidebars, and bullets along with comments from leading experts.
>
> (trade paper) ISBN 0914984489 $16.95   AVAILABLE NOW

Revelation—God's Word for the Biblically-Inept™ TITLE CODE: GWRV
Daymond R. Duck

> **Revelation—God's Word for the Biblically-Inept**™ is the first in a new series designed to make understanding and learning the Bible as easy and fun as learning your ABC's. Reading the Bible is one thing, understanding it is another! This book breaks down the barrier of difficulty and helps take Revelation off the pedestal and into your hands.
>
> (trade paper) ISBN 0914984985 $16.95   AVAILABLE NOW

The Bible—God's Word for the Biblically-Inept™   TITLE CODE: GWBI
Larry Richards

> **The Bible—God's Word for the Biblically-Inept**™ is the third book in a series designed to make understanding and learning the Word of God as simple and fun as your ABC's. Each chapter contains select verses from books of the Bible along with illustrations, definitions, and references to related Bible passages.
>
> (trade paper) ISBN 0914984551 $16.95   AVAILABLE OCTOBER '98

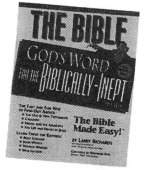

Health and Nutrition —God's Word for the Biblically-Inept™
Kathleen O'Bannon Baldinger   TITLE CODE: GWHN

Health and Nutrition—God's Word for the Biblically-Inept™ gives
scientific evidence that proves that the diet and health principles outlined in the Bible are the best diet for total health. Experts include
Pamela Smith, Julian Whitaker, Kenneth Cooper, and TD Jakes.

(trade paper) ISBN 0914984055 $16.95   **AVAILABLE FEBRUARY '99**

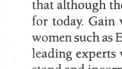

Women of the Bible —God's Word for the Biblically-Inept™
Kathy Collard Miller   TITLE CODE: GWWB

Women of the Bible—God's Word for the Biblically-Inept™ shows
that although the Bible was written many years ago, it is still relevant
for today. Gain valuable insight from the successes and struggles of
women such as Eve, Esther, Mary, Sarah, and Rebekah. Comments from
leading experts will make learning about God's Word easy to understand and incorporate into your daily life.

(trade paper) ISBN 0914984063 $16.95   **AVAILABLE MARCH '99**

Purchasing Information

www.starburstpublishers.com

Books are available from your favorite bookstore, either from current
stock or special order. To assist your bookstore in locating your selection,
be sure to give title, author, and ISBN #. If unable to purchase from a
bookstore, you may order direct from **STARBURST PUBLISHERS** by mail,
phone, fax, or through our secure sebsite at **www.starburstpublishers.com**.

When ordering enclose full payment plus $3.00 for shipping and han-
dling ($4.00 if Canada or Overseas). Payment in U.S. Funds only. Please
allow two to three weeks minimum (longer overseas) for delivery.

Make checks payable to and mail to:

Starburst Publishers
P.O. Box 4123
Lancaster, PA 17604

Credit card orders may also be placed by calling 1-800-441-1456 (credit
card orders only), Mon–Fri, 8:30 A.M.–5:30 P.M. (Eastern Time). Prices subject to change without notice. Catalog available for a 9 x 12 self-addressed
envelope with 4 first-class stamps.

INTRODUCTION

Welcome to *Daniel—God's Word for the Biblically-Inept™*. It is the second book (*Revelation* was the first) in a new series that takes the Bible and makes it fun and educational. This is not the traditional hum-drum, boring Bible study or commentary you are used to seeing. It is a REVOLUTIONARY COMMENTARY™ that will change your outlook on the Bible forever. You *will* Learn The Word!™

To Gain Your Confidence

Daniel—God's Word for the Biblically-Inept™ is for those who are not interested in all that complicated stuff. You can be sure that I have tried to take an educational approach, but much effort has gone into keeping things simple. I always end up making things so complicated when I try to explain them, so I make every effort to use the "KISS" method.

> Keep **I**t **S**imple **S**tupid

Jesus promised a blessing to all those who *read, hear* and *keep* those things written in Revelation (Revelation 1:3). He also promised a curse on all those who *add to*, or *take away* from it (Revelation 22:18, 19). I am sure that God also intended this same blessing and curse for the Book of Daniel, so I take them seriously and have undertaken this project with great care. To help explain things in the Book of Daniel I will use the age-old *Golden Rule of Interpretation* which states: *When the plain sense of Scripture makes common sense, seek no other sense. . . .* The Bible explains itself. You don't need to go anywhere else. That is why I have included other verses of Scripture from the Bible to explain difficult areas of the Book of Daniel.

A Word About The Bible

The Bible is divided into two major sections called the "Old"

CHAPTER HIGHLIGHTS

(Chapter Highlights)

Let's Get Started

(Let's Get Started)

> **Daniel 11:15**
> Then the king of the North will come . . .

(Verse of Scripture)

☞ **GO TO:**

Jeremiah 25:8-11
(Judah destroyed)

(Go To:)

Testament and the "New" Testament. The word "Testament" means covenant. The Old Testament deals with the "old covenant" that God had with *his* Hebrew people, the Jews. The New Testament deals with the "new covenant" that God has with *all* people.

The Old Testament is the first, oldest, and longest section of the Bible. It contains 39 books that were written over a period of about 1500 years. The New Testament is the second, newest, and shortest section of the Bible. It contains 27 books that were written over a period of less than 100 years. All of the books in the Bible were written by men, but the source of their writings was God. Men wrote what God *inspired* them to write—nothing more and nothing less. For this reason the entire Bible is called the Word of God.

Why Study Daniel?

The Book of Daniel is the only apocalyptic book in the Old Testament. The word "apocalyptic" comes from the Greek word "apocalypse," which means *revelation* or *uncovering of something hidden*. Daniel is the book of revelation in the Old Testament (Revelation is the only apocalyptic book in the New Testament.) and it may well be the greatest "prophetic" (what will happen in the future) book in the entire Bible.

More and more it seems like we are living in perilous times. The revelations found in the Book of Daniel are of particular interest today because they prophesy world events that are now coming to pass, and world events that will signal the Tribulation Period, the Second Coming of Christ, and the arrival of God's Millennium.

There is much to learn from the life of Daniel. Daniel had to endure trials just like all of us, but he knew his God was always in control. In him alone Daniel put his trust, and because of his faithfulness he prospered. He was a man of *faith and prayer*; a man of *intelligence and wisdom*; a man of *courage and humility*, and a man we can learn much from. Here are seven good reasons to study the Book of Daniel:

1) It is part of the Word of God (the Bible).

2) It teaches us many things about God, politics, and faith.

3) Jesus said Daniel was a prophet (Matthew 24:15), and we are to listen to God's prophets.

4) It accurately revealed many things about the past, present and future.

---

demon possession: *being under the control of an evil spirit*

Seventieth-Week of Daniel: *another name for the Tribulation Period*

(What?)

KEY POINT

Everything comes from God. He can take it away or restore it anytime he chooses.

(Key Point)

KEY Symbols:

God's Statue
head
- gold

chest and arms
- silver

(Key Symbols:)

What Others are Saying:

(What Others are Saying:)

5) Because so much of the Book of Daniel has accurately been fulfilled, we can logically expect the rest to be fulfilled.

6) It gives us details not found in any other book of the Bible.

7) If we do not study the Book of Daniel our understanding of the entire Bible will remain *Biblically-Inept*.

How To Study Daniel

As you study the Book of Daniel keep in mind it has two main sections:

Chapters 1–6 (Part I) are "historic" in nature and are called **Events in the Life of Daniel and His Friends**. These chapters show how Daniel and his friends survived in a pagan society by trusting in their God. The message for all of us is that we can do the same. It is more important to obey God than it is to obey man.

Chapters 7–12 (Part II) are "prophetic" in nature and are called **Daniel's Prophecies**. These chapters cover some very interesting things about the future, and we see some of these future events coming on the scene today.

Also Keep In Mind Four Other Main Points:

1) The theme of the Book of Daniel is the *sovereignty of God*. No matter who rules on earth God has the final say.

2) Some things in the Book of Daniel are *sealed* (hidden away). The book is protected by God and not everything in it will be fully understood until the End of the Age (the Tribulation Period). Remember, "the main things are the plain things, and the plain things are the main things."

3) Daniel's main focus is the *Jews*. He ignores the Church (the followers of Jesus Christ).

4) What Daniel prophesies about the end-times is often explained by other books in the Bible, particularly Revelation.

Which Book Should I Study?

You need to study both Revelation and the Book of Daniel to

Illustration #1

Modern day map of the Middle East showing the location of ancient cities.

(Illustrations)

Something to Ponder

(Something to Ponder)

Remember This . . .

(Remember This)

RELATED CURRENT EVENTS

(Related Current Events)

have a good understanding of Bible prophecy. They are like Siamese twins; joined together, but different. Their subjects are similar, but each book contains details not found in the other book. They are the two most important prophetic books in the Bible and together they reveal more information about the closing scenes of this age than any other portion of the Bible. Here are just a few reasons why this is true:

1) The Book of Daniel accurately reveals the First Coming of Jesus, his death, and the destruction of Israel, Jerusalem and the Temple. Revelation begins with events that will take place after these.

2) The Book of Daniel gives an outline of world history from King Nebuchadnezzar to the First Coming of Jesus not found in Revelation. But Revelation gives an outline of what will happen after the Second Coming of Jesus not found in the Book of Daniel.

3) The Book of Daniel will be helpful to those who miss the Rapture to know how to identify the beginning of the Tribulation Period, what group of nations will rule the world, and who will be their last leader.

4) The Book of Daniel gives us a clearer understanding of God's ability to protect the Jews than any other book in the Bible.

5) The Book of Daniel gives us information about the influence of evil spirits on nations and their leaders.

6) The Book of Daniel gives us the *skeleton* of the end-times (an outline). Revelation gives us the *flesh* (many of the details). They combine to give us a more complete picture.

The Book of Daniel and Revelation enhance each other. They are like the bookends of prophecy. Each book will help you understand the other, as well as all the other prophetic books in the Bible. How amazing to have two different books, written by two different authors hundreds of years apart, that are in complete agreement with each other.

Who Wrote Daniel?

Prophecy experts do not believe it was a fictitious Daniel as many critics claim. We still think the entire Book of Daniel was written by the real Daniel who lived about 600 years before the birth of Christ. He was a member of the royal family of Israel and was captured by King Nebuchadnezzar as a teenager, car-

(Warning)

Study Questions

(Study Questions)

CHAPTER WRAP-UP

(Chapter Wrap-Up)

INTRODUCTION

ried off to Babylon, and trained to serve in the King's palace. He was a brilliant and godly man who, because of his faithfulness, was given special insight and visions by God.

Symbols, Symbols, And More Symbols

The Book of Daniel is filled with symbols because Daniel had several visions of the future. Depending upon the Bible translation we use, the singular word "vision" occurs about twenty-two times and the plural word "visions" occurs about ten times. King Nebuchadnezzar's dreams and Daniel's visions were pictures or symbols of things to come. God chose to do it this way so Nebuchadnezzar would have to rely upon Daniel for help, and to keep many future events sealed up until the End of the Age. As you read this book you will find that the unsealing has begun. We do not fully understand all of the symbols, but we now know what most of them mean.

So Many Critics And Different Viewpoints

Critics have spent an incredible amount of energy questioning the authenticity and historicity of the Book of Daniel. According to some, the miracles in the Book of Daniel, such as the deliverance of Shadrach, Meshach and Abednego from the fiery furnace, could not have happened; prophesying the future is impossible; and there is no evidence that many of the events found in the Book of Daniel ever occurred. But these same critics have not been able to prove their claims, and their efforts to discredit the Book of Daniel have only resulted in embarrassment to themselves and their faulty brand of reasoning. The surprising thing is not that some keep trying to destroy this book, but rather that their record of failure is so long. Let's study the Book of Daniel with confidence and leave the critics to face the God who revealed it.

I have tried to look at the Book of Daniel as the experts would, but have also tried to write it for the *Biblically-Inept*. I want it to be easy to read and understand. That's why I chose to use the *New International Version (NIV)* of the Bible. It is a scholarly translation that accurately expresses the original Bible in clear and contemporary English, while remaining faithful to the thoughts of Biblical writers. That is what I would want and think you, too, would want.

A Word About Dates

Many experts have differing opinions about dates in the Book of Daniel. Variations of one to two years in some cases are not uncommon. But archaeologists keep making new discoveries so that many of the dates are now known and thought to be accurate. Where discrepancies occur the most commonly recognized date is given.

How To Use Daniel—God's Word For The Biblically-Inept

The chapter divisions in this book correspond to the chapter divisions in the Bible. There are 12 chapters in the Book of Daniel and 12 chapters in this book. First you will find each verse of the Book of Daniel. Then you will find my thoughts and lots of icons and tidbits of information to help you in the sidebar. Here's what you will see:

Sections and Icons	What's it for?
CHAPTER HIGHLIGHTS	the most prominent points of the chapter
Let's Get Started	a chapter warm-up
Verse of Scripture	what you came for—the Bible
Commentary	my thoughts on what the verse means
GO TO:	other Bible verses to help you better understand (underlined in text)
What?	the meaning of a word (bold in text)
KEY POINT	a major point in the chapter
KEY Symbols:	mini-outlines to help you
What Others are Saying:	if you don't believe me, listen to the experts
Illustrations	a picture is worth a thousand words
Something to Ponder	interesting points to get you thinking
Remember This . . .	don't forget this
RELATED CURRENT EVENTS	tidbits from today's news
WARNING	red lights to keep you from danger
Study Questions	questions to get you discussing, studying, and digging deeper
CHAPTER WRAP-UP	the most prominent points revisited

There are several interchangeable terms: Scripture, Scriptures, Word, Word of God, God's Word, Gospel, etc. All of these mean the same thing and come under the broad heading called the Bible. I will use each one at various times, but I will use Bible most of the time. Also, keep in mind that the Book of Daniel is a *book* of the Bible, and Daniel is the *man* (the prophet) whose life the Book of Daniel records.

One Final Tip

God gave the Book of Daniel for us to study and with his help, through prayer, he will help us in our understanding. You will be surprised at how much you will learn when you put your heart and mind into it.

CHAPTERS AT A GLANCE

PART II: Daniel's Prophecies

Part One

EVENTS IN THE LIFE OF DANIEL AND HIS FRIENDS

*Say, do you think you could be a good guard and fetch us some more marshmallows? . . .
Shadrach keeps eating them all before we can finish putting our smores together.*

DANIEL 1

CHAPTER HIGHLIGHTS

- Babylon's Attack
- Daniel's Qualifications
- Daniel's Great Decision
- A Ten Day Test
- God Rewards the Faithful

Let's Get Started

When <u>Moses led</u> the Hebrews (the Jews) out of Egypt God made a special **covenant** with them. He promised to be their God and to bless them, but there was a condition. They would have to obey him by keeping his laws, offering sacrifices, and letting the <u>land</u> rest every seventh year. The Hebrews agreed to do this, but they soon forgot their promise and slowly abandoned their God. Over the years they turned toward a life of wickedness, so that by Daniel's time only a few people were keeping God's commandments.

God's **prophets** warned the people of Judah (see Illustration #4, page 36) that he was growing weary of their wickedness. These prophets admonished the people to repent of their sins or <u>their nation would be destroyed by Babylon</u>. But the people's ears were tickled by the sweet sounding words of many **false prophets**, and they refused to heed the dire warnings of <u>his true prophets</u>.

The Hebrew word for *prophet* means "one who is inspired by God." The Greek word means "one who foretells future events." Prophets are also called "Seers" and "Men of God" in the Scriptures. They were *divinely inspired* men who were commissioned by God to speak and/or record his messages. They often revealed his will on moral issues, exhorted people to be faithful to him, warned people of the consequences of sin, and called on people to repent. True prophets were expected to have a 100% success rate when foretelling future events. False prophets made mistakes. Some of what they said might be true, but not all of it.

 **GO TO:**

Exodus 6–14 (Moses)

Exodus 19:5–8 (covenant)

Leviticus 25, 26 (land)

Jeremiah 25:8–11 *four exile* (Judah destroyed)

Jeremiah 14:14; Matthew 7:15 (false)

II Chronicles 36:16 (true)

Jeremiah 36:30–31 (Judah's wickedness)

Something to Ponder

covenant: an agreement between two or more parties

prophet: one who is inspired by God

false prophets: those who claim to speak for God but actually spread false teachings

Bel: the chief god of the Chaldeans

KEY Symbols:

Land of Shinar
  cradle of civilization

Septuagint: Greek translation of the Bible written in 3rd century B.C.

Dead Sea Scrolls: a large library of scrolls found in a cave near the Dead Sea

The Book of Daniel opens around the year 605 B.C. (see Time Line 1, Appendix A). It begins by telling us what happened to Judah and how Daniel wound up in Babylon. It tells us about a crisis that came into Daniel's life, how he handled it, and his resultant rise to power and prominence in Babylon.

Who Was Daniel?

Daniel was a Hebrew and a member of the royal family of Judah. We do not know the exact place or year of his birth, but he was probably born in Jerusalem around the year 620 B.C. He was about 13 or 14 years old when King Nebuchadnezzar captured him at Jerusalem (a city in Judah), along with the other Israelites (the people of Israel and Judah), and carried them off to Babylon (around 605 B.C.). Even though Daniel was already well-educated, he was selected for additional training in the language and literature of the Babylonians. His name Daniel which means "God is my judge" was changed to Belteshazzar which means "whom **Bel** favors" or "keeper of the treasures of the prince of Bel." Daniel quickly distinguished himself because of his determination to be faithful to God. He gained the blessings of God and reaped the confidence and favor of those around him. When he interpreted a troubling dream for the hot-tempered Nebuchadnezzar he was promoted to a position of authority over all the wise men of Babylon. He spent the rest of his life as one of the most powerful men in the world, faithfully served several world leaders, and is widely recognized as one of the greatest men of all time.

Some Background On Babylon

When Noah, his three sons and their wives, came out of the ark they began to multiply and migrate. Noah's son, Ham, bore a son named Cush. Cush bore a son named Nimrod who settled in a flat, fertile plain between the Tigris and Euphrates rivers called the Land of Shinar (later called Mesopotamia or Chaldea) and also affectionately called "the cradle of civilization" (see Illustration #2, page 19). This is the same area where the Garden of Eden was located.

Nimrod established a great kingdom that the Bible says began with the cities of Babylon, Erech, Akkad, and Calneh. He is even credited with establishing several great cities in Assyria. He was astute, powerful, and wicked. His city of Babylon is mentioned more than 300 times in the Bible. Because of all the evil in Babylon, some Bible experts have started referring to it as the "City of Satan" as opposed to the "City of God" (Jerusalem).

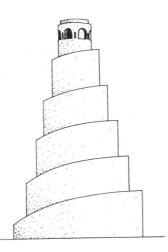

Nimrod built several towers in the area. The most famous one, called the <u>Tower of Babel</u> (see Illustration #1, this page), was built at Babylon. He made it the focus of his rebellion against God. He welcomed pagan religions, catered to the occult (Satanic practices), and promoted sexual gratification and prostitution. He merged his city-states, put them all under his control and took over their education systems. Because of the religious harlotry (unfaithful practices) he began at Babylon, the city is called the "Mother of Harlots." And because of the love for big government he began at Babylon, the city is recognized as the beginning of world government.

Alexander the Great: *head of the Greek Empire*

Ezekiel: *Jewish prophet who wrote the book of Ezekiel and was also a captive in Babylon*

Abomination of Desolation: *statue or* <u>**Image of the Beast**</u>

Image of the Beast: *a statue or image of the Antichrist*

Jack W. Hayford: Daniel found himself as a teenager far from home and in negative circumstances. He had been abducted from his homeland and taken to the conquering country of Babylon, where he was selected to become a trainee in the king's court. There his personal character and religious convictions were immediately tested. His personal integrity sustained him and secured a position in the king's palace and a place of prominence through the parade of two world powers and four kings.[1]

What Others are Saying:

KEY Symbols:

City of Satan
Babylon
the Mother of Harlots

City of God
Jerusalem

Chaldeans

The Chaldeans were Semitic nomads who lived near the Persian Gulf in what is now Kuwait and southeastern Iraq (see Illustration #2, page 19). Starting around 1100 B.C. there were several different tribes that were wandering in and out of Babylon at will, but by 875 B.C. some had permanently settled in Babylon. During the 700's B.C. some Chaldean leaders ruled as kings of Babylon. One of their leaders, a man named Nabopolassar, united all the Chaldean tribes and was

Remember This . . .

God's "True" Prophets

Seers
Men of God
divinely inspired
commissioned by God
100% accurate

False Prophets

make mistakes

KEY Symbols:

Daniel
God is my judge

Belteshazzar
whom Bel favors
keeper of the treasures
of the prince of Bel

Jeremiah: a Jewish prophet who predicted the fall of Judah

☞ **GO TO:**

Ezekiel 1:1–3 (Ezekiel)

subjugation: process of conquering, subduing, and bringing under complete control

---

crowned king of Babylon in 626 B.C. He was succeeded by his son Nebuchadnezzar around 605 B.C. Today, the terms "Chaldean" and "Babylonian" mean essentially the same thing.

• • •

Israelites

The nation of Israel divided into a Northern Kingdom and a Southern Kingdom (see Illustration #4, page 36). The Northern Kingdom retained the name "Israel" and was taken captive by the Assyrians. The Southern Kingdom was called "Judah" and was taken captive by the Babylonians. The people in both kingdoms were called Israelites.

The author identifies himself as <u>Daniel</u> more than a dozen times. But in spite of this, many critics vehemently deny Daniel's authorship. Why? Because they do not believe in the supernatural, and the prophecies that have already been fulfilled are so accurate they have no other explanation. So they declare the Book of Daniel is a forgery. But modern Bible-believing experts are not fooled by the critics. We know that the Book of Daniel was included in the **Septuagint**, that a good copy was found with the **Dead Sea Scrolls** in 1947, and that Josephus, a Jewish historian, mentions that **Alexander the Great** 356–323 B.C. read it. We know that the prophet **Ezekiel** lived at the same time as Daniel and he wrote about Daniel. Even the reference of Jesus to the ***Abomination of Desolation*** spoken of through the prophet Daniel implies that Daniel is the author. So there is little doubt that Daniel is the author and the last recorded event was probably written before 530 B.C. when, if he was alive, Daniel would have been almost 90 years old.

> **Daniel 1:1** In the third year of the reign of Jehoiakim king of Judah, Nebuchadnezzar king of Babylon came to Jerusalem and besieged it. *606 BC*

Off They Went

Daniel's initial words identify several historical facts about Babylon's first attack on Jerusalem: 1) It was in the third year of Jehoiakim's reign, 2) Jehoiakim was king of Judah, 3)

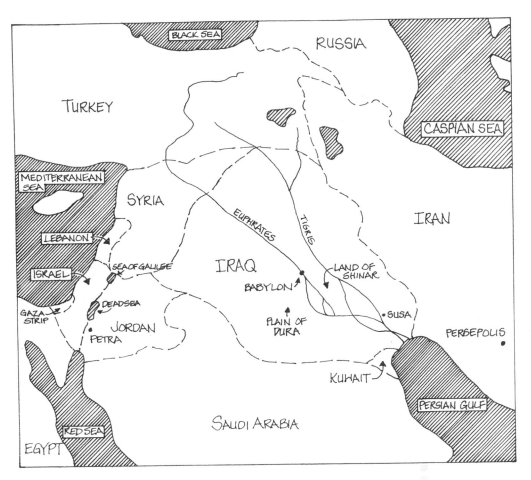

Nebuchadnezzar was king of Babylon, and 4) Nebuchadnezzar attacked Jerusalem. Based on these facts, most experts date the first strike against Jerusalem as beginning in 606 B.C. and ending in 605 B.C.

A Babylonian tablet found by archeologists states that Nebuchadnezzar's father was king of Babylon (see illustration #2, this page) in 605 B.C., but the king died in August of that year. Nebuchadnezzar had not completed the attack, but he broke off and returned home to be crowned king.

Illustration #2

Babylon—Modern day map of the Middle East showing the location of ancient cities.

Uriah Smith: **Jeremiah** places this captivity in the fourth year of Jehoiakim, Daniel in the third. This seeming discrepancy is explained by the fact that Nebuchadnezzar set out on his expedition near the close of the third year of Jehoiakim, from which point Daniel reckons. But he did not accomplish the **subjugation** of Jerusalem till about the ninth month of the year following; and from this year Jeremiah reckons.[2]

What Others are Saying:

*Nabonidus cylinder: one of several **cuneiform** cylinders unearthed in Babylon*

cuneiform: the symbols used in the writings of ancient Babylon, Assyria, and Persia

Remember This . . .

Many claim God's statue in Chapter 3 never existed. Then archaeologists uncovered the base of the statue. They said nothing has ever been found in secular history about Belshazzar which means he was a fictitious person who never existed. Then archaeologists found the **Nabonidus cylinder**, proving the Book of Daniel right and the critics wrong. The critics also said Daniel was written in the 2nd century B.C. not the 6th century B.C. Then a scroll of Daniel was found with the Dead Sea Scrolls which contained a style and phrasing of words that is much older than the 2nd century B.C.[2]

Major Jewish Captivities

Event	Approximate Date
Egyptian Captivity	1875–1445 B.C.
Assyrian Captivity of Northern Kingdom (Israel)	722 B.C.
1st Babylonian Captivity—Jerusalem (Daniel and Friends)	605 B.C.
2nd Babylonian Captivity—Ten Thousand Jews (Ezekiel)	597 B.C.
3rd Babylonian Captivity—Southern Kingdom (Judah) First destruction of Jerusalem	586 B.C.
Jews from Judah returned in three phases:	
1st Return	536 B.C.
2nd Return	458 B.C.
3rd Return	445 B.C.
Domination by Greece	331–63 B.C.
Domination by Rome	63 B.C.–500 A.D.
Second destruction of Jerusalem by the Romans	70 A.D.

☞ **GO TO:**

Leviticus 25:1–7 (rest)

delivered: allowed them to be defeated

pagan king: a ruler who worships anything other than Almighty God

Temple: the main religious center of the Jews

> **Daniel 1:2** And the Lord delivered Jehoiakim king of Judah into his hand, along with some of the articles from the temple of God. These he carried off to the temple of his god in Babylonia and put in the treasure house of his god.

A Broken Covenant

This was a dark day in Judah's history. It was a day when our loving God showed his great displeasure with the Jews for constantly breaking his covenant. He had been patient with them for 490 years, but he refused to be patient or protect them any longer. He **delivered** them into the hands of Nebuchadnezzar and Babylon. He used a **pagan king** to defeat his own nation.

70 x 7 *from before?*

KEY Symbols:

Nebuchadnezzar's Chief God

Bel / Baal / Marduk / Merodach

Temple treasures: *580 items of gold, silver and bronze used at the Temple*

iniquities: *sins; breaking or not keeping God's laws*

Sabbath: *God's command to let the land <u>rest once every seven years</u>*

But that is not all. God added insult to injury. He showed the Jews that by breaking the covenant they had also set aside his promise to be their God. He allowed the **Temple** (see Illustration #17, page 299) to be plundered and some of the **Temple treasures** to be taken back to Babylon and placed in the house of Nebuchadnezzar's god. Nebuchadnezzar worshipped many gods, but his chief god was Bel who was sometimes called Baal, Marduk, or Merodach (see Illustration #3, this page).

Ed Young: In this second verse we see that God was involved in the affairs of the world.[3]

What Others are Saying:

Uriah Smith: Such was God's passing testimony against sin. Not that the Chaldeans were the favorites of heaven, but God made use of them to punish the **iniquities** of his people. Had the Israelites been faithful to God, and kept his **Sabbath**, Jerusalem would have stood forever.[4]

> **Daniel 1:3** Then the king ordered Ashpenaz, chief of his court officials, to bring in some of the Israelites from the royal family and the nobility—

☞ **GO TO:**

II Chronicles 36:11–21 (disobey)

Bring Me The Best

At the same time Nebuchadnezzar captured king Jehoiakim, he also captured several members of the royal family. He ordered the prince of his **eunuchs**, a man named Ashpenaz, to take them back to

eunuchs: *men who have parts of their genitals removed*

Babylon. Although it is not stated, it appears that they were also made eunuchs and placed under Ashpenaz's supervision.

Hal Lindsey: It was a common practice of the kings of that day to take parts of the royal family back to their capital in order to hold as hostages so they could keep the king they left in place in check.[5]

Peter and Paul Lalonde: The Israelites did disobey God, and true to his word, he allowed them to be taken captive into Babylon. Ever since the Babylonian captivity, about 2,500 years ago, the Jews have been scattered about in nations all around the world. Still, in all of that time, the Jews have never lost their identity and we all know that today the phrase, 'the wandering Jew' has even become a cliché.[6]

KEY Symbols:

the wandering Jew
Israel

astrology: *the study of heavenly bodies to forecast their supposed effect upon people and events*

black magic: *supposed magic that is performed with the help of evil spirits*

omens: *something that seems to be a sign of things to come*

indoctrinating: *teaching certain beliefs and principles*

> **Daniel 1:4** young men without any physical defect, handsome, showing aptitude for every kind of learning, well informed, quick to understand, and qualified to serve in the king's palace. He was to teach them the language and literature of the Babylonians.

Teach Them Our Ways

This reveals the kind of people Nebuchadnezzar wanted Ashpenaz to take back to Babylon. It also tells us about the qualifications of Daniel and his friends. Nebuchadnezzar wanted young males who were perfect physical specimens, sharp intellectuals, and had already been taught a wide variety of subjects. They needed to meet the high requirements for service in his palace. He did not want these young men to be used for low or base things. He wanted them to be educated in the language and literature of Babylon. It included astronomy, **astrology**, **black magic**, the interpretation of dreams, history, medicine, **omens**, and philosophy.

counterculture: *group of people who oppose the traditional customs and standards of society*

Ed Young: We first meet Daniel when he was about a 13 or 14-year-old boy. Just think about a 13 or 14-year-old boy you know; a man beginning to grow up, voice changing, growing fast, maybe a few pimples, a little awkward.[7]

David Jeremiah with C.C. Carlson: Mind control begins with the young. By destroying their beliefs and **indoctrinating** them into a **counterculture**, the ruling forces of evil can capture a generation for their purposes. Today our children are being **subverted** in a more subtle fashion than the Hitler Youth, but the **web of control** is just as strong.[8]

subvert: to cause the downfall of something

web of control: method used to control many at one time.

World Book Encyclopedia: Hitler also set up organizations for young people between the ages of 6 and 18. These groups included the Hitler Youth for boys 14 years and older and the Society of German Maidens for girls 14 years and older. The organizations were designed to condition German children to military discipline and to win their loyalty to the Nazi government. All German children were required to join such groups from the age of 10. They wore uniforms, marched, exercised, and learned Nazi beliefs. The Nazis taught children to spy on their own families and report anti-Nazi criticism they might hear.[9]

```
At [a] lesbian caucus [National Education Associa-
tion Gay Lesbian Caucus], the big feature was a
90-minute video entitled "It's Elementary: Teach-
ing About Gay Issues in School." The video shows
how psychological manipulation in the classroom
can be used to change children's home-taught
attitudes and beliefs about homosexuality.[10]
```

RELATED CURRENT EVENTS

> **Daniel 1:5** The king assigned them a daily amount of food and wine from the king's table. They were to be trained for three years, and after that they were to enter the king's service.

☞ **GO TO:**

Colossians 2:6–8 (captive)

Give Them The Best

Most captives would be glad to receive just a little to eat, and they would not expect a high quality of food. However, these captives were to receive food and drink from Nebuchadnezzar's own table, and, as was the regular practice, it was probably food and drink that had been offered as an **oblation** to the Babylonian gods.

Most captives would not expect to receive an education. But Nebuchadnezzar commanded that these captives be trained for three years. He wanted them to receive the best education money could buy in those days, and after three years, these highly educated 16 and 17-year-old captives were to be given good jobs. They were to be given positions of honor and trust in the Babylonian kingdom.

oblation: an offering or sacrifice that has been presented to God or a god

humanist: one who deifies humans instead of God

inner self: the mental and spiritual part of a person

David Jeremiah with C.C. Carlson: He wanted them to look like Jews on the outside but be Babylonians on the inside. This is the aim of most secular universities if the professors do not know Christ; they don't care if you look like a Christian on the outside, attending church or marking a denominational choice on your college application, as long as they can teach you to think like a **humanist** on the inside.[11]

Grant R. Jeffrey: Archaeologists recently discovered, next to the ruined palace in Babylon, the elaborate ruins of the special schools for training the "wise men."[12]

Jack Van Impe: There's a virtual "culture war" against the values of the Bible in the United States. While Christians are not yet being locked up for their beliefs in our country, they are being broadly discriminated against in the public square. Is it so difficult to imagine what the next phase might be?[13]

John Hagee: Parents of America believe their children go to school to be educated in the disciplines of reading, writing, and arithmetic. Not so! Other countries are teaching their children this core curriculum; in America our children are being taught how to get in touch with their **inner selves** and to become subservient pawns of a global society.[14]

**RELATED
CURRENT
EVENTS**

Try to imagine the New Testament without the resurrection or miracles of Jesus. It simply wouldn't be the New Testament, would it? Yet, that is precisely what America's new censors at the ACLU as well as other extremist groups are trying to force on a high school in Florida. According to the ACLU, the resurrection account in the New Testament is too "controversial" to be included in a high school curriculum on the Bible. As if that's not enough, imagine, for a moment, what Christmas would be like without Christmas carols celebrating the birth of Christ. Well, that's exactly what a high school principal in New Mexico wants. She believes singing Christmas carols in a school choral program is offensive, insensitive, and unbalanced.[15]

> **Daniel 1:6** Among these were some from Judah: Daniel, Hananiah, Mishael, and Azariah.

Four Hebrew Boys

This verse reveals the Hebrew names of four members of King Jehoiakim's family who were taken captive by King Nebuchadnezzar and placed under the supervision of Ashpenaz.

Hebrew Names and Their Meanings

Hebrew Name	Hebrew Meaning
Daniel	God is my Judge
Hananiah	God is gracious; God's gift
Mishael	Who is like God?; God is great
Azariah	God is my helper

J. Vernon McGee: These four young men from Judah are singled out and identified to us, and the reason is that they are going to take a stand for God.[16]

What Others are Saying:

> **Daniel 1:7** The chief official gave them new names: to Daniel, the name Belteshazzar; to Hananiah, Shadrach; to Mishael, Meshach; and to Azariah, Abednego.

☞ **GO TO:**

Genesis 10:10 KJV; 11:9 (Babel)

monotheism: *the belief in one God*

polytheism: *the belief in more than one god*

ancient Babel: *the old Hebrew name for Babylon*

New Names

The Hebrew names of these four young men identified some of the characteristics of their God. As long as they went by those names they would remember him, which is exactly what Ashpenaz didn't want. He wanted to switch their allegiance from the true God to the Babylonian gods, so he changed their names.

Babylonian Names and Their Meanings

Hebrew Name	Babylonian Name	Babylonian Meaning
Daniel	Belteshazzar	whom Bel favors; keeper of the treasures of the prince of Bel
Hananiah	Shadrach	illumined by Shad (a sun god)
Mishael	Meshach	who is like Shach (a love goddess)
Azariah	Abednego	the servant of Nego (a fire god)

What Others are Saying:

KEY Symbols:

Hebrew Names Reveal:

monotheism (one God)

judgment of God

grace of God

greatness of God

provision of God

Babylonian Names Reveal:

polytheism (many gods)

Satanism

goddess worship

☞ **GO TO:**

Leviticus 7:19-27 (Law)

Leviticus 11 (forbidden)

Law of God: *the rules God gave to Moses*

holiness: *sincere conformity to the nature and will of God*

These names are important. The Hebrew names reveal the judgment of God, the grace of God, the greatness of God, and the provision of God. The Babylonian names reveal Satanism and goddess worship. The Hebrew names reveal **monotheism**, and the Babylonian names reveal **polytheism**.

Noah Hutchings: These names of religious significance carried over from **ancient Babel** offer substantiation to the belief that Babylon was actually a revival of the program which started at Babel for man to join Satan in his rebellion against the Most High [God] in the heavens.[17]

M.R. DeHaan: This [the name of Daniel], then, is one of the first lessons in Daniel: God will judge sin and evil.[18]

Jay Alan Sekulow: In 1990 the outrage case that stood out involved students who were suspended for "possession" of Christian literature on campus. In 1991 it was Luanne Fulbright who was told that her report on baby Jesus violated the "Separation of Church and State" and could not be displayed in the classroom. 1992 saw an outrage which took us to the Supreme Court when a church was denied access to school facilities in the evening because it wanted to show a film on family issues from a Christian perspective. . . . Adam Villa in 1993 caused a stir when he wanted to sing the Christian song, *Shepherd Boy*, in a school talent show. School officials said "no" until our legal teams intervened. In 1994 it was Emily Hsu, a high school student from New York who wanted to make sure her Christian Bible Club was led by Christians. School officials said "no," and we [the American Center for Law and Justice] are still in court.[19]

> **Daniel 1:8** But Daniel resolved not to defile himself with the royal food and wine, and he asked the chief official for permission not to defile himself this way.

Not Me!

Changing Daniel's name did not change his character nor did it make him forget what he had learned from the Scriptures. He knew that partaking of these royal delicacies would ceremonially defile him according to the **Law of God**, so he determined in his heart that he would not eat them. Then he respectfully asked Ashpenaz for permission to remain true to his God. It's hard to believe that Daniel had such integrity and steadfastness at the age of 13 or 14.

Oliver B. Greene: The crowning day of his [Daniel's] experience with God was the day he purposed in his heart to remain clean and separate and he did it under the most trying conditions one could imagine! Everything seemed against him; from the human standpoint he could not win, he could only suffer loss. But with dark clouds all around him, seemingly fighting a losing battle, he faced it all.[20]

separation: withdrawal from worldly things

David Jeremiah with C.C. Carlson: The same strength that armed Daniel to be a tough-minded teenager and a man of courage is available to us. The marvelous thing is how God blesses when a person is committed.[21]

RELATED CURRENT EVENTS

```
Despite dire warnings by politicians and doctors
of [Israel's] medical system's impending financial
collapse, Israel is the second healthiest country
in the world, according to a statistical analysis
compiled by the Economist Intelligence Unit in
London and published in the Healthcare Interna-
tional quarterly.22
```

Daniel was willing to live in a foreign land, serve a pagan king, and change his name, so why was he unwilling to eat the king's food? The answer may lie in the fact that the Scriptures did not forbid these activities, but they did <u>forbid him from eating certain foods</u>. These Scriptures teach **holiness** and **separation**; some things are wholesome and some things defile; we should make healthy choices, right decisions, and avoid carelessness. When confronted with a tough decision about the king's food, Daniel decided that obeying God was more important than obeying man.

Something to Ponder

• • •

At least some of America's health problems are related to poor eating habits (fad diets, overeating) and poor nutrition (junk foods, unbalanced diet). Other problems are lack of exercise, lack of sleep, uncleanness, poor dental care, stress, and use of things like tobacco, alcohol, and drugs. Good health starts with good food and a commitment to healthy living.

KEY POINT

Good health starts with good food and commitment to healthy living.

☞ **GO TO:**

Romans 8:31 (God)

> **Daniel 1:9** Now God had caused the official to show favor and sympathy to Daniel,

Daniel And God Together

Daniel had the right stuff and the God who was really in charge on his side. When he determined to be faithful, <u>God worked on his behalf</u> by giving Ashpenaz an understanding and sympathetic heart.

What Others are Saying:

Ed Young: You have convictions. That's how you live a godly life in an ungodly culture.[23]

> **Daniel 1:10** but the official told Daniel, "I am afraid of my lord the king, who has assigned your food and drink. Why should he see you looking worse than the other young men your age? The king would then have my head because of you."

He'll Have My Head

Ashpenaz was on the spot. He reminded Daniel that it was Nebuchadnezzar who had commanded the young captives to eat and drink from the king's table. He let Daniel know that he was afraid of Nebuchadnezzar and believed he would be risking his life by granting the request. Ashpenaz speculated that Nebuchadnezzar would see Daniel looking more pale and haggard than the other captives, hold him personally responsible, and have him killed. If that happened, it would be Daniel's fault.

☞ **GO TO:**

John 14:15 (you will obey)

> **Daniel 1:11** Daniel then said to the guard whom the chief official had appointed over Daniel, Hananiah, Mishael, and Azariah,

Why Not Do This

Daniel did not want to be responsible for the death of Ashpenaz. However, he loved God and was <u>determined not to defile himself</u>, so he made a suggestion to the guard Ashpenaz had appointed to watch over him and his friends.

> **Daniel 1:12** "Please test your servants for ten days: Give us nothing but vegetables to eat and water to drink."

☞ **GO TO:**

Romans 12:1, 2 (offer)

demarcation: *setting and marking limits*

the world: *the secular world, people who are not Christians*

A Vegetarian? I Don't Think So.

Daniel wanted to <u>offer himself</u> to God by doing God's will and, by faith, he was expecting God to help him. So, he wisely proposed a test: he and his friends would eat nothing but vegetables and water for ten days.

What Others are Saying:

M.R. DeHaan: The line of difference and **demarcation** between the Church and **the world** has almost been wiped out, and those few of Christ's followers who dare to be different and refuse to go along with the crowd are so small in number that they are looked upon as odd and peculiar, and even fanatical and narrow-minded. It does cost something to be different and separate, but it is the only way which leads to the highest reward.[24]

Oliver B. Greene: He [Daniel] did not refuse the king's meat because he was a vegetarian or a religious fanatic, but because he was an obedient child of God—and God had forbidden the eating of certain meats which were termed unclean to his chosen people.[25]

The Church versus a church

The Church consists of the followers of Jesus Christ, as opposed to a church which is a building where people meet to worship.

Remember This . . .

> **Daniel 1:13** Then compare our appearance with that of the young men who eat the royal food, and treat your servants in accordance with what you see."

A Ten Day Test

After ten days, Daniel and his three friends wanted to be compared to those who ate the kings choice food. He wanted Ashpenaz to base his decision on the outcome of that comparison.

What Others are Saying:

David Hocking: If we know what God says, and we agree with it in our hearts, then we can depend on the Lord to take care of us. If we get off that, we get a little shaky.[26]

☞ **GO TO:**

Revelation 2:10
(Smyrna)

Luke 19:12–27 KJV
(parable)

parable: *a story about familiar things that teaches or illustrates unfamiliar things*

KEY POINT

When you say "No" to what is wrong, God says "Yes! Bless that person!"

> **Daniel 1:14** So he agreed to this and tested them for ten days.

So Be It

Ashpenaz was still laying his life on the line, but he liked Daniel so he consented to the ten day test.

David Hocking: When you say "No" to what is wrong, God says "Yes! Bless that person!" Many of us are not growing and experiencing the blessing of God because we won't say "No!" to the world.[27]

Charles Halff: "Ten" in the Bible is symbolic of testing. The ten commandments were the special test that God gave to Israel. God told the church at <u>Smyrna</u> [see GWRV, page 31] that they would be tested for ten days with severe persecution. The **parable** of the ten pounds illustrates how the Lord will test our service when he returns.[28]

> **Daniel 1:15** At the end of the ten days they looked healthier and better nourished than any of the young men who ate the royal food.

Now Look At Us

Here we have the outcome of the test. The ten days passed and now Daniel and his friends stand before Ashpenaz. They are examined and found to look healthier and better fed than any of those who had eaten the king's food which was the best in the land.

> **Daniel 1:16** So the guard took away their choice food and the wine they were to drink and gave them vegetables instead.

All The Vegetables You Want

Because Daniel and his friends passed the test, Ashpenaz felt safe in letting them refuse the king's food and drink. They would not be forced to defile themselves. The guard was instructed to stop giving them the royal delicacies and to provide them with vegetables instead.

Dare to be a Daniel,
Dare to stand alone;
Dare to have a purpose firm!
Dare to make it known!

Something to Ponder

☞ **GO TO:**

Deuteronomy 13:1-4
(Satan)

> **Daniel 1:17** To these four young men God gave knowledge and understanding of all kinds of literature and learning. And Daniel could understand visions and dreams of all kinds.

Knowledge Beyond Human Understanding

God rewarded the faithfulness of these four teenagers by giving them special knowledge and understanding in the literature and languages of the various nations comprising the Babylonian empire. It was not self-attained but a gift from God. It was not ordinary knowledge and understanding but superior knowledge and understanding. Daniel and his friends had wisdom and knowledge beyond the sharpest minds in Babylon.

Still Daniel received an even greater gift: the ability to understand **visions** and **dreams**. Explaining visions was a science in Babylon to which much importance and esteem was attached. Yet God knew Daniel would soon have need of such a gift, so he supplied it beforehand.

visions: *dreams, trances, and/or pictorial revelations that stimulate the mind and are regarded as omens of future events*

dream: *in the Old Testament a vision of spiritual or prophetic significance*

Christians: *believers in Jesus Christ*

David Hocking: We don't have anything that we haven't received from the Lord. When we determine to follow him and walk in his way, God himself gives us extra portions of his ability.[29]

Noah Hutchings: Regardless of how much education a person has or how much knowledge he has amassed, knowledge and all the degrees in the world will avail him little unless he has the wisdom to make use of that which he knows. It is not so much what you know, but rather how you use it.[30]

Rick Joyner: Visions can come on the impression level also. They are gentle and must be seen with "the eyes of our heart." These, too, can be very specific and accurate, especially when received and/or interpreted by those who are experienced. The more the "eyes of our hearts" are opened, as Paul prayed in Ephesians 1:18, the more powerful and useful these can be.[31]

What Others are Saying:

KEY POINT

It is not so much what you know, but rather how you use it.

Visions and dreams do not belong to any particular age or group of people. The Bible records Jews, Egyptian pharaohs, Babylonian kings, **Christians**, and others who had them in Old and New Testament times. The world has always had people who claimed to have them, whether true or counterfeit. God said the visions and dreams of those who are true will always be right, but the visions and dreams of counterfeiters will sometimes be right and sometimes wrong. So how do we recognize counterfeiters? God says we are not to believe them if they do or say things that deny the truths of the Bible. God does not send dreams or visions to people who contradict his Word, but <u>Satan does</u>.

Something to Ponder

Examples Of People Who Had Visions And Dreams

Abimelech (Genesis 20:1-17)
Jacob (Genesis 31:10-13, 22-24)
Joseph (Genesis 37:5-11)
Pharaoh (Genesis 41:1-40)
Solomon (I Kings 3:5-15)
Joseph (Matthew 1:20-25; 2:13-15, 19)
Pilate's Wife (Matthew 27:11-19)
Peter (Acts 10:10)
Paul (Acts 22:17)

God

Remember This . . .

delivered Jehoiakim into Nebuchadnezzar's hand (Daniel 1:2).
caused Ashpenaz to show favor and sympathy to Daniel (Daniel 1:9).
gave gifts to Daniel and his friends (Daniel 1:17).

> **Daniel 1:18** At the end of the time set by the king to bring them in, the chief official presented them to Nebuchadnezzar.

KEY Symbols:

God Gave to All Four
knowledge
understanding

God Also Gave to Daniel
ability to understand visions and dreams

Here They Are, My Lord

When the three years of schooling ordered by Nebuchadnezzar was completed, it was the responsibility of Ashpenaz to take Daniel and his friends before the king. This implies that the king took a personal interest in his captives and that he was careful to see his orders were carried out. Also, it is not too hard to speculate that it was an anxious moment for these youngsters. After all, how often does one stand before the most powerful man in the world?

They were to be trained for three years, and after that they were to enter the king's service (Daniel 1:5).

Remember This . . .

> **Daniel 1:19** The king talked with them, and he found none equal to Daniel, Hananiah, Mishael, and Azariah; so they entered the king's service.

The Wisest In The Land

King Nebuchadnezzar wanted to make his own determination of the condition and learning of these teenagers, so he personally interviewed them. Following the examination, it was his finding that these four were superior to everyone else, and that they would be of great value to his government.

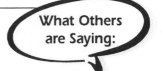

What Others are Saying:

Oliver B. Greene: We need more Daniels today. We need the spirit of Daniel, the conviction and determination of Daniel, and we need the love for God that Daniel had. Believers today are not captives in Babylon, literally speaking, but we ARE in the Babylon of worldliness and pleasure.[32]

David Jeremiah with C.C. Carlson: Daniel was "our man in the palace" to the POW's.[33]

> **Daniel 1:20** In every matter of wisdom and understanding about which the king questioned them, he found them ten times better than all the magicians and enchanters in his whole kingdom.

☞ **GO TO:**

Psalm 119:97-100 (wiser than all others)

Ten Times Wiser

God had exceedingly blessed them. <u>Whatever the king asked they knew.</u> And he found them not just a little better than all of his so-called wise men, but *ten times better.*

> **Daniel 1:21** And Daniel remained there until the first year of King Cyrus.

☞ **GO TO:**

Daniel 10:1 (Cyrus)

90 Years

Couple this with Daniel 1:1 and we gain insight into the approximate length of Daniel's life—about ninety years. We can also determine several other things: 1) that he served four major kings: Nebuchadnezzar, Belshazzar, Darius, and Cyrus (see Time Line #1, Appendix A); 2) that he held his position in government at least until the first year of King Cyrus; 3) that he was alive at least two years after he vacated his office.

Study Questions

1. Who caused Jerusalem to be captured and what did he use?
2. How did Nebuchadnezzar change Daniel's life and what was he unable to change?
3. Daniel 1:9 says Daniel found favor with Ashpenaz, so why didn't Ashpenaz want Daniel to change his diet?
4. Other than not defiling himself with the king's food, what evidence do we have that Daniel trusted God?
5. What changes occurred as a result of Daniel's (and his friends') faithfulness to God?

CHAPTER WRAP-UP

- Babylon attacked Jerusalem, captured the royal family, and seized the Temple treasures. (Daniel 1:1, 2)

- Daniel was a perfect physical specimen, healthy, good-looking, intelligent, and well-informed. (Daniel 1:4)

- Daniel resolved not to defile himself with the king's food. (Daniel 1:8)

- Daniel suggested that he and his friends be given nothing but vegetables and water for ten days—then be compared to those who ate the king's food. Daniel and his friends were found to be ten times better. (Daniel 1:12–15)

- God rewarded Daniel and his friends with unusual knowledge and understanding. He also gave Daniel the ability to understand visions and dreams. (Daniel 1:17)

DANIEL 2

CHAPTER HIGHLIGHTS

- A Disturbing Dream
- A Deadly Command
- Daniel Prays
- Daniel's Prayer Answered
- A Destroying Rock

Let's Get Started

God made a covenant with <u>Abraham</u>, <u>Isaac</u>, <u>Jacob</u>, <u>David</u>, and <u>many of the prophets</u> to establish a kingdom that will never end. Many people call that kingdom Israel, "God's covenant nation." Following the <u>death of King Solomon</u>, ten of the twelve tribes of Israel seceded (broke away) and formed the Northern Kingdom called Israel. The other two tribes formed the Southern Kingdom called Judah.

Both kingdoms failed to keep the covenant and continued to sin. First, the Northern Kingdom was taken captive by Assyria, then the Southern Kingdom was taken captive by Babylon. According to Scripture, these captivities were temporary. God's covenant had not been abolished; it had only been set aside for a period of time.

When Babylon captured Judah the world began a temporary period of time known in the Bible as the ***Times of the Gentiles*** (see Time Line #2, Appendix A). Just as the captivities were temporary, so will be this period. It will not last forever. It will end at the **Battle of <u>Armageddon</u>** (see GWRV, pages 239–240) with the **<u>Second Coming of Jesus</u>**. God will return Jerusalem to the Jews and establish the kingdom of his covenant. The modern restoration of Israel as a nation in 1948, the rebuilding of Jerusalem as a city, the current Arab/Israeli conflict over Jerusalem, the restoration of Europe as a Gentile world power, and many other signs indicate that the Times of the Gentiles is about over. It seems that the world is now in a transition period—between the Times of

☞ **GO TO:**

Genesis 12:1–3 (Abraham)

Genesis 26:1–5 (Isaac)

Genesis 28:1–22 (Jacob)

II Samuel 7:8–16 (David)

Deuteronomy 30:1–10; Jeremiah 31:31–40 (prophets)

I Kings 11:41–43 (Solomon)

Luke 21:24 (Times)

Revelation 16:12–16 (Armageddon)

Revelation 22:6, 7 (Second Coming)

Illustration #4

Jewish Kingdoms—The Northern Kingdom was called Israel and the Southern Kingdom was called Judah.

☞ **GO TO:**

I Kings 11:29–34 (promise to David)

I Kings 12:1-9 (Rehoboam)

I Kings 11:29-33 (Jeroboam)

Times of the Gentiles: the period Gentiles exercise some control over Jerusalem from the Babylonian captivity to the Second Coming of Jesus

Battle of Armageddon: a great battle on earth during the **Tribulation Period**

What Others are Saying:

Second Coming of Jesus: his coming at the end of the Tribulation Period to establish his eternal kingdom

Tribulation Period: seven years of God's wrath against the wicked on earth

Something to Ponder

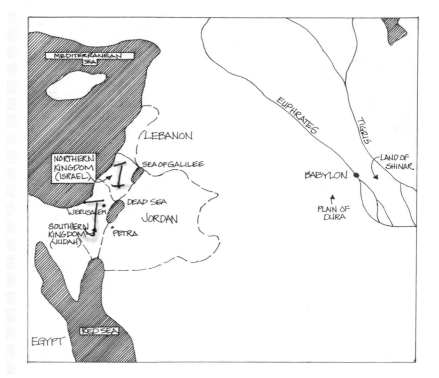

the Gentiles and the Second Coming of Jesus. This chapter will detail the first dream of King Nebuchadnezzar, and provide some amazing and important information about how God will establish his kingdom on earth.

Jack W. Hayford: Dreams always had a prominent place in the lives of ancient peoples. They were considered to convey messages from God and were frequently thought to be predictive in nature.[1]

Wallace Emerson: Dreams are one of the means by which, in Old Testament times, God spoke to men, especially in the absence of written Scripture or without the presence of a prophet of God.[2]

King Solomon

King Solomon was a failure in many ways: he had hundreds of wives and concubines, got involved in false religions, and greatly increased taxes to fund his large building projects. His failures angered God and provoked him to declare that the kingdom would be divided. But God waited until after Solomon died because of a <u>promise he made to Solomon's father, King David</u>.

When Solomon died, <u>Rehoboam</u> (Solomon's son) took the throne. It wasn't long until <u>Jeroboam</u> (a high ranking official to Solomon) visited Rehoboam with a delegation to ask for lower taxes. Rehoboam's advisors suggested he lower them, but instead he raised taxes. This angered the people and caused a rebellion that divided the nation in which Jeroboam left with ten of the twelve tribes to form Israel, the Northern Kingdom.

Twelve Tribes

Israel originally was made up of twelve tribes. It was sometimes called the United Kingdom and Jerusalem was its capital. Then Israel divided. The ten tribes in the north were called the Northern Kingdom, or Israel. The two tribes in the south were called the Southern Kingdom, or Judah. Jerusalem was in the Southern Kingdom. In fact, it was the capital of the Southern Kingdom. A small minority of people disagree, but modern day Israel is made up of all twelve tribes. People do not talk about it, but the nation is again a United Kingdom. It is a problem for the nations of the world, because Israel calls the rebuilt Jerusalem their capital, and the Palestinians are trying to also claim it as their capital.

Remember This . . .

> **Daniel 2:1** In the second year of his reign, Nebuchadnezzar had dreams; his mind was troubled and he could not sleep.

The First Dream

Nebuchadnezzar had not reigned very long and Daniel was still a teenager when the king began to have disturbing dreams (see Time Line #1, Appendix A).

David Hocking: Nebuchadnezzar's concern is told to us in the Bible so that we can know that God can trouble the greatest kings of the world any time he wants to.[3]

What Others are Saying:

Something to Ponder

In spite of the fact that this verse tells us this dream occurred in the second year of king Nebuchadnezzar's reign, some debate exists among Bible experts about the exact time of this event. Most experts believe Daniel and his friends were actually captured *before* Nebuchadnezzar became the official king of Babylon. After Nebuchadnezzar's father died, he was recognized as the "acting king," but he was not officially crowned until later. If Nebuchadnezzar was officially king when Daniel and his friends began their three years of schooling, as some experts believe, then this event occurred before they graduated. But, on the other hand, if he was only the "recognized king," and had not been officially crowned, this event occurred after they graduated.

☞ **GO TO:**

Isaiah 48:1–15 (magicians)

Revelation 9:21 (magic)

Revelation 14:8; 17:1–18 (spirit of Babylon)

> **Daniel 2:2** So the king summoned the magicians, enchanters, sorcerers, and astrologers to tell him what he had dreamed. When they came in and stood before the king,

Bring In My Wise Men

The troubled king called in several of his special advisors. He summoned: 1) <u>magicians</u> who were skillful in tricks and illusions (slight of hand), and understood mysteries and black <u>magic</u> (using secret charms and spirits to make unnatural things happen); 2) enchanters who were chanters of evil spells and incantations (sets of words spoken as a magic charm); 3) sorcerers who talked to the dead and practiced magic with the aid of evil spirits; and 4) astrologers who read horoscopes and studied the stars and other heavenly bodies to foretell the future. When they arrived they stood before the powerful Nebuchadnezzar.

What Others are Saying:

trance channeler: one who goes into an altered state of consciousness to communicate with evil spirits

New Age: false religious movement

psychic: a spiritualist who claims special insight

Peter and Paul Lalonde: Today, countless thousands of people around the world are ready and willing to seek the advice of spirits from another time and place. People, including famous people like actresses Shirley MacLaine and Linda Evans, spend thousands of dollars at a time to listen to spirit entities speak through so-called **trance channelers** like J.Z. Knight or Kevin Ryerson.[4]

John Hagee: Former First Lady Nancy Reagan planned the White House calendar with the advice of her astrologer. During his term as governor of Massachusetts presidential candidate Michael Dukakis was featured in *National Geographic* as honoring the state's leading witch. As I mentioned in Chapter 1 [of *Day of Deception*], Hillary Clinton talks to the dead with the assistance of **New Age psychic** Jean Houston.[5]

Hal Lindsey: The New Age is dominated by the <u>spirit of Babylon</u>.[6]

> **Daniel 2:3** he said to them, "I have had a dream that troubles me and I want to know what it means."

A Troubling Dream

Nebuchadnezzar told his special advisors that he had a troubling dream, and he wanted to know what it meant.

Noah Hutchings: Even in his best mood, Nebuchadnezzar was not to be crossed, but on that morning he was completely out of sorts. He had experienced many sleepless nights, and probably that previous night he had not slept at all.[7]

What Others are Saying:

> **Daniel 2:4** Then the astrologers answered the king in Aramaic, "O king, live forever! Tell your servants the dream, and we will interpret it."

☞ **GO TO:**

Deuteronomy 4:19; 17:2-5 (abomination)

zodiac: the 12 imaginary signs in heaven

Tell Us Your Dream

The astrologers' statement indicates that they thought this would be a simple matter. All they wanted to know was the dream. Once that was revealed they would give the interpretation.

David Jeremiah with C.C. Carlson: Does God still speak through dreams today? If we have dreams that we think are inspiration, they are more likely to be indigestion. . . . We have God's full revelation, and there is a big period at the end of it.[8]

What Others are Saying:

```
A CNN news report estimates at least 300 of
today's Fortune 500 companies use astrologers in
one way or another.[9]
```

RELATED CURRENT EVENTS

The Zodiac

The ancient occultic practice of astrology is still popular today. Astrologers relate the time of one's birth to one of the 12 signs of the **zodiac**. Then, based upon the position of celestial objects, they profess to predict people's futures. They have had thousands of years to prove their theories scientifically valid but have never managed to do so. If this pagan practice was an abomination to God in ancient times and something he condemned, is it not still <u>an abomination</u> and something that we should condemn today?

Something to Ponder

Remember
This . . .

WARNING

horoscope: *a diagram of the heavens, showing the relative positions of planets and the signs of the zodiac, used to predict events in a person's life*

Which Language Is It?

Daniel's native tongue was Hebrew, but the commercial language of his day was Aramaic. The astrologers were not Jews. They stood before the Babylonian king, and they spoke Aramaic. Up to Daniel 2:4, Daniel wrote in Hebrew, but beginning with this verse he wrote in Aramaic. He switched back to Hebrew at Daniel 8:1.

The use of **horoscopes** is one of the most common occultic practices of our time. Even though most scientists tell us there is no scientific basis for believing in them, multitudes still use horoscopes to determine things about their character and future. Some even use them to make important decisions. The idea that the position of the sun, moon and planets influence one's character, fortune, future and personality was an abomination unto God during Old Testament times and nothing has changed. God wants us to commit our life to him, to give him charge of our character and future, and to pray for guidance before making important decisions. Instead of reading the horoscope published in the newspaper he would have us read the Bible. Those who use horoscopes are making the terrible mistake of ignoring the will of God.

> **Daniel 2:5** The king replied to the astrologers, "This is what I have firmly decided: If you do not tell me what my dream was and interpret it, I will have you cut into pieces and your houses turned into piles of rubble.

I'll Cut You Into Little Pieces

frauds: *fakes; dishonest people who are not what they claim to be*

augury: *the art of predicting events based upon the study of dreams, signs and omens*

What a scene this must have been. We talk about lowering the boom, but this must have filled the wicked hearts of the king's advisors with terror. On the throne was a powerful world ruler not used to being denied or refused anything; in front of him was a cowering bunch of **frauds** who knew they were being asked to do the impossible. The angry king issued a decree; a decree that he would not, and could not, go back on. By law what he said could not be reversed. These advisors would have to tell him his dream and interpret it, or their heads would roll and their houses would be leveled.

What Others are Saying:

The Pulpit Commentary: Brought up in an absolute faith in astrology and **augury**, the king never doubted their ability to tell him his dream; it could only be a treasonable desire to hinder him from taking the suitable steps to avoid whatever danger might be threatened by it, or to gain whatever advantage might be promised.[10]

RELATED CURRENT EVENTS

```
Ford executives consulted astrologer Joyce
Jillson of Sherman Oaks, California, for good
dates to introduce their redesigned Taurus, it-
self named after the second sign of the zodiac.[11]
```

> **Daniel 2:6** But if you tell me the dream and explain it, you will receive from me gifts and rewards and great honor. So tell me the dream and interpret it for me."

Riches To The One Who Knows

Nebuchadnezzar really wanted to know the dream, have it interpreted, and be sure he had been told the truth. So this is the carrot: he would give gifts, rewards, and honor to his advisors if they did what he asked. He also wanted them to believe that he did not want to kill them, so he encouraged them to reveal the dream and its interpretation.

What Others are Saying:

Wallace Emerson: In the king's speech to his wise men, there is first a threat and then a promise of a reward—certainly, a very strange way of dealing with a group whose place in Babylonian society was one of honor and prestige. Threats are usually reserved for enemies.[12]

> **Daniel 2:7** Once more they replied, "Let the king tell his servants the dream, and we will interpret it."

A Second Request

A second time Nebuchadnezzar's special advisors courteously asked him to tell them the dream, and they promised to interpret it.

Everyone dreams, but some people never recall dreaming. Others remember only a little about a dream they had just before awakening and nothing about earlier dreams. No one recalls every dream and, in general, dreams are very easily forgotten.

Something to Ponder

> **Daniel 2:8** Then the king answered, "I am certain that you are trying to gain time, because you realize that this is what I have firmly decided:

I Warn You!

This dream was becoming a nightmare for Nebuchadnezzar's advisors. He was accusing them of trying to buy time because they knew he would carry out his decree and have them killed and their houses leveled.

The possibility also remains that Nebuchadnezzar believed this dream signified that he would be overthrown. He could have been accusing his advisors of treason or trying to stall until a successor took over.

> **Daniel 2:9** If you do not tell me the dream, there is just one penalty for you. You have conspired to tell me misleading and wicked things, hoping the situation will change. So then, tell me the dream, and I will know that you can interpret it for me."

Another Threat

It was time to "put up or shut up." Nebuchadnezzar gave these advisors a choice: tell him his dream or die. He would not accept any excuses. However, he explained that if they would tell him the dream, he would also believe their interpretation. But, he implied that if they did not, he would consider them fakes.

What Others are Saying:

The Pulpit Commentary: In his own mind he [Nebuchadnezzar] was warped and confused by his overmastering belief in omens and auguries, in gods and demons, in magicians and astrologers. With this faith in his heart, his only explanation of the silence of these **soothsayers** was treason.[13]

> **Daniel 2:10** The astrologers answered the king, "There is not a man on earth who can do what the king asks! No king, however great and mighty, has ever asked such a thing of any magician or enchanter or astrologer.

No One Can Do What You Ask

These trapped men were desperately struggling to preserve their lives. This was a veiled admission that they were imposters and could not do what the king asked. They were saying the king's demand was impossible and implying that he was being unreasonable.

```
Abadie [a New York psychotherapist, psychic counse-
lor, and professional astrologer] cites trade
publications showing that Americans spend more than
$12 million per month calling psychic hotlines, an
average of about 10,000 calls per day.[14]
```

> **Daniel 2:11** What the king asks is too difficult. No one can reveal it to the king except the gods, and they do not live among men."

Only The Gods Could Possibly Know

Nebuchadnezzar's advisers were nervously restating their defense: the king's request was impossible. They were also admitting that they were out of touch with the <u>gods</u> and they added something today's **New Agers** would very much disagree with: the gods *do not live among men.*

The Pulpit Commentary: This excuse of the wise men is a preparation for Daniel's claim to reveal the secret of the king by the power of a higher God than any that communicated with the Babylonian soothsayers.[15]

It is not their intent to get involved with dangerous cults, but a lot of good people are doing so by taking up New Age beliefs. They do not seek to be involved in sin, but without realizing it they are being enticed by people holding doctrines as dangerous as Satan himself. One such doctrine is the New Age idea that we are all gods. Unfortunately, one's New Age trek toward godhood always winds up hurting that individual because it winds up being a walk away from the one true God. Thinking they are gods they trust in themselves instead of the God who can make them better and secure their future. Millions now claim that they are gods, but there is no evidence that the world is getting better.

RELATED CURRENT EVENTS

☞ **GO TO:**

I Corinthians 8:5, 6 (gods)

What Others are Saying:

WARNING

New Ager: *follower of a false religious movement interested in astrology, fortune telling, metaphysics, occultism, re-incarnation, witchcraft, etc.*

KEY POINT

There is but *one* God.

> **Daniel 2:12** This made the king so angry and furious that he ordered the execution of all the wise men of Babylon.

Off With Their Heads

The edgy king probably decided that his advisers really were traitors or, at least, imposters. Either way, he was so upset he ordered they be put to death. Unfortunately, this wide-ranging order included Daniel and his friends, Hananiah (Shadrach), Mishael (Meshach), and Azariah (Abednego).

What Others are Saying:

Uriah Smith: While we cannot justify the extreme measures to which he resorted—dooming them to death and their houses to destruction—we cannot but feel a hearty sympathy with him in his condemnation of a class of miserable imposters.[16]

David Breese: Beware of false teachers. Even though they profess religion, they are not of God! Like these soothsayers, they come up empty when there is a real need for truth.[17]

> **Daniel 2:13** So the decree was issued to put the wise men to death, and men were sent to look for Daniel and his friends to put them to death.

Search Them Out

The command was given to execute the wise men. And from this verse we learn that Daniel and his friends were included in that group. They were innocent victims in this sordid affair, but trifles like this did not matter to the fiery Nebuchadnezzar.

> **Daniel 2:14** When Arioch, the commander of the king's guard, had gone out to put to death the wise men of Babylon, Daniel spoke to him with wisdom and tact.

A Word Of Wisdom

The commander of the king's guard took his troops and went forth to round up the wise men for execution. It wasn't long before he located Daniel, who was just a teenager, but he already possessed a godly character beyond his young years. He did not act like an unjustly condemned man by arguing or protesting, but instead used his head, was composed, and had good manners.

Oliver B. Greene: The only thing that keeps the judgment of God from falling upon this great land of ours are the few godly, God-fearing men and women left in the United States of America. God spares this country for the sake of the righteous.[18]

> **Daniel 2:15** He asked the king's officer, "Why did the king issue such a harsh decree?" Arioch then explained the matter to Daniel.

What Is The Problem?

Daniel was unaware of what had transpired until Arioch arrived with the arrest warrant. One thing Daniel wanted to know was why Nebuchadnezzar had issued such a cruel command. Arioch, being commander of the king's guard, had probably witnessed the entire matter, so he took the time to explain everything to Daniel.

> **Daniel 2:16** At this, Daniel went in to the king and asked for time, so that he might interpret the dream for him.

☞ **GO TO:**

James 5:16 (pray)

psychoanalyst: a person who studies someone's mind to discover unconscious desires, fears, or motivations

Take Me To Your Leader

Daniel's *first step* was to obtain permission to speak to Nebuchadnezzar. Then his *second step* was to ask him for time. He was not stalling out of a desire for the king to be overthrown or change his mind, but because he was acting on his unshakable faith in God. He obviously believed that he could reveal the dream if he had time to <u>pray</u>.

What Others are Saying:

Oliver B. Greene: All hell cannot stop the program of Almighty God. He always has his representative in the right place at the right time.[19]

David Jeremiah with C.C. Carlson: Daniel needed time, not to look up answers in a dream manual, consult the stars, or the nearest **psychoanalyst**, but to do what all of us should do in tense situations, and that is to pray.[20]

KEY POINT
Take time to pray.

David Breese: More things are wrought by prayer than the world has ever dreamed of![21]

> **Daniel 2:17** Then Daniel returned to his house and explained the matter to his friends Hananiah, Mishael, and Azariah.

☞ **GO TO:**

Matthew 18:20 (friends)

Isaiah 10:20-22 (Jews)

Listen To Me My Friends

Daniel's *third step* was to go home and tell his <u>friends</u> what had happened. They are identified here by their Hebrew names which is a reminder that they were still <u>Jews, followers of Jehovah</u>.

> **Daniel 2:18** He urged them to plead for mercy from the God of heaven concerning this mystery, so that he and his friends might not be executed with the rest of the wise men of Babylon.

☞ **GO TO:**

Matthew 18:20 (prayer)

James 5:16 (praying)

God of heaven: *Jehovah God of Israel. He created the heavens.*

Pray!

Daniel's *fourth step* was to ask his friends to join him in <u>prayer</u>. The *fifth step* was for them to actually pray. They prayed to the **God of heaven** and specifically asked him for mercy concerning this dream. If he granted it, they would live. If he did not, they would die.

What Others are Saying:

Ed Young: Pray specifically. Tell God exactly what you're <u>praying for</u>.[22]

☞ **GO TO:**

Amos 3:7 (revealed)

> **Daniel 2:19** During the night the mystery was revealed to Daniel in a vision. Then Daniel praised the God of heaven

So That's It

Daniel and his friends prayed and went to bed. It is impossible to say exactly what happened, but the dream was probably <u>revealed</u> as Daniel dreamed the same dream Nebuchadnezzar dreamed. Then he woke up and his *sixth step* was to praise the same God he and his friends had prayed to: the God of heaven.

KEY POINT

Tell God exactly what you're praying for.

Ed Young: God answers every prayer that is offered by a member of his family. Sometimes he says, "Yes!" Sometimes he says, "No!" Sometimes he says, "Maybe!" Sometimes he says, "Wait!"[23]

Daniel's Six Steps to His Three P's

Step 1—Daniel obtained permission to speak to the king.

Step 2—Daniel asked for time. **Pleading**

Step 3—Daniel went home and told his friends.

Step 4—Daniel asked his friends to join him in prayer.

Step 5—Daniel and his friends prayed. **Prayer**

Step 6—Daniel and his friends praised God. **Praise**

> **Daniel 2:20** and said: "Praise be to the name of God for ever and ever; wisdom and power are his.

Wisdom And Power

This is Daniel's first reaction in response to God answering his prayer. It is a prayer of praise and thanksgiving. Daniel called for the name of his God to be praised forever and ever, and he acknowledged that wisdom *and* power are Divine qualities of his God. His God's great name should be praised because he is the sole source of wisdom and strength. He has all authority because he is both **omniscient** and **omnipotent**.

☞ **GO TO:**

James 1:5 (wisdom)

Matthew 28:18 (authority)

omniscient: God knows everything

omnipotent: God has power over everything

David Hocking: We often forget to bless God—even when he does something wonderful. Before Daniel went in to see Nebuchadnezzar, he was already praising the Lord.[24]

God is:

Omniscient (all-knowing)
   I John 3:20 (God knows everything)
   Psalm 147:5 (God's understanding has no limit)
Omnipotent (all-powerful)
   Job 42:1, 2 (the Lord can do all things)
   Matthew 19:26 (with God all things are possible)
Omnipresent (everywhere)
   Psalm 139:7–10 (you are there)
   Jeremiah 23:24 (I fill heaven and earth)

☞ **GO TO:**

Psalm 75:7 (down)

Proverbs 1:7 (knowledge)

Daniel 1:17 (understanding)

discernment: the act of showing good judgment

> **Daniel 2:21** He changes times and seasons; he sets up kings and deposes them. He gives wisdom to the wise and knowledge to the discerning.

He Can Give And He Can Take

Daniel praised God because God is in control:

1) of the *times and seasons*—he can end one age and begin another
2) of *kings and rulers*—he can raise them up or <u>bring them down</u>
3) of *wisdom*—he can give people the ability to rightly use their knowledge
4) of <u>knowledge</u>—he can impart information and the ability to learn

Remember, God is in control of everything!

What Others are Saying:

KEY POINT

Discernment comes from God alone, not from astrologers, psychics, or sorcerers.

Remember This . . .

Oliver B. Greene: Times and seasons are not under the control of chance, but are regulated by established laws; yet God, who appointed these laws, has power to change them, and all the changes which occur under these laws are produced under his power and control.[25]

Ed Young: History has a purpose in it and God is in the middle of that purpose. History is *his story*.[26]

To these four young men God gave <u>knowledge and understanding</u> of all kinds of literature and learning.

☞ **GO TO:**

Hebrews 4:13 (hidden)

I John 1:5 (God is light)

> **Daniel 2:22** He reveals deep and hidden things; he knows what lies in darkness, and light dwells with him.

Nothing Is Hidden From God

Daniel praised his God because:

1) he reveals deep and complex secrets
2) he reveals <u>hidden</u> things that no one else knows
3) he is the source of **revelation** and **enlightenment**

Daniel knew that it was his God who revealed to him Nebuchadnezzar's dream that was hidden from everyone else. All of Nebuchadnezzar's wise men were in *darkness*, but light was found in God.

> **Daniel 2:23** I thank and praise you, O God of my fathers: You have given me wisdom and power, you have made known to me what we asked of you, you have made known to us the dream of the king."

☞ **GO TO:**

Deuteronomy 6:10 (fathers)

We, Not Me

Daniel gave his God thanks and praise for answering prayer. It is the God of his fathers, Jehovah God of Israel, the God of Abraham, Isaac and Jacob, who gave him wisdom and power. And notice that Daniel did not take all the credit for gaining God's favor. He thanked God and praised him for *what we asked,* and for making *known to us the dream of the king.* He knew that God's answer was in response, not only to his prayer, but to that of his companions as well.

Noah Hutchings: This is the God whom Daniel acknowledged, and it is the God of Daniel whom we also address in our prayers. He is the God who is all-sufficient.[27]

What Others are Saying:

☞ **GO TO:**

Ezekiel 33:11 (death of the wicked)

> **Daniel 2:24** Then Daniel went to Arioch, whom the king had appointed to execute the wise men of Babylon, and said to him, "Do not execute the wise men of Babylon. Take me to the king, and I will interpret his dream for him."

Spare Them

After taking time to give thanks and praise to God, Daniel went to Arioch, the commander of the king's guard. He told Arioch to stop putting the wise men to death, because he could interpret the king's dream if Arioch would take him to the king.

☞ **GO TO:**

Nehemiah 7:6 (exiles)

1 Chronicles. 9:1 (Judah)

exiles from Judah: Jews taken from Jerusalem

> **Daniel 2:25** Arioch took Daniel to the king at once and said, "I have found a man among the exiles from Judah who can tell the king what his dream means."

Pride And Humility

There seems to be a contrast here between the humble Daniel and the proud Arioch. When God revealed Nebuchadnezzar's dream to Daniel, he did not claim all the credit. Instead Daniel included his companions when he thanked and praised God for giving what we asked for. But the warrior Arioch was made from a different mold. He had done nothing, but yet he rushed Daniel to the king and said, *I have found a man among the **exiles from Judah** who can tell the king what his dream means.* God revealed the dream to Daniel, but Arioch tried to make it look like he should get all the credit.

What Others are Saying:

David Hocking: The problem moved Daniel to *prayer*. The answer moved him to *praise* God. Also, the opportunity moved Daniel to *action*! That should be our response.[28]

☞ **GO TO:**

Matthew 19:26 (all things are possible)

> **Daniel 2:26** The king asked Daniel (also called Belteshazzar), "Are you able to tell me what I saw in my dream and interpret it?"

Let Me Have It

Apparently Nebuchadnezzar did not think this was <u>possible</u>. He was somewhat skeptical of either Arioch's claim or Daniel's ability to do what Arioch said.

What Others are Saying:

Oliver B. Greene: Whether the king realized it or not, he was asking Daniel, "Was *your* God able to help you? Did he hear *your* prayers? Is *your* God more powerful and wiser than the gods of the astrologers and wise men of Babylon?"[29]

☞ **GO TO:**

I Corinthians 1:20 (wisdom of this world)

> **Daniel 2:27** Daniel replied, "No wise man, enchanter, magician, or **diviner** can explain to the king the mystery he has asked about,

No Man Knows The Answer

Daniel made no boasts about his ability or that of his friends. He began by politely letting the hotheaded king know that he was asking the impossible of his <u>wise men</u>. This answer could even be considered a mild rebuke to the fiery Nebuchadnezzar.

The astrologers answered the king, there is not a man on earth who can do what the king asks (Daniel 2:10).

> **Daniel 2:28** but there is a God in heaven who reveals mysteries. He has shown King Nebuchadnezzar what will happen in days to come. Your dream and the visions that passed through your mind as you lay on your bed are these:

A Prophecy Of Things To Come

This tells us both the source and purpose of Nebuchadnezzar's dream. Daniel let the king know that the source of this dream was the God in heaven—a reference to Daniel's God, the God of Israel. He also let the king know that the purpose of this dream was God's desire to reveal the future.

J. Vernon McGee: Daniel now has the unique privilege of introducing to the darkened mind of this pagan king the living and true God.[30]

What Others are Saying:

Noah Hutchings: The essence of Daniel's opening remarks was that the King's dream concerned a great prophecy, a prophecy that extended from his day to the very last days.[31]

> **Daniel 2:29** "As you were lying there, O king, your mind turned to things to come, and the revealer of mysteries showed you what is going to happen.

The Revealer Of Mysteries

Daniel began by reminding Nebuchadnezzar that the king was lying in bed thinking about the future. It is reasonable to assume he went to bed speculating about what kind of king he would be, how he would be remembered, what kind of decisions he should make, and who his successor might be. With the future on his

☞ **GO TO:**

Matthew 13:11 (mysteries)

KEY Symbols:

God
Revealer of Mysteries

mind the king fell asleep, and God, who is the *Revealer of <u>Mysteries</u>*, gave him a revelation about the future.

What Others are Saying:

David Jeremiah with C.C. Carlson: God communicated to a pagan king not only the future events in his life, but also in the life of the world. Understanding the prophetic truths in the Bible hinges on the second chapter of Daniel.[32]

☞ **GO TO:**

I Kings 14:7–11 (David)

house / line of David: *family, lineage, or descendants of King David*

scepter: *a special rod that kings held to signify their authority or sovereignty*

> **Daniel 2:30** As for me, this mystery has been revealed to me, not because I have greater wisdom than other living men, but so that you, O king, may know the interpretation and that you may understand what went through your mind.

So That You May Know

Daniel's thoughts turned from the king's dream to himself. He was humbly saying something like this, "This mystery has been revealed to me not because of my ability, my greatness, my understanding or my wisdom, but because God wants you to know what went through your mind and what it means."

What Others are Saying:

Uriah Smith: God would not work for the king independently of his own people; though he gave the dream to the king, he sent the interpretation through one of his own acknowledged servants.[33]

J. Vernon McGee: Because of the failure of the **house of <u>David</u>**, God is now taking the **scepter** of this universe out from the hands of the line of David [the Jews], and he is putting it into the hands of the Gentiles. It will be there until Jesus Christ comes again to this earth.[34]

☞ **GO TO:**

Matthew 24:15 (prophet)

> **Daniel 2:31** "You looked, O king, and there before you stood a large statue—an enormous, dazzling statue, awesome in appearance.

God's Statue

As Daniel began to tell what the dream was, he reminded Nebuchadnezzar that he was looking into the future when he saw a great statue (see Illustration #5, page 53) standing before him. It was an *enormous, dazzling statue, awesome in appearance;* as we shall soon see, it was an unusual statue of a man.

KEY Symbols:

First Dream
a great statue

Oliver B. Greene: If we will bear in mind that Jesus declared <u>Daniel to be a prophet</u>, and therefore, the book that bears his name is a prophetic book, we will be more likely to keep in mind the prophetic aspect of Nebuchadnezzar's dream.[35]

Gold, Silver, And Bronze

The head of the statue was made of pure gold, the most precious of metals. Its chest and arms were made of silver, a significantly less precious metal. Its belly and thighs were made of bronze, a metal less expensive than silver but still precious in Nebuchadnezzar's lifetime.

KEY Symbols:

God's Statue
head
- gold gold

chest and arms
- silver

belly and thighs
- bronze

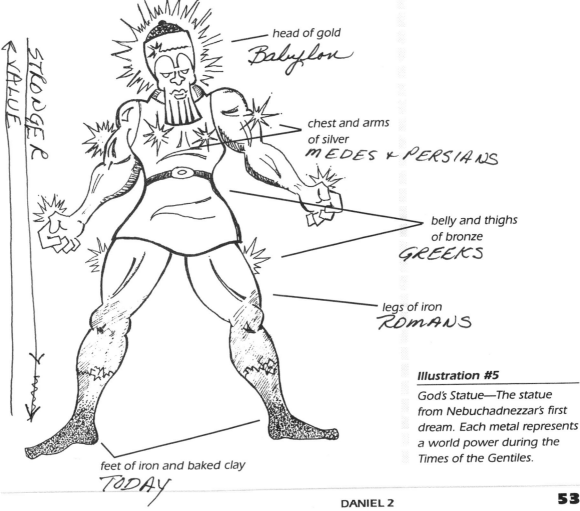

head of gold — *Babylon*

chest and arms of silver — *MEDES + PERSIANS*

belly and thighs of bronze — *GREEKS*

legs of iron — *ROMANS*

feet of iron and baked clay — *TODAY*

STRONGER VALUE

Illustration #5

God's Statue—The statue from Nebuchadnezzar's first dream. Each metal represents a world power during the Times of the Gentiles.

KEY POINT

Each segment of the statue decreased in value and weight, but increased in hardness (strength).

What Others are Saying:

KEY Symbols:

God's Statue

legs

- iron

feet

- iron and baked clay

RELATED CURRENT EVENTS

> **Daniel 2:33** its legs of iron, its feet partly of iron and partly of baked clay.

Iron And Baked Clay

The legs of the statue were made of iron, a metal less expensive than bronze but still valuable 2,600 years ago. Its feet were made of a mixture of iron and baked clay, a crude conglomeration that would be brittle and easy to shatter and the least expensive of all the materials. Thus we see that each segment of the statue decreased in value.

Another interesting point is the fact that the metals decrease in weight starting with the head and going down to the feet. Gold is heavier than silver. Silver is heavier than bronze. Bronze is heavier than iron. Iron is heavier than a mixture of iron and baked clay. This means the statue was top heavy, unstable, and poorly constructed.

Notice too, that the metals in the statue increased in hardness starting with its head and going down to its feet. Gold is not as hard as silver. Silver is not as hard as bronze. Bronze is not as hard as iron.

Grant R. Jeffrey: The metals symbolized the course of **world gentile rule** [see Time Line #2, Appendix A] for the next two-and-a-half thousand years. The progression from gold to silver to bronze to iron indicated that each of the following empires would be progressively stronger in military power but of lesser value as they degenerated from a monarchy to military rule and finally ended with democracy and dictatorship.[36]

John Hagee: You'll notice that as Daniel's eye traveled down the image, the strength of the metals progressed from soft (gold) to very hard (iron). This is a prophetic picture of the military strength of nations that would develop in years to come. Mankind has progressed from relatively weak weapons such as spears and **cudgels** to smart bombs, scud missiles, and **thermonuclear devices** that could leave earth a spinning graveyard in space.[37]

The big issue at stake here [in the 1998 crisis with Iraq] is nothing more or less than world government. Will the world government, born under the name New World Order after the fall of the

Berlin Wall, succeed in imposing its will on
Iraq, or will the International Community lose
its resolve and allow all the advances made toward world government to be squandered? . . . If
Iraq is allowed to disobey the United Nations,
then all the world's nations will know that the
UN can be disregarded. But if the International
Community acts with resolve, forcing Iraq to bow
to its edicts, then the world will know that
international law as defined by the UN must be
feared and obeyed. We are witnessing the rein-
forcing and the showcasing of world government.
And it is world government the Bible prophesies
will appear in the end-time![38]

> **Daniel 2:34** While you were watching, a rock was cut
> out, but not by human hands. It struck the statue on its
> feet of iron and clay and smashed them.

supernaturally: it did not come into being in a normal way

Watch Out For That Rock

As Nebuchadnezzar was looking at the statue in his dream, a rock
was **supernaturally** cut out without the help of human beings. It
streaked like a missile at the brittle feet of the statue and shattered
them.

> **Daniel 2:35** Then the iron, the clay, the bronze, the
> silver, and the gold were broken to pieces at the same
> time and became like **chaff** on a **threshing floor** in the
> summer. The wind swept them away without leaving a
> trace. But the rock that struck the statue became a huge
> mountain and filled the whole earth.

☞ **GO TO:**

Psalm 1:4 (chaff)

Jeremiah 51:33 (threshing floor)

Timber!

When the feet shattered the entire statue broke into chunks of
iron, clay, bronze, silver, and gold. Then the chunks broke into
smaller particles of the same materials, and the smaller particles
were pulverized into powder. A wind came up and blew all the
powder away, but the rock began to grow. It grew into the size of
a boulder, then into the size of a mountain, and it continued to
grow until it covered *the whole earth.*

chaff: bits of straw and grain husk that is removed by threshing

threshing floor: stomping floor used to separate grain from the chaff

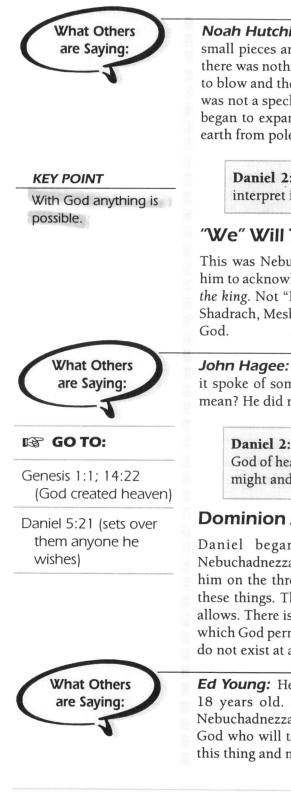

What Others are Saying:

Noah Hutchings: Then the entire image began to break up in small pieces and then the pieces broke up and subdivided until there was nothing left but a pile of dust, and then the wind began to blow and the dust was carried away through the air until there was not a speck left. And as Nebuchadnezzar watched, the stone began to expand and increase in size until it covered the entire earth from pole to pole.[39]

KEY POINT

With God anything is possible.

> **Daniel 2:36** "This was the dream, and now we will interpret it to the king.

"We" Will Tell You What It Means

This was Nebuchadnezzar's dream, but Daniel did not wait for him to acknowledge it. He immediately said, *We will interpret it to the king.* Not "I," but "we." Daniel included his prayer partners: Shadrach, Meshach, and Abednego. But, most of all, he included God.

What Others are Saying:

John Hagee: Yes, he remembered the image, and yes, he knew it spoke of something dreadfully important! But what did it all mean? He did not interrupt as Daniel continued to speak.[40]

☞ **GO TO:**

Genesis 1:1; 14:22 (God created heaven)

Daniel 5:21 (sets over them anyone he wishes)

> **Daniel 2:37** You, O king, are the king of kings. The God of heaven has given you dominion and power and might and glory;

Dominion And Power From God

Daniel began interpreting the dream by reminding Nebuchadnezzar where the king got his kingdom and who put him on the throne. Daniel told the king the <u>God of heaven</u> did these things. There are no kings or kingdoms except those God allows. There is no dominion, power, might, or glory except that which God permits. <u>All of them exist with his permission</u>, or they do not exist at all.

What Others are Saying:

Ed Young: Here is Daniel before the monarch. He's now 17 or 18 years old. . . . And he is saying, "I want you to know Nebuchadnezzar it is God who has put you on the throne, it is God who will take you off the throne, it is God who is running this thing and not you."[41]

> **Daniel 2:38** in your hands he has placed mankind and the beasts of the field and the birds of the air. Wherever they live, he has made you ruler over them all. You are that head of gold.

The First Kingdom

This reveals just how extensive Nebuchadnezzar's kingdom (see Illustration #6, page 58) was. God had given all men, all wild animals, and all the birds of the air into *his* hands. God had made Nebuchadnezzar ruler over all he had made. He had given Nebuchadnezzar a worldwide government—a government that included every living creature.

Daniel used the words "king" and "kingdom" interchangeably. He informed Nebuchadnezzar that he (and his kingdom) was the statue's head of gold.

David Jeremiah with C.C. Carlson: Israel, God's own people, except for a remnant, had literally pushed him aside. They had said, "We don't want you to rule over us." So God allowed the pagan Gentile rulers and kingdoms to move into center stage. The focus of influence moved from Jerusalem to Babylon.[42]

The <u>Times of the Gentiles</u> (see Time Line #2, Appendix A) is that period of time when the city of Jerusalem is under the control of Gentile governments. Not everyone agrees, but it is generally recognized to be that period of time that runs between Babylon's capture of Jerusalem and the Second Coming of Christ at the end of the Tribulation Period.

> **Daniel 2:39** "After you, another kingdom will rise, inferior to yours. Next, a third kingdom, one of bronze, will rule over the whole earth.

The Second And Third Kingdoms

After Nebuchadnezzar and his world kingdom, there would be a second world kingdom (see Illustration #7, page 59) inferior to Babylon. Then there would be a third world kingdom (see Illustration #8, page 59), a kingdom of bronze, that would rule the whole earth.

Daniel did not identify these world kingdoms, but we do not

☞ **GO TO:**

Luke 21:24 (Times)

KEY Symbols:

First Kingdom
BABYLON

head of gold

Nebuchadnezzar
ruler over all
- mankind, beasts, and birds

What Others are Saying:

Remember This . . .

☞ **GO TO:**

Daniel 5:28; Daniel 8:1-21 (Medes and Persians)

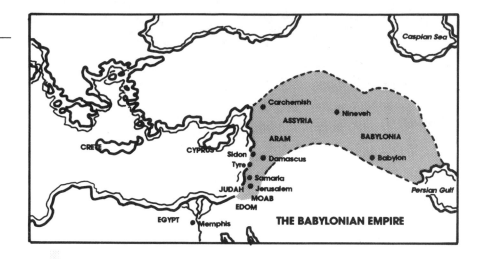

have to speculate about who they are. The Bible and history make clear that the second world kingdom was the silver empire led by the <u>Medes and Persians</u>. And the third world kingdom was the brass empire led by the nation of Greece under Alexander the Great.

What Others are Saying:

Grant R. Jeffrey: Beginning in 608 B.C. [or 606–605 B.C.] the Babylonian Empire, led by King Nebuchadnezzar, became the head of gold with overwhelming wealth and power. Seventy years later the confident but wicked kingdom fell to the new empire of the Medes and Persians.[43]

David Jeremiah with C.C. Carlson: Notice that there are two arms to the silver section of the image, indicating the **divided nature** of the second empire.[44]

divided nature: the two main divisions (the Medes and the Persians)

> **Daniel 2:40** Finally, there will be a fourth kingdom, strong as iron—for iron breaks and smashes everything—and as iron breaks things to pieces, so it will crush and break all the others.

A Fourth Kingdom

There was a fourth world kingdom (see Illustration #9, page 60) in Nebuchadnezzar's dream. Daniel did not identify it, but there is general agreement that the iron kingdom was the Old Roman Empire. That empire replaced the Greeks. The Romans literally crushed all their enemies. It was the major power on earth when Jesus first came.

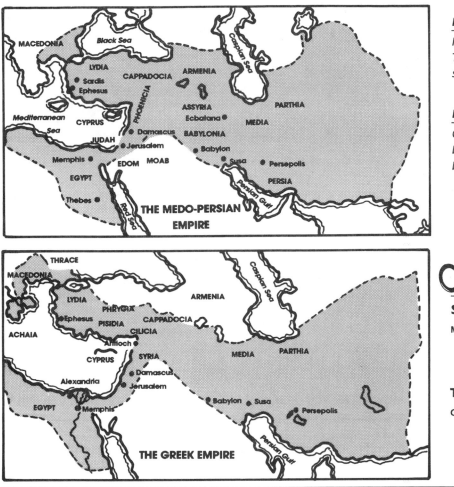

 **KEY Symbols:**

Second Kingdom

MEDES AND PERSIANS

chest of silver
arms of silver

Third Kingdom

GREECE

belly of bronze
thighs of bronze

Charles H. Dyer: The four—Babylon, Medo-Persia, Greece, and Rome—form an unbroken line of descent from Daniel's day till the time of Christ.[45]

What Others
are Saying:

David Hocking: There was no empire in world history that so crushed all of its enemies as Rome did. They were not satisfied just to take over a country and make them pay taxes, they slaughtered them. Rome crushed the peoples so that they would never even consider rebelling.[46]

David Breese: He [Daniel] gives us the **scenario** of history in a few short verses and reminds us of the triumph of God over it all. Because of the emphasis given on this fourth kingdom, we need to think further about Rome and the role it will play as we move toward the **consummation of history**.[47]

scenario: overall outline

consummation of history:
the End of the Age (the End
of the Times of the Gentiles)

Illustration #9

Old Roman Empire—
The legs of iron in
God's Statue.

KEY Symbols:

Fourth Kingdom
OLD ROMAN EMPIRE

legs of iron

☞ **GO TO:**

Revelation 19:11–21
(Second Coming)

Revelation 13:1; 17:12
(ten minor divisions)

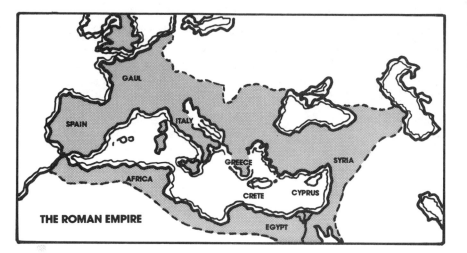

GAUL

SPAIN

ITALY

GREECE

SYRIA

AFRICA

CRETE

CYPRUS

THE ROMAN EMPIRE

EGYPT

> **Daniel 2:41** Just as you saw that the feet and toes were partly of baked clay and partly of iron, so this will be a divided kingdom; yet it will have some of the strength of iron in it, even as you saw iron mixed with clay.

A Fifth Kingdom

Up to this point in Nebuchadnezzar's dream we have been looking at events that are history to us—events that, although they were future to Daniel, are past to us because they have now been fulfilled. In the remainder of Chapter 2 we are going to be looking at a prophecy about the future—events that are now coming on the scene; they have yet to arrive, but we can see them approaching.

Daniel's interpretation moved from an explanation of the legs of iron down to an explanation of the feet and toes made from a mixture of iron and baked clay. This will be a fifth Gentile world kingdom. It will be the last Gentile world kingdom, and shortly after it comes to power it will be destroyed by the <u>Second Coming of Christ</u> (see GWRV, pages 285–292).

Daniel revealed that the last Gentile world kingdom will be a divided world kingdom. Based upon what we have already learned, it is reasonable to assume this fifth kingdom will organize into two main divisions at first corresponding to the two feet of the statue. Later on, it will sub-divide into <u>ten minor divisions</u> (see GWRV, pages 183–185) corresponding to the ten toes of the statue.

Daniel also told us it will be a mixture of iron and baked clay. It

KEY Symbols:

Past History
the first four kingdoms

Future History
the last two kingdoms

is difficult to say exactly what he meant, but it seems it will be a mixture of iron nations coming out of the **Old Roman Empire** and non-iron (baked clay) nations that existed apart from the Old Roman Empire. Those non-iron nations could include countries from Central Europe. It is even possible that the mixture of iron and baked clay could be the United Nations.

The fact that this fifth Gentile world kingdom will have some of the strength of the iron in it means that much of its power will come from the iron nations that were in the Old Roman Empire. They will give the fifth world kingdom power by transferring their weapons, resources and military to it.

Noah Hutchings: According to the prophecy of Daniel, and related prophecies in Revelation, Rome would not be revived through conquest, but rather by common agreement. This prophecy has been fulfilled in our day through the [European] **Common Market Alliance**.[48]

Old Roman Empire: *that part of the world controlled by Rome at the time of Christ*

Peter and Paul Lalonde: Today, a world which feared communism sweeping westward is finding that instead, democracy ("of the people, by the people, for the people") is sweeping eastward. As the two systems adapt to embrace each other, as is the case in Eastern Europe, we may be beginning to see the formative stages of one empire made "partly of iron and partly of clay."[49]

Common Market Alliance: *group of nations in Europe that have joined together for economic reasons*

RELATED CURRENT EVENTS

"The **UN bureaucracy** sees itself as a sort of world government in the making," says Dr. Justus Thurman, a sociologist who studies international organizations at Columbia University. "The Senate [U.S. Senate] wants it to give up that vision. It's a furtive but ferocious fight. I am betting on the UN to come out on top."[50]

According to press reports President Clinton has made promises to some of his colleagues in Europe to help establish a permanent United Nations army. Many in the U.S. Senate are opposed to the idea of American taxpayers funding a world army, but Mr. Clinton gave the UN $200,000 in September 1997 for start-up costs. Experts are now predicting that American contributions will soon reach hundreds of millions of dollars. The "New Roman Empire" now has a fledgling world military.[51]

UN bureaucracy: *United Nations leaders who want to regulate all governments*

Something to Ponder

Some people limit the scope of this government with its two main divisions and ten sub-divisions to Europe. However, this will be a world government. Europe may not rule every nation with an iron fist, but it will try. And its military and economic power will be so great that it will be the major power and influence in the world. Nothing precludes the United Nations from being the world government and Europe taking it over.

KEY Symbols:

Fifth Kingdom

REVIVED ROMAN EMPIRE

*last Gentile kingdom
feet and toes of iron
and baked clay
partly strong and partly
brittle*

Gentile Kingdoms	**Ten Divisions**
1 Babylonian (gold)	
2 Medo-Persian (silver)	
3 Greek (bronze)	
4 Old Roman Empire (iron)	
5 Revived Roman Empire	1
	2
	3
	4
Nations from Europe and the Old Roman Empire (iron and clay)	5
	6
	7
	8
	9
	10

> **Daniel 2:42** As the toes were partly iron and partly clay, so this kingdom will be partly strong and partly brittle.

Strong But Brittle

The fifth and final Gentile world kingdom will lack uniformity. It will be *partly strong and partly brittle* signifying a precarious mixture of strong Old Roman Empire nations and weaker non-Roman Empire nations. They will be brought together by treaties and agreements that will have the outward appearance of unity, but these treaties and agreements will fail to tightly bind the nations together.

Charles H. Dyer: The Achilles' heel of this **military juggernaut** will be its **factionalism**.[52]

Jack Van Impe: It's now official. A United Nations agency is openly advocating the need for a one-world government and global taxation. This declaration by the UN Development Program came to light during the recent World Summit for Social Development in Denmark [March 1995].[53]

```
Another pro-expansion [NATO expansion] point the
internationalists make is: "NATO expansion is
sound strategic policy. By bringing in three
countries now and keeping the door open to fur-
ther enlargement, NATO will prevent the national-
ization of armed forces in new members by
integrating them into a multilateral and trans-
parent defense planning process." So, by expand-
ing NATO we also crush any nationalist movements
in the newly admitted member countries. . . .This
is your international army, then. . . . Countries
are not going to be allowed to have their own
armies; [they will] only have soldiers who par-
ticipate in an international force.[54]
```

> **Daniel 2:43** And just as you saw the iron mixed with baked clay, so the people will be a mixture and will not remain united, any more than iron mixes with clay.

military juggernaut: a powerful military

factionalism: internal differences and dissension

NATO: North Atlantic Treaty Organization

What Others are Saying:

RELATED CURRENT EVENTS

multilateral: a military made up of forces from several countries; a world army

United We Fall

The people in the last Gentile world government will be just like the unstable mixture of iron and baked clay. They will be forced into a one-world government, but they will not stay united.

What Others are Saying:

Grant R. Jeffrey: The basic point to remember is that democracy and citizen input can only occur on a local or national level. Once our nations sign these complicated international agreements, the ability of the public to influence the economic or political situation is nil.[55]

RELATED CURRENT EVENTS

```
The Clinton administration has acted speedily on
the dual goals outlined at the latest Bilderberg
meeting: eliminating racial and ethnic distinc-
tions and letting NATO forces patrol the world as
the UN army. Just days after a Bilderberg par-
ticipant said intermarrying means "racial and
cultural distinctions will blissfully blur"—
leading Americans to accept a "world without
borders," President Clinton picked up the theme
in the oval office. "We want to become a multira-
cial, multiethnic society," Clinton told a group
of black journalists. "This will arguably be the
third great revolution—to prove we literally can
live without having a dominant European culture,"
Clinton said.[56]
```

Bilderberg: a group of European high financiers who meet secretly and promote world government

The Bilderberg group is sometimes referred to as a "World Shadow Government" because they apparently tell world leaders what to do. They are the real force behind the New World Order. Specifically, the group includes Heads of State, European royalty, and heads of multi-national banks and corporations. They are so powerful the major media does their bidding and silences almost all reports on their activities.

Remember This . . .

> **Daniel 2:44** "In the time of those kings, the God of heaven will set up a kingdom that will never be destroyed, nor will it be left to another people. It will crush all those kingdoms and bring them to an end, but it will itself endure forever.

☞ **GO TO:**

Revelation 17:12 (ten)

Psalm 72:11 (bow down)

I John 2:18, 22; 4:3; II John 1:7 (Antichrist)

A Sixth And Final Kingdom

Here is an important clue concerning the Second Coming of Christ and his subsequent reign here on earth. He will return to establish his own kingdom on earth while the one-world government is organized into ten sub-divisions under the leadership of <u>ten kings</u>. And his world kingdom will be different from the Gentile world kingdoms in two ways: 1) it *will never be destroyed*, and 2) it will never be taken over by anyone else.

The kingdom that is to be established by Jesus will bring an end to all rebellion against God. It will bring an end to all sin. All kings will <u>bow down</u> to him, and his kingdom will endure forever.

Grant R. Jeffrey: The Club of Rome, the Trilateral Commission, and the Council on Foreign Relations each use a "ten kingdom" administrative model in their plans for the coming world government. In the Book of Revelation the prophet John revealed that the **<u>Antichrist</u>**, the **Beast** (the first beast of Revelation), and his ten-nation confederacy will rule the world for seven years during the coming Tribulation Period until the **Messiah** returns to establish the Kingdom of God on earth.[57]

Richard Booker: Many people think the world is going to end when Messiah Jesus comes. But the world is not going to end. What is going to end is the present age in which we live. But first, this present world order must come to an end. It must come to an end because it is an anti-God system. The Tribulation Period will bring it to an end. Then Messiah Jesus will come and establish a new world order based on justice and righteousness.[58]

> **Daniel 2:45** This is the meaning of the vision of the rock cut out of a mountain, but not by human hands—a rock that broke the iron, the bronze, the clay, the silver, and the gold to pieces. "The great God has shown the king what will take place in the future. The dream is true and the interpretation is trustworthy."

The Rock

Here is some important information concerning the <u>rock</u>. *Cut out of a mountain, but not by human hands* means the rock will be the work of God. As a world kingdom, it will not come into being

Antichrist: an enemy of Christ who will come during the Tribulation Period

Beast: a person who is full of evil (i.e. the Antichrist)

Messiah: the Christ; Jesus

What Others are Saying:

☞ **GO TO:**

Deuteronomy 32:3, 4, 15 (rock)

KEY Symbols:

Sixth Kingdom
KINGDOM OF GOD ON EARTH

never be destroyed
never be taken over

through the hard work of men. It will come into being through the divine power of God.

It is again stated that the rock will break the other world kingdoms. It is added that God himself revealed these things to the king; that absolutely nothing can change them, and that they will definitely be fulfilled.

J. Vernon McGee: The Lord Jesus himself made it clear that he is that Stone. In his day there were probably more people who understood what he was saying than there are today. In Matthew 21:44 he said, *And whosoever shall fall on this stone shall be broken: but on whomsoever it shall fall, it will grind him to powder* [KJV, King James Version].[59]

> **Daniel 2:46** Then King Nebuchadnezzar fell prostrate before Daniel and paid him honor and ordered that an offering and incense be presented to him.

Flat On His Face

An extraordinary thing happened when Daniel finished revealing the dream and its interpretation. The arrogant and powerful Nebuchadnezzar fell down on his face *before* Daniel and worshiped him. When he got up he commanded that an **offering and incense** be given to Daniel.

Oliver B. Greene: Daniel had purposed in his heart that he would not deny his God, he would not bow to the king, he would not defile himself with the king's meat and wine. Whatsoever he did in Babylon, he would do to the glory of God and not to the glory of the heathen king. Daniel remembered God—and God remembered Daniel.[60]

> **Daniel 2:47** The king said to Daniel, "Surely your God is the God of gods and the Lord of kings and a revealer of mysteries, for you were able to reveal this mystery."

The Father, Son, And Holy Spirit

This does not appear to be a **confession of faith** on the part of Nebuchadnezzar. Notice that he spoke of Daniel's God as *your God* and not *my God*. But it does appear to be an unwitting acknowledgment of the **Trinity**. The *God of gods* is Jehovah God or God the

Father. The *Lord of kings* is the King of kings and Lord of lords or God the Son. The *revealer of mysteries* is the one who <u>searches</u> all things or God the Holy Spirit. Nebuchadnezzar also acknowledged that Daniel had succeeded in revealing the mystery.

> **Daniel 2:48** Then the king placed Daniel in a high position and lavished many gifts on him. He made him ruler over the entire province of Babylon and placed him in charge of all its wise men.

confession of faith: *a public acknowledgment that a person* <u>accepts God and his Son</u>

Trinity: *a word not found in the Bible, but it refers to the idea that God exists in three ways: as God the Father, as God the Son, and as God the Holy Spirit*

Power And Riches I Give To You

Nebuchadnezzar rewarded Daniel by giving him the two things in life that most of society thinks will make a man great: power and riches. When a man has both he is respected, whether he deserves it or not. Daniel was made ruler over the entire province of Babylon; he was put in charge of all the so-called wise men, and he was lavished with many gifts. That would swell the heads of many people, but as we continue we will see that it did not affect the **God-fearing** Daniel.

God-fearing: *submitting to the power and authority of God*

> **Daniel 2:49** Moreover, at Daniel's request the king appointed Shadrach, Meshach, and Abednego administrators over the province of Babylon, while Daniel himself remained at the royal court.

KEY Symbols:

Given to Daniel
power
riches

Remember My Friends

As soon as Daniel was rewarded, he began to reward his friends. One of his first acts was to request some changes. He wanted new appointments for Shadrach, Meshach, and Abednego who had been his prayer partners in this whole matter. They were made administrators over the province of Babylon, so Daniel could remain at the royal court.

KEY Symbols:

God's Statue	Metal	Gentile Kingdom
Head	Gold	Babylonian
Chest and Arms	Silver	Medo-Persian
Belly and Thighs	Bronze	Greek
Legs	Iron	Old Roman Empire
Feet	Iron and Clay	Revived Roman Empire

Study Questions

1. Why did Nebuchadnezzar decree that the astrologers tell him both what the dream was and what it meant?
2. Why were the magicians, enchanters and astrologers unable to tell Nebuchadnezzar his dream and interpret it for him?
3. What six steps did Daniel go through to get an interpretation for Nebuchadnezzar's dream?
4. Who will set up the only kingdom that will never be destroyed?
5. Did Nebuchadnezzar become a believer as a result of Daniel's amazing feat?

CHAPTER WRAP-UP

- Nebuchadnezzar dreamed a disturbing dream that troubled him and interfered with his sleep. (Daniel 2:10)
- Nebuchadnezzar summoned his wise men to reveal the dream and its meaning. In spite of offers of rewards, the wise men were unable to reveal the dream and its meaning. Consequently, Nebuchadnezzar ordered the wise men to be executed.(Daniel 2:2–12)
- When Daniel heard of the king's decree he asked for time, so that he might interpret the dream. Then he went to his friends and urged them to pray for God's mercy. (Daniel 2:13–18)
- God revealed the king's dream and its interpretation to Daniel. It concerned a great statue with a head of gold, chest and arms of silver, belly and thighs of bronze, legs of iron, and feet of part iron and part clay. Each part of the statue represented a different Gentile world kingdom. (Daniel 2:19–43)
- A great rock smashed the statue. The rock (Jesus) grew and filled the earth (representative of the Kingdom of God on earth). (Daniel 2:34, 35, 44, 45)

DANIEL 3

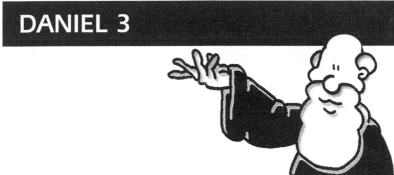

CHAPTER HIGHLIGHTS

- Statue of Gold
- One-World Worship Service
- Three Faithful Jews
- Our God is Able
- A Fourth Man

Let's Get Started

The Bible does not say when the fiery furnace occurred, but according to the Septuagint it took place somewhere between sixteen and twenty years after the events described in Chapter 2. Chapter 1 opens around 605 B.C. when Daniel and his friends were about 13 or 14 years old. Chapter 2 probably took place after the young Jews had completed a few years of schooling; when they were about 17 or 18 years old. All this leads us to believe the events of Chapter 3 occurred around the year 585 B.C., when Shadrach, Meshach, and Abednego were in their early thirties (see Time Line #1, Appendix A).

Not much else had changed. Nebuchadnezzar is still the king and just as arrogant, demanding, and dangerous as ever. The so-called wise men are still serving under Daniel and his friends. They, of course, have forgotten that Daniel knew and interpreted Nebuchadnezzar's dream when they could not. Now they are stewing with jealousy and hurt pride.

M.R. DeHaan: Remember what Jesus said about Daniel; he tells us that Daniel was a prophet and that his prophecies deal with future events. So beyond the immediate lesson of God's care for his own, we look also for a prophetic lesson concerning the future.[1]

What Others are Saying:

Hal Lindsey: I believe the Holy Spirit has selected these true historical incidences out of all of those years that they [the Jews] were under Babylonian captivity, and one incident is under Medo-Persian captivity, to show how God would protect the Jew in the midst of the time when Gentiles would be in power over the whole world. It also shows by application how God will preserve those who believe in him in the midst of the most desperate situation caused by an alien government that is against the true faith.[2]

> **Daniel 3:1** King Nebuchadnezzar made an image of gold, ninety feet high and nine feet wide, and set it up on the plain of Dura in the province of Babylon.

☞ **GO TO:**

Daniel 2 (troubling dream)

Matthew 24:15 (Abomination)

Revelation 7:3–8 (144,000)

Jeremiah 30:7 (Jacob's trouble)

144,000: *marked men from the twelve tribes of Israel*

KEY Symbols:

Nebuchadnezzar's Statue
made of gold
ninety feet high and nine feet wide
very tall and very thin

Illustration #10

Nebuchadnezzar's Statue— Nebuchadnezzar's attempt at immortality.

A Tall Golden Statue (Nebuchadnezzar's Statue)

Sixteen to twenty years had passed, but Nebuchadnezzar still had that <u>troubling dream</u> on his mind. It seems that he was obsessed with it, and I'm sure he did not want his kingdom to come to an end. He obviously liked Daniel, but Nebuchadnezzar probably hoped Daniel was wrong. He wanted Babylon to be the kingdom that would never be destroyed.

So Nebuchadnezzar decided to make a great statue of his own (see Illustration #10, this page). He could have the statue like the one in his dream—a statue of gold, silver, bronze, iron, and clay. But he did not want that. He did not want the kingdom of Babylon to be overthrown. He did not want those other Gentile world kingdoms to appear. He did not want the Times of the Gentiles to come to an end or Jesus to come and set up his own kingdom.

Gold represented the kingdom of Babylon in the king's dream so he made this statue entirely of gold. Obviously Nebuchadnezzar refused to believe his kingdom would be overthrown. He made a statue to contradict his dream, a statue to signify that his kingdom would last forever, a statue to signify that the prophecies of God would not come to pass.

The statue was ninety feet high and nine feet wide. Something that tall could easily be seen from a great distance, especially something placed in a wide open space and made of glistening gold. It would also be disproportionate, very tall and very thin.

GOD'S WORD FOR THE BIBLICALLY-INEPT

It was set up in the Plain of Dura (see Illustration #2, page 19). *Smith's Bible Dictionary* tells us an archeologist named Oppert found the site almost a century ago. It is southeast of Babylon and at a place now called Duair.

What Others are Saying:

M.R. DeHaan: Now remember that with the captivity of Israel and the ascendancy of the empire of Babylon, the "Times of the Gentiles" began, which was to run until the coming again of the Messiah the Christ at the end of the Tribulation. This age (Times) of the Gentiles begins and ends with a great image, a false god. . . .

Nebuchadnezzar is one of many types and shadows of this coming superman, the Antichrist. Babylon is a forerunner of the great world empire over which [the Antichrist] will rule in the Tribulation Period. The image Nebuchadnezzar erected is a type of the image of Revelation 13 [see GWRV, pages 196–197] and is called in Scripture the "Abomination of Desolation." The three young Hebrews represent the remnant of the Tribulation, the **one hundred forty-four thousand** [144,000; see GWRV, page 108]. Because they refuse to bow before Satan they are cast into a fiery furnace on the Day of Jacob's Trouble [the Tribulation Period], but delivered by the Lord and highly exalted.[3]

J. Vernon McGee: The Plain of Dura was like an airport—flat and expansive—allowing a great multitude to assemble for the worship of the image, actually the worship of the king.[4]

> **Daniel 3:2** He then summoned the **satraps**, **prefects**, governors, advisers, treasurers, judges, magistrates, and all the other provincial officials to come to the dedication of the image he had set up.

All Must Come

Nebuchadnezzar called on the government leaders in the top seven levels (or offices) of his world kingdom plus many more to attend a dedication service for the *image*. It would be the greatest gathering of politicians and bureaucrats the world had ever seen.

☞ **GO TO:**

Exodus 20:4–6 (image)

satrap: *an office just below the king (similar to a prince or vice-president)*

What Others are Saying:

David Jeremiah with C.C. Carlson: The basic reason King Nebuchadnezzar had this image set up in the desert is that he was doing his best to unite his kingdom religiously. He ruled over a vast empire, and he decided the way to unify his empire was to

bring it together and have everyone bow down before this image. In the end-times the Antichrist will do the same.[5]

J. Vernon McGee: There are many who are working toward a world religion today, including the denominations which make up the **World Council of Churches**. They are moving toward a world religion, and, my friend, they are going to leave Jesus out altogether.[6]

```
In the spirit of the 1993 Parliament, held in
Chicago, the Council for a Parliament of the
World's Religions (CPWR) works to convene a new
Parliament of the World's Religions at a new site
every five years. The 1999 Parliament will be
held in early December, in Cape Town, South
Africa.[7]
```

Not everyone agrees on what these government offices actually were, but there is little question that they were the top offices in Babylon's world government.

> **Daniel 3:3** So the satraps, prefects, governors, advisers, treasurers, judges, magistrates, and all the other provincial officials assembled for the dedication of the image that King Nebuchadnezzar had set up, and they stood before it.

A One-World Worship Service

We can logically assume that the city of Babylon began to bustle as the great dedication day approached. With important dignitaries arriving from all over the world the level of excitement probably reached a new high. Then the well-planned-for dedication arrived and a great crowd moved to the Plain of Dura. They stood before the image like the multitudes who stand before our flag at a baseball game.

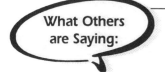

What Others are Saying:

Oliver B. Greene: We are not in ignorance concerning Nimrod and his attempt to build a tower to heaven, as recorded in the tenth and eleventh chapters of Genesis—and Nebuchadnezzar was at this point walking in the footsteps of Nimrod, by-passing the God of heaven to set up his own god, drawing his own blueprints for a world-wide kingdom that should never crumble and fall.[8]

The Bible does not say whether or not Daniel was present during this worship service, but many Bible experts hold the position that he wasn't. Their reasoning being that if Daniel had been present he would have refused to bow and also been thrown into the fiery furnace. Since that did not happen most experts contend he was away tending to the king's business.

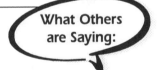

Something to Ponder

• • •

Nimrod was the <u>great-grandson of Noah</u>. He lived after the flood and was a lawless person who tried to establish a world religion and a world government. He is credited with founding several new cities including Babylon, and as the head of the first great anti-God civilization, he is a forerunner of the Antichrist.

> **Daniel 3:4** Then the herald loudly proclaimed, "This is what you are commanded to do, O peoples, nations, and men of every language:

☞ **GO TO:**

Revelation 13:7, 8 (earth)

Revelation 16:13 (False Prophet)

The First Decree

One of Nebuchadnezzar's **heralds** made an announcement. It was a loud command that <u>people from all the earth</u> had to follow.

What Others are Saying:

David Hocking: The Bible says that all the world will worship him (the Antichrist). He will be inspired by Satan himself, to deceive the world. He will have a <u>false prophet</u>, a religious leader, who will stir up the hearts of the people of the world to worship him.[9]

herald: a messenger similar to a master of ceremonies

KEY Symbols:

The Pulpit Commentary: True religion is nothing less than the purest love of the human heart pouring itself out, in service or in speech, unto the living God; and if love, must ever be spontaneous and free, in order to be love at all, so must be the piety of the human soul. Spontaneity is a necessity in religion. If compulsion be employed, its essence evaporates, its spirit disappears.[10]

Decrees
Nebuchadnezzar
- herald

Antichrist
- False Prophet

☞ **GO TO:**

Revelation 13:8 (image)

> **Daniel 3:5** As soon as you hear the sound of the **horn**, **flute**, **zither**, **lyre**, **harp**, **pipes**, and all kinds of music, you must fall down and worship the image of gold that King Nebuchadnezzar has set up.

lyre: an ancient hand-held instrument similar to a small harp

harp: a large stringed instrument

pipes: musical tubes of some type

angel: a heavenly being who serves God; usually a messenger

Remember This . . .

☞ **GO TO:**

Revelation 13:15 (refuse to worship)

II Timothy 3:12-17 (evil men)

False Prophet: the spiritual leader of the one-world religion

All Must Bow

The herald told everyone that at the sound of music they were commanded to fall down and worship the golden <u>image</u>. With the music coming from many different kinds of instruments (see Illustration #11, page 75) being played at the same time, it appears that the musicians were acting similar to a band or orchestra in a modern church service. But this was no church service, and there may have been many who wished they didn't have to be there.

David Hocking: The Babylonians loved music. In the celebrations of the rebuilt city that Saddam Hussein had, to which he invited guests from all over the world in 1988-89, he did exactly the same thing. He had all of these instruments (ancient instruments) being played, big processionals and big spectacular programs to display the glory of rebuilt Babylon. He tried to duplicate what Nebuchadnezzar did.[11]

David Jeremiah with C.C. Carlson: Almost every major cult and -ism, every false religion, has found some way to use music for its perverted purposes. It's a type of mind control. I believe with all of my heart that music belongs to God. It belongs to the **angels**. It belongs to God's people. The world will take what belongs to God and prostitute it for its own purposes.[12]

Not everyone agrees on what these instruments were, but there is little question that music was an important part of this worship service.

> **Daniel 3:6** Whoever does not fall down and worship will immediately be thrown into a blazing furnace."

Oops! A Little Too Hot for Me

Everything was fast and furious. Freedom of religion and <u>worship</u> was suspended. An <u>evil man</u> commanded that all who did not immediately fall down and worship the image would die. There would be no delay. A giant furnace was set to swiftly carry out the sentence. In essence the command was "bow or burn." What a choice! Many would rather bow and try to justify what they did at a later time.

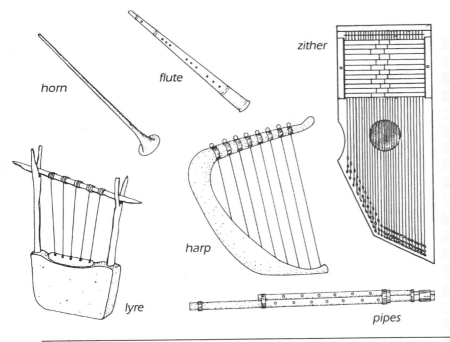

horn

flute

zither

harp

lyre

pipes

David Breese: The Scripture specifically predicts the coming of the anti-Christ and warns us that he will invent a global religion where everyone will be forced to worship. . . . The religion of the anti-Christ will be:

Satanic—People will worship the dragon [Satan] which is another name in Scripture for the devil.

Humanistic—They will worship the beast [Antichrist] who is the anti-Christ himself.

Universal—All the world will be involved.

Ecumenical—Every religion in the world, except Christianity will be involved.

Phenomenalistic—The anti-Christ will work miracles and even call down fire from heaven.

Pagan—The world will worship the Image of the Beast.

Cruel—All who do not worship will be killed.[13]

```
In June 1941, it [Auschwitz] became an extermina-
tion center when four huge gas chambers were
installed. Rudolf Hess, who directed the camp for
more than three years, testified at the Nuremberg
trials that over 2 ½ million people were executed
at Auschwitz and 500,000 more starved to death.
Most people who died at Auschwitz were Jews from
German-controlled countries.[14]
```

What Others are Saying:

KEY Symbols:

Bow and Worship

Nebuchadnezzar
- his great statue

Antichrist
- the Image of the Beast

RELATED CURRENT EVENTS

Forcing people to worship this image is similar to what the spiritual leader called the **False Prophet** (see GWRV, pages 194–198) will do during the Tribulation Period. As the head of the one-world religion during that time he will force people to worship the Image of the Beast and give all allegiance to the Antichrist (the one-world political leader). All who refuse will be killed.

☞ **GO TO:**

II Timothy 3:1–5
(form of godliness)

> **Daniel 3:7** Therefore, as soon as they heard the sound of the horn, flute, zither, lyre, harp, and all kinds of music, all the peoples, nations, and men of every language fell down and worshiped the image of gold that King Nebuchadnezzar had set up.

So Much Music

What an event. Most people knew what they were going to do in this worship service. There was very little hesitation or reluctance, if any. As soon as the music started people from all over the world hit the ground and the prayers to this idol started to flow. But this was just a form of godliness. It was not true worship and about the only positive thing it accomplished was the appeasement of Satan and Nebuchadnezzar.

**What Others
are Saying:**

Noah Hutchings: This was the plan which the devil put into Nebuchadnezzar's head to prevent Christ's glorious reign over the earth, and the devil has not changed his plan because this was the best one that he could come up with. And this is why the Antichrist will again try to succeed where Nebuchadnezzar failed.[15]

**RELATED
CURRENT
EVENTS**

A measure awaits action in Congress that would, also for the first time, create a White House office to monitor religious persecution. "The persecution of people of faith is the great untold human rights story of the decade," says Rep. Frank Wolf (R-VA), sponsor of the "Freedom from Religious Persecution Act of 1997." Legislation to address this problem is long overdue, but so is prayer. That is why organizers of The International Day of Prayer for the Persecuted Church (IDOP)—actually a "season of prayer" from September 28 to November 16—hope to enlist 50,000 churches to join in collective prayer for the persecuted Church. Believers in 110 nations will join in prayer and action on behalf of believers victimized by Islamic and communist regimes.[16]

> **Daniel 3:8** At this time some astrologers came forward and denounced the Jews.

☞ **GO TO:**

Daniel 2:24
(lives spared)

Down With The Jews

This may have been an act of jealousy, a power grab, an effort to stamp out religious competition or just plain old **anti-Semitism**. Some of the astrologers were acting as spies at this event. Their lives had been spared about sixteen years earlier when Daniel and his three friends prayed to their God and received the revelation of Nebuchadnezzar's dream. Whatever the reason, the astrologers ignored what the Jews had done for them and reported the Jews for disobeying this new command.

anti-Semitism: prejudice or hostility against Jews

Hal Lindsey: There is one thing that you will find about religion. Religion does not like any competition. And religion will do away with competition in the most bloody barbaric way. Some of the worst crimes in history have been committed by religion.[17]

What Others are Saying:

Communist regimes, having learned from the role faith played in the downfall of Marxist rulers in Eastern Europe, severely restrict religious expression. In China, for example, where more Christians are imprisoned for their faith than in any other country, "house church" leaders suffer imprisonment, torture, and death. The most severe repression takes place in Sudan where the Islamic regime, under the influence of militant Islamic extremists, is pursuing a *Jihad*, or "holy war," against the nation's Christian and non-Muslim population. Sudanese military attack the Christian civilian population, subjecting men to abduction and torture, while kidnaping women and children who are sold into slavery for as little as $15.[18]

RELATED CURRENT EVENTS

Daniel said, *Destroy not the wise men of Babylon: bring me in before the king, and I will show unto the king the interpretation* (Daniel 2:24). *Then the king placed Daniel in a high position and lavished many gifts on him. He made him ruler over the*

Remember This . . .

entire province of Babylon and placed him in charge of all its wise men. Moreover, at Daniel's request the king appointed Shadrach, Meshach, and Abednego administrators over the province of Babylon, while Daniel himself remained at the royal court (Daniel 2:48, 49).

> **Daniel 3:9** They said to King Nebuchadnezzar, "O king, live forever!

O King, You're The Best!

adoration: admiration, love or worship

dispatches: letters, messages, official communications

The astrologers approached the haughty Nebuchadnezzar with an expression of **adoration** that was often used to flatter rulers in ancient times. It was also sometimes used in **dispatches** like the modern day "Dear Sir." But the fact is that it was pretty ridiculous and something everyone knew to be untrue. In essence they were saying, "O king, you are so great, and we love you so much, we hope you will live forever."

What Others are Saying:

The Pulpit Commentary: The politics and warfare of that period proceeded on the assumption that the gods directly interfered in the affairs of the nations. Any slight done to the national god would—as it was believed—be avenged on the nation who had suffered it to pass unpunished.[19]

☞ **GO TO:**

Isaiah 54:17 (no weapon)

> **Daniel 3:10** You have issued a decree, O king, that everyone who hears the sound of the horn, flute, zither, lyre, harp, pipes, and all kinds of music must fall down and worship the image of gold,

Remember Your Word

The astrologers reminded Nebuchadnezzar of his decree. It was not that they thought that he was getting senile. No, it was that they wanted him to be embarrassed and angered at what appeared to be an element of disrespect, ingratitude, and outright rebellion. The astrologers wanted to make sure that a confrontation took place and that Nebuchadnezzar was sufficiently stirred up when it happened. In this case, we see that they were using the hotheaded king to their own advantage. He was their <u>weapon</u> against any Jews who would not bow with Shadrach, Meshach, and Abednego among them.

David Hocking: We know very clearly that it [the evidence against Shadrach, Meshach and Abednego] was based on the decree of Nebuchadnezzar and the Chaldeans saw their opportunity. They didn't like those Jewish captives being in power and they were going to do whatever they could to get them out. They knew, because of their allegiance to the Lord God of Israel, that they were not going to do what Nebuchadnezzar commanded. So, they mentioned it to him.[20]

What Others are Saying:

While dedicated Christians around the world are in favor of Israel's existence, their governments are not. The only political ally on the side of Israel is the United States—and many in Washington are wavering. In light of these developments let us appeal to the court of heaven for the final verdict in the case.[21]

RELATED CURRENT EVENTS

> **Daniel 3:11** and that whoever does not fall down and worship will be thrown into a blazing furnace.

Into The Fire They Must Go

This is a remainder of Nebuchadnezzar's **Satanic** decree. The astrologers were making sure that he remembered what he said the penalty for disobedience would be. They did not want any mistakes. They wanted to see their immediate rulers (Shadrach, Meshach, and Abednego) dead.

Satanic: inspired by Satan

David Jeremiah with C.C. Carlson: Solomon said, *Jealousy . . . burns like blazing fire, a mighty flame* (Song of Songs 8:6), and the Chaldean crowd wanted to smell the seared flesh of Shadrach, Meshach, and Abednego.[22]

What Others are Saying:

A homemade video televised Thursday [October 23, 1997] shows German army officers giving the Hitler salute, talking about killing Jews, and making anti-Semitic comments.[23]

RELATED CURRENT EVENTS

> **Daniel 3:12** But there are some Jews whom you have set over the affairs of the province of Babylon— Shadrach, Meshach, and Abednego—who pay no attention to you, O king. They neither serve your gods nor worship the image of gold you have set up."

☞ **GO TO:**

Acts 5:27–29 (obey God instead of men)

II Timothy 3:1–4 (the Bible says)

KEY Symbols:

Last Days

people will be like the astrologers

- abusive
- slanderous
- treacherous

people will be like Nebuchadnezzar

- rash
- without self-control

Something to Ponder

last days: *the last days of the Times of the Gentiles*

☞ **GO TO:**

Psalm 2:12 (moment)

Three Faithful Jews

This is a list of accusations and a plain statement of who was being accused. It was alleged that Shadrach, Meshach, and Abednego:

1) *pay no attention to you*

2) *neither serve your gods*

3) *nor worship the image of gold you have set up*

Pay attention to the fact that the astrologers mentioned the political position—*you have set over the affairs of the province of Babylon*—of Shadrach, Meshach, and Abednego. Their point is that, in their opinion, the three Jews, being high officials in Nebuchadnezzar's one-world kingdom, should have been examples of <u>obedience</u>.

<u>The Bible says</u> in the **last days** terrible times will come because people will be *abusive, slanderous, and treacherous* [characteristics of the astrologers], *rash, and without self-control* [characteristics of Nebuchadnezzar]. How bad do you think it will get for Christians and Jews trying to live in a world like that, a world that embraces a one-world religion and a one-world dictator?

> **Daniel 3:13** Furious with rage, Nebuchadnezzar summoned Shadrach, Meshach, and Abednego. So these men were brought before the king,

Come To Me At Once

Nebuchadnezzar was like a stick of dynamite with a short fuse. He had a real anger problem, was easily upset, and quick to fly into a rage. It was during one of these rages that he summoned Shadrach, Meshach, and Abednego.

Something to Ponder

Most of us would be afraid of a powerful man like Nebuchadnezzar. We would be careful around him and try to stay on his good side. But how many of us realize that the Bible says, *the wrath of God can flare up in a <u>moment</u>*? And how many of us are careful to please him?

> **Daniel 3:14** and Nebuchadnezzar said to them, "Is it true, Shadrach, Meshach and Abednego, that you do not serve my gods or worship the image of gold I have set up?

Say It Isn't So

Here we learn what Nebuchadnezzar thought about the character of his astrologers versus the character of Shadrach, Meshach, and Abednego. It shows that he did not wholeheartedly believe his astrologers, and he was willing to give Daniel's three friends the benefit of the doubt.

RELATED CURRENT EVENTS

```
The United Religions' structure will be patterned
after the structure of the United Nations. The
goal will be to produce consensus among religions
in the same way that the United Nations has been
able to bring about a consensus among the nations
of the World Community. The danger is that, once a
strong enough consensus among the major religions
of the world is produced, any religion unwilling
to conform to the will of the majority will be
considered guilty of religious extremism. . . .
Already it has been stated that one of the main
advantages of the UR will be to eradicate reli-
gious extremism. How much religious control (sup-
pression) will the world be willing to accept for
the cause of achieving world peace?[24]
```

☞ **GO TO:**

Genesis 3:14, 15 KJV (seed of Satan, seed of woman)

blasphemy: irreverence for God

> **Daniel 3:15** Now when you hear the sound of the horn, flute, zither, lyre, harp, pipes, and all kinds of music, if you are ready to fall down and worship the image I made, very good. But if you do not worship it, you will be thrown immediately into a blazing furnace. Then what god will be able to rescue you from my hand?"

Come On, Just One Little Bow

Nebuchadnezzar's confrontation with Shadrach, Meshach, and Abednego continued. He must have loved these three men because he was giving them a second chance to redeem themselves. If they would reconsider and bow down to his image, he would put out the fire. If they would not reconsider, disown their God, and bow down, he would cast them into the fire. He was turning this into a religious competition, a war of the gods so to speak.

KEY Symbols:

powers of darkness
*Satanic forces, wicked
people*

powers of light
*heavenly forces, godly
people*

KEY Symbols:

Seed of the Woman
Jesus

Seed of the Serpent
*the followers of Satan;
the unsaved*

RELATED
CURRENT
EVENTS

*Remember
This . . .*

WARNING

Noah Hutchings: Music had a role in creating this kind of **blasphemy** in the minds of German youth, and today music is being used to help destroy our country. It does make a difference what kind of music your children listen to; and it does make a difference what kind of music you have in your church. Music that is uplifting and soul-building is a gift of God and leads man to seek the one who will put a new song in his life.[25]

David Jeremiah with C.C. Carlson: The history of the church has been written in blood. There will always be warfare between the powers of darkness and the powers of light, and there will always be pagan rulers who will cry out in sarcasm, *Who is that god?*[26]

M.R. DeHaan: From all this you will see that the history of man is not a succession of isolated events. It is all part of one grand plan, a struggle between God and Satan, the <u>seed of the woman and the seed of the serpent</u>. History is a unit and while we see the events as isolated occurrences, underneath it all is one great line and program, the struggle of Satan against the Christ and God's people.[27]

According to the April 4, 1994 issue of *The Vancouver Sun*, the feminists [at a New Age conference called "Re-imagining 1993"] considered passages from pop singer Helen Reddy and novelist Alice Walker to have the same authority as Scripture. . . . The Presbyterian Church (USA) donated $66,000 to sponsor the event according to *The Christian American*. The music at the conference reflected New Age concepts. For instance, participants sang, "Oh great spirit, earth and wind and sea, you are inside and all around me."[28]

About 16 to 20 years earlier Daniel interpreted the king's first dream. Nebuchadnezzar fell on his face before Daniel and said, *Surely your God is the God of gods and the Lord of kings and a revealer of mysteries, for you were able to reveal this mystery* (Daniel 2:46, 47). He knew the Jewish God then. Now Nebuchadnezzar is pretending he has forgotten him.

Jesus said, *Do not put the Lord your God to the test* (Matthew 4:7).

> **Daniel 3:16** Shadrach, Meshach, and Abednego replied to the king, "O Nebuchadnezzar, we do not need to defend ourselves before you in this matter.

☞ **GO TO:**

Exodus 20:3–6 (bow down)

Matthew 22:21 (God)

Answer #1

This is the first of a threefold response to the fiery king. Their minds were made up. They did not have to think about it. They did not have to pray about it. There was no need to reconsider their actions. They had purposed in their hearts that they would not <u>bow down</u> under any circumstances. Their worship would go to <u>God</u>.

What Others are Saying:

Noah Hutchings: The answer that these three young faithful Jews gave this heathen monarch is a classic, and it should be the Christian's answer to every temptation we are called to face. In essence, they told the king that his question about God being able to deliver them from the fiery furnace required no great wisdom or deliberation to answer, because the answer was self-evident.[29]

KEY Symbols:

Answer #1
We do not need to defend ourselves.

David Jeremiah with C.C. Carlson: This is what this world is crying for: men and women, boys and girls, who have conviction of heart and who do not change their convictions on the basis of their circumstances. These three men knew what God wanted them to do, and they weren't afraid of the consequences.[30]

Do you think it took courage for Shadrach, Meshach, and Abednego to stand up to this violent king? Where do you think their courage came from? If they were afraid of him, nothing is said about it.

Something to Ponder

> **Daniel 3:17** If we are thrown into the blazing furnace, the God we serve is able to save us from it, and he will rescue us from your hand, O king.

☞ **GO TO:**

Isaiah 26:3, 4 (trust)

Matthew 22:37–39 (love)

Micah 4:5 (for ever)

Answer #2

This is the second part of the threefold response. These men <u>trusted</u> in their God. They knew he could save their lives and actually believed he would. It seems obvious that they <u>loved</u> him very much and were committed to following him <u>for ever and ever</u>.

What Others are Saying:

Hal Lindsey: There are some things that are worth dying for. There are some things where if your life is put on the line, you put it on the line.[31]

Ed Young: How did they know this was worth dying for? They had made a lifetime commitment to love God and keep his commandments. It involved their mind, their heart, and their will.[32]

KEY Symbols:

Answer #2

God is able to save us

RELATED CURRENT EVENTS

```
In the mid 1960s Christians were sent to
forced-labor camps [in Cuba], where many were
tortured. Official repression of religious activ-
ity continues today. Private houses of worship
face harassment; churches cannot operate schools,
use television or radio, or buy printing supplies
or equipment from any Cuban business; missionary
activity is forbidden.33
```

Something to Ponder

Nebuchadnezzar asked, *What God will be able to rescue you from my hand* (Daniel 3:15)? Shadrach, Meshach, and Abednego responded, *the God we serve is able to save us from it, and he will rescue us from your hand, O king* (Daniel 3:17). Why don't *we* have this kind of faith?

> **Daniel 3:18** But even if he does not, we want you to know, O king, that we will not serve your gods or worship the image of gold you have set up."

☞ **GO TO:**

Hebrews 4:16 (grace)

Joshua 1:8, 9 (successful)

Answer #3

This is the third part of the threefold response. The **grace of God** was upon Shadrach, Meshach, and Abednego. Even if God did not deliver them they would not change their minds; they would not worship any other god or anyone's image.

grace of God: the undeserved favor of God

Does success by the world's standards ruin people? Some stop serving the Lord when they prosper enough to afford vacations, boats, or a membership in the Country Club. Are they really <u>successful</u>? Did success by the world's standards affect Shadrach, Meshach, and Abednego? Were they failures?

Something to Ponder

• • •

There is something more important than life—*Who* we serve.

> **Daniel 3:19** Then Nebuchadnezzar was furious with Shadrach, Meshach, and Abednego, and his attitude toward them changed. He ordered the furnace heated seven times hotter than usual

☞ **GO TO:**

Jeremiah 29:22 (burned in the fire)

I Peter 4:12–19 (trial)

Seven Times Hotter

In modern language, Nebuchadnezzar *blew his top*. He exploded in anger at Shadrach, Meshach and Abednego. We have already noted that he must have loved them and was giving them a second chance, but his whole attitude toward them changed at this point. He was so angry he ordered the great furnace heated *seven times hotter*. He was burning with rage and he wanted their bodies to be totally <u>burned up in the fire</u>.

Wallace Emerson: It is entirely characteristic that Nebuchadnezzar should react with rage and fury at the public resistance of these men. After all, these very men have been promoted by him and ought, above all others, to remember that they were picked, even though foreigners and captives, for promotion to high office . . . they owed their preeminence to Nebuchadnezzar alone. Their refusal to worship is not only a public affront to the authority of a powerful king but is an insult to his god and a challenge to the very stability of his empire.[34]

What Others are Saying:

KEY Symbols:

Answer #3
We will not serve your gods.
We will not worship your image of gold.

Noah Hutchings: The Babylonians used a particular type of smelting furnace [see Illustration #12, page 86]. The furnace would be heated to a certain temperature, depending upon the type of metal they desired to melt. The metal would be thrown in at the top from a ramp, and the molten mass would be extracted at the bottom and poured into molds. It is evident that Nebuchadnezzar used this type of furnace to dispose of undesirables and those who questioned his absolute sovereignty over the empire.[35]

> **Daniel 3:20** and commanded some of the strongest soldiers in his army to tie up Shadrach, Meshach, and Abednego and throw them into the blazing furnace.

☞ **GO TO:**

Matthew 9:2 (faith)

Into The Fire They Must Go

We must wonder if Nebuchadnezzar was afraid of Shadrach, Meshach, and Abednego or if he feared their God. Perhaps he <u>noticed their faith</u> and was afraid their God would help them es-

Illustration #12

Fiery Furnace—Babylonian furnaces were used to melt metal.

KEY Symbols:

Faith (in Jesus)

substance of things hoped for (will turn such things as going to heaven and eternal life into reality)

evidence of things not seen (changed lives and good works) point to the existence of God)

Something to Ponder

cape. Whatever the case, it appears he did not want to take any chances, so he issued a command for his strongest men to tie them up and cast them into the blazing furnace.

The Bible says, *Faith is the substance of things hoped for, the evidence of things not seen* (Hebrews 11:1 KJV). To further explain, divide this faith into two parts:

1) The substance of things hoped for—*substance* is something that is real. *Things hoped for* are such things as going to heaven and having eternal life. So faith in Jesus is how the Christian's hopes in heaven and eternal life become a reality.

2) The evidence of things not seen—*evidence* is a clue, sign, or proof of something. *Things not seen* include God, Jesus, and the Holy Spirit. A detective may not see who committed a crime but he looks for clues that will help him identify the criminal. He tries to find things he can see that will point him to what he cannot see. Faith is the same way because faith in Jesus (which can be seen through changes in people and the production of good works) is the evidence of things not seen (God, Jesus, and the Holy Spirit).

It seems likely that Nebuchadnezzar thought the faith of Shadrach, Meshach, and Abednego could be evidence of the existence or reality of their God. That would explain why he ordered his strongest men to tie them up. He saw their faith and was afraid of what he could not see.

> **Daniel 3:21** So these men, wearing their robes, trousers, turbans, and other clothes, were bound and thrown into the blazing furnace.

royal occasion: an event attended by the king

turbans: scarves they wore around their hats or heads

No Time To Change

This was a **royal occasion**, so Shadrach, Meshach, and Abednego were properly dressed in their official attire for such an event. Their formal wear included some expensive robes, **turbans**, and fancy silk garments. They were not even given time to change out of these outfits or do anything else. Nebuchadnezzar's best men quickly seized them, tied them up, and threw them into the furnace. We can almost visualize it in our mind. When the king gave this terrible command his top soldiers moved with great haste.

> **Daniel 3:22** The king's command was so urgent and the furnace so hot that the flames of the fire killed the soldiers who took up Shadrach, Meshach, and Abednego,

Mark of the Beast: the mark, number, or name of the Antichrist

Oops! I Didn't Mean Them Too

The upset king went overboard with his demands. His command was extreme and insistent. The furnace was roaring, and the flames were so high that his best soldiers died when they took Shadrach, Meshach, and Abednego to the top. They gave their life for this angry tyrant.

KEY Symbols:

Fiery Furnace
lake of burning sulfur
Lake of Fire

David Hocking: When you serve the Lord, the wicked are going to be taken care of by the Word of God. Nobody is going to get away with anything.[36]

What Others are Saying:

Remember This . . .

Those who oppose God and his people during the Tribulation Period will not get away with anything either. In Revelation their fiery furnace is called "the lake of burning sulfur." John said, *Then I saw the beast (the Antichrist) and the kings of the earth and their armies gathered together to make war against the rider on the horse (Jesus) and his army (God's people). But the beast was captured, and with him the false prophet who had per-*

KEY Symbols:

Rider on the Horse
Jesus

His Army
God's people

☞ **GO TO:**

Romans 8:28 (good)

Revelation 6:9 (kill
multitudes)

formed the miraculous signs on his behalf. With these signs he had deluded those who had received the **mark of the beast** (see GWRV, pages 198–202) *and worshiped his image. The two of them were thrown alive into the fiery lake of burning sulfur. The rest of them* (the wicked) *were killed with the sword that came out of the mouth of the rider on the horse, and all the birds gorged themselves on their flesh* (Revelation 19:19–21).

> **Daniel 3:23** and these three men, firmly tied, fell into the blazing furnace.

In They Went

The intense heat did not kill Shadrach, Meshach, and Abednego, but they were still tied up when they fell into the furnace. Nothing is said about the great crowd who witnessed all of this, but we can guess that many were stunned. It is likely that some even screamed when this happened. On the surface, it looks like a terrible thing, but <u>good</u> things did come out of it.

What Others
are Saying:

*Remember
This . . .*

David Breese: I think that God has told us this because he wants to remind us of the beautiful possibilities of trusting him no matter what may be the circumstance of our life.[37]

Standing firm in our faith will not keep Christians out of persecution. Jesus said, *If you belonged to the world, it would love you as its own. As it is, you do not belong to the world, but I have chosen you out of the world. That is why the world hates you* (John 15:19). The Antichrist and his followers <u>will kill multitudes</u> of Christians during the Tribulation Period because of their strong obedience to the Word of God and their testimony of faith.

> **Daniel 3:24** Then King Nebuchadnezzar leaped to his feet in amazement and asked his advisers, "Weren't there three men that we tied up and threw into the fire?" They replied, "Certainly, O king."

What Is Going On Here?

The furnaces in those days had a large opening in the side so they could be stoked and fueled. Nebuchadnezzar could probably see Shadrach, Meshach, and Abednego through such an opening. As

☞ **GO TO:**

Matthew 24:21; Revelation 2:22 KJV; 7:14 (Tribulation Period)

Revelation 16:13 (False Prophet)

Daniel 3:4 (herald)

he looked, he was expecting, and hoping, to see his three godly advisors burned to a crisp. That did not happen, and he could not believe his eyes.

Ed Young: There are two things that are generally present when you see a display of the supernatural work of God with man and in history. First of all, you see the kingdom of God is in some sort of crisis in the human domain. The second thing you see, the children of God, the sons and daughters of God, are under tremendous pressure. And when you see a kingdom crisis and the children of God under pressure, so many times there you see an outbreak of the supernatural.[38]

Daniel 9:27; 11:31; Matthew 24:15 (Abomination)

Although this is a true story about an actual event, we have seen that it is filled with prophetic significance. The <u>Tribulation Period</u> will be like this blazing furnace. The Antichrist will be like Nebuchadnezzar—a proud, godless, violent, out-of-control, one-world, Gentile leader. The <u>False Prophet</u> will be like the <u>herald</u> who told everyone to worship the statue, and the <u>Abomination of Desolation</u> will be like Nebuchadnezzar's grotesque, odd-shaped statue. Shadrach, Meshach, and Abednego will be like the Jews (and possibly others who follow God) who go through the Tribulation Period. The Fourth Man in the furnace will be like Jesus who helps his people. But who or what will be like Daniel and why is he not present? Could it be that the Church is like Daniel and it will not be present during the Tribulation Period because of the **Rapture** (see GWRV, pages 63–67)?

Something to Ponder

Rapture: when the Church is removed from the earth

> **Daniel 3:25** He said, "Look! I see four men walking around in the fire, unbound and unharmed, and the fourth looks like a son of the gods."

☞ **GO TO:**

Matthew 17:1–13 (Jesus transfigured)

A Fourth Man

Nebuchadnezzar was counting and what he saw startled him. There were four men walking around in the fire, not three. No one was tied up and no one was harmed, but the Fourth Man looked like a son of the gods. This was a perceptive statement to be coming from a pagan king, and most experts think he was looking at the **pre-incarnate** Christ.

pre-incarnate: before Jesus was born to Joseph and Mary

theophany: a visit from God

Mount of Transfiguration: the mountain where <u>Jesus was transfigured</u>

KEY Symbols:

Tribulation Period
furnace

Antichrist
Nebuchadnezzar

False Prophet
herald

Abomination of Desolation
Nebuchadnezzar's golden statue

Shadrach, Meshach, and Abednego
144,000 Jews

Something to Ponder

Pentecost: a holy day celebrated 50 days after Easter

Never in living memory has a fascination with the paranormal been so epidemic. Psychic hot lines have mushroomed into a billion-dollar industry since their debut in the mid-80's. . . . Mainstream publishers churn out scores of books with titles like *The Executive Mystic*, touting the usefulness of psi in office politics or mate hunting. This year's hottest nonfiction best-seller is *Talking to Heaven*, by a man who claims to converse telepathically with the dead. Web sites advertise courses in clairvoyance . . . at hundreds of dollars a pop. Although polls have shown for decades that up to two thirds of the population believe in psychic phenomena, unprecedented millions are now willing to validate their faith with a Visa card. This upsurge surely derives momentum from the New Age movement, with its shifting search for esoteric antidotes to premillennial anxieties. But it also reflects some startling developments in parapsychology—developments that present the scoffers with their toughest challenges ever.[39]

The appearance of the Fourth Man in the furnace is called a **theophany**. Some other theophanies in the Bible are:

1) The appearance of God to Moses as the burning bush (Exodus 3:2).
2) The appearance of God to lead the Jews as a pillar of cloud and a pillar of fire (Exodus 13:21).
3) The appearance of God to Moses and the Jews as thunder, lightning, and smoke on Mount Sinai (Exodus 19:18-20).
4) The appearance of Jesus to Peter, James, and John as dazzling white clothes on the **Mount of Transfiguration** (Mark 9:2–7).
5) The appearance of the Holy Spirit to the 120 believers as wind and tongues of fire on **Pentecost** (Acts 2:2, 3).

There is wide agreement among Bible experts that the Fourth Man in the fire was Jesus. The Son of God visited earth during this world-wide religious service and took control of the fire. This shows that the supernatural world is real and a power to be reckoned with by everyone.

> **Daniel 3:26** Nebuchadnezzar then approached the opening of the blazing furnace and shouted, "Shadrach, Meshach, and Abednego, servants of the Most High God, come out! Come here!" So Shadrach, Meshach, and Abednego came out of the fire,

☞ **GO TO:**

Isaiah 43:2 (walk through the fire)

Romans 8:31 (God is for us)

Most High God: the Supreme God

Dancing Before The Lord

Nebuchadnezzar was probably sweating and nervous as he approached the opening in the side of the blazing furnace. He could see that the ropes used to bind these men had burned away. He could see them walking around in the <u>fire</u>, and it seemed like <u>God</u> was with them. They were, however, in no hurry to get out. This confirmed something Nebuchadnezzar already knew—they were servants of the **Most High God**. He asked them to leave the furnace and come to him.

Ed Young: If you are a son or daughter of God, you will not be in there (the fiery furnace of trials, persecution, sickness, etc.) alone. You will never be alone because the Lord Jesus Christ will be in the middle of the fire with you.[40]

What Others are Saying:

Hal Lindsey: I would rather be running amok in the furnace with the Son of God than to be walking around bound outside the furnace.[41]

> **Daniel 3:27** and the satraps, prefects, governors, and royal advisers crowded around them. They saw that the fire had not harmed their bodies, nor was a hair of their heads singed; their robes were not scorched, and there was no smell of fire on them.

☞ **GO TO:**

Revelation 13:15–17 (take his mark)

Not Even A Singed Hair

This startling event had completely changed directions. It was so filled with tension that worship of the great image had long been forgotten. Everyone was crowding around Shadrach, Meshach, and Abednego to inspect them. Fire had killed Nebuchadnezzar's best soldiers, and burned the ropes off the other three men, but fire had not:

1) burned their bodies,
2) singed their hair,
3) scorched their robes, or
4) left its smell on them.

What a tremendous testimony to the power of God! Nebuchadnezzar had tried to start a one-world religion by giving glory to his statue, but before it was all over, God got all the glory instead.

Many will choose to die during the Tribulation Period rather than worship the image of the Antichrist, <u>take his mark</u>, his number, or the number of his name.

Remember This . . .

guardian angels: angels assigned to help children and believers

> **Daniel 3:28** Then Nebuchadnezzar said, "Praise be to the God of Shadrach, Meshach, and Abednego, who has sent his angel and rescued his servants! They trusted in him and defied the king's command and were willing to give up their lives rather than serve or worship any god except their own God.

Praise Be To God

This miracle changed things dramatically. Nebuchadnezzar was the powerful leader of a one-world government, but he quickly accepted defeat and began to praise God. He was somewhat confused not knowing the difference between *the Most High God*, one like a *son of the gods*, and *his angel*, but he knows that he had seen a heavenly visitor. He acknowledged the great faith and faithfulness of Shadrach, Meshach, and Abednego, their trust in God, and their courage to stand firm and be faithful in the face of death.

What Others are Saying:

David Breese: Daniel and his friends became a fabulous testimony for the Lord so that the kingdom of Babylon was profoundly affected by their testimony and the impact of their lives. Your testimony, the impact of your life, can produce a result in the world. . . .[42]

Do angels watch over us? Jesus was warning us about teaching or doing things that lead little children astray or into sin when he said, *See that you do not look down on one of these little ones. For I tell you that their angels in heaven always see the face of my Father in heaven* (Matthew 18:10). Many scholars think this means each one of us has one or more **guardian angels**.

Remember This . . .

> **Daniel 3:29** Therefore I decree that the people of any nation or language who say anything against the God of Shadrach, Meshach, and Abednego be cut into pieces and their houses be turned into piles of rubble, for no other god can save in this way."

The Second Decree

Nebuchadnezzar issued another decree. If anyone said anything against the God of Shadrach, Meshach, and Abednego:

1) they would be cut into pieces, and

2) their houses would be destroyed.

The reason behind this decree is very important. The most powerful man in the world said, *no other god can save in this way*. This is an acknowledgment before the world of the omnipotence and superiority of the Jew's God.

David Breese: I believe that we (the United States) must come back to the place where we live by the kind of faith that is absolutely sure that God walks with us every step that we take, and whatever may be the adversity that we face, Jesus Christ will make us equal to the occasion.[43]

Nebuchadnezzar's first decree stated, *everyone who hears the sound of the horn, flute, zither, lyre, harp, pipes, and all kinds of music must fall down and worship the image of gold, and that whoever does not fall down and worship will be thrown into a blazing furnace* (Daniel 3:10, 11). It was very difficult for a king to change or rescind a decree, but here, Nebuchadnezzar came close to doing that. Here is a small step away from paganism and idolatry and a giant step toward the True and Living God.

> **Daniel 3:30** Then the king promoted Shadrach, Meshach, and Abednego in the province of Babylon.

Rewards For The Worthy

God let these three young men endure a terrible test, and because of their faithfulness he let them be rewarded. They received promotions giving them even more power than they had held before. This was a great upset for those who had tried to eliminate Shadrach, Meshach, and Abednego.

KEY Symbols:

First Decree
bow down to my statue or die

Second Decree
say anything against their God and you will die

What Others are Saying:

Something to Ponder

KEY POINT

God's will and purpose for man and this earth cannot be changed by human will or power.

Noah Hutchings: The overall object lesson of Chapter 3 is that God's will and purpose for man and this earth cannot be changed by human will or power. Nebuchadnezzar, though it had been revealed to him the course of history by Daniel, still sought to change God's plan and purpose.[44]

Study Questions

1. What motive did the astrologers have for telling the king that Shadrach, Meshach, and Abednego did not obey his decree? Why is that bad, and how does it apply to us?

2. What decree did Nebuchadnezzar issue and what was the penalty for disobedience? If given this choice during the Tribulation Period, what would you do?

3. Do you think the three Jews would have worshiped the golden image if they had believed God would not save them from the fire?

4. What amazing sight did Nebuchadnezzar see in the fire? Why was it amazing and what did he ask the three Jews to do?

5. How did Nebuchadnezzar change his decree? What does it show about free speech and freedom of worship in Babylon?

CHAPTER WRAP-UP

- Nebuchadnezzar was hoping to prove that his disturbing dream in Chapter 2 was not true, so he built a great statue. It was gold from head to foot and contradicted Daniel's interpretation of the dream. Nebuchadnezzar was trying to show that his kingdom would last forever. (Daniel 3:1)

- Nebuchadnezzar held a worldwide worship service to dedicate his great statue. The service began with music. People from all nations were present and ordered to bow or suffer a terrible punishment—being thrown into a blazing furnace. (Daniel 3:2–6)

- Nebuchadnezzar was furious when he was told that three Jews did not obey his command. Although he gave them a second chance, they still refused. (Daniel 3:8–18)

- The answer given by the Jews angered the king even more. He had the furnace heated to its maximum capacity, then commanded some of his best men to tie up the Jews and throw them into the fire—but the fire had no effect on them. (Daniel 3:19–21, 27)

- When Nebuchadnezzar saw a Fourth Man in the fire he was amazed. He saw that the fire had no effect on Shadrach, Meshach, and Abednego, so he asked them to come out of the furnace. Then he praised their God and promoted them. (Daniel 3:24–30)

DANIEL 4

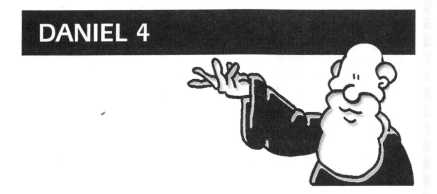

CHAPTER HIGHLIGHTS

- Written Testimony
- Another Terrible Dream
- Refusal to Repent
- The King is Humbled
- The King is Healed

Let's Get Started

Time is passing (see Time Line #1, Appendix A). Daniel has been in Babylon for more than 40 years and is now well past 50 years old. Nebuchadnezzar is in his early 70's, nearing the end of his reign, and the end of his life. A big change has come over him, and we are now going to see what caused it.

To better understand this change in the king's life, this chapter is told by the king himself. It is his personal written testimony.

> **Daniel 4:1** King Nebuchadnezzar, To the peoples, nations and men of every language, who live in all the world: May you prosper greatly!

Hear Me, Hear Me

We are beginning to look at one of the most ancient written testimonies known to mankind. It appears to have been written by the great king himself. He presents it as a true historical event. Could this once violent king have become a **saved** man? At one time he would have been a poor role model as a wild barbarian, but at this time he was setting a good example for everyone to follow. Here he tells the whole world what God did for him.

It is a tragedy that so many people today, even church members, will not do what Nebuchadnezzar did—tell the world about what God has done. God deserves better.

☞ **GO TO:**

Ephesians 2:8, 9 (saved)

Daniel 3:29 (people)

saved: to receive forgiveness of sins and eternal life

Something to Ponder

☞ **GO TO:**

Genesis 9:12, 13 (sign)

Exodus 3:20 (wonders)

signs: evidence of things like miracles and covenants

wonders: supernatural events

> **Daniel 4:2** It is my pleasure to tell you about the miraculous signs and wonders that the Most High God has performed for me.

The Most High God

It is my pleasure indicates he was sharing this testimony out of his own desire to do so. He was not being coerced or forced. It was his genuine desire and a pleasing thing to him to be able to reveal these things to the world. Miraculous **signs** and **wonders** had taken place—amazing things that the Most High God had performed for Nebuchadnezzar personally.

What Others are Saying:

Remember This . . .

David Jeremiah with C.C. Carlson: He didn't stand at a podium and mumble, he shared his testimony with enthusiasm. He wanted the whole world to know what God had done for him.[1]

The Most High God is the same God Shadrach, Meshach, and Abednego worshipped. When Nebuchadnezzar approached the opening in the side of the fiery furnace he said, *Shadrach, Meshach, and Abednego, servants of the Most High God, come out!* (Daniel 3:26).

☞ **GO TO:**

Hebrews 2:3 (great)

Psalm 145:13 (dominion)

Matthew 25:46; John 3:16 (eternal)

dominion: power and authority

> **Daniel 4:3** How great are his signs, how mighty his wonders! His kingdom is an eternal kingdom; his dominion endures from generation to generation.

Signs And Wonders

The evidence of God is revealed through <u>great</u> signs. The amazing miracles of God are mighty wonders. The kingdom of God is a spiritual kingdom, not a physical kingdom, and his **dominion** is <u>eternal</u>.

The *death of Jesus* is a great sign of God's love; the *miracle of Jesus' resurrection* could be called a mighty wonder; and *heaven* is a part of his spiritual (or eternal) kingdom. These three great signs provide evidence of God.

Remember This . . .

The Antichrist, the False Prophet, and some of their followers will perform great signs and wonders during the Tribulation Period. Jesus said, *false Christs and false prophets will appear and perform great signs and miracles to deceive even the elect—if that were possible* (Matthew 24:24).

> **Daniel 4:4** I, Nebuchadnezzar, was at home in my palace, contented, and prosperous.

A New Man?

This is the opening statement in Nebuchadnezzar's testimony. It tells us where he was, and how he perceived himself. He looked at his life and said he was pleased. He was happy and prospering. He had soldiers to guard him, servants to wait on him, and wise men to advise him; he had anything money could buy. He even built one of the seven greatest wonders of the world.

The Seven Wonders of the Ancient World
1) Pyramids of Egypt at Giza
2) Hanging gardens of Babylon
3) Temple of Artemis at Ephesus
4) Statue of Zeus at Olympia, Greece
5) Mausoleum at Halicarnassus in southwestern Turkey
6) Colossus of Rhodes on the island of Rhodes
7) Lighthouse of Alexandria on the island of Pharos near Alexandria, Egypt

Noah Hutchings: Nebuchadnezzar, materially and politically speaking, was a self-satisfied man. But spiritually, he was greatly troubled. He had peace in his kingdom, but there was no peace within his soul. He was financially wealthy but spiritually destitute. He believed there was a God because he had personally witnessed his mighty works, but there had been no personal acceptance of God as King of kings and Lord of lords.[2]

David Hocking We have a lot of archaeological evidence about Nebuchadnezzar and Babylon at that time. The Greek historians refer to Nebuchadnezzar's building of Babylon as one of the seven wonders of the ancient world. . . . He built seventeen temples within the city of Babylon not counting the great walls around Babylon and the famous Ishtar Gate (see Illustration #13, p. 98).[3]

Uriah Smith: [Nebuchadnezzar] had subdued Syria, Phoenicia, Judea, Egypt, and Arabia. It was probably these great conquests that puffed him up and betrayed him into such vanity and self-confidence. And this very time, when he felt most at rest and secure, when it was most unlikely that he would allow a thought

☞ **GO TO:**

Luke 16:19-31 (rich)

Ishtar Gate: the main gate leading into the city of Babylon and dedicated to their goddess of fertility

hell: a place of eternal punishment

KEY POINT

Earthly kingdoms and kings are only temporary, but God's kingdom will last forever.

What Others are Saying:

KEY Symbols:

Death of Jesus
a great sign of God's love

Resurrection of Jesus
one of God's amazing miracles

to disturb his self-complacent tranquillity—this very time God takes to trouble him with fears and forebodings.[4]

Jesus talked about a <u>rich man</u> who *dressed in purple and fine linen and lived in luxury every day*. This man had the best the world had to offer, but great riches and fine living are not everything. The rich man died without God. He left all his worldly possessions behind and wound up begging for mercy in **hell**. When death comes the man who has a good relationship with God is rich, but the man who has no relationship with him is a pauper.

Remember This . . .

Illustration #13

Ishtar Gate—The main entrance to Babylon which Saddam Hussein has rebuilt. Note the depictions of Babylonian gods like Marduuk.

> **Daniel 4:5** I had a dream that made me afraid. As I was lying in my bed, the images and visions that passed through my mind terrified me.

A Second Dream

In Chapter 5 we will learn that Babylon was an armed fortress with very high and very thick walls, massive gates, soldiers constantly on guard, a deep moat surrounding the city, and drawbridges that could quickly be closed. It would seem that Nebuchadnezzar had nothing to be afraid of, but not so. Something scared him, even terrified him. It was not enemy troops, but **images** and **visions** that passed through his head while he was lying in his bed.

☞ **GO TO:**

Acts 10:1–23 (Peter)

Deuteronomy 13:1–5 (rebellion)

Deuteronomy 18:9–14 (astrologers)

What Others are Saying:

Rick Joyner: Another higher level prophetic experience is a **trance**, such as <u>Peter</u> had when he was first instructed to go to the house of Cornelius and preach the gospel to the Gentiles for the first time, and such as Paul had when he prayed in the Temple in Acts 22.

Trances were a common experience of the Biblical prophets. Trances are like dreaming when you are awake. Instead of just seeing a "screen" like in an open vision, you feel like you are in the movie, that you are actually there in a strange way.[5]

God warned the Jews to beware of people who foretell by dreams and to put them to death if they used dreams to <u>teach rebellion</u> against him. He did <u>not want them to listen to astrologers</u>, diviners, magicians, soothsayers, interpreters of dreams, or those who contact the dead. He instructed them to <u>listen to his prophet</u>. But he gave Daniel the <u>ability to understand</u> visions and dreams. Could it be that the interpretations of vision and dreams can be demonic or Satanic, and the only safe interpretations are those that come directly from God through his special prophets?

Jesus was talking about the End of the Age when he said, *For false Christs and false prophets will appear and perform great signs and miracles to deceive even **the elect**—if that were possible. See I have told you ahead of time* (Matthew 25:24, 25). Beware of modern-day "prophets" with ear-tickling "prophecies" and "great signs." Their messages may be partly right, but multitudes will be deceived by that which is wrong. Messages, prophecies, and visions are false if:

1) they contradict anything in the Bible
2) they approve of anything the Bible calls sin
3) they speak against Jesus (anything from his virgin birth to his resurrection)
4) they approve or call for harm to those who believe in Jesus
5) they stress political correctness above Biblical correctness
6) they call for worship of any god, goddess, or being other than the God of Heaven
7) they come from other religions or ignore the Bible

> **Daniel 4:6** So I commanded that all the wise men of Babylon be brought before me to interpret the dream for me.

Deuteronomy 19:15–19 (his prophet)

Daniel 1:17 (ability to understand)

Something to Ponder

WARNING

images: *here it refers to mental pictures*

visions: *images that occur while in a* **trance**

trance: *a dazed or stunned condition similar to sleep*

the elect: *true Christians*

KEY POINT

If God gives the dream only God can give the interpretation, and he will not give the interpretation to anyone who is not one of his servants.

☞ GO TO:

Daniel 2:2, 12 (wise men)

Not Again!

It seems that Nebuchadnezzar had to learn some lessons the hard way—by experience. He should have called for Daniel to come in and interpret the dream, but he did not. He did the same worthless thing he did about 40 years earlier. He called for his _wise men_.

What Others are Saying:

David Hocking: We can dream strange things and it may be because of what we ate, or we're not feeling well. We need to be careful about that. However, in Old Testament times before God's written revelation, God literally spoke to people and he used dreams. Dreams had to be interpreted.[6]

Something to Ponder

Nebuchadnezzar may have thought he did not need Daniel because this was a different situation. He could not remember the dream he had 40 years earlier, but he could remember this one. Perhaps he thought all these great wise men from all over the world could explain at least this dream since they would know what it was.

Daniel 4:7 When the magicians, enchanters, astrologers, and diviners came, I told them the dream, but they could not interpret it for me.

☞ **GO TO:**

Daniel 2:2–11 (before)

channeler: *person through whom evil forces or spirits communicate*

apostle: *someone commissioned by God to represent Christ*

We Couldn't Do It Then, So How Can We Do It Now?

Nebuchadnezzar tells us that the result was the same as before. These supposedly gifted people came in, listened to the dream, and still couldn't interpret it.

What Others are Saying:

Ron Carlson and Ed Decker: The number one television program in Russia today features a New Age psychic and **channeler** who is on every morning in Moscow. His program has captivated the nation.[7]

Something to Ponder

Acts 16:16–19 tells us about a slave girl who was possessed by an evil spirit. She was very good at telling fortunes and predicting the future. She even earned a lot of money for her owners. But after the **Apostle** Paul commanded the evil spirit to come out of her *in the name of Jesus Christ,* she lost the ability to do these things. Some psychics and fortune tellers may be successful because they are demon-possessed.

> **Daniel 4:8** Finally, Daniel came into my presence and I told him the dream. (He is called Belteshazzar, after the name of my god, and the spirit of the holy gods is in him.)

Holy Before The Lord

After the wise men failed miserably again there was one last resort—the **true prophet** of God. Daniel went in to see the king and Nebuchadnezzar told him the dream. This was the same Daniel whose name was changed to <u>Belteshazzar</u>. Nebuchadnezzar confirmed that Daniel had a special spirit in him that was holy.

The *only spirit* in the Bible that is called "holy" is the **<u>Holy Spirit</u>**, the *only god* that is called "holy" is the *God of heaven*, and the *only person* who is called "holy" is the <u>Holy One of God</u>—*Jesus*.

Ron Carlson and Ed Decker: Historical antecedents [the roots or ancestry] of the New Age Movement can be found in several major religious groups:

1) witchcraft and **shamanism** (prehistoric)
2) astrology (circa 2000 B.C.)
3) **Hinduism** and **Yoga** (circa 1800 B.C.)[8]

Some of the Characteristics of the New Age Movement Include:

astrology—The study of the stars and planets to determine their supposed influence on persons or events (Deuteronomy 4:19; 17:2–5; Isaiah 47:12–15).

fortune telling—The effort to predict events in one's life before they happen (Deuteronomy 18:9–14; Jeremiah 14:14; Acts 13:6–10).

metaphysics—The study of hard to understand metaphors, and fanciful or elaborate images (Genesis 41:8).

occultism—Belief in Satanic or evil powers (Leviticus 20:6–27; Acts 16:16; 19:13–19).

reincarnation—The passing of a soul into another body (Hebrews 9:27).

witchcraft—The effort to obtain power to do evil (Deuteronomy 18:9–14; Acts 8:9–24).

☞ **GO TO:**

Daniel 1:7 (Belteshazzar)

Luke 4:1 (Holy Spirit)

Mark 1:24 (Holy One)

Psalm 51:11; Isaiah 63:10 (Old)

true prophet: *one who speaks under the influence of God*

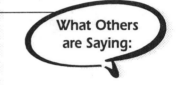

What Others are Saying:

Holy Spirit: *the Spirit of God or God himself*

Something to Ponder

shamanism: *a primitive religion that believes certain priests can influence spiritual powers that control things*

Hinduism: *the common religion of India*

Yoga: *a Hindu technique designed to help a person reach the state of union with the Hindu concept of God (a.k.a. enlightenment)*

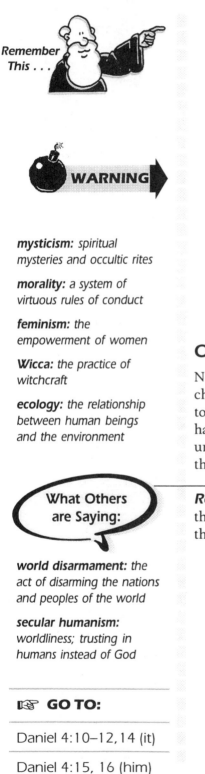

Remember This . . .

Some people think the existence of the Holy Spirit is solely a New Testament concept, but he is <u>mentioned in the Old Testament</u> too. Some Old Testament writers visualized God as an invisible spirit. They could not see him, but they believed he was just as real as the wind or our breath. They even believed he could live in people. Because of the special abilities that Daniel had displayed, Nebuchadnezzar believed that the Holy Spirit lived in him.

WARNING

Jesus said, *"Watch out for false prophets. They come to you in sheep's clothing, but inwardly they are ferocious wolves"* (Matthew 7:15).

> **Daniel 4:9** I said, "Belteshazzar, chief of the magicians, I know that the spirit of the holy gods is in you, and no mystery is too difficult for you. Here is my dream; interpret it for me.

mysticism: *spiritual mysteries and occultic rites*

morality: *a system of virtuous rules of conduct*

feminism: *the empowerment of women*

Wicca: *the practice of witchcraft*

ecology: *the relationship between human beings and the environment*

Only You Know The Answer

Nebuchadnezzar told the world that he addressed Daniel as the chief of his wise men and that he complemented Daniel before he told him what he wanted. He expressed his certainty that Daniel had a special spirit of the holy gods in him and praised him on his understanding of mysteries or hidden truths. Then he explained that he had a dream he wanted Daniel to interpret.

What Others are Saying:

Ron Carlson and Ed Decker: The immediate beginnings of the New Age Movement can be found in the cultural ferment of the 1960's:

1) the hippie counterculture

2) interest in drugs and **mysticism**

3) destruction of traditional **morality**

4) **feminism**, **Wicca**, and **ecology**

5) **world disarmament** and various "hunger" projects

7) **secular humanism**[9]

world disarmament: *the act of disarming the nations and peoples of the world*

secular humanism: *worldliness; trusting in humans instead of God*

> **Daniel 4:10** These are the visions I saw while lying in my bed: I looked, and there before me stood a tree in the middle of the land. Its height was enormous.

☞ **GO TO:**

Daniel 4:10–12, 14 (it)

Daniel 4:15, 16 (him)

A Tree In The Middle

Here we are told what the dream was. Later we will be told its interpretation. But it will be helpful, at this time, to understand that a tree is sometimes used in Scripture as a symbol of something else. For example:

1) A tree can symbolize a man. *He* [the man who follows God] *is like a tree planted by streams of water, which yields its fruit in season and whose leaf does not wither* (Psalm 1:3). *He* [the man who trusts God] *will be like a tree planted by the water that sends out its roots by the stream* (Jeremiah 17:8).

2) A tree can symbolize a nation. *Consider Assyria, once a cedar in Lebanon, with beautiful branches overshadowing the forest; it towered on high, its top above the thick foliage* (Ezekiel 31:3).

KEY Symbols:

Tree (it)
a man (him), or a nation (it)

Uriah Smith: Babylon, where Nebuchadnezzar reigned, was about in the center of the then known world.[10]

What Others are Saying:

David Jeremiah with C.C. Carlson: The strange thing is that in the beginning of the dream the tree was an "<u>it</u>," but before the end of the description it becomes "<u>him</u>."[11]

> **Daniel 4:11** The tree grew large and strong and its top touched the sky; it was visible to the ends of the earth.

It Reaches To The Heavens

The tree became so large and so strong that its highest branches reached into the heavens allowing it to be seen all over the world. Never before had there been such a great tree.

Keep in mind the fact that this tree can be a symbol of a man, and if it is, then it is easy to see how this part of the dream refers to a man's accomplishments—his authority, power, and fame. This would be a man whose achievements and notoriety far exceeded those of most men. He would be a man of <u>sovereignty, greatness, glory and splendor</u>. A man known to all the world.

☞ **GO TO:**

Daniel 4:25 (sovereign)

I Chronicles 29:11 (greatness)

Isaiah 61:3 (splendor)

KEY Symbols:

Tree (it)
large and strong
- great power and authority

visible to the ends of the earth
- famous

☞ **GO TO:**

Jeremiah 27:6 (wild animals)

> **Daniel 4:12** Its leaves were beautiful, its fruit abundant, and on it was food for all. Under it the beasts of the field found shelter, and the birds of the air lived in its branches; from it every creature was fed.

A Tree Of Protection And Plenty

This tree was covered with beautiful leaves. It was a fruit tree loaded with enough delicious fruit to feed everyone. It was also a shade tree with strong thick branches. <u>Wild animals</u> could stand under it for protection from the sun, wind, and rain, and the birds could nest in its branches.

What Others are Saying:

Uriah Smith: What could represent more plainly and forcibly the fact that Nebuchadnezzar ruled his kingdom in such a way as to afford the fullest protection, support, and prosperity to all his subjects? Really to accomplish this is the perfection of earthly governments, and the highest glory of any kingdom.[12]

☞ **GO TO:**

Matthew 1:20; Luke 1:26 (angel)

> **Daniel 4:13** "In the visions I saw while lying in my bed, I looked, and there before me was a messenger, a holy one, coming down from heaven.

A UFO?

This is a complex verse surrounded in controversy. It is plain that Nebuchadnezzar was lying on his bed and that he saw someone coming down from heaven, but there is much disagreement about who or what that someone was. Some experts believe the *messenger* and the *holy one* are two different types of angelic beings. Others think the *messenger* is a *holy one*. Here it looks like there is just one "holy messenger," but when we get to Daniel 4:17 we will discover *messengers* (plural).

KEY Symbols:

Tree (it)

its leaves were beautiful

its fruit abundant

under it the beasts of the field found shelter

the birds of the air lived in its branches

from it every creature was fed

RELATED CURRENT EVENTS

American-born **Beit Shemesh** [a city in Israel] resident Barry Chaimish, a self-professed UFOlogist, says, "Israel is recognized as an international UFO hot spot—with an unsurpassed quantity and quality of evidence." In January 1995, a crew from Paramount TV's "Sightings" program came to Israel to film an episode and ended up with enough material for three, two of which have aired to a global audience estimated at 60 million. UFOlogists are at a loss to explain their lack of sightings in Israel's near neighbors; it is as if the aliens, unlike most earthlings, are aware of Israel's borders.[13]

The Jewish **Talmud** teaches that God has a council of angels who rule over matters and issue decrees in much the same fashion as the Jewish **Sanhedrin** did during the earthly life of Jesus. There even seems to be a hierarchy of angels who rule over some or all of the nations. Could it be that Nebuchadnezzar saw an <u>angel</u> coming down to earth?

> **Daniel 4:14** He called in a loud voice: 'Cut down the tree and trim off its branches; strip off its leaves and scatter its fruit. Let the animals flee from under it and the birds from its branches.

Timber!

It would be wise to pay attention to the sequence of events here. The messenger said:

1) The tree would be <u>cut down</u>.
2) The branches would be cut off.
3) The leaves would be stripped off.
4) The fruit would be scattered.
5) The animals would flee.
6) The birds would be scattered.

This shows that the tree would go through a great calamity, but it would be worse than that. There would be consequences that would affect every living thing dependent upon it.

Angels, Angels, Angels

Up until just a few years ago, very little was said in our modern society about the ministry of angels. But all of that has changed. In recent years, we have rediscovered the existence and activity of angels. As the morals of our society decline and we approach the coming Tribulation Period, we are becoming more aware of the activity of angelic beings. According to the Bible, angels will be very active during the Tribulation Period. Not all, but most will be involved in carrying out the judgments of God. The following angels are part of the Book of Revelation:

Talmud: a book of Jewish sacred writings

Something to Ponder

☞ **GO TO:**

Luke 13:1-9 (cut down)

Sanhedrin: a council of Jews similar to the U.S. Supreme Court

KEY Symbols:

Tree (it)
cut down
branches cut off
leaves stripped off
fruit scattered
animals flee
birds scattered

Remember This . . .

four horsemen of the Apocalypse: *riders on the four horses mentioned in the sixth chapter of Revelation*

winds of earth: *air breezes coming from any point on the compass*

seal of the Living God: *a mark or symbol used by God to identify and protect his people*

Abyss: *a deep pit where demons are kept*

Euphrates River: *a great river in Iraq known as the dividing line between east and west*

archangel: *a leader or angel of the highest rank*

sickle: *an implement for cutting grain*

millstone: *a large round, flat stone (doughnut-shaped) used for grinding corn, wheat, or other grain*

Four Living Creatures—restrain and command the **four horsemen of the Apocalypse** and worship God (4:6, 8)

Four Angels—control the **winds of the earth** (7:1)

Angel from the East—carries the **seal of the Living God** (7:2)

Angel with Trumpet #1—brings hail, fire, and blood to burn up one-third of the plants (8:7)

Angel with Trumpet #2—throws a huge mountain into the sea to pollute one-third of the sea, kill one-third of the sea creatures, and sink one-third of the ships (8:8, 9)

Angel with Trumpet #3—causes a blazing object to fall to earth causing one-third of the fresh water to be polluted (8:10, 11)

Angel with Trumpet #4—causes heavenly bodies to be struck causing one-third of the sun, moon, and stars to be darkened (8:12)

Angel with Trumpet #5—opens the **Abyss** which releases the demon-possessed locusts (9:1)

Angel with Trumpet #6—causes the four angels to be released at the **Euphrates River**, and one-third of mankind killed (9:13)

Four Fallen Angels—four powerful allies of Satan (9:14)

Mighty Angel—claims the earth for his King (10:1)

Angel with Trumpet #7—sounds a heavenly declaration of praise (11:15)

Michael—God's head **archangel** in battle (12:7)

Angel #1—proclaims the eternal Gospel to all people (14:6)

Angel #2—declares the fall of Babylon (14:8)

Angel #3—warns against worshiping the Antichrist or taking the Mark of the Beast (14:9)

Angel #4—takes his **sickle** and reaps the earth because the harvest is ready (14:15)

Angel #5—brings a second sickle from God (14:17)

Angel #6—tells the fourth angel to take his sharp sickle and gather the clusters of grapes (14:18)

Angel with Bowl #1—brings ugly and painful sores (16:2)

Angel with Bowl #2—causes the sea to turn to blood, and everything in it to die (16:3)

Angel with Bowl #3—causes rivers and springs of water to turn to blood (16:4)

Angel with Bowl #4—causes the sun to scorch people with fire (16:8)

Angel with Bowl #5—brings darkness over all the earth (16:10)

Angel with Bowl #6—causes the Euphrates River to dry up (16:12)

Angel with Bowl #7—proclaims "It is done!" (16:17)

Angel that Illuminates the Earth—sheds light since he was in the presence of God (18:1)

Angel Throwing **Millstone** into Sea—symbol of Babylon being destroyed forever (18:21)

Angel that is Unnamed—has the key to open the Abyss and a great chain to bind Satan (20:1)

> **Daniel 4:15** But let the stump and its roots, bound with iron and bronze, remain in the ground, in the grass of the field. " 'Let him be drenched with the dew of heaven, and let him live with the animals among the plants of the earth.

A Hedge Of Protection

Here we have an act of mercy. It shows that the coming calamity would not be permanent. The messenger said:

1) Leave the stump in the ground.
2) Leave the roots in the ground.
3) Bind them with iron and brass.
4) Do not disturb the grass around them.
5) Let him be watered with the dew of heaven.
6) Let him live.
7) Let him dwell with the animals among the plants of the earth.

In essence, the instruction is to cut the tree down but not to kill it. Surround the stump and its roots with a <u>hedge</u> or fence of iron and bronze, so they cannot be harmed. Preserve and protect the life of the tree. Give him water and let him live.

The last sentence provides an important clue about this verse because it starts referring to the tree as a *him*. This dream about a tree is actually a dream about a man.

KEY POINT

Notice the change starting in verse 15. All of a sudden this tree is a *him* instead of an *it*. This may be one of the things that terrified Nebuchadnezzar. He must have wondered if he was the *him*.

☞ **GO TO:**

Job 1:10 (hedge)

Acts 17:28 (in him)

KEY Symbols:

Tree (it)
> *leave the stump in the ground*
> *leave its roots in the ground*
> *bind them with iron and brass*
> *do not disturb the grass around them*

KEY Symbols:

Tree (him)
> *watered with the dew of heaven*
> *will live*
> *will dwell with the animals*

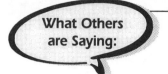
David Breese: We are not autonomous. We are not masters of our own destiny. *In him we live* and *move and have our being.*[14]

Oliver B. Greene: The idea is that the mighty tree would fall, yet there would remain life in its root, and this would spring up again—a most striking image of what would happen to Nebuchadnezzar after he should be cast down from his throne, and then restored to his reason and to power.[15]

 **GO TO:**

Revelation 12:14
(Tribulation Period)

> **Daniel 4:16** Let his mind be changed from that of a man and let him be given the mind of an animal, till seven times pass by for him.

Seven Years

The messenger turned his thoughts to the man's mind. He decreed that the man's mind would be changed. It would no longer be the mind of a man but would be transformed into the mind of an animal. This mental affliction would last for seven years.

What Others are Saying:

KEY Symbols:

Tree (him)
his mind changed to that of an animal for seven years

Uriah Smith: "Let seven times pass over him," said the decree. This is plain, literal narration; hence the time is here to be understood literally. How long a period is denoted? This may be determined by ascertaining how long Nebuchadnezzar, in fulfillment of this prediction, was driven out to have his dwelling with the beasts of the field; and this, Josephus [a first century historian] informs us, was seven years. A *time* then, denotes one year.[16]

David Hocking: Seven years is not much. We see a lot of people going longer than that. I spoke to a man who has wasted (in his own terms) twenty-six years running away from God.[17]

Remember This . . .

It is very important to remember that *seven times* means seven years. From that we calculate that "one time" equals one year; also that "one-half time" equals one-half year; also that the "dividing of a time" equals the dividing of a year or one-half year; and last of all, that "times" equals two years. It is important to remember this because it explains other major verses in the Bible. *He* [the Antichrist] *will speak against the Most High and oppress his saints and try to change the set times and the laws. The saints will be handed over to him for a time* [one year], *times* [two more years], *and half a time* [one-half year] which will be the last 3 1/2 years of the Tribulation Period (Daniel 7:25). *The woman [Israel] (see GWRV page 178) was given the two wings of a great eagle, so that she might fly to the place prepared for her in the desert* (probably Petra—see GWRV, page 174), *where she would be taken care of for a time* [one year], *times* [two more years], *and a half time, out of the serpent's* [Satan's] *reach* which will be the last 3 1/2 years of the Tribulation Period.

> **Daniel 4:17** " 'The decision is announced by messengers, the holy ones declare the verdict, so that the living may know that the Most High is sovereign over the kingdoms of men and gives them to anyone he wishes and sets over them the lowliest of men.'

God, The Decision-Maker

Keep in mind the fact that this is Nebuchadnezzar's testimony to the whole world about what a messenger from heaven told him in a dream. Let's break it down because it seems so important. He said:

1) *The decision is announced by messengers, the holy ones declare the verdict.* There was a council of angelic beings involved in Nebuchadnezzar's affairs. They had made a decision concerning him and his one-world kingdom. This was the announcement of their decision and we will see that it contains implications for the whole world.

2) *So the living may know* gives the purpose of their decision. The council of angels sent a message to Nebuchadnezzar, so every living person can know:

   a) That *the Most High is* **sovereign** *over the kingdoms of men.* God is the ultimate ruler of nations not presidents, kings, or dictators. God's rank and power are paramount and no one can change that.

   b) That God *gives them* [the nations or control over the nations] *to anyone he wishes.* God decides who will be in power.

   c) That God *sets over them the lowliest of men.* God sometimes gives us idiots and fools to rule over us. When we complain about our leaders we should remember that God gives us what he thinks we deserve. They are a reflection of our relationship with him.

☞ **GO TO:**

Psalm 7:1-17 (Most High)

Psalm 34:7; Jude 1:9 (angels)

KEY Symbols:

Time
one year

Times
two years

Half a Time
one-half year

sovereign: *the Supreme Ruler*

KEY POINT

God rules nations and chooses their leaders. Sometimes he chooses weak leaders to teach us to follow him.

KEY POINT

Angels guide, comfort, and provide for the people of God in the midst of suffering and persecution.

ancient wisdom: the accumulated knowledge of all their past generations

Billy Graham: The Bible teaches that <u>angels</u> intervene in the affairs of nations. God often uses them to execute judgment on nations. They guide, comfort and provide for the people of God in the midst of suffering and persecution. Martin Luther once said . . . , "An angel is a spiritual creature without a body created by God for the service of christendom and the church."[18]

J. Vernon McGee: If you think our nation happens to be his special little pet, you are entirely wrong. I believe we have already been put on the auction block: we are already judged. The downward course which this nation is traveling is going to take us right to the judgment of God. He rules in the kingdom of men.[19]

> **Daniel 4:18** "This is the dream that I, King Nebuchadnezzar, had. Now, Belteshazzar, tell me what it means, for none of the wise men in my kingdom can interpret it for me. But you can, because the spirit of the holy gods is in you."

Now, What Does It Mean?

Nebuchadnezzar has concluded the telling of his dream. Now he appeals to Daniel [Belteshazzar] to solve this mystery. He pointed out to the world a second time the failure of his wise men. And he also repeated to the world why he believed Daniel could interpret this dream: because Daniel had the spirit of the holy gods in him.

What Others are Saying:

Wallace Emerson: This must have been a bitter pill [for the wise men] to swallow, the more so since Daniel had once saved them from death (which they were powerless to prevent) and their efforts to railroad Daniel's companions to their death had not only failed but had magnified the power of Daniel's God against whom they were powerless. These are the men in whom was reposed all the learning of the Chaldeans, the **ancient wisdom**.[20]

> **Daniel 4:19** Then Daniel (also called Belteshazzar) was greatly perplexed for a time, and his thoughts terrified him. So the king said, "Belteshazzar, do not let the dream or its meaning alarm you." Belteshazzar answered, "My lord, if only the dream applied to your enemies and its meaning to your adversaries!

Daniel's Interpretation

When Daniel heard the dream he understood its meaning and was perplexed or stunned. For a while, he sat silently in the presence of Nebuchadnezzar. He loved his king and had to confront him with the answer, an answer he found awesome and terrifying. Nebuchadnezzar recognized Daniel's reluctance to reveal the interpretation. But he wanted to know, so he implored Daniel not to let it bother him. Daniel began by wishing these bad things applied to Nebuchadnezzar's enemies instead of his beloved king, but they did not.

> **Daniel 4:20** The tree you saw, which grew large and strong, with its top touching the sky, visible to the whole earth,

Restating the Dream

Daniel is simply restating the dream for Nebuchadnezzar. He is reminding the king that he dreamed about a magnificent tree; the tallest tree known to man, touching the sky, and visible to the whole earth.

M.R. DeHaan: Now in studying this interpretation of the king's dream, we must bear in mind that [the Book of] Daniel is, indeed, a prophecy, and while all of these accounts contain many, many valuable moral and ethical lessons which can be very profitable to us and which we should not overlook, nevertheless the purpose of Daniel is to prophesy concerning the things which are to come.[21]

What Others are Saying:

> **Daniel 4:21** with beautiful leaves and abundant fruit, providing food for all, giving shelter to the beasts of the field, and having nesting places in its branches for the birds of the air—

Continuing The Restatement

This is more of Daniel's restatement of the dream. The magnificent tree had not only grown strong and visible to the whole world, but it had gained great glory (become beautiful) and had prospered (was providing food and shelter for the people and creatures of the earth).

☞ **GO TO:**

Judges 9:6–15 (tree)

Daniel 2:41–45 (Bible tells us)

> **Daniel 4:22** you, O king, are that tree! You have become great and strong; your greatness has grown until it reaches the sky, and your dominion extends to distant parts of the earth.

You Are That Tree

We could do no better than the wise men without this information, but now we know. Daniel told Nebuchadnezzar he was that <u>tree</u>. He had become great and strong. His greatness reached to the heavens, and his dominion covered the earth. Some question it, but as far as God was concerned, Nebuchadnezzar's kingdom was a world kingdom. Nebuchadnezzar had won all his wars, put down all his enemies, rebuilt all his cities, invigorated his nation's agriculture, built great buildings such as temples and places of worship, and gained so much wealth his kingdom had become known as the "kingdom of gold." For a pagan king ruling a pagan people it was an amazing record. But remember God's people, the Jews, had abandoned him, so he put this man in power and gave great glory to this pagan king.

KEY Symbols:

Tree

NEBUCHADNEZZAR

his greatness reached to the heavens
his dominion covered the earth

What Others are Saying:

M.R. DeHaan: Just as Nebuchadnezzar succeeded in conquering the entire world and uniting all the people under one great Babylonian system of government, so too <u>the Bible tells us</u> that toward the end of this age there will emerge a world government, a world federation of nations under one federal headship which shall guarantee unto man a man-made prosperity, a time when war shall cease, when there will be no poverty, no strife, no disagreement, but the Utopia of man's dreams, the millennium of man's making shall find its fulfillment [the Tribulation Period].[22]

Remember This . . .

Forty years earlier Daniel interpreted a dream for the king and said, *You O king, are the king of kings. The God of heaven has given you dominion and power and might and glory; in your hands he has placed mankind and the beasts of the field and the birds of the air. Wherever they live, he has made you ruler over them all. You are the head of gold* (Daniel 2:37, 38).

> **Daniel 4:23** "You, O king, saw a messenger, a holy one, coming down from heaven and saying, 'Cut down the tree and destroy it, but leave the stump, bound with iron and bronze, in the grass of the field, while its roots remain in the ground. Let him be drenched with the dew of heaven; let him live like the wild animals, until seven times pass by for him.'

 **GO TO:**

Romans 14:10; II Corinthians 5:10 (God's judgment seat)

Revelation 20:11–15 (judged)

Revelation 13:1 (beast)

Judgment And Grace

This is a continuation of Daniel's recounting of the dream. The heavenly messenger said:

1) *Cut the tree down and destroy it* which symbolized God's plan to <u>judge</u> Nebuchadnezzar.

2) *Leave the stump* symbolized the grace of God in his desire to judge, but not reject, the king. It shows God's desire to preserve what was left of Nebuchadnezzar's life after he was judged (punished).

3) *Let him be drenched with the dew of heaven and live like the wild animals* reveals what the king's judgment would be. He would be driven out of his palace where his body would get wet from the dew of heaven, and his mind and life would be like that of an animal.

4) *Until seven times pass by him* is a statement showing how long this <u>judgment</u> would last—seven years.

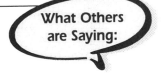 **KEY Symbols:**

Cut Tree Down
God will judge

Leave Stump
grace of God

Drenched with Dew and Live Like Animal
king's judgment

Seven Times
seven years

Billy Graham: Though some see the ranking of celestial powers as conjectural, it seems to follow this pattern: archangels, angels, **seraphim**, **cherubim**, principalities, authorities, powers, thrones, might, and dominion (Colossians 1:16).[23]

What Others are Saying:

M.R. DeHaan: And so the voice that came from heaven and commanded that the tree representing Nebuchadnezzar, the king, be hewed down and cut to the ground, is a picture of the coming of the Lord who will cause the nations to become stark mad in their insane delusion of self-achievement and self-grandeur, and then will follow seven years of the greatest confusion the world has ever known.[24]

seraphim: an angel of praise that guards the Temple of God

cherubim: an angel of insight that guards the Temple of God

Some experts see a double fulfillment in this prophecy about Nebuchadnezzar. They believe it was literally fulfilled the first time when Nebuchadnezzar went out of his mind and

Something to Ponder

Nebuchadnezzar

insane for seven years

Antichrist

his rule will last for seven years

☞ **GO TO:**

II Corinthians 11:1–15 (false)

KEY POINT

Every person is accountable to God for his actions.

What Others are Saying:

WARNING ➤

KEY POINT

Messengers of God (angels) never draw attention to themselves but ascribe the glory to God.

acted like a beast in the field. But they also think there is reason to believe it will be fulfilled a second time when the Antichrist comes on the scene. The Antichrist will be a world leader just like Nebuchadnezzar was. His deceit, treachery, wars, and persecution of Christians and Jews will be the deeds of a mad man. He will be so evil the <u>Bible calls him a beast</u>. Nebuchadnezzar went insane for seven years, and the folly of the Antichrist will last for seven years in the Tribulation Period.

> **Daniel 4:24** "This is the interpretation, O king, and this is the decree the Most High has issued against my lord the king:

So Let It Be Done

This is the prophecy about what would happen to Nebuchadnezzar. Notice that it is by decree of the Most High, a decree that he personally issued against the King of Babylon. If this was the decision of a council of angels, it was also the decision of God. They were in perfect agreement.

Billy Graham: Reports continually flow to my attention from many places around the world telling of visitors of the angelic order appearing, ministering, fellowshipping, and disappearing. They warn of God's impending judgment; they spell out the tenderness of his love; they meet a desperate need; then they are gone. Of one thing we can be sure: angels never draw attention to themselves but ascribe the glory to God and press his message upon the hearers as a delivering and sustaining word of the highest order.[25]

It would be good if we could trust everyone who claims to speak for Christ or in the name of God, but we simply cannot. Concerning the End of the Age Jesus said, *many false prophets will appear and deceive many people* (Matthew 24:11). The Apostle Paul warned that, *Satan himself masquerades as an angel of light* (II Corinthians 11:14). Beware of people who preach a Jesus other than the Jesus of the Bible, a gospel other than the gospel of the Bible, or a Christianity other than historical Christianity. Beware of people who boast of special revelations, private knowledge, or previously uncovered secrets.

Beware of people who want to involve you in a fantastic new movement that ties you to their organization. These are the kinds of things <u>false prophets</u> will do.

> **Daniel 4:25** You will be driven away from people and will live with the wild animals; you will eat grass like cattle and be drenched with the dew of heaven. Seven times will pass by for you until you acknowledge that the Most High is sovereign over the kingdoms of men and gives them to anyone he wishes.

Driven From His Home

The king would be driven out of his palace. He would be driven away from the people and attention he loved so much, away from the power and glory he exalted in, away from all the delicacies, comforts, and servants. Where would he go? He would live in the fields with the wild animals, cattle, sheep, camels, and donkeys. His body would be wet from being outside in the dew. Seven years would pass before he would finally acknowledge that God rules over the nations and puts in power anyone he wishes.

Wallace Emerson: King Nebuchadnezzar is to be stricken in his reason. The very mind that has envisioned and produced the walls of Babylon, the magnificence of the **sacred street** (see Illustration #14, page 127), the conquest of strong nations is to become the mind of a beast.[26]

The Bible refers to the Antichrist (see GWRV, pages 183–202) as a beast. He is the (the first beast of Revelation) <u>beast coming out of the sea</u> and his number (666) is <u>the number of the beast</u>. The Bible also refers to the False Prophet as a beast. He is (the second beast of Revelation) *another beast, <u>coming out of the earth</u>*; he is the one who will set up an image to honor the first beast (Antichrist) and the one who will order people to worship the Antichrist. He will also force people to take the <u>Mark of the Beast</u>.

> **Daniel 4:26** The command to leave the stump of the tree with its roots means that your kingdom will be restored to you when you acknowledge that Heaven rules.

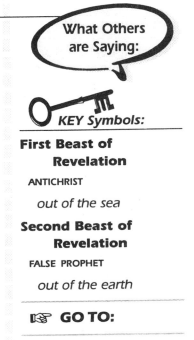

☞ **GO TO:**

Revelation 13:1 (sea)

Revelation 13:18 (number)

Revelation 13:11 (earth)

Revelation 13:14–17 (Mark)

sacred street: the main street leading into Babylon that was often used for processions—Processional Way

What Others are Saying:

KEY Symbols:

First Beast of Revelation

ANTICHRIST

out of the sea

Second Beast of Revelation

FALSE PROPHET

out of the earth

☞ **GO TO:**

I Corinthians 4:7 (receive)

He Will Return

After reading the harsh judgments of Daniel 4:25 who could imagine that Nebuchadnezzar would ever get his throne back? Who could imagine the people of Babylon accepting him back and trusting his decisions as king, after seeing him going out of his mind and living like an animal? But that was Daniel's interpretation of the dream. Nebuchadnezzar would be out of his mind for seven years, and would eventually acknowledge that heaven rules. Only then would he <u>receive</u> his kingdom back.

Nebuchadnezzar

will be driven away from people

will live with the wild animals

will eat grass like the cattle

will be drenched with the dew of heaven

☞ **GO TO:**

Proverbs 16:18 (pride)

Revelation 6:7, 8; 8:10, 11; 9:15, 18; 11:13; 13:15 (perish)

KEY POINT

God always gives ample warning—grace before judgment.

> **Daniel 4:27** Therefore, O king, be pleased to accept my advice: Renounce your sins by doing what is right, and your wickedness by being kind to the oppressed. It may be that then your prosperity will continue."

Grace Before Judgment

If we tried we could compile a fairly long list of sins in Nebuchadnezzar's life—abuse of power, anger, arrogance, cruelty to Israel, idolatry, oppression of the poor, <u>pride</u>, etc.—but that is not needed. The most important thing is that Nebuchadnezzar was in the presence of a man of God, the chief of all his wise men, and he knew it. This man of God, leader of the wise men, and friend offered him some kindly advice.

God always gives ample warning. Preachers call it "grace before judgment." God does not enjoy using the paddle, and only true repentance can turn away his wrath.

Something to Ponder

Remember This . . .

In spite of everything he had seen and heard, the king did not take the advice of his good friend and advisor Daniel. There is no indication that he changed anything. It seems that many people are making the same mistake today. What do you think?

God's judgments will fall upon the earth during the Tribulation Period. In just seven years <u>millions will perish</u>, but the grace of God will come into play before these judgments. This grace is called the Rapture. It is possible to leave in the Rapture and miss God's terrible judgments. Anyone can do that by repenting of their sins and sincerely accepting Jesus as their Savior.

> **Daniel 4:28** All this happened to King Nebuchadnezzar.

So Be It

Again, we should keep in mind that this is Nebuchadnezzar's personal testimony written for all the world to read. He does not say that he <u>foolishly</u> ignored Daniel's advice, but apparently he must have since God's judgment fell. The following is his own account of what happened to him.

> **Daniel 4:29** Twelve months later, as the king was walking on the roof of the royal palace of Babylon,

God Never Forgets

God's judgment did not come <u>quickly</u>. One week passed after Daniel advised the king to repent and nothing happened. Soon one month was gone, then six months, and then one year later Nebuchadnezzar was walking around his royal palace. It was the custom in those days to build a flat roof on at least part of the building and use it for a patio, which is where we find Nebuchadnezzar.

Oliver B. Greene: Since judgment did not fall at once, perhaps Nebuchadnezzar thought Daniel was mistaken or that God had forgotten; but God's prophet, speaking under inspiration, is never wrong, and the God of Daniel never forgets. He does not always pay off on Saturday night nor at the end of the month, but he never fails to pay. *And when God pays, he always pays in full.*[27]

Noah Hutchings: We know from archaeological discoveries that the palace of Nebuchadnezzar covered six square miles. Never had a king had such a palace. Twelve months after he had resolved to change his ways, he was walking about the palace, and its enormity and beauty began to overwhelm him.[28]

M.R. DeHaan: As such, Nebuchadnezzar represented the course of the history of the nations until at the end-time, after man's day has run its course, they shall be lifted up with pride at their own achievements, imagining, foolishly imagining, that they have finally brought about the Utopian condition of world security, world peace, and world prosperity; then God is going to come and strike

☞ **GO TO:**

Proverbs 1:7; 19:29;
  Ephesians 5:15–17
  (foolish)

☞ **GO TO:**

Ecclesiastes 8:11
  (quickly)

What Others are Saying:

KEY POINT

Everything comes from God. He can take it away or restore it anytime he chooses.

☞ **GO TO:**

I Thessalonians 5:18 (give thanks)

Deuteronomy 8:6–18; Psalm 9:17 (forget)

Psalm 96:1–13 (glory)

Proverbs 16:5; 29:23 (pride)

self-exaltation: elevate one's own self, brag, boast

exalt: give glory to, praise

Remember This . . .

☞ **GO TO:**

Psalm 94:11; I Corinthians 3:20 (thoughts)

Matthew 12:36 (word)

Matthew 3:17; John 12:28; Acts 11:9 (voice from heaven)

What Others are Saying:

down the world powers and set up his own King, the Lord Jesus Christ, upon the throne, and he shall reign forever and forever.[29]

> **Daniel 4:30** he said, "Is not this the great Babylon I have built as the royal residence, by my mighty power and for the glory of my majesty?"

Wow, Look What I've Done

Nebuchadnezzar was out on his patio admiring the beautiful kingdom God had already said was given to him. He should have been <u>thanking</u> God for what he saw and received, but he had <u>forgotten God</u>. He should have done these things for God's <u>glory</u>, but he did them for his own glory. This <u>proud</u> king was patting himself on the back.

Self-exaltation runs contrary to the teachings of Jesus. He said, *whoever* **exalts** *himself will be humbled, and whoever humbles himself will be exalted* (Matthew 23:12). True greatness is service to God and others.

> **Daniel 4:31** The words were still on his lips when a voice came from heaven, "This is what is decreed for you, King Nebuchadnezzar: Your royal authority has been taken from you.

Gone In A Word

The Bible teaches that God knows our very <u>thoughts</u>, even every <u>word</u> we speak. These words were not even off the lips of Nebuchadnezzar when there came a <u>voice from heaven</u>. The heavenly council had decided that the time to dethrone the king had come.

Hal Lindsey: What happened to Nebuchadnezzar was an act of supreme grace on the part of God. The fact that he was put into a catastrophe personally was grace not judgment, because God could have just let him go on like an Adolph Hitler, or some other ruler of the past like Alexander the Great. Many of them [had] built empires and beautified their capitols, cities, etc., and yet, they died lost in their pride.[30]

Then Daniel praised the God of heaven and said: "Praise be to the name of God for ever and ever; wisdom and power are his. He changes times and seasons; he sets up kings and deposes them (Daniel 2:19-20).

Remember This . . .

☞ **GO TO:**

I Corinthians 15:24 (authority)

Psalm 47:1-9 (Most High)

> **Daniel 4:32** You will be driven away from people and will live with the wild animals; you will eat grass like cattle. Seven times will pass by for you until you acknowledge that the Most High is sovereign over the kingdoms of men and gives them to anyone he wishes."

No Repentance

Look at the list! He could have **repented**. Perhaps, the angelic council would have changed its mind if he had, but he did not.

repented: turned away from sin and turned toward God

1) *Your royal <u>authority</u> has been taken from you* (Daniel 4:31).

2) *You will be driven away from people* (Daniel 4:32).

3) *You will live with the wild animals.*

4) *Seven times* (years) *will pass by for you.*

5) *You will acknowledge that the <u>Most High</u> is sovereign over the kingdoms.*

6) *You will acknowledge that he gives kingdoms to anyone he wishes.*

M.R. DeHaan: The thing to remember is that Nebuchadnezzar was stricken with this madness for a period of exactly seven years, which we believe to be prophetic of the seven years of tribulation, between the Rapture of the Church and the Second Coming of the Lord Jesus. This seven-year period is called "the Great Tribulation," "the Time of Jacob's Trouble," "the Day of Indignation."[31]

What Others are Saying:

> **Daniel 4:33** Immediately what had been said about Nebuchadnezzar was fulfilled. He was driven away from people and ate grass like cattle. His body was drenched with the dew of heaven until his hair grew like the feathers of an eagle and his nails like the claws of a bird.

☞ **GO TO:**

I Samuel 19:9 (Saul)

Matthew 4:24 (demon possession)`

Birdman Of Babylon

The instant the heavenly voice ceased speaking the defiant king received exactly what God said. This rebellious man was driven out of his wonderful palace where he became a monstrosity of a man. He crawled around on his hands and knees, ate grass like ordinary cattle, and his body stayed wet all the time. He was covered with hair—hair so thick it looked like the feathers of an eagle. His fingernails and toenails grew out and looked like the claws of a bird. He would not repent and for seven long years he paid a terrible price.

We are not told where he lived or anything about his interim government during the seven years of his insanity. We suspect that everyone knew from Daniel's interpretation of the dream that his illness would be only temporary. From Daniel 4:15, *let the stump and its roots, bound with iron and bronze, remain in the ground, in the grass of the field,* we would assume that he was confined to a well-cared-for field, surrounded by an iron fence decorated with brass. Daniel and the king's other advisors probably ran things until he recovered.

Wallace Emerson: Nebuchadnezzar's insanity, if it can be called such, does not follow the usual mental dynamics and is obviously an "act of God" and unique. It has no affinity with Saul's madness with its murderous overtones nor with any Old or New Testament pattern of **demon possession**, though it more closely resembles the latter than it does ordinary paranoid conditions. Daniel tells us that Nebuchadnezzar's madness was a direct visitation from God and Nebuchadnezzar, in this most unusual, original document confirms this.[32]

Oliver B. Greene: During the **Seventieth-Week of Daniel's** seventy weeks of prophecy (see Time Line #3, Appendix A), the Antichrist will reign from the temple in Jerusalem which will have been rebuilt. The Holy Spirit will be taken out with the Church at the Rapture (II Thessalonians 2:7); and when the restraining power of the Holy Spirit is gone, the earth will be left to the mercy of demons. *And for this cause God shall send them strong delusion, that they should believe a lie: That they all might be damned who believed not the truth, but had pleasure in unrighteousness* (II Thessalonians 2:11, 12 KJV).[33]

> **Daniel 4:34** At the end of that time, I, Nebuchadnezzar, raised my eyes toward heaven, and my sanity was restored. Then I praised the Most High; I honored and glorified him who lives forever. His dominion is an eternal dominion; his kingdom endures from generation to generation.

☞ **GO TO:**

Deuteronomy 32:39–43 (heal)

Philippians 2:11 (confess)

I Was Wrong

At the end of that time means there was no parole. Nebuchadnezzar served his full sentence before he finally raised his eyes toward heaven. Then he was <u>healed</u>, and while in his right mind, he understood that God is in charge. So he began to praise God—the eternal God who lives forever, the God who will always reign, the God whose kingdom will never end.

M.R. DeHaan: All this came to pass historically. But prophetically, this stump means that after the seven years of the madness of the nations in the Tribulation, the Gentile nations, too, will be converted. While Israel will be restored in the land, these Gentile nations will occupy the countries of the world, acknowledge the Lord Jesus Christ as Saviour, and every knee shall bow to him and every tongue <u>confess</u> that Jesus Christ is Lord to the glory of God the Father.[34]

What Others are Saying:

When Daniel interpreted Nebuchadnezzar's dream he said, *The command to leave the stump of the tree with its roots means that your kingdom will be restored to you when you acknowledge that Heaven rules* (Daniel 4:26).

Remember This . . .

> **Daniel 4:35** All the peoples of the earth are regarded as nothing. He does as he pleases with the powers of heaven and the peoples of the earth. No one can hold back his hand or say to him: "What have you done?"

☞ **GO TO:**

Romans 8:38; Colossians 1:15, 16 (powers)

Ephesians 6:12 (heavenly realms)

Genesis 1:1 (Creator)

No One But Me

God is great. All the peoples of the earth are nothing compared to him. He does as he pleases whether it be with spiritual <u>powers</u> in <u>heavenly realms</u> or with peoples of the earth. He is so powerful no one can resist him, not even a strong world leader. He has done such marvelous things no one can ask, *What have you done?* Nebuchadnezzar learned his lesson. God is the <u>Creator</u>; he is in charge, and he does what he wants to do.

☞ **GO TO:**

Proverbs 22:1–4 (good name)

> **Daniel 4:36** At the same time that my sanity was restored, my honor and splendor were returned to me for the glory of my kingdom. My advisers and nobles sought me out, and I was restored to my throne and became even greater than before.

Greater Than Before

God always does what he says he will do. Nebuchadnezzar got his <u>good name</u> back and his kingdom. His officials did not shun him, and for the remainder of his life (about one year), he was greater than ever.

What Others are Saying:

David Jeremiah with C.C. Carlson: It is almost unbelievable that after seven years, his kingdom was still secure. No foreign power had come and confiscated it; there had been no national uprising or coup to depose him.[35]

☞ **GO TO:**

Psalm 33:4 (right)

Deuteronomy 32:4 (just)

Deuteronomy 8:1–5; Matthew 18:1–4; Luke 14:7–11 (humble)

> **Daniel 4:37** Now I, Nebuchadnezzar, praise and exalt and glorify the King of heaven, because everything he does is right and all his ways are just. And those who walk in pride he is able to humble.

Humble Thyself Before The Lord

This testimony shows the great change that came about in Nebuchadnezzar. He turned away from the false gods of Babylon, and to the world he wrote, *I, Nebuchadnezzar, praise and exalt and glorify the King of heaven.* Why? Because:

1) *Everything God does is <u>right</u>.*
2) *All his ways are <u>just</u>.*
3) *All those who walk in pride he is able to <u>humble</u>.*

What Others are Saying:

Noah Hutchings: Nebuchadnezzar had received as much light and knowledge of God as any man could receive, yet he had to be brought low in judgment before he would believe and receive the God of whom Daniel witnessed. He was like most Americans today who have been preached to so much that they have become Gospel-hardened. But there is a limit to the patience and mercy of God. To this truth, Nebuchadnezzar testified to the world.[36]

A King's Understanding of God

1) He called him Daniel's God. *The king said to Daniel, "Surely your God is the God of gods and the Lord of kings and a revealer of mysteries, for you were able to reveal this mystery"* (Daniel 2:47).

2) He called him the God of Shadrach, Meshach, and Abednego. *Then Nebuchadnezzar said, "Praise be to the God of Shadrach, Meshach, and Abednego, who has sent his angel and rescued his servants! They trusted in him and defied the king's command and were willing to give up their lives rather than serve or worship any god except their own God"* (Daniel 3:28).

3) He recognized that God is great. *It is my pleasure to tell you about the miraculous signs and wonders that the Most High God has performed for me. How great are his signs, how mighty his wonders! His kingdom is an eternal kingdom; his dominion endures from generation to generation* (Daniel 4:2, 3).

KEY Symbols:

God is

the God of Daniel

the God of Shadrach, Meshach, and Abednego

great

everybody's God

Nebuchadnezzar's God

4) He recognized that God is everybody's God. *Then I praised the Most High; I honored and glorified him who lives forever. His dominion is an eternal dominion; his kingdom endures from generation to generation. All the peoples of the earth are regarded as nothing. He does as he pleases with the powers of heaven and the peoples of the earth. No one can hold back his hand or say to him: "What have you done"* (Daniel 4:34–35)?

5) He recognized that God is his God. *Now I, Nebuchadnezzar, praise and exalt and glorify the King of heaven, because everything he does is right and all his ways are just. And those who walk in pride he is able to humble* (Daniel 4:37).

Study Questions

1. How could Daniel interpret the dream when the other wise men could not?
2. Who said, *Cut down the tree*? Who or what are they? How was mercy shown?
3. What important thing does God want the living to know? Why?
4. Are we in charge of our own destiny?
5. What control does God have over the proud? Does he do wrong? How did this help Nebuchadnezzar?

CHAPTER WRAP-UP

- This chapter is an account of Nebuchadnezzar's personal written testimony of one who initially was contented, prosperous, and proud of his accomplishments. (Daniel 4:1–4)

- Nebuchadnezzar had a second dream. Again he called in his wise men, but they could not explain it. Then, he called in Daniel. At first, Daniel was stunned, but then explained the dream. (Daniel 4:5-8; 19–26)

- Daniel recommended that the king repent, but Nebuchadnezzar ignored the advice. God's judgment came when, one year later, the king went insane and lived in the fields like a wild animal. This affliction of madness lasted seven years. (Daniel 4:27–33)

- The king's affliction eventually humbled his pride, causing him to look toward heaven, acknowledge God, and repent. (Daniel 4:34)

- When Nebuchadnezzar looked to God he was healed of his insanity. Then his throne was restored and he became greater than ever. (Daniel 4:34–36)

DANIEL 5

CHAPTER HIGHLIGHTS

- A Big Party
- A Big Boast
- A Big Hand
- A Big Invasion
- A Big Change

Let's Get Started

A little more than 20 years has now passed (see Time Line #1, Appendix A) since Nebuchadnezzar's testimony; much has changed. Nebuchadnezzar is dead and Daniel is about 80 years old. Infighting has struck the royal family and the crown has changed heads several times. The palace has been declared off limits to Daniel and many of the advisors who served former kings. The winds of change have blown hard on Babylon.

Chapter 5 details the last night of Babylon's existence, the last night of the *empire of gold* on God's Statue (see Illustration #5, page 53) of Nebuchadnezzar's famous dream about Gentile world kingdoms. A combined army of Medes and Persians has surrounded the city (see Illustration #14, page 127). They represent the *empire of silver* in Nebuchadnezzar's famous dream. Before dawn the empire of gold will be gone and the empire of silver will rule the world.

The main character is now one of Nebuchadnezzar's **despotic** grandsons, a man named Belshazzar. He is serving as **co-regent** with his father, Nabonidus, who had taken an army outside the walls to engage the Medes and Persians in battle. But Nabonidus was defeated, then fled, and is now in hiding. Major changes have taken place since the death of Nebuchadnezzar. Keep in mind that Nebuchadnezzar was Belshazzar's *grandfather*. This is important in order to understand Daniel 5:2, 11, 13, and 18.

despotic: *a tyrant; a cruel, unjust ruler*

co-regent: *a co-ruler; an acting ruler in the absence of the main ruler*

Rulers of Babylon

Beginning of Reign	King	Years Reigned	Death	Replaced by
626 B.C.	Nabopolassar	21	??????	His son, Nebuchadnezzar
605 B.C.	Nebuchadnezzar	44	Natural	His son, Evil-merodach
561 B.C.	Evil-merodach	2	Murdered by Neriglissar	His brother-in-law, Neriglissar (married to Nebuchadnezzar's daughter)
559 B.C.	Neriglissar	4	Killed in battle	His son, Labosoar-chad (Nebuchadnezzar's grandson)
556 B.C.	Labosoar-chad	9 mos.	Murdered by Nabonidus	His step-grandfather, Nabonidus (married to Neriglissar's widow)
555 B.C.	Nabonidus	16	Not dead, in hiding	Not replaced. Belshazzar, his son is co-regent
544 B.C.	Belshazzar	5	Killed when Babylon fell	Darius, King of the Medes and Persians

What Others are Saying:

J. Vernon McGee: Nabonidus was on the field of battle while Belshazzar his son remained in Babylon. We will notice that when Belshazzar offers Daniel a position in the kingdom, it is to be the third ruler in the kingdom. Why not second to Belshazzar? Well, Belshazzar himself was number two—his father was really the king.[1]

Ed Young: When we see the decline of a man or a woman, or the decline of a nation, we should learn from their experience. Those who do not learn from history always have to pay the price of history repeating itself in their business, their state, their nation, and in their lives.[2]

Remember This . . .

When Daniel interpreted Nebuchadnezzar's first dream about the great statue he told the king, *After you another kingdom* [the chest and arms of silver] *will rise, inferior to yours* (Daniel 2:32, 39).

> **Daniel 5:1** King Belshazzar gave a great banquet for a thousand of his nobles and drank wine with them.

A BIG Party

KEY Symbols:

Belshazzar
son of Nabonidus
grandson of
Nebuchadnezzar

The Medes and the Persians had joined forces in an effort to defeat Babylon. Nabonidus had come out of the city to attack them, but he was defeated. Cyrus now had the city of Babylon under siege. His combined army of Medes and Persians was just outside the city walls, and he was preparing to attack. Belshazzar, however, did not seem to care because he undoubtedly had been told

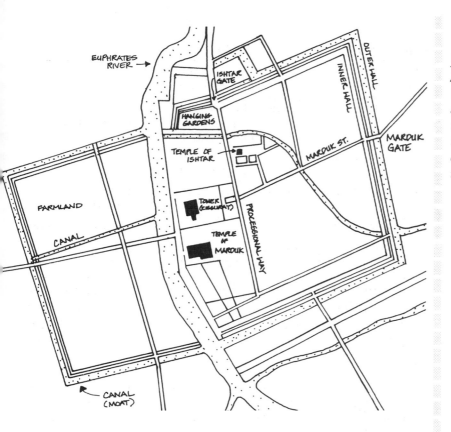

Illustration #14

Ancient City of Babylon—
One of the greatest cities of
all times. The palace alone
took up six square miles, and
the Hanging Gardens were
one of the Seven Wonders of
the Ancient World.

KEY Symbols:

Cyrus, Son of
King Cambyses I of
Persia, and
Queen Mandan,
daughter of King
Astyages of the
Medes

**Something
to Ponder**

that he was secure behind the walls of Babylon. He seemed to believe it, because he was proud and defiant. He feared no one; not his enemies, not Cyrus, not the empire of silver, not even God. He even decided to show everyone how unafraid he was. He threw a big party while enemy troops were outside his beautiful city. He invited a thousand nobles from his kingdom, brought out the best wine, and they drank together.

Cyrus was the son of King Cambyses I of Persia and Queen Mandan, daughter of King Astyages of the Medes. Their marriage was a major factor in the alliance between the Medes and the Persians. Cyrus was the "commander" of the combined army of the Medes and Persians that conquered Babylon. He was a shrewd, compassionate leader who would come to be known as "Cyrus the Great." After Cyrus captured Babylon, Darius, who was then King of the Medes, became king of the new world empire. When Darius died two years later, Cyrus replaced him on the throne.

☞ **GO TO:**

Daniel 1:2; II Chronicles 36:11–21 (vessels)

Daniel 4:17 (sovereign)

sacred: *belonging to, or set apart for, God*

concubines: *his least-favored wives*

> **Daniel 5:2** While Belshazzar was drinking his wine, he gave orders to bring in the gold and silver goblets that Nebuchadnezzar his father had taken from the temple in Jerusalem, so that the king and his nobles, his wives and his concubines might drink from them.

Bring In Those Hebrew Goblets

As the evening wore on, the wine became both a comfort and a curse to Belshazzar. With each drink he seemed to become more bold and more foolish. In a moment of daring he sent for the **sacred** vessels his grandfather, Nebuchadnezzar, had plundered from the Jewish Temple. He decided to defy the God who is sovereign over the kingdoms of men by drinking wine out of these vessels. He wanted his nobles, his wives, and his **concubines** to do the same. It was a grave **sacrilege**. We will learn in Daniel 5:22 that he knew better.

What Others are Saying:

Union Gospel Press: Some rulers, in spite of their vices, have redeeming qualities that give their lives some worth. This brief glimpse of Belshazzar, however, reveals nothing to be admired. He was a carefree **reveler**, an immoral **polygamist**, an arrogant **blasphemer**.[3]

sacrilege: *disrespect for God*

reveler: *pleasure seeker*

polygamist: *has more than one wife*

blasphemer: *shows contempt for God*

longsuffering: *patient*

M.R. DeHaan: We have continually been reminding you of the fact that Babylon represents more than a physical kingdom. Babylonianism is a system, an anti-Christian, anti-God system of man's endeavor to dethrone Almighty God and to bring about, in this world, an ideal utopian kingdom and federation which shall not need the direction and the revelation of God in any sense whatsoever.[4]

Oliver B. Greene: The God of heaven is great in mercy and slow to anger. He is **longsuffering**, not willing that any should perish, but that all should come to repentance. But there is a deadline, even with the God of divine compassion. When Belshazzar and his guests poured wine into the sacred vessels and lifted those vessels to drunken lips, the cup of iniquity was filled to the brim! That second, Belshazzar stepped across God's deadline and plunged into eternal doom.[5]

Remember This . . .

Remember, Nebuchadnezzar was Belshazzar's grandfather and not his father as this verse says. This is not an error in the Bible. It should be understood that we are using a translation of an original text, and in the original language (Aramaic) there is no word for "grandfather" or "grandson." The word "father" in the original language means "ancestor." Nebuchadnezzar was Belshazzar's ancestor—his grandfather.

> **Daniel 5:3** So they brought in the gold goblets that had been taken from the temple of God in Jerusalem, and the king and his nobles, his wives and his concubines drank from them.

☞ **GO TO:**

Luke 12:16-21 (foolish)

A Big Boast

There is much in the Bible about the love of God. He is love, but He is also to be feared (respected) of above all else. And while He is loving and longsuffering there is usually a line that no man should cross. It is that line that the <u>foolish</u> Belshazzar crossed. He made a big mistake when he requested the sacred vessels for use at his drunken party and drank from them. In doing so, he openly mocked God.

> **Daniel 5:4** As they drank the wine, they praised the gods of gold and silver, of bronze, iron, wood, and stone.

Praise Be To Our Gods

This was the crowning event in Belshazzar's contempt for God. It shows just how far he was willing to go with his anti-God attitude. The golden vessels had not come from some pagan temple but from God's own house. It was a foolish thing to do, but Belshazzar used the sacred vessels to praise the false gods of Babylon.

David Jeremiah with C.C. Carlson: Visualize yourself in church as communion is being served. On the communion table are the little glasses in which the juice is poured, honoring the death of our Lord. Suddenly an inebriated man swerves up the center aisle, grabs a cup from the tray, throws the juice on the floor, and fills it up with a shot of whiskey. He then turns around and shouts to the congregation, "Here's a toast to the devil!"[6]

What Others are Saying:

David Breese: It is spiritual things and the defilement of them that become the ultimate reality, the ultimate iniquity of man.[7]

☞ **GO TO:**

Daniel 4:31;
I Thessalonians 5:1–3
(suddenly)

Exodus 8:19 (finger)

I Chronicles 28:15
(lampstand)

Exodus 8:19
(magicians)

Exodus 31:18 (wrote)

John 8 1–11 (sand)

What Others are Saying:

plaster: a soft chalky
covering on the wall

golden lampstand: a
seven-branched candlestick
that stood in the Temple at
Jerusalem

Ten Commandments: ten
laws for Israel which God
revealed to Moses

Alcohol is a depressant. Specifically, alcohol affects the control centers of the brain. As a result, intoxicated people may lose their self-control and behave in ways that are unacceptable to others. They may experience mental confusion and an inability to walk steadily or talk clearly.

> **Daniel 5:5** Suddenly the fingers of a human hand appeared and wrote on the plaster of the wall, near the lampstand in the royal palace. The king watched the hand as it wrote.

A Big Hand

Suddenly, the fingers of a man's hand appeared and, as the king watched, they wrote on the wall. Were these drunken idolaters hallucinating? Was this the product of their intoxicated imagination? No. This was painfully real.

The hand wrote on the **plaster** *near the lampstand in the royal palace.* This may have been the **golden lampstand** (see Illustration #15, page 131) taken from the Jewish Temple. Archaeologists have discovered that it was used by the Babylonians as a trophy or a symbol of their victory over Israel. It is also possible that God wants us to know that the hand appeared in a well-lit area of the banquet hall.

David Hocking: Back in ancient Egypt in the plagues those magicians said, *This is the finger of God.* When God gave the **Ten Commandments**, he wrote them with his own finger—a spectacular display to Moses as he saw a revelation of the power of God.[8]

J. Vernon McGee: God would not endure this impious insult to heaven, so he writes on the wall of the banqueting hall. Is it done in anger? Very frankly, I think it is, and I believe the one who wrote this is the same one who wrote in the sand when they brought a sinful woman before him. At that time, it was a message of forgiveness; here, for Belshazzar, it is a message of doom.[9]

> **Daniel 5:6** His face turned pale and he was so frightened that his knees knocked together and his legs gave way.

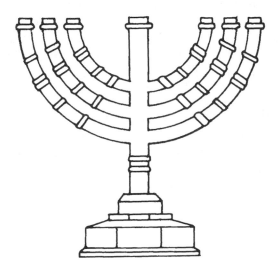

Illustration #15

Golden Lampstand—Before the Temple was destroyed, Jewish priests kept this lit day and night.

His Knees Were A' Knockin'

I imagine there was no more tinkling of glasses and no more loud laughter. It appears Belshazzar now realized that he had made a terrible mistake. The color drained from his face, he began to tremble, and his knees started knocking. He was so weak with fear that his legs gave way.

Ed Young: Why did Belshazzar respond with such staggering fear when he knew a message from God was coming his way? I'll tell you why. It was because he had a guilty conscience. Guilt makes cowards of us all.[10]

Noah Hutchings: Inasmuch as there is a prophetic significance for the Gentile nations at the End of the Age in the fall of Babylon, we must conclude that this drunken and immoral party is quite symbolic of the degenerate condition of the Gentile world just before Christ returns.[11]

What Others are Saying:

Daniel 5:7 The king called out for the enchanters, astrologers, and diviners to be brought and said to these wise men of Babylon, "Whoever reads this writing and tells me what it means will be clothed in purple and have a gold chain placed around his neck, and he will be made the third highest ruler in the kingdom."

☞ **GO TO:**

Daniel 2:2 (summoned)

Daniel 4:6 (wise men)

I John 1:9 (sin)

Bring In My Wise Men

It was time for Belshazzar to confess his sin, repent, and pray, but he did not. He was too defiant and proud. So he made the same mistake his once pagan grandfather Nebuchadnezzar often made. He <u>summoned</u> his ever-failing <u>wise men</u>.

He needed to know what the writing was all about—what it said and what it meant. His wise men were called, and he offered rewards of expensive clothing, jewelry, power, and position to anyone who could tell him. He was desperate, scared, and willing to pay any price except the one that might possibly work—acknowledging his <u>sin</u> and recognizing God.

What Others are Saying:

Union Gospel Press: Much discussion has surrounded the word for "third" here, since it is different from the usual one. It is possible that it was a technical political title like "triumvir," indicating an equal rank with two others. If "third ruler" is the meaning, it may have been an offer to make the person third in authority, after Nabonidus (first) and Belshazzar (second).[12]

> **Daniel 5:8** Then all the king's wise men came in, but they could not read the writing or tell the king what it meant.

What Does It Mean?

In came the unfortunate crew of so-called wise men. They looked at the message, but it was from God, so they obviously didn't understand it. The Bible says, *The man without the Spirit does not accept the things that come from the spirit of God, for they are foolishness to him, and he cannot understand them, because they are spiritually discerned* (I Corinthians 2:14). So, once again, the enchanters, astrologers, and diviners failed.

KEY POINT

Once again, the enchanters, astrologers, and diviners failed.

> **Daniel 5:9** So King Belshazzar became even more terrified and his face grew more pale. His nobles were baffled.

This Can't Be Happening Again

The failure of Belshazzar's wise men drove the intensity of the crisis even higher. The pale, knee-knocking king was now terrified. The ashen color of his face grew even whiter than before. No one there could claim his great rewards because no one could tell him what he wanted to know.

David Jeremiah with C.C. Carlson: Of all the stupid parties in history, this one takes the prize. At the very moment Belshazzar and his guests were becoming more and more inebriated, slopping down their liquor from the holy vessels of the God of Jerusalem, their mortal enemies were coming under the walls of the city.[13]

What Others are Saying:

> **Daniel 5:10** The queen, hearing the voices of the king and his nobles, came into the banquet hall. "O king, live forever!" she said. "Don't be alarmed! Don't look so pale!

O King, Take It Easy

There may have been some shouting and yelling going on and perhaps some shrieks of terror, because the queen heard the voices of Belshazzar and his rulers as she went to the banquet hall to learn what was going on.

Notice something here. This queen was probably not the wife of Belshazzar. Daniel 5:3 tells us that his wives and concubines were already present. So, although it cannot be said for certain, this queen who was most likely the Queen Mother—the daughter of Nebuchadnezzar, the one who first married Neriglissar and later Nabonidus.

This queen, whoever she was, entered the banquet hall, quickly sized up the situation, and began to try to calm Belshazzar down. She had seen other crises, other times when the wise men were baffled, and knew this mystery was not impossible to solve.

> **Daniel 5:11** There is a man in your kingdom who has the spirit of the holy gods in him. In the time of your father he was found to have insight and intelligence and wisdom like that of the gods. King Nebuchadnezzar your father—your father the king, I say—appointed him chief of the magicians, enchanters, astrologers, and diviners.

☞ **GO TO:**

Daniel 2:48 (in charge)

Daniel 4:8, 9, 18 (spirit)

Don't You Remember Daniel?

The Queen Mother's calmness grew out of her knowledge of Daniel and his God-given ability to solve mysteries for her father Nebuchadnezzar. She informed the king that he had a man in his

Remember This . . .

kingdom who could help. She reminded him that Daniel had proven his **insight**, **intelligence**, and **wisdom** during the days of Nebuchadnezzar, and that Daniel was placed in charge of all the wise men. This is another great testimony about Daniel and the things he had done—the Queen Mother knew all about him.

Nebuchadnezzar placed <u>Daniel in charge</u> of all the wise men. He knew that <u>Daniel had the spirit of the holy gods</u> in him.

> **Daniel 5:12** This man Daniel, whom the king called Belteshazzar, was found to have a keen mind and knowledge and understanding, and also the ability to interpret dreams, explain riddles, and solve difficult problems. Call for Daniel, and he will tell you what the writing means."

He'll Know The Answer

In essence the Queen Mother told Belshazzar that Daniel had proven himself, and he should be called to explain this. Daniel was up to the task, but it might be worth noting that the situation was a little different this time. This was not a dream, riddle, or difficult problem. It was a plain statement of fact written by the hand of Almighty God.

> **Daniel 5:13** So Daniel was brought before the king, and the king said to him, "Are you Daniel, one of the exiles my father the king brought from Judah?

Are You The One?

Belshazzar took the Queen Mother's advice. He called for Daniel to be brought before him. It is obvious that Daniel was living within the city walls, and he was probably not far away. It wasn't long until someone brought him to the palace where he entered the banquet hall.

As he entered, we learn something strange: the drunken king did not even know him. He had to ask Daniel if he was one of the exiles Nebuchadnezzar had brought from Judah. We wonder why but can only speculate. Maybe Daniel had been shoved aside at some point during the power struggle following Nebuchadnezzar's death. Whatever the case, it is obvious that he did not currently hold the high position he once held and that Belshazzar definitely had not been consulting with him about anything.

> **Daniel 5:14** I have heard that the spirit of the gods is in you and that you have insight, intelligence, and outstanding wisdom.

Insight, Intelligence, And Wisdom

Belshazzar told Daniel that his reputation had preceded him. He explained that he had heard of Daniel and began to praise him for his abilities. He had been neglecting Daniel, but now he wanted something and was trying to butter him up. There can be little doubt that Daniel, with all his abilities, was well aware of what this hypocrite was doing.

Oliver B. Greene: Belshazzar knew nothing of the eternal God of Daniel. He spoke in terms of *gods*—many gods.[14]

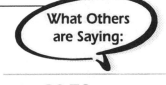

☞ **GO TO:**

Daniel 2:10, 11; Daniel 4:7 (wise men)

> **Daniel 5:15** The wise men and enchanters were brought before me to read this writing and tell me what it means, but they could not explain it.

Those Buffoons Don't Know

The king summarized the events for Daniel:

1) He summoned the wise men and enchanters.
2) He showed them the message on the wall.
3) He asked them to interpret it.
4) They failed.

The wise men were frauds having no knowledge of the things of God.

There were two other times when <u>the wise men of Babylon could not do what the king asked</u>.

Remember This . . .

> **Daniel 5:16** Now I have heard that you are able to give interpretations and to solve difficult problems. If you can read this writing and tell me what it means, you will be clothed in purple and have a gold chain placed around your neck, and you will be made the third highest ruler in the kingdom."

earthly minded: *only concerned about the things of this life*

☞ **GO TO:**

Acts 8:17–20 (money)

KEY POINT

A true man of God will not use the things of God for his own glory.

KEY POINT

Every good thing is a gift from God.

What Others are Saying:

Remember This . . .

☞ **GO TO:**

I Samuel 13:13, 14 (foolish)

Money, Position, And Power

This is the same offer that Belshazzar made to his unenlightened wise men: expensive gifts, a prominent position in the kingdom, and power. These are the things that most **earthly minded** people want—money, position and power. All Daniel had to do to receive them was interpret the handwriting.

> **Daniel 5:17** Then Daniel answered the king, "You may keep your gifts for yourself and give your rewards to someone else. Nevertheless, I will read the writing for the king and tell him what it means.

Keep Your Gifts

Daniel was unusually disrespectful to the king. He did not answer with, "O King, live forever" but immediately rejected the king's gifts and rewards. He probably knew they wouldn't be worth much, because he wouldn't be keeping them very long. What good is a raise and promotion the day before your company folds?

However, there is another point here: when God gives someone a gift, such as Daniel's gift of interpreting dreams, that gift is meant to be used for God's glory and not for the profit or glory of the one who receives it. Daniel did not want to make <u>money</u> with the gift God had given him, so he told the king to keep the gifts. It seems obvious that Daniel did not like the king, but he assured Belshazzar that he would still read the message and interpret it.

David Hocking: That's what I call integrity. Right off the bat, he said, "Let your gifts be for yourself, and give your rewards to another." I don't need them and I don't want them—my ministry is not for sale! That was a powerful point.[15]

This was not the first time Daniel refused something. *Daniel resolved not to defile himself with the royal food and wine, and he asked the chief official for permission not to defile himself this way (Daniel 1:8).*

> **Daniel 5:18** "O king, the Most High God gave your father Nebuchadnezzar sovereignty and greatness and glory and splendor.

Remember Old Nebuchadnezzar

Daniel let Belshazzar tremble a little longer. Before reading the message to him, he reminded the <u>foolish</u> king of a few things. *First*, he reminded him of the source of Nebuchadnezzar's sovereignty, greatness, glory, and splendor. Nebuchadnezzar did not earn or deserve the things he had. They were gifts from the Most High God.

> **Daniel 5:19** Because of the high position he gave him, all the peoples and nations and men of every language dreaded and feared him. Those the king wanted to put to death, he put to death; those he wanted to spare, he spared; those he wanted to promote, he promoted; and those he wanted to humble, he humbled.

The Greatest Of Them All

Second, Daniel reminded Belshazzar that <u>Nebuchadnezzar</u> had absolute power. He was known and feared all over the earth. He killed those he wanted to kill and spared those he wanted to spare. He was so powerful no human being could prevent him from doing whatever he wished.

> **Daniel 5:20** But when his heart became arrogant and hardened with pride, he was deposed from his royal throne and stripped of his glory.

God Sat Him Down

Third, Daniel pointed out Nebuchadnezzar's sin. His heart was filled with arrogance and <u>pride</u>. He took sole credit for all his accomplishments and believed everything he did was for his own <u>glory</u>. It was only after God <u>humbled</u> him that he developed a right perspective and began to glorify God. The purpose of Daniel's words was to show the trembling king that he had made the same mistake his grandfather made, and Belshazzar had no right to expect to get away with it.

 KEY Symbols:

Nebuchadnezzar
all he had was from the Most High God

☞ **GO TO:**

Jeremiah 27:6, 7 (Nebuchadnezzar)

 KEY Symbols:

Nebuchadnezzar
absolute power

☞ **GO TO:**

Proverbs 16:18 (pride)

Daniel 4:30 (glory)

Daniel 4:37 (humbled)

 KEY Symbols:

Nebuchadnezzar
filled with arrogance and pride
God humbled him
he repented

David Hocking: Belshazzar listened to this story: he wasn't dumb. He was a little drunk, but he was listening to this story and realizing what the punch line was going to be. "It was pride," Daniel said. This old man [Daniel] was looking at [the king] knowing that Belshazzar could have him executed. "It was pride that caused your ancestor Nebuchadnezzar to lose his throne. Do you think God's going to be any different with you?"[16]

God cannot lead people who will not submit. If we would humble ourselves and submit to him, he would reward instead of having to humble us. The Bible says, *God opposes the proud but gives grace to the humble* (I Peter 5:5).

☞ **GO TO:**

Daniel 4:30–33 (grass)

milquetoast: *very timid*

> **Daniel 5:21** He was driven away from people and given the mind of an animal; he lived with the wild donkeys and ate grass like cattle; and his body was drenched with the dew of heaven, until he acknowledged that the Most High God is sovereign over the kingdoms of men and sets over them anyone he wishes.

Out To Pasture

Fourth, Daniel reminded Belshazzar of what happened to Nebuchadnezzar. God deposed him and caused him to go insane. He had the mind of a beast, lived with the wild donkeys, and ate grass like an ordinary cow. His body was always wet with dew, and his mental illness continued until he admitted that the Most High God controls all kingdoms and chooses all rulers.

David Jeremiah with C.C. Carlson: Most sermons from our pulpits today are **milquetoast** renditions compared to those given by the holy men of the Bible. Daniel told it like it was.[17]

☞ **GO TO:**

II Peter 3:3–7 (deliberately)

Psalm 119:105 (light)

light: *knowledge of God*

> **Daniel 5:22** "But you his son, O Belshazzar, have not humbled yourself, though you knew all this.

Oh Foolish You

Fifth, Daniel reminded Belshazzar that he was a descendant of Nebuchadnezzar which is a way of saying he had personal knowledge of the things that happened to him. Also, that Belshazzar had committed the same sin Nebuchadnezzar committed by not humbling himself before God. And to make matters worse,

Belshazzar was fully aware of all these things. Daniel was making the point that Belshazzar could not plead ignorance; he had <u>deliberately</u> ignored these things.

Ed Young: In other words, you have not responded to the **light** that you have been given. And those who have the <u>light</u> of God in Jesus Christ and don't respond to it are much more accountable than those who do not have a clear word from God and a clear light from God.[18]

Hal Lindsey: We [America] have the witness of how God has protected this country and we have the witness of how great the light was given here. And yet, we are forsaking it. We have pushed the knowledge of God out of the public consciousness.[19]

> **Daniel 5:23** Instead, you have set yourself up against the Lord of heaven. You had the goblets from his temple brought to you, and you and your nobles, your wives and your concubines drank wine from them. You praised the gods of silver and gold, of bronze, iron, wood, and stone, which cannot see or hear or understand. But you did not honor the God who holds in his hand your life and all your ways.

desecrating: abusing or showing contempt for the things of God

How Could You Be So Stupid

Sixth, Daniel charged Belshazzar with being an enemy of God by opposing and setting himself against him. He charged the king with committing a grave *sacrilege* by sending for the Temple vessels and **desecrating** them at his drunken feast. He also charged the king with *idolatry* by praising man-made gods that are deaf and dumb while ignoring the God who held the king's life and ways in his hands.

These harsh and embarrassing charges were leveled against Belshazzar in front of all his guests and family. He could have had Daniel killed for saying these things, but Daniel did not soften his words. He laid it on the line.

KEY Symbols:

Nebuchadnezzar
the mind of a beast
lived with the wild donkeys
ate grass like an ordinary cow
always wet with dew

Oliver B. Greene: When we look around us, it seems that percentage wise we are in the same position as were Daniel and his friends in Babylon. We are in the Babylon of the world, a world that has but one desire: to build a world empire, with one-world government, one-world religion, one-world language, and world currency. The rulers of today are striving to make one giant Babylon from this earth which is the Lord's.[20]

Belshazzar's grandfather Nebuchadnezzar had said, *I decree that the people of any nation or language who say anything against the God of Shadrach, Meshach, and Abednego be cut into pieces and their houses be turned into piles of rubble, for no other god can save in this way* (Daniel 3:29). He decreed the death penalty and the destruction of their house. Who would have thought Nebuchadnezzar's own grandson would have violated it?

Daniel Reminded Belshazzar:

1) that God was the source of Nebuchadnezzar's sovereignty, greatness, glory, and splendor,
2) that God gave Nebuchadnezzar absolute power,
3) of Nebuchadnezzar's sin—a heart filled with arrogance and pride,
4) of what happened to Nebuchadnezzar—God deposed him and caused him to go insane,
5) that he was a descendant of Nebuchadnezzar so he should remember what happened to him, and
6) that he was acting as an enemy of God by opposing and setting himself against him.

> **Daniel 5:24** Therefore he sent the hand that wrote the inscription.

The Hand

Because of what Daniel has already said, God sent the hand that wrote on the wall. In short, God made Belshazzar's grandfather great and gave him absolute power. But his grandfather became arrogant and proud, ignoring God and glorifying himself, So God humbled him. Belshazzar knew this but did not care. He did not use the information God had placed before him or take advantage of the opportunities he had. And, to make matters worse, he even made himself an enemy of God by defiling the sacred vessels taken from the Temple. This is what provoked the handwriting on the wall.

> **Daniel 5:25** "This is the inscription that was written: MENE, MENE, TEKEL, PARSIN

What Was That?

The hand had disappeared, but the message remained on the wall. Daniel looked at it and read it. No one can definitely say what language it was written in, but it was certainly not that of the Babylonians. If it had been, Belshazzar would have read it himself. It was probably not Hebrew either, since some of his wise men could have read it. All that can be said for sure is that it was written by God, and the Holy Spirit revealed it to Daniel.

> **Daniel 5:26** "This is what these words mean: Mene: God has numbered the days of your reign and brought it to an end.

☞ **GO TO:**

Psalm 90:12 (numbered)

Your Number Is Up

This is Daniel's interpretation of the message. Each word has a short definition. The word *Mene* is similar to the English words "number" or "<u>numbered</u>." It meant that God had numbered the days of Belshazzar's reign, and they were all used up. His reign was over.

The word *Mene* was repeated (Mene, Mene or numbered, numbered) to add emphasis to the decision or to show that it was final. Belshazzar may not have been afraid of that army outside his walls when he drank the wine out of the Temple vessels, but he should have been. God was emphatic about bringing him down.

KEY Symbols:

Mene, Mene
your days are numbered
it is final

Union Gospel Press: Here the term [Mene] stood for the fact that God had fixed a time limit on the Babylonian Empire and now reckoned that it had reached this limit. The word was repeated to show the certainty of the judgment.[21]

What Others are Saying:

> **Daniel 5:27** Tekel: You have been weighed on the scales and found wanting.

You Don't Measure Up

The word *Tekel* is similar to the English words "<u>weigh</u>," "weight" or "<u>weighed</u>." It meant that God had put Belshazzar on his divine scales and found that he did not measure up. He was undeserving of the blessings he was enjoying and not qualified to lead a world government.

☞ **GO TO:**

Job 31:6 (weigh)

I Samuel 2:3; Psalm 62:9 (weighed)

Exodus 32:33; Revelation 3:5; 20:12; 22:19 (recording)

Noah Hutchings: God weighed Belshazzar, and though he may have made a good dishwasher, a stable keeper, or a bartender, a king he was not. He was not even worth saving. The people of Babylon were guilty with him in his folly, because they approved of the moral standards. In other words, they liked the king because he did the things which they also liked to do.[22]

David Hocking: Any act that we have ever done and every word that we have ever said, God has numbered. All the hairs of our head are numbered, all the days of our lives are numbered, all the tears that we have shed are numbered. The Bible has wonderful things to say about how <u>God is recording everything</u> that we have ever done or said. That can be a wonderful thought in the sense of our security in the Lord or it can be an awesome thing if you are not walking with the Lord.[23]

> **Daniel 5:28** Peres: Your kingdom is divided and given to the Medes and Persians."

A Double Meaning

KEY POINT

God has recorded
everything we have
ever done

Here the word is *Peres.* In Daniel 5:25 it was *Parsin.* Most scholars say *Peres* and *Parsin* are the same word with *Peres* being the singular form and *Parsin* being the plural form. Like most words, it had more than one meaning. The first meaning is similar to the English words "divide," "divided," or "division," and the second meaning is a reference to the kingdom of Persia. The thought is that Babylon would be divided and given to the Persians. At that time, the Persians formed a dual empire with the Medes (see Something to Ponder at Daniel 5:1, page 127), so Daniel rightly interpreted the word to mean *your kingdom is divided, and given to the Medes and Persians.*

Now, we ask "Could God really do that?" It seems impossible. Belshazzar was the head of a world power and the city of Babylon was an armed fortress. It was one of the most fantastic and greatest cities of all time. It's hanging gardens were among the seven wonders of the world (see Commentary at Daniel 4:4, page 97). The city was essentially a square (see Illustration #14, page 127). Each side was 14 miles long. If you set out to walk around it, you would walk 14 miles across the front, 14 miles down one side, 14 miles across the back, and 14 miles up the other side for a total of 56 miles.

You have heard of the Great Wall of China. The city of Babylon was circled by two great walls. The outer wall was 311 feet high,

87 feet thick, and 56 miles long. There was a road on top of the wall. It was wide enough for six chariots to ride side by side. There were 250 towers on top of that wall. Each tower was manned with troops.

Down below, on the outside of the wall, was a canal or moat. It surrounded the city and was filled with water. People crossed it on drawbridges. Huge gates closed off the city. There was a second wall inside the outer wall with more soldiers and another road that was used for the rapid deployment of troops and supplies. The river Euphrates flowed under these walls. It went through the city and out the other side. It provided a constant supply of drinking water.

Several hundred acres of land had been set aside for farming inside the walls. Vegetables and cattle were grown to support the inhabitants of the city. There was enough food and provisions in storage to last for years, and more food could be grown if needed. At the time of Belshazzar's big feast, the ever-flowing Euphrates river was full of water, the drawbridges were raised, the gates were closed, sentinels were posted on the walls, and a great army was entrenched behind them. This is why Belshazzar felt so secure. He believed he was safe and had all he needed, but God had other plans.

Could it happen? Belshazzar must have given it some thought. He knew the Medes and Persians had an army outside the city, but how could they get across the moat? It was filled with water. How could they get over the first wall? It was 311 feet high. How could they get through the wall? It was 87 feet thick. And even if they did get past it, they still had to penetrate the second wall and defeat the Babylonian army. But God said Belshazzar's time was up, so even the most impressive defenses in the world couldn't save him.

KEY Symbols:

Peres
a divided kingdom given to the Medes and Persians

Hal Lindsey: When God is through with a nation there is no defense. We can't defend ourselves with missiles or anything else if God is through with us. So the most important thing is that this nation [America] repent and turn back to God.[24]

What Others are Saying:

> **Daniel 5:29** Then at Belshazzar's command, Daniel was clothed in purple, a gold chain was placed around his neck, and he was proclaimed the third highest ruler in the kingdom.

☞ **GO TO:**

Judges 8:26; Luke 16:19 (purple)

Take Your Gifts, You Have Them Coming

If Belshazzar was angry with Daniel for his bold denunciation, nothing is said about it. His word was law, and he kept it. He ignored Daniel's suggestion to keep the gifts and give the rewards to someone else. A **purple** robe was placed on Daniel's shoulders, a gold chain was placed around his neck, and he was proclaimed the third highest ruler in Babylon.

Remember This . . .

The first ruler and true king was Nabonidus. The second ruler and co-regent was Belshazzar. That is why Daniel was made the third highest ruler. Belshazzar could not replace his father, and would not replace himself, so he put Daniel in the next highest position.

☞ **GO TO:**

I Corinthians 6:19, 20 (temple)

> **Daniel 5:30** That very night Belshazzar, king of the Babylonians, was slain,

A Big Invasion

Here we have the end result, but we have to rely on secular history for the details. About two weeks before the drunken party Cyrus, Commander of the Medes and Persians, started preparing for an invasion. He divided his army and sent several thousand troops to the south side of the city. It was their job to stay near the place where the Euphrates River exited the city, to watch for the river to stop flowing, and stay out of sight. He sent several thousand more troops to the north side of the city. It was their job to stay near the place where the Euphrates River entered the city. They were also supposed to watch for the river to stop flowing and stay out of sight (see Illustration #14, page 127).

About ten miles north of the city there was a very large swamp not far from the river. Cyrus had his troops dig a channel from the river to within just a few feet of the swamp. He also had the dirt piled on the banks of the river, so he could dam it up at the time of his choosing.

On the night of the invasion, he had some of his troops complete the unfinished part of the channel to the swamp. He had thousands of other troops pushing dirt into the river to block the flow of water. All of that sent the water flowing in a different direction. The river bed emptied and the moat drained. That left only the river bed under the wall with no water. When the troops on each side of the city saw the water drop, they went under both walls of the city, killed the guards, lowered the drawbridges, and let in the rest of the army.

This caught Belshazzar and his lords by complete surprise. The handwriting on the wall had them rattled, the wine had them drunk, and as a result, they were unable to direct their army. Belshazzar was a proud, unrepentant pleasure seeker who was living under a false sense of security. He assumed he had everything under control. He provoked God, and in one night his world empire fell. He failed to consider the power of God and was killed.

What Others are Saying:

Noah Hutchings: The city experienced little battle damage, and the conquest was so swift and complete, history records that it was several days before many citizens knew that there had been a change in the government.[25]

Ed Young: History tells us that not a spear was thrown—not a spear was thrown when Babylon was defeated.[26]

David Jeremiah with C.C. Carlson: It was curtains for Belshazzar when he took the holy vessels of God and desecrated them. What about us? We don't have personal access to the ancient cups of gold. But the Bible says our bodies are <u>temples</u> of the Lord, the vessels of God. When we take holy things that belong to God and corrupt them with drugs, alcohol, and the degrading things of the world, God's judgment is soon at the door. That's a pretty sobering thought.[27]

> **Daniel 5:31** and Darius the Mede took over the kingdom, at the age of sixty-two.

A Big Change

After Cyrus and his troops captured the city, several weeks passed. Eventually, his uncle, Darius the Mede, went to Babylon and took over the world kingdom (see Time Line #1, Appendix A). He was 62 years old at the time. Later we will learn that this seems to be **foreordained** by God because this new empire will release the Jewish captives Nebuchadnezzar had taken years before and allow them to return home to rebuild Jerusalem and the Temple.

It is an interesting fact of history that the mother of Cyrus was a Mede and his father a Persian. It was their marriage that brought this coalition together.

KEY POINT

Our bodies are the temple of God

☞ **GO TO:**

Daniel 2:39 (inferior)

II Peter 1:19 (light)

foreordained: decreed by God before it happened

light: spiritual light such as knowledge of the Bible and Jesus

J.G. Hall: Two prophecies were fulfilled as Darius entered the reveling city and conquered it that night. The head of gold on Nebuchadnezzar's dream-image gave way to the breast and arms of silver as an inferior kingdom came to power, and the handwriting on the wall was fulfilled to the letter.[28]

Hal Lindsey: The course of every empire in history, of every great nation, has been that it will start and it will have some good men at the beginning, and then it will decline. The moral character, moral fiber of the government eventually declines, and when that happens, you will find that there is . . . eventually the judgment of God. And especially that is true when a nation is given a lot of light.[29]

KEY POINT

The course of every empire in history, of every great nation, has been that it will start and it will have some good men at the beginning, and then it will decline. The moral character, moral fiber of the government eventually declines, and when that happens, you will find that there is . . . eventually the judgment of God.

Study Questions

1. What rewards were offered to Daniel to interpret the handwriting? What was his response, and what happened?
2. Did Daniel respect his king or gloss over Belshazzar's terrible sin?
3. Are people secure in an armed fortress? Were the Babylonians?
4. Are people and nations accountable to God for what they do? What happened to Babylon?
5. How did Belshazzar change when the hand wrote the message on the wall? Did he repent?

CHAPTER WRAP-UP

- The Medes and Persians had Babylon surrounded, so Belshazzar threw a big party to show everyone that he was not afraid. He invited a thousand of his top leaders, his wives, and his concubines. (Daniel 5:1)
- Belshazzar decided to demonstrate that he was not even afraid of Israel's God, so he stupidly committed a sacrilege by drinking wine out of the vessels taken from the Temple in Jerusalem. All his guests foolishly joined in. (Daniel 5:2–4)
- Suddenly a supernatural event took place at the party. A ghostly hand appeared, and its finger wrote a strange message on the wall. Everyone was dumbfounded. (Daniel 5:5–12)
- When no one at the party could interpret the message, Daniel was summoned. He told the king that the message meant the king's reign was over, he had been judged and found lacking, and the Medes and Persians would take control of the kingdom. (Daniel 5:13–28)
- Although Daniel was rewarded for his service to the king, it meant little to him. For that same night Babylon fell, Beshazzar was killed, and the Medes and Persians took over the empire. (Daniel 5:29–30)

DANIEL 6

CHAPTER HIGHLIGHTS

- A Plan to Promote
- A Plot to Eliminate
- Prayer and Protection
- Punishment of Accusers
- King's Decree

Let's Get Started

Now we come to the best-known chapter in Daniel. In fact, the story of Daniel in the lions' den, and the story in Chapter 3 about Shadrach, Meshach, and Abednego are two of the most popular children's stories in the entire Bible. Many Christians have probably never heard of God's Statue (Nebuchadnezzar's dream statue) in Chapter 2 or the Seventy Weeks of Daniel in Chapter 9, but they are well aware of the courage and faith of Daniel as he stood before the den of lions, and that of Shadrach, Meshach, and Abednego as they stood before the fiery furnace. We can learn a great deal from these stories about God's **sustaining grace**.

Not much time has passed since the handwriting on the wall, but there are many dramatic changes taking place in Babylon. The head of gold, Babylon (the first Gentile world kingdom), on God's Statue (see Illustration #5, page 53) is gone. Medo-Persia (the second Gentile world kingdom), the chest and arms of silver, are now in power. Belshazzar, the last and most foolhardy king of Babylon, is dead, and Darius, the 62 year-old king of Medo-Persia, is on the throne. However, he is sick, and this is how we know that not much time has passed. Historians tell us Darius died about two years after he became king of the empire. Daniel was still about 80 years old (see Time Line #1, Appendix A).

☞ **GO TO:**

Nehemiah 9:21; Psalm 55:22 (sustain)

I Corinthians 1:4; 15:10 (grace)

sustaining: the helping power of God

grace: the undeserved favor of God

☞ **GO TO:**

Daniel 3:2, 3 (satraps)

satraps: princes or people of authority

KEY Symbols:

Darius

*three administrators
  including Daniel*
  - protect the interests
    of the king
120 satraps
  - 40 in each group
  - one for each
    division of the
    kingdom

What Others
are Saying:

☞ **GO TO:**

Genesis 41:39–44
(second in command)

> **Daniel 6:1** It pleased Darius to appoint 120 satraps to rule throughout the kingdom,

Divvy It Up

This is another reason why we know not much time had passed since the handwriting on the wall. Darius was in the process of setting up his government. He divided his newly-conquered kingdom into 120 divisions or provinces. Then came the political appointments which usually, but not always, went to members of the royal family. It pleased Darius to make 120 appointments, one ruler for each division or province of his kingdom. These rulers were called **satraps**.

> **Daniel 6:2** with three administrators over them, one of whom was Daniel. The satraps were made accountable to them so that the king might not suffer loss.

Daniel Finds Favor

The 120 divisions or provinces of the kingdom were divided up into three groups, probably 40 in each group. Then three administrators were appointed, one over each group, and Daniel was one of the three. It was the job of these administrators to protect the interests of the king. They were probably told to watch the satraps for things like corruption, disloyalty, theft, and poor administration.

Noah Hutchings: History records that Cyrus crucified three thousand Babylonian political enemies. Doubtless all of the one thousand lords of Babylon who attended Belshazzar's party were included in this number. . . . We would certainly expect Daniel, the third ruler of Babylon, to have been included in this execution of high political Babylonian officials; however, not only was he spared, but he was made one of the three presidents of the empire.[1]

> **Daniel 6:3** Now Daniel so distinguished himself among the administrators and the satraps by his exceptional qualities that the king planned to set him over the whole kingdom.

Promote Daniel

Daniel was superior to everyone else Darius had appointed. He quickly distinguished himself among the other leaders, and it did not go unnoticed. The king made plans to set Daniel over the whole kingdom. He would have Daniel <u>second in command</u> only to himself.

What Others are Saying:

Hal Lindsey: The reason Daniel was great was that he learned by faithfully following the will of God that integrity and honesty is always our responsibility, not just before men and what they can see, but before the Lord.[2]

Noah Hutchings: With the institution of Daniel in the government of the Medo-Persian Empire, we witness the fall of one empire and the rise of another. Now, the question often arises: "Will Babylon ever rise again?" As we have brought out many times, the city of Babylon will be rebuilt. The Babylonian system will spread to all Gentile nations, the foremost of which is our own country, but the city itself will be rebuilt on its old site.[3]

Remember This . . .

To these four young men [Daniel, Shadrach, Meshach, and Abednego] God gave knowledge and understanding of all kinds of literature and learning (Daniel 1:17). In every matter of wisdom and understanding about which the king [Nebuchadnezzar] questioned them, he found them ten times better than all the magicians and enchanters in his whole kingdom (Daniel 1:20). There is a man in your [Belshazzar's] kingdom who has the spirit of the holy gods in him. In the time of your father he was found to have insight and intelligence and wisdom like that of the gods (Daniel 5:11).

> **Daniel 6:4** At this, the administrators and the satraps tried to find grounds for charges against Daniel in his conduct of government affairs, but they were unable to do so. They could find no corruption in him, because he was trustworthy and neither corrupt nor negligent.

We've Got To Get Rid Of Him

The idea of making Daniel second in command found opposition among the other two administrators and all 120 satraps. They organized and tried to formulate <u>charges</u> to bring against Daniel.

☞ **GO TO:**

Acts 24:13-21 (charges)

Philippians 2:15 (blameless)

Luke 23:4 (no basis)

Romans 12:17 (what is right)

Daniel 6:2 (strict accounting)

Daniel 6:4 (faultless)

They wanted to discredit his service to the king, but could not find a way to do it. His conduct was <u>blameless</u>, and they had <u>no basis for a charge</u>. He was trustworthy, honest, and always did <u>what was right</u>.

Union Gospel Press: While Daniel's competence and honesty pleased the king, they infuriated the other officials. There may have been several reasons for this. First, jealousy is a normal reaction in people who are passed over when promotions are made. Second, some may have considered Daniel's high status unfair since he was advanced in years, a hold-over from the enemy administration, and a Jew. Furthermore, since his office involved a <u>strict accounting of money</u> and since <u>Daniel himself was faultless</u>, he may have been thwarting other officials' corrupt schemes for enriching themselves.[4]

Hal Lindsey: You can look through one empire after another and you can see anti-Semitism always raises its ugly head. It is like an infection. . . . It is always just underneath the surface.[5]

Noah Hutchings: Greedy and incompetent employees always hate a dedicated and efficient employee because the good worker will show them up for the lazy loafers that they are.[6]

Concerning the End of the Age, the Apostle Paul said, *There will be terrible times in the last days. People will be lovers of themselves, lovers of money, boastful, proud, abusive, disobedient to their parents, ungrateful, unholy, without love, unforgiving, slanderous, without self-control, brutal, not lovers of the good, treacherous, rash, conceited, lovers of pleasure rather than lovers of God—having a form of godliness but denying its power. Have nothing to do with them* (II Timothy 3:1-5).

※ ※ ※

During the Tribulation Period the False Prophet will use the Mark of the Beast (see GWRV, pages 198–202) to make Christians appear **subversive**. He will use it to create a conflict between world government and Christianity thereby trying to justify the execution of Christians.

> **Daniel 6:5** Finally these men said, "We will never find any basis for charges against this man Daniel unless it has something to do with the law of his God."

Something Must Be Done

Look at the steps of this determined group. First, they tried to find something wrong with Daniel's service to the king, but they found no errors. Second, they tried to find something wrong with Daniel's character, but they found no flaws. Finally, they came to the conclusion that the only way to get him was to attack his commitment to God.

This was not a new idea. It comes from Satan and it was used before. *At this time some astrologers came forward and denounced the Jews. They said to King Nebuchadnezzar, "O king, live forever! You have issued a decree, O king, that everyone who hears the sound of the horn, flute, zither, lyre, harp, pipes, and all kinds of music must fall down and worship the image of gold, and that whoever does not fall down and worship will be thrown into a blazing furnace. But there are some Jews whom you have set over the affairs of the province of Babylon—Shadrach, Meshach, and Abednego—who pay no attention to you, O king. They neither serve your gods nor worship the image of gold you have set up"* (Daniel 3:8–12).

> **Daniel 6:6** So the administrators and the satraps went as a group to the king and said: "O King Darius, live forever!

O Gracious Darius, Listen To Us

The administrators and satraps assembled themselves together in or near the palace. They probably selected a spokesperson, and then they went in as a group to have an audience with the king. They were very <u>crafty</u> and **subtle**. They approached the king like <u>angels of light</u> with sweet-sounding words: *O King Darius, live forever!*

Hal Lindsey: Apart from Bible-believing Christians who believe prophecy is the Word of God, the Jews would have already been wiped out of the United States. And all we need for the United States to be wiped out is for us to turn officially against the Jews because God says, "I will bless that nation that blesses you, and I will curse that nation that curses you."[7]

KEY Symbols:

Daniel
nothing wrong with his service to the king
nothing wrong with Daniel's character
- then attack his commitment to his God

Remember
This . . .

☞ **GO TO:**

Genesis 3:1 (crafty)

II Corinthians 11:14 (angel of light)

subtle: *cunning, clever, tricky, sly*

What Others are Saying:

Most Islamic Arabs are taught from the time they are children to hate and kill Jews. Islamic religious leaders teach their young people that the greatest thing they can do is to die killing a Jew, which will ensure their immediate entrance into heaven. Terrorist groups within Islam actively recruit young men without wives or children to support to go on many of these suicide missions.[8]

☞ **GO TO:**

Psalm 62:4 (lies)

Daniel 6:4 (conspiracy)

Isaiah 45:5, 21, 22; 46:9 (God)

Psalm 59:3; 64:2–4 (conspiracy)

Sanhedrin: the highest legal and religious authority of the ancient Jewish nation

KEY Symbols:

Decree
  not pray
  recognize Darius as god
  or break the law

Penalty
  death in the lions' den

> **Daniel 6:7** The royal administrators, prefects, satraps, advisers, and governors have all agreed that the king should issue an edict and enforce the decree that anyone who prays to any god or man during the next thirty days, except to you, O king, shall be thrown into the lions' den.

Even Daniel Wants This

They exaggerated the situation and even <u>lied</u>. This was <u>a conspiracy</u> of the administrators and satraps. They exaggerated the situation by telling the king that the prefects, advisors, and governors were in on it too, so they lied by acting like Daniel was included in the decision.

They wanted two things: a decree and a penalty. The decree would forbid all prayers for 30 days except those directed to Darius. This would force everyone to do one of three things: not pray, recognize Darius as a <u>god</u>, or break the law. The penalty they wanted called for violators to be thrown into the lions' den. This was similar to the <u>conspiracy</u> against Jesus: *The chief priests and the whole **Sanhedrin** were looking for false evidence against Jesus so that they could put him to death* (Matthew 26:59).

Alabama Judge Ira DeMent has ordered paid anti-religious "monitors" to enter classrooms and assemblies in a rural school district. In a permanent injunction, this federal judge:

- ORDERED A CRACK DOWN on any student observed discussing their faith or praying out loud—even quiet, private, voluntary prayers!
- ORDERED A CRACK DOWN on prayers traditionally given at graduation assemblies, and by players and coaches before football games;

- ORDERED A CRACK DOWN on so-called "religious harrassment." This mandate has been interpreted by some frightened school officials as a ban on Christian students witnessing to others, even at lunchtime—or Christian students wearing Jesus T-shirts and bracelets. Penalties will be severe.[9]

> **Daniel 6:8** Now, O king, issue the decree and put it in writing so that it cannot be altered—in accordance with the laws of the Medes and Persians, which cannot be repealed."

KEY POINT

They were asking the king to establish a world religion for 30 days.

So Let It Be Written

They not only asked the king to issue this decree, they also asked him to put it in writing. According to the law of the Medes and Persians, if he put it in writing, it could not be changed, not even by him. It was a very sinister plan.

☞ **GO TO:**

Malachi 3:6 (change)

Genesis 3:5 (like God)

Isaiah 45:5, 14, 21, 22 (no other)

David Jeremiah with C.C. Carlson: In that culture, they believed their monarchs were infallible; therefore, they could never make a mistake. The king himself could not change what he had written, because that would be admitting his fallibility. . . .[10]

Most religions believe their gods are infallible and <u>changeless</u>. And since their gods are infallible and changeless, the decrees of their gods are infallible and changeless. Apply this to our time because some modern New Age cults teach that we are gods. If it is true then why do we make so many mistakes? Why do we age? Why aren't we surrounded by millions of infallible and changeless people? How many god-men or god-women do you know? The fact is that none of us are infallible or changeless. Satan is the first one to say humans can be <u>like God</u>. God says there are <u>no other</u> gods.

What Others are Saying:

Something to Ponder

KEY POINT

We can *never* be like God.

> **Daniel 6:9** So King Darius put the decree in writing.

So Let It Be Done

The king was deceived. He did not see the diabolical plan behind the decree. He thought his advisors and satraps were asking for a good thing, so he gave in, put the decree in writing, signed it, and was stuck with it.

anointed: *a person chosen by God to do something special*

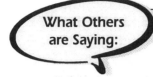

What Others are Saying:

Oliver B. Greene: I imagine that as the presidents and princes left the meeting, they thought their troubles would soon be over. Their scheme had worked perfectly (so they thought), and Daniel would soon be dead. But they reckoned without considering that they were dealing with God's prophet, and God had said, *Touch not mine **anointed**, and do my prophets no harm* (I Chronicles 16:22).[11]

RELATED CURRENT EVENTS

The practice [in Saudi Arabia] of any religion besides Islam is banned and conversion to another faith is punishable by execution. Non-Muslims caught worshiping (even in private), and wearing religious symbols such as crosses, or uttering prayers have faced arrest, imprisonment without trial, torture, and in some cases death.

☞ **GO TO:**

I Kings 8:44-45 (city)

Ephesians 3:14 (kneel)

Psalm 55:17 (three)

I Thessalonians 5:17, 18 (give thanks)

Romans 13:1–7 (obey)

Daniel 3:17, 18; Acts 5:29 (interfere)

> **Daniel 6:10** Now when Daniel learned that the decree had been published, he went home to his upstairs room where the windows opened toward Jerusalem. Three times a day he got down on his knees and prayed, giving thanks to his God, just as he had done before.

Back On His Knees

Daniel did not know about the decree until after it had been published. But learning about it did not change anything. It seemed, from a human standpoint, that his life was on the line, but he did not back down. He did not stop praying. He did not pray in secret, nor did he pray to Darius. He simply did what he had always done—went home, opened a window facing the <u>city</u> of Jerusalem, and humbly <u>knelt</u> and prayed. <u>Three times</u> a day he <u>prayed and gave thanks</u> to God.

What Others are Saying:

Hal Lindsey: When there is a law, a civil law, that diametrically opposes a law of God, guess which one you choose? God's law! Daniel didn't do anything violent. He didn't go out and murder someone or something like that, but Daniel did practice civil disobedience because there was a ridiculous law that said he couldn't pray to his God.[12]

Remember This . . .

As a general rule Christians are supposed to <u>obey their government</u>. But when government <u>interferes with the worship of God</u> civil disobedience is both acceptable and necessary.

Daniel prayed on his knees three times each day, and gave thanks to God.

> **Daniel 6:11** Then these men went as a group and found Daniel praying and asking God for help.

Just Like We Thought

It is only speculation, but it seems almost certain that at least some of these men knew how many times a day Daniel <u>prayed</u> and when. The two administrators and the 120 satraps went as a group to catch Daniel disobeying the law. They were out to make things hard for God's man, so he wouldn't get the promotion he so well deserved.

Uriah Smith: It only remained for these men, having set the trap, to watch their victim that they might ensnare him therein. So they again came tumultuously together, this time at the residence of Daniel, as though some important business had called them suddenly together to consult the chief of the presidents; and lo, they found him, just as they intended and hoped, praying to his God. So far all had worked well.[13]

David Breese: There are many people who ask the foolish question, "If there is a God, why is there so much evil in the world?" "Why is life so hard?" The answer to this is that life is supposed to be hard . . . because it is not final reality but the prelude to reality. Ultimate joy, peace, and fulfillment will only come when we arrive on the **shining shores of eternity**.[14]

```
The government [of China] restricts the practice
of religion to those groups and places of worship
it has authorized. Leaders of groups that do not
comply have been arrested and beaten by police.
Tibetan Buddhist monks and nuns protesting reli-
gious oppression have been tortured, and their
temples and shrines destroyed. The estimated 40
million Chinese Christians worship in underground
churches, and more Christians are imprisoned or
detained than in any other country.[15]
```

☞ **GO TO:**

Matthew 6:9–15 (pray)

shining shores of eternity: heaven

What Others are Saying:

KEY POINT

Daniel would not compromise any of his beliefs.

RELATED CURRENT EVENTS

Something to Ponder

KEY Symbols:

Daniel

prayed daily
at the same time
in the same place
knelt in humbleness
showed thankfulness
was persistent

Daniel was one of the chief administrators in a world kingdom. He had many important and pressing responsibilities. And he also had a group of corrupt individuals to supervise, but he was never too busy to pray. Daniel:

1) Prayed regularly (daily).
2) Had a set time of prayer (three times a day).
3) Had a set place of prayer (upstairs by the window facing Jerusalem).
4) Was humble (he kneeled).
5) Showed gratitude (he gave thanks to God).
6) Was persistent (he prayed just as he had done before).

> **Daniel 6:12** So they went to the king and spoke to him about his royal decree: "Did you not publish a decree that during the next thirty days anyone who prays to any god or man except to you, O king, would be thrown into the lions' den?" The king answered, "The decree stands—in accordance with the laws of the Medes and Persians, which cannot be repealed."

The Law Stands

They did not waste any time. They had what they wanted, and they rushed back to the king. Notice the hypocrisy of their question. They are the ones who got the king to publish the fiendish decree, but they asked, *Did you not publish a decree that during the next thirty days anyone who prays to any god or man except to you, O king, would be thrown into the lions' den?* Of Course the king did, and he made it clear that the decree still stood. He even confirmed that the law of the Medes and Persians would not allow the decree to be repealed.

RELATED CURRENT EVENTS

"Millions of American Christians pray in their churches each week, oblivious to the fact that Christians in many parts of the world suffer brutal torture, arrest, imprisonment, and even death—their homes and communities laid waste—for no other reason than that they are Christians," writes Nina Shea, director of Puebla Program of Freedom House, in her book *In the Lion's Den*. "The shocking untold story of our time is that more

Christians have died this century simply for being Christians than in the first 19 centuries after the birth of Christ. They have been persecuted and martyred before an unknowing, indifferent world and a largely silent Christian community."[16]

— — —

Prominent American Christian leaders from many faith traditions launched a vigorous campaign a year ago to get the government to speak out about the persecution faced by Christians. Last January, the National Association of Evangelicals, a membership organization with 42,000 congregations across the United States, issued a "statement of conscience" declaring "dismay that the United States government has been indifferent to its obligation to speak out against the reigns of terror now being plotted and waged against Christians."[17]

> **Daniel 6:13** Then they said to the king, "Daniel, who is one of the exiles from Judah, pays no attention to you, O king, or to the decree you put in writing. He still prays three times a day."

Islamization:
indoctrination or brainwashing into the religion of Islam

Three Times A Day

Notice several things here about the conspirators:

1) They are guilty of anti-Semitism for unnecessarily pointing out that Daniel was one of the exiles from Judah.
2) They tried to cause a rift between Daniel and the king by pointing out that Daniel was ignoring the king.
3) They tried to put pressure on the king by pointing out that Daniel was ignoring the decree.
4) They tried to pressure the king even more by pointing out that the decree was in writing.

What was Daniel's crime? He was still praying three times a day. That is almost as bad as praying in school.

Oliver B. Greene: Note the utter contempt and disrespect with which the conspirators made the announcement to the king: *That Daniel, which is of the children of the captivity of Judah.* . . . (KJV)—

What Others are Saying:

---

as if to say: "That old foreigner, that Jew, who is no more than a captive and a slave and who is in a position of prominence because of you, is very ungrateful for the power you gave him and the position to which you promoted him."[18]

RELATED CURRENT EVENTS

Christian families are broken up [in Sudan] by abduction, imprisonment, torture, and execution of men. Women and children are kidnapped, sold into slavery for as little as $15, and forced to work as slaves or concubines for their Muslim masters. Other children are sent to re-education camps for forced **Islamization**. Young boys undergo military-type training and become cannon fodder on the front lines of Sudan's civil war. And all this from a country that has signed and ratified the U.N. Convention on the Rights of the Child.[19]

— — —

After I [Richard H. Schneider, Guideposts Senior Staff Editor] read a statement by Michael Horowitz, senior fellow of the Hudson institute, a think tank in Washington, D.C., I felt even more strongly that I had to take action. "I am speaking out on behalf of persecuted Christians precisely because I am a Jew in the most deeply rooted sense," Horowitz said. "I see eerie parallels between the way the elite of the world are dealing with Christians (who have become the scapegoats of choice for thug regimes around the world) and the way the elite dealt with the Jews as Hitler was coming to power."[20]

> **Daniel 6:14** When the king heard this, he was greatly distressed; he was determined to rescue Daniel and made every effort until sundown to save him.

Time Has Run Out

The administrators and satraps were unsuccessful with their attempt to cause a rift between Daniel and the king. He fully understood what had happened and instead of being angry with Daniel, he was distressed with himself for being duped into creating this dilemma. He was determined to keep Daniel out of the lions' den and made every effort to find a way to do so. But the trap was firmly set, and both Daniel and the king were caught in it.

It was only last year when two reporters from the *Baltimore Sun* went to Sudan in northern Africa and were able to buy two Christian slaves for $500 each. This provided front-page verification of the slave trade in Sudan, confirming a series the newspaper ran in 1995. The reporters returned the young Sudanese men to their families.

A group of doctors associated with the Voice of the Martyrs traveled to Sudan and purchased 19 Christian children from Muslim slave traders for $250 each. They were also returned to their parents.[21]

> **Daniel 6:15** Then the men went as a group to the king and said to him, "Remember, O king, that according to the law of the Medes and Persians no decree or edict that the king issues can be changed."

Remember Your Word

Daniel's enemies were still assembled together at sundown and went as a group to see the king. They reminded him that the law of the Medes and Persians would not permit him to change the decree.

What Others are Saying:

Noah Hutchings: Most ancient laws stipulated execution of sentence within a matter of hours, usually the same day. Daniel had to be thrown into a den of angry, hungry lions. As the sun went down, the conspirators appeared before the king to again remind him that it was time for the sentence against Daniel to be carried out.[22]

Oliver B. Greene: Daniel was an old man—probably ninety—but I picture him as tall and straight, walking toward the king's palace as the sun set in the western sky. It was not only sundown in Babylon, but from the human standpoint, it was sunset in Daniel's life.[23]

☞ **GO TO:**

Psalm 34:7,19; 37:39–40; 50:15; I Thessalonians 1:10; II Peter 2:9 (rescue or deliver)

> **Daniel 6:16** So the king gave the order, and they brought Daniel and threw him into the lions' den. The king said to Daniel, "May your God, whom you serve continually, rescue you!"

Daniel never stopped serving God regardless of what came his way.

Something to Ponder

☞ **GO TO:**

Esther 3:12; 8:8–10 (signet ring)

Matthew 27:35–56 (Jesus on the cross)

signet ring: *a ring used to make an official stamp or mark on something*

Something to Ponder

Into The Lions' Den

Darius had no choice but to give the order. He reluctantly ordered Daniel to be taken and thrown into the lions' den (see Illustration #16, page 161). The king loved Daniel and went along, so he could be with Daniel. When his friend was thrown in he said, *May your God, whom you serve continually, <u>rescue</u> you!*

Are we accomplishing what God wants us to accomplish? Christians are not only the objects of God's love, we are also the means through which he works to show others his love. Our behavior impacts others and we are witnesses whether we intend to be or not. If Daniel's faith, loyalty, and service could greatly impact two powerful heathen kings like Nebuchadnezzar and Darius, shouldn't we also be a factor in changing our society for the better?

> **Daniel 6:17** A stone was brought and placed over the mouth of the den, and the king sealed it with his own signet ring and with the rings of his nobles, so that Daniel's situation might not be changed.

Roll In The Stone

After shoving Daniel into the lions' den, a large stone was rolled over the opening. Next, a layer of warm wax was poured between the stone and the den wall to make sure it was sealed. Then, the king used his **signet ring** to make an impression in the wax. Finally, some of the administrators and satraps also used their <u>signet rings</u> to make impressions in the wax. All of this was done to make sure the rock was not moved during the night. When the administrators and satraps returned the next morning, they wanted to be sure that Daniel had not been set free.

When Daniel was thrown into the lions' den, Darius said, *May your God, whom you serve continually, rescue you* (Daniel 6:16)! When Jesus hung on the cross the chief priests, teachers of the law, and elders mocked him saying, *Let God rescue him now if he wants him* (Matthew 27:43). When Daniel was thrown into the lions' den, they rolled a large stone over the opening and sealed it. When Jesus was crucified, *Joseph took the body, wrapped it in a clean linen cloth, and placed it in his own new tomb that he had cut out of the rock. He rolled a big stone in front of the entrance to the tomb and went away. Mary Magdalene and the other*

Illustration #16

Lions' Den—Where Daniel trusted God for his deliverance.

*Mary were sitting there opposite the tomb. The next day, the one after **Preparation Day**, the chief priests and the Pharisees went to Pilate. "Sir," they said, "we remember that while he was still alive that deceiver said, 'After three days I will rise again.' So give the order for the tomb to be made secure until the third day. Otherwise, his disciples may come and steal the body and tell the people that he has been raised from the dead. This last deception will be worse than the first." "Take a guard," Pilate answered. "Go, make the tomb as secure as you know how." So they went and made the tomb secure by putting a seal on the stone and posting the guard* (Matthew 27:59–66).

Preparation Day: the day before the Sabbath (people prepared for the Sabbath because they could not work on the Sabbath)

> **Daniel 6:18** Then the king returned to his palace and spent the night without eating and without any entertainment being brought to him. And he could not sleep.

No Sleep

Darius left the site of the lions' den grieving and worried. He returned to his palace and spent the restless night **fasting**. He even refused all entertainment and pleasure.

Fasting

Many Christians fast by going without food, but not because they want to lose weight. They do it for spiritual reasons. They want to demonstrate:

☞ **GO TO:**

Isaiah 58:4–7 (fasting)

fasting: the act of denying oneself something such as food or drink to show humility, mourning or sorrow before God, and to gain his favor

Something to Ponder

1) Sincerity before God (sincere grief, humility, repentance, or faith).
2) That they are willing to exchange things they need or enjoy for a closer relationship with God.
3) That spiritual things are more important to them than physical things.
4) That the answer to their prayers is more important to them than their own comfort.

They seek things like forgiveness of their sins, a revelation from God, help with problems they cannot solve, deliverance from a national crisis, and healing for someone. They fast for different periods of time: one day (Judges 20:26), three days (Esther 4:16), forty days (Luke 4:1, 2), or a period of time of their own choosing. They usually spend a great deal of time in prayer when they are fasting and they often read their Bibles. It is even possible for groups of Christians to fast. However, it is best to see a doctor before fasting. People with diseases like diabetes should not fast without a doctor's approval.

KEY POINT

It is best to see a doctor before fasting.

• • •

During the lifetime of Isaiah, the Jews were noted for fasting, but they were not fasting to draw closer to God. They were fasting for their own glory, to gain a reputation and to gain the applause of men. Fasting that is done for selfish reasons is worthless. Instead of giving up a few meals, a candy bar and a coke, God would prefer that we give up our sins. Instead of putting on ashes and sackcloth, God would prefer that we put on a genuine attitude of holiness and caring. It is far better to stop living a self-centered life, to stop using the Lord's Day for our business and pleasure, and to stop trying to bring religious glory to ourselves than it is to stop eating a particular treat for a while. This is not to say that fasting is wrong, but it does mean that we can fast for the wrong reasons.

Fasting is good, but we can fast for the wrong reasons.

☞ **GO TO:**

Matthew 28:1 (dawn)

> **Daniel 6:19** At the first light of dawn, the king got up and hurried to the lions' den.

Back To The Lions' Den

The king could have sent legions of soldiers to check on Daniel, but he did not. He wanted to do that personally. So early the next morning, at the first light of <u>dawn</u>, he rushed out of his palace and headed to the lions' den.

> **Daniel 6:20** When he came near the den, he called to Daniel in an anguished voice, "Daniel, servant of the living God, has your God, whom you serve continually, been able to rescue you from the lions?"

☞ **GO TO:**

Romans 14:4 (able)

Living God: the giver of life, the one who is alive, the eternal God

A Hedge Of Protection

Darius was so anxious to find out about Daniel's condition he could not wait until he arrived at the lions' den. He started calling out as soon as he got close enough for Daniel to hear. There was anguish in his voice. He called Daniel's God the **Living God**. He repeated the fact that Daniel constantly—not part of the time or when he felt like it—served the Living God, and he asked if Daniel's God was <u>able</u> to save him.

Jesus said, *If you remain in me and my words remain in you, ask whatever you wish, and it will be given you* (John 15:7). Daniel *continually* served God.

> **Daniel 6:21** Daniel answered, "O king, live forever!

KEY POINT

Daniel's God is the Living God.

Remember This . . .

Yes, I Am Here

This is the fourth time we have seen this expression in Daniel. It seems to be the usual way of addressing kings in Babylon. It was supposed to convey **adulation** or respect. But it seems a little ridiculous because, regardless of the way the kings were addressed, they all died.

We see the words *O king, live forever* also in Daniel 2:4; 3:9; 5:10.

> **Daniel 6:22** My God sent his angel, and he shut the mouths of the lions. They have not hurt me, because I was found innocent in his sight. Nor have I ever done any wrong before you, O king."

adulation: praise or flattery

Remember This . . .

☞ **GO TO:**

Romans 4:20, 21 (power)

☞ **GO TO:**

Jeremiah 32:17
(nothing too hard)

Daniel 3:19–25
(furnace)

What Others
are Saying:

KEY POINT

We should worship
God alone (Matthew
4:10).

Remember
This . . .

☞ **GO TO:**

Matthew 24:15;
   Revelation 12:13–16
   (flee to mountains)

foreshadows: illustrates or
pictures

Petra: an ancient city south
of the Dead Sea in Jordan

He Shut The Mouths Of The Lions

What Darius desperately wanted to do, but could not, God had
the <u>power</u> to do. <u>Nothing is too hard</u> for him. God sent an angel
(some say this angel was Jesus) to shut the mouths of the lions.
Daniel told the king he was not hurt because he was innocent in
God's eyes; not according to the man-made laws of the Medes and
Persians, but according to the laws of God. Daniel also added that
he was innocent before the king. He could honestly claim this
because he was not supposed to worship any human being.

Billy Graham: Spiritual forces and resources are available to all
Christians. Because our resources are unlimited, Christians will
be winners. Millions of angels are at God's command and at our
service. The hosts of heaven stand at attention as we make our
way from earth to glory, and Satan's BB guns are no match for
God's heavy artillery. So don't be afraid. God is for you. He has
committed his angels to wage war in the conflict of the ages—and
they will win the victory.[24]

When Shadrach, Meshach, and Abednego were thrown into
the fiery <u>furnace</u> Nebuchadnezzar looked into the fire and
said, *I see four men walking around in the fire, unbound and
unharmed, and the fourth looks like a son of the gods* (Daniel
3:25). When Daniel was thrown into the lions' den *God sent
his angel, and he shut the mouths of the lions.*

> **Daniel 6:23** The king was overjoyed and gave orders
> to lift Daniel out of the den. And when Daniel was lifted
> from the den, no wound was found on him, because he
> had trusted in his God.

Not Even A Scratch

The administrators and satraps had tricked Darius into signing a
devilish decree. They even forced him into condemning Daniel
and carrying out the penalty it prescribed. The sentence was executed, but Daniel survived. The king was truly delighted and
immediately commanded his troops to lift Daniel out of the lions'
den. Daniel was pulled up and examined. They didn't find even
one scratch on him *because he had trusted in his God.*

David Breese: Is there an application we can make today? Daniel, of course, from here on out is going to give us marvelous prophetic things from God. But in my opinion, here we have an illustration of something that is going to happen as we move toward the End of the Age. The righteous will be persecuted by the wicked, but in the final analysis the righteous will triumph and the wicked will be destroyed.[25]

Many students of prophecy believe the deliverance of Daniel from the lions' den **foreshadows** the deliverance of the Jews from the Antichrist during the Tribulation Period. Those Jews who trust in their God and <u>flee into the mountains</u> will be saved. The mountains referred to here are probably those at the ancient site of **Petra** (see Illustration #2, page 19).

Remember This . . .

> **Daniel 6:24** At the king's command, the men who had falsely accused Daniel were brought in and thrown into the lions' den, along with their wives and children. And before they reached the floor of the den, the lions overpowered them and crushed all their bones.

Throw Them In

Darius did not see through the plot when his administrators and satraps first approached him seeking the decree, but before this event was over he figured it out and did not like being used. Not once did he get angry with Daniel, but now he was furious with the conspirators. He sent his troops to round up the conspirators and their families. They were taken to the lions' den and given the same treatment they so eagerly sought for Daniel. And the lions were so vicious and hungry they attacked and killed their victims while they were still falling through the air.

Oliver B. Greene: Critics have suggested that the reason the lions did not devour Daniel was because the king had previously filled their den with choice meats and they were so gorged that they were not hungry when Daniel was cast in among them; but these claimants fail to explain why the lions so quickly devoured the group of men and their families who were cast into the den for conspiring against Daniel.[26]

David Hocking: All the way through the Psalms it presents the revenge of God upon unbelievers who have falsely accused believers with God as our confidence and our hope. God's not going to let anybody get away with anything.[27]

Wallace Emerson: Does the king, in his desire to do justice to these plotters, commit a greater injustice in sacrificing their children and their wives? We do not have to defend Persian justice. (It is not Biblical justice after the admonition of Ezekiel 18:20.) It was the custom of the orient to assume a man's unity with his family and also to assume that if the husband and father was guilty, the wives and the children were implicated. This assumption might or might not be true, but it can be said that children grow up with ideas of avenging their parents and wives can themselves foster their vengeance in their children and even take part in other conspiracies.[28]

GO TO:

Daniel 4:1 (prosper)

Those in power should understand that it is a mistake to unjustly mistreat people who trust in the Living God.

> **Daniel 6:25** Then King Darius wrote to all the peoples, nations, and men of every language throughout the land: "May you prosper greatly!

Prosper Greatly

This incident prompted another decree from Darius. It went to everyone in his worldwide kingdom. It began in the normal way: *May you prosper greatly!*

> **Daniel 6:26** "I issue a decree that in every part of my kingdom people must fear and reverence the God of Daniel. "For he is the living God and he endures forever; his kingdom will not be destroyed, his dominion will never end.

fear: respect

reverence: respect mixed with wonder, awe and love

The Living God

The decree then gave a warning to everyone in the kingdom; everyone was required to **fear** and **reverence** the God of Daniel. King Darius gave several reasons:

1) *He is the Living God* (not a dead god, false god, or idol).
2) *He endures forever* (is alive and well in every generation).
3) *His kingdom will not be destroyed* (earthly kingdoms will end, but his spiritual kingdom will never end).
4) *His dominion will never end* (nothing can replace him or prevail against him).

Uriah Smith: In this case, and in the case of the three Hebrews in the fiery furnace, the seal of God is set in favor of two great lines of duty: 1) As in the case of the three in the fiery furnace, not to yield to any known sin; and 2) As in the present case, not to omit any known duty. And from these instances, the people of God in all ages are to derive encouragement.[29]

What Others are Saying:

> **Daniel 6:27** He rescues and he saves; he performs signs and wonders in the heavens and on the earth. He has rescued Daniel from the power of the lions."

He Does It All

Here are more reasons why everyone should fear and reverence Daniel's God:

1) *He rescues* (He rescued Daniel from his enemies; also, Shadrach, Meshach, and Abednego).
2) *He saves* (He saved Daniel from the lions and Shadrach, Meshach, and Abednego from the fiery furnace).
3) *He performs signs and wonders in the heavens and on the earth* (He has the power to perform miracles not just in heaven, but also on earth).
4) *He rescued Daniel from the power of the lions.*

> **Daniel 6:28** So Daniel prospered during the reign of Darius and the reign of Cyrus the Persian.

So Daniel Lives On

Daniel was safe, secure, and successful during the reign of Darius and also that of Cyrus. There were no more conspiracies or attempts to overthrow and kill him.

KEY Symbols:

The God of Daniel
is the Living God
endures forever
his kingdom will not be destroyed
his dominion will never end

The God of Daniel
rescues
saves
performs signs and wonders

☞ **GO TO:**

Acts 4:19 (obey)

Psalm 9:17 (nations)

Ephesians 3:20 (ask)

What Others are Saying:

David Hocking: We ought to <u>obey</u> God rather than man—that's the point of this story.[30]

David Breese: Remember the principle—in the last analysis those who follow God . . . prosper into eternity, [but] the wicked shall be sent to hell [along with] all the <u>nations</u> that forget God. [This] is the equation by which we understand the overarching providence of God working in history.[31]

Oliver B. Greene: The God of Daniel is still able to do . . . all that we think or <u>ask</u>![32]

Remember This . . .

Trust and obey, for there's no other way, to be happy in Jesus, but to trust and obey.

Study Questions

1. Why did the administrators and satraps object to Daniel being in charge?
2. What is wrong with having a one-world religion?
3. Which is more important, the laws of man or the laws of God?
4. Why was Daniel delivered from the lions?
5. Was Daniel's deliverance a miracle?

CHAPTER WRAP-UP

- After capturing Babylon, Darius made several political appointments. One of them was Daniel, who excelled to where the king planned to promote him over everyone else. (Daniel 6:1–3)

- Daniel's honesty and integrity worried the administrators and satraps. They could not find any flaws in his character or the way he did his job, so they devised a plan to use his religion against him. They proposed an unjust law that they knew Daniel would not obey. Then they got the king to make it official. (Daniel 6:4–9)

- The administrators and satraps caught Daniel breaking the new law by praying to God instead of Darius. They turned Daniel over to the king and had him thrown into the lions' den. But God protected Daniel; he survived and was released. (Daniel 6:10–23)

- The administrators and satraps, along with their wives and children, were given the same treatment they sought for Daniel—they were killed by the lions. (Daniel 6:24)

- The king issued a decree honoring Daniel's God. Daniel prospered during the remainder of Darius' reign and through the reign of King Cyrus. (Daniel 6:25–28)

Part Two

DANIEL'S PROPHECIES

REVEREND FUN

DANIEL 7

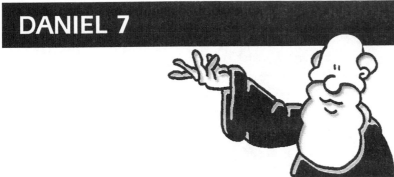

CHAPTER HIGHLIGHTS

- Four Beasts
- The Heavenly Court
- A Heavenly Being
- Daniel's Interpretation
- The End of Things

Let's Get Started

The Book of Daniel has twelve easily divided chapters: Chapters 1–6 are are **historical** and Chapters 7–12 are **prophetic** (see Time Line #1, Appendix A). Because Daniel divided them into these two simple sections, he did not put them in chronological order. Insead, he used the *first verse* of each chapter to let us know how they fit chronologically. Notice the chronology for the last six chapters on the time line. The visions found in these chapters were all given after the death of Nebuchadnezzar. Chronologically, Chapters 7 and 8 took place before Chapter 5 (the handwriting on the wall and death of Belshazzar), but Chapters 9 through 12 took place after Chapter 5 (during the reign of the Medo-Persian Empire).

All of this means we have come to a turning point in the Book of Daniel. Chapters 7–12 deal with prophecy. It was future prophecy to Daniel, but it is partly future and partly past prophecy to us. For example, the rise of the Old Roman Empire was future to Daniel but past to us. And the rise of the Revived Roman Empire was future not only to Daniel but to us as well. Concerning that which is future to us, a very important thing to remember is the fact that at least some of it may be sealed and not yet explained. Keep in mind the instructions to Daniel near the end of this book, *close up and seal the words of the scroll until the time of the end* (Daniel 12:4). The word *until* is a key. It implies that some mysteries will be unexplainable for a while, but they will start to unravel as we approach the End of the Age of the Gentiles.

historical: *about past events*

prophetic: *about future events*

KEY POINT

The word *until* is a key. It implies that some mysteries will be unexplainable for a while, but they will start to unravel as we approach the End of the Age of the Gentiles.

Two Viewpoints

Viewpoint #1—Chapter 7 may be one of those unexplainable chapters. It tells about four strange beasts Daniel saw in a series of visions from God. Many great Bible experts believe these four strange beasts represent the same four world kingdoms Nebuchadnezzar saw in his scary dream found in Chapter 2, and therefore also relate to God's Statue (Nebuchadnezzar's dream statue; see Illustration #5, page 53) as follows:

1) The head of gold is the kingdom of Babylon.
2) The breast of silver is the kingdom of Medo-Persia.
3) The belly and thighs of bronze is the kingdom of Greece.
4) The legs of iron and feet of partly iron and partly clay are the kingdoms of the Old Roman Empire and Revived Roman Empire.

Viewpoint #2—But this author and a few other prophecy experts disagree. Because there are so many experts on both sides of the issue it is recommended that careful consideration be given to the following:

1) The *symbols* are different. Chapter 2 is about materials in a statue, but Chapter 7 is about beasts.
2) The *number of symbols* is different. Chapter 2 has five materials (gold, silver, brass, iron, a mixture of iron and clay), but Chapter 7 has four beasts (lion, bear, leopard, terrifying animal).
3) The *timing* is different. Chapter 7 was given *in the first year of Belshazzar* (Daniel 7:1) and the four beasts *are four kingdoms that "will" rise from the earth* (Daniel 7:17). The first beast (lion) cannot be the first material (gold) because Babylon had "already" risen and, in fact, was near its demise.
4) The *end of the kingdoms* is different. In Chapter 2, the first material (head of gold) did not outlive the last material (feet of iron and clay); the second material (breast and arms of silver) did not outlive the last material (feet of iron and clay); nor did the third material (belly of brass). But in Chapter 7, the first three beasts will outlive the fourth beast (see Daniel 7: 11–12).
5) The *relationship between the kingdoms* is different. In Chapter 2, the five materials of the statue lived at different times. The gold kingdom existed, then the silver kingdom existed, then the bronze kingdom existed, etc. But in Chapter 7, the four

beasts all live at the same time. The first three even witness the destruction of the fourth.

6) In Chapter 2, the gold, silver, and brass kingdoms *will not exist* when Jesus returns. They are past history. But in Chapter 7 all the beasts will be alive when Jesus returns.

7) In Chapter 2, Daniel knew who the head of gold was (Babylon). But in Chapter 7, he *did not know* who the winged lion was.

8) The first three beasts in Chapter 7 appear to be the same kingdoms associated with the kingdom of Antichrist in Revelation 13:2 (see GWRV, page 186) and *all of them are future*, not past.

9) In Chapter 8, a *two-horned ram* represents Medo-Persia not a bear (Daniel 8:20). And a *shaggy goat* represents Greece not a four-winged, four-headed leopard (Daniel 8:21).

So what does all of this mean? First, there is no question that those who think Chapter 2 and Chapter 7 deal with the same thing have excellent reasons for believing so. They can accurately point to many historical fulfillments that seem to bare their viewpoint out. Second, while that is true we still have the differences in the list above. And, although we might be able to find an explanation for some of them, there is no explanation for all of them. Third, we should keep in mind the fact that the Bible often gives us an initial partial fulfillment of a prophecy, but there is a greater, more complete fulfillment in the future. That will work. The four beasts do correspond to the materials in God's Statue (Nebuchadnezzar's dream statue) up to a point. But the final fulfillment is at the Time of the End.

KEY POINT

The Bible often gives us an initial partial fulfillment of a prophecy, but there is a greater, more complete fulfillment in the future.

David Hocking: You may ask me, "Are you sure, David [that Chapter 2 and Chapter 7 are about different things]?" I must answer, "Absolutely not!" However, I'll tell you one thing, because of certain details, I cannot believe the standard view [that Chapter 2 and Chapter 7 are about the same thing] because it doesn't match with what the Bible says! I don't know if what I'm saying is right or not, but I believe that these visions [in Chapter 7] apply to the Time of the End before the Messiah comes to set up his kingdom. So this is more likely to refer to something in the end-time than to three kingdoms that fell long before Rome was ever in existence. There's something wrong here with **traditional** interpretation.[1]

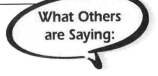

What Others are Saying:

traditional: the usual interpretation

Edward Tracy: I am of the opinion that the seventh chapter cannot be simply another view of the same world powers fully treated in the second chapter of [Daniel's] prophecy.[2]

Wallace Emerson: The first vision (Chapter 7), seen by Daniel in the first year of Belshazzar, carries us directly to the Time of the End, as we interpret it. It exhibits to our eyes four empires that will occupy the world stage at the End of the Age [not four empires that existed hundreds of years ago].[3]

Noah Hutchings: It is difficult to understand how anyone could be so dogmatic as to say that the lion has to be ancient Babylon, the bear has to be Medo-Persia, and the leopard has to be Greece. The forces of Satan deceiving the nations, and preparing them to be drawn into the Middle East at the battle of Armageddon; the waves and the seas roaring; wars and rumors of wars; the major world powers' interest in the Mediterranean—all these things would place the setting entirely in the last generation [not a previous generation].[4]

☞ **GO TO:**

Revelation 9:17 (vision)

Revelation 1:19 (write)

substance: *the main points*

Isle of Patmos: *a small island in the Mediterranean Sea*

> **Daniel 7:1** In the first year of Belshazzar king of Babylon, Daniel had a dream, and visions passed through his mind as he was lying on his bed. He wrote down the substance of his dream.

Daniel's Dream

In Chapter 5, it was stated that Nabonidus became king of Babylon around 555 B.C. and Belshazzar, his son, was a co-regent when Babylon fell around 539 B.C. Depending upon what source we use, Belshazzar reigned for about three to five years. From that we can deduce that the first year of his reign as co-regent and the date of these visions was approximately 544–542 B.C. (see Time Line #1, Appendix A).

So far as we can tell, Daniel was asleep and dreaming when these visions started passing through his mind. The word *visions* suggests more than one. The following chart explains what this means.

When the dream and <u>visions</u> ended, Daniel awoke. Realizing that something significant had occurred, he <u>wrote</u> down the **substance** of what he saw. This is the practice (see GWRV, page 24) John followed when he recorded Revelation on the **Isle of Patmos**.

Visions of the Four Beasts

Part	Verse	Phrase	Vision
1	2	*I looked*	the four beasts (kingdoms) will rise up
2	9	*as I looked*	God will sit on the throne
3	11	*I kept looking*	the four beasts (kingdoms) will be judged
4	13	*I looked*	Jesus will receive dominion

David Breese: Nothing is clearer in the Word of God than the fact that God wants us to understand himself and his working in the lives of men.[5]

> **Daniel 7:2** Daniel said: "In my vision at night I looked, and there before me were the four winds of heaven churning up the great sea.

Wind, Wind, Everywhere Wind (Visions of the Four Beasts, Part 1)

1) One of the names of the Tribulation Period is *a day of darkness and gloom*, and it will come *as a thief in the night*, so some interpreters think this vision is something that will be fulfilled during the Tribulation Period. There are other reasons to think that they may be right, but here, *at night* probably refers to the time of day when Daniel had the vision.

2) The Bible talks about the four winds of the earth (see GWRV, page 105) coming from the four corners of the earth (north, south, east, and west), so a small minority of prophecy experts think this is a reference to the natural winds causing a storm. Since these are called "the four winds of heaven" a few argue that the winds are caused by heavenly forces. But *the four winds of heaven* probably refers to demonic forces because Satan is *the ruler of the kingdom of the air, the spirit who is now at work in those who are disobedient* (Ephesians 2:2).

3) *The great sea* is a Bible expression with more than one meaning. It sometimes refers to the Mediterranean Sea and it sometimes refers to the sea or waters of humanity (people).

What Others are Saying:

☞ **GO TO:**

Zephaniah 1:14–16; Joel 2:2 (darkness)

I Thessalonians 5:2 (night)

Revelation 7:1 (winds)

Jeremiah 25:32, 33 (storm)

Joshua 15:12; Isaiah 57:20; Revelation 13:1–10; 15:2 (sea)

Revelation 17:1, 15; 19:6 (waters)

We should not be dogmatic about the exact meaning of this verse, but it probably means that demonic forces will cause war in the Middle East at the End of the Age. Those demonic forces will upset nations all over the earth, but the main focus of their disturbance will be concentrated around the Mediterranean Sea as the Times of the Gentiles runs out. The Mediterranean is approximately 2,200 miles long. Europe lies to the north, Africa to the south, Asia to the east, and the Atlantic Ocean to the west.

What Others are Saying:

Wallace Emerson: Some have interpreted the *great sea* literally as meaning the Mediterranean and as indicating that the action in the vision will take place around this sea. Others regard it as symbolic of humanity at large; i.e., the nations. There may even be a double reference here since there is no incompatibility between these two meanings. The action may, indeed, take place around the *great sea* and involve all nations.[6]

J. Vernon McGee: Customarily the wind blows from only one direction at a time, but here it is a tornado of great violence with the wind coming from all directions. It refers not only to the disturbed conditions out of which these four nations arose, but particularly to the last stage of the fourth kingdom (Daniel 7:11, 12, 17) in which certain ideologies shall strive to capture the thinking of the disturbed masses of all nations and tribes.[7]

Hal Lindsey: There has hardly been an era where there has not been war. And some of the greatest achievements of mankind have been achieved in connection with building machines of war. . . . Like ravenous beasts the Gentile powers of the earth have continued in carnage.[8]

RELATED CURRENT EVENTS

The "mother of all winters" devastated North America and Europe throughout 1996/1997 with whiteouts, wind chills dropping to minus 80 and flooding cities. . . . Scientists at the World Watch Institute blame the Pacific Ocean warming known as El Niño, for global warming and the "greenhouse effect." . . . Other strange happenings: London experienced its hottest summer since 1659; Moscow and Siberia recorded its warmest year on record; World-wide tropical storms and hurricanes the worst since 1933; Worst heat and drought in Europe and Australia in 300 years;

Unprecedented snowfall in Japan; Mexico City saw its first-ever snowfall. The largest insurance underwriter in the world, Munich Re in Germany (also facing bankruptcy) points out there have been 70 "major natural catastrophes" during the past 10 years. There were only 16 in the 1960s and 29 during the 1970s.[9]

In Daniel 7:2 we see the "four winds of heaven" churning up the great sea. This could mean demonic forces from every direction on the compass would cause a struggle around the Mediterranean Sea at the End of the Age. Daniel 7:3 points out that four beasts *came up* out of the sea. Daniel 7:4 shows the first beast located west of the Sea, Daniel 7:5 shows the second beast located north and east of the Sea, and Daniel 7:6 shows the third beast located south of the Sea. The fourth beast is the rise of the final Gentile world kingdom.

Something to Ponder

Jesus was talking about the signs of the End of the Age when he said, *Nation will rise against nation, and kingdom against kingdom. There will be great earthquakes, famines and pestilences in various places, and fearful events and great signs from heaven. He also said, There will be signs in the sun, moon, and stars. On the earth, nations will be in anguish and perplexity at the roaring and tossing of the sea* (Luke 21:10, 11, 25).

Remember This . . .

> **Daniel 7:3** Four great beasts, each different from the others, came up out of the sea.

☞ **GO TO:**

Daniel 7:17 (four)

Four Big Beasts

One result of this worldwide disturbance will be the rise of <u>four great beasts</u>. These beasts will be four kingdoms and this verse tells us they are different from each other.

ideology: beliefs, opinions, doctrines, etc.

The important thing to remember is that some kind of strife will cause four kingdoms (probably four groups or four coalitions of nations) to appear on the scene near the end of the Gentile Age. We are not told what will cause their appearance or the disturbing strife, but we are told some of the characteristics of the four kingdoms and there is reason to believe that the greatest turmoil will be in the Middle East.

Edward Tracy: The next thing [Daniel 7:3] we note is that there is a difference between these powers on the earth in the end-time. This difference may be expressed in their **ideology**, their form of government, or pride of race, but whatever it is, the basic "difference" between them is what leads to the strife of the previous verse. . . . The manner of their striving would not be limited to war alone, but to all forms of political intrigue and power politics which are so characteristic of nations today. There is struggling for supremacy and predominance among these four world powers [at the end-time].[10]

GO TO:

Jeremiah 4:7–13;
  Ezekiel 38:13 KJV
  (lion)

Jeremiah 17:9 (heart)

KEY Symbols:

Four Great Beasts
  four kingdoms
  different from each
    other
  out of the sea

KEY POINT

The United States lies west of the Mediterranean Sea and, along with England, was very instrumental in the re-establishment of Israel as a nation.

> **Daniel 7:4** "The first was like a lion, and it had the wings of an eagle. I watched until its wings were torn off and it was lifted from the ground so that it stood on two feet like a man, and the heart of a man was given to it.

The First Beast

The symbol used to represent this empire is not that of a lion. It is something that looks *like a lion*. And it does not look like an ordinary <u>lion</u>. It looks like a lion with the *wings of an eagle*.

This beast will have its wings torn off and will stand on its hind legs *like a man*. It will be given the wicked <u>heart</u> of a man. But it will still be a beast (a nation or coalition of nations).

In general, experts agree that the wings represent the rapid movement, victory, and expansion of this kingdom while the plucking of the wings represents an inability to continue to do these things. At first this kingdom will be very powerful and unrestrained. Then it will weaken and become somewhat restrained. Many also agree that *standing on its feet* represents a decline militarily. A lion on the attack crouches low, runs on all fours, and leaps or pounces. It does not stand up and walk on its hind legs because it would lose power and speed in that position.

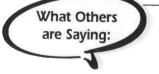

What Others are Saying:

Wallace Emerson: No names are given to these beasts. Could it be, as we have indicated elsewhere, that these are not identified because at that time the kingdoms (if kingdoms they are) did not exist? And hence, if named by their subsequent names, would cause confusion and cast doubt on the prophecy as a whole? If this be granted for the time being at least, we must then identify them if at all, by the symbolism used and by descriptive marks. (It would be well to assume that all of these beasts are delineated here because of their significance to Israel and to Israel's land.)[11]

Edward Tracy: In spite of the brevity of the description of the lion, the identification of this world power at the end-time is quite obvious. It unmistakably suggests the British Empire. In support of this, consider that the coat of arms of the throne of England bears two standing lions—yea, standing on their hind feet as would a man![12]

Noah Hutchings: The United States, since World War I, has been England's protective wings. This nation had to come to England's aid in World War I and again in World War II, but England and the United States have drifted apart and England has declined as a world colonial power. . . . With the withdrawal of England from the Mediterranean after World War II, the eagle's wings that were plucked off, the United States, controlled the great sea. Thus, for twenty years the Mediterranean was an American sea and the United States dictated policy in the Middle East.[13]

David Hocking: All it [the lion] will become is a political voice in the world, saying what it wants to say but without its past glory. That would explain Daniel 7:12 where *the lives were prolonged for a season and a time* (KJV). It may have existed for a time as a great nation, but its wings were plucked and all of a sudden it was lifted up from the earth—no longer having the effectiveness it once had. It becomes nothing more than a man speaking and acting like he has power when, in fact, he does not have it anymore.[14]

"In that sense [in the sense that the U.S. cannot get the U.N. to agree to force Iraq to open certain sites to weapons inspectors], the United States has lost, or at least lost something," said David Albright, President of the Institute for Science and International Security. Albright is a leading authority on Iraq's efforts to build weapons of mass destruction.[15]

KEY Symbols:

First Beast / First Kingdom (West)

BABYLON OR ENGLAND?

like a lion (possibly England)

wings of an eagle (possibly the United States)

- rapid movement, victory, and expansion

wings torn off

like a man

standing on it feet

- decline militarily

wicked heart

RELATED CURRENT EVENTS

WARNING

Some experts believe Babylon's symbol was the <u>lion</u> while others claim it wasn't. In either case, Babylon's symbol was not a standing lion. England is the only nation to ever use the standing lion for its symbol, and since the United States largely came out of England, it is possible that our nation is *like a lion* in its language and culture.

☞ **GO TO:**

Ezekiel 38:10–13 (invade)

Ezekiel 38:13 KJV (lion empire)

rapacious: *predatory, hungry, grasping, greedy*

warlike: *belligerent, willing to fight*

Gog and Magog: *Russia and her allies*

> **Daniel 7:5** "And there before me was a second beast, which looked like a bear. It was raised up on one of its sides, and it had three ribs in its mouth between its teeth. It was told, 'Get up and eat your fill of flesh!'

The Second Beast

The symbol used to represent this empire is not that of a bear. It is something that looks *like a bear*. But it will not be like a cuddly teddy bear. It will be like an angry or hostile grizzly bear threatening anything in its path. It will have three ribs (parts of other beasts or empires) in its mouth between its huge teeth (representing a **rapacious** and **warlike** nature). It will be told to eat its fill of flesh (attack and devour other beasts or empires).

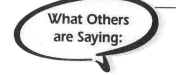
What Others are Saying:

Wallace Emerson: The first thought that comes to one when Russia is mentioned is the Russian bear. For generations, this animal has been used to designate this vast, ungainly country. Can any one country on the face of the earth be so aptly described as having devoured much flesh? Even Hitler, with his demonic lust for power and willingness to shed much blood, cannot equal the human loss of Russia in the First World War, the Russian Revolution, the prison camps of Siberia (20,000,000), the Volga famines (6,000,000), the murders and liquidations that took place under Stalin (wholesale murder of Polish officers), and the human loss during the Second World War. How could anyone describe Russia in better terms?[16]

Edward Tracy: Other expositors have painstakingly investigated the identification of **Gog and Magog**, etc. of Ezekiel 38–39. It is their considered consensus, with scarcely a dissent, that the nations referred to are Russia and her satellites in league with Islamic nations who pose the final threat to Israel's sovereignty.[17]

David Hocking: I have never seen the bear being utilized in the history of Persia. I have a question in my mind about the lack of this figure in history. Yet, we all know that Russia has long referred to itself as a bear. The commentators prior to this century all held that this was Russia even before the Bolshevik Revolution and the devastation of Communism. Millions of people have been murdered under the banner of the great Russian bear.[18]

Hal Lindsey: If you are in a time of constant conflict, if you want to stay a free and peaceful nation, what do you have to do? You have to prepare for war. And you have to be willing to use it if you have to. That's been the order of the day during the "Times of the Gentiles." Only the strong have stayed free.[19]

```
The cold war may be over and the Soviet empire
extinct, but Russia is working on a new jet
fighter that some aerospace experts say will
counter the best planes the U.S. Air Force has on
its drawing board. In late September, 1997 the
fabled Sukhoi fighter design bureau, which devel-
oped the lethal SU-27 Flanker began test flights
at Zhukovsky air base near Moscow of its new
S-32, according to Pentagon sources and reports
from the Russian news agency ITAR-Tass. . . . The
new Russian fighter will be a leap ahead of any
tactical fighter the Russians or Soviets have
flown in the past, say Air Force officials who
would speak only on condition of anonymity.[20]
```

Ezekiel 38 and 39 record an unfulfilled prophecy about a future attack on Israel in the last days. The list of experts who say the aggressors will be Russia and some of her allies is very impressive. These nations will prepare for war and decide to devour and plunder the land of Israel. Several nations, including those from the lion empire, will question the attack but not stop it. Since Russia will be the leader, and main supplier of troops, weapons, and fighter planes in this group of nations, could we not say the group will be *like a bear*?

KEY POINT

Russia and some of the nations that will join her (Iran, Iraq, etc.) in an end-time invasion of Israel lies to the north and east of the Mediterranean Sea. (see Illustration #2, page 19)

RELATED CURRENT EVENTS

KEY Symbols:

Second Beast / Second Kingdom (North and East)

MEDO-PERSIA OR RUSSIA?

like a bear (possibly Russia)

raised up

three ribs in its mouth
- parts of other nations

between its teeth
- rapacious, warlike nature

Something to Ponder

Some prophecy experts say Medo-Persia's symbol was the bear while others claim it wasn't. While there may be some basis for agreeing with those who say Medo-Persia's symbol was the bear, we must still keep in mind the fact that many prophecies have an initial, partial fulfillment, and then later they have a final, total fulfillment. And we must not forget that this empire will be on the scene when the Antichrist arrives.

☞ **GO TO:**

Revelation 12:3; 13:1; 17:3, 7–10 (heads)

> **Daniel 7:6** "After that, I looked, and there before me was another beast, one that looked like a leopard. And on its back it had four wings like those of a bird. This beast had four heads, and it was given authority to rule.

The Third Beast

KEY POINT

If the four winds of heaven churning the great sea in Daniel 7:2 represent turmoil coming from all directions around the sea, we must, at some point, expect trouble from a coalition of nations in the South (see Illustration #2, page 19). That could only mean Africa and Arab nations.

The symbol used to represent this empire is something that looks *like a leopard*. It will be a strange leopard indeed with four wings and four heads. Instead of seizing authority as a conqueror, it will be given authority by someone or something more powerful than it is (perhaps an alliance of nations such as NATO or the United Nations).

The traditional interpretation says this strange leopard was Greece, the belly and thighs of bronze on God's Statue from Nebuchadnezzar's dream. As with the lion beast in Daniel 7:4, the wings are supposed to represent rapid movement and conquest, but with one difference: this beast with four wings would have to be faster than the lion with just two wings. So the traditional interpretation is that Alexander the Great fulfilled this by conquering the world in a short time. And the final aspect of that view says the four heads represent the generals who divided up Alexander's empire after he died.

There are several problems with that. And it seems more likely that this beast represents a four-nation Arab/African coalition of the future. The coalition has not yet appeared nor can it until after the second beast of Daniel 7:5 (Russia and her allies) invades the Middle East. Notice that it receives its power between the decline of the second beast and the rise of the fourth beast.

What Others are Saying:

Wallace Emerson: Could the leopard be an alliance of Arab nations? Most especially those that are closer to the old Babylonian world and which are found in the areas now designated as Iraq, Syria, Jordan, Egypt, Libya, and Arabia? Some of these Arabian states in North Africa belonged to the Old Roman Empire in its greatest extent and might conceivably belong to the new one but not necessarily so. . . . That some fourfold federation could rather suddenly appear in the Arab world should not seem too far-fetched or impossible.[21]

Edward Tracy: I submit that the four-headed and four-winged leopard of Daniel's vision suggests the age-old symbol of the East—the dragon! Its four heads may suggest its political divisions, perhaps the alignment will be China, Indonesia, India, and Japan. Just which nations of the East will constitute the four heads is not critical.[22]

Noah Hutchings: After the bear is chased from the Mediterranean, the four-headed leopard with four wings on its back appears. We cannot tell a great deal about this particular beast because it has not made its appearance yet, and it cannot appear until after the battle of Ezekiel Chapters 38 and 39. Leopards are not native to Palestine; however, from the Song of Solomon 4:8, it is evident that there were some of these animals in the mountains to the south of Israel. . . . The nature and characteristics of this third beast are indicative of the African bloc of nations, or an Afro-Asian alliance.[23]

David Hocking: The heads of the beast certainly represent empires as they do in Revelation where we find <u>the beast with seven heads and on the seventh head, there are ten horns</u> (see GWRV, pages 170–171, 183–185. If they represent empires or kingdoms, why don't they represent that here? So who in the world might this third beast be? Is it not possible that this leopard that comes to power in the midst of the continuance of the lion and the bear nations (although they have lessened powers) is something different than we have ever thought before? Could this refer to some sort of Arab alliance of the end-time? Could the leopard who strikes very quickly be someone like Saddam Hussein? Could the result of handling the difficult Middle East problems be the emergence of an Arab empire with four powerful nations all looking at the question of domination? We simply don't know.[24]

KEY Symbols:

Third Beast / Third Kingdom (South)

GREECE OR ARAB / AFRICAN COALITION?

like a leopard (possibly a coalition of four African and Arab nations)

four wings

like that of a bird

- *rapid movement and conquest*

four heads (four generals or nations)

"given" authority to rule

RELATED CURRENT

The long-range outlook for the current Egyptian government, headed by President Hosni Mubarak, is not good. Many believe that the likelihood of the outbreak of civil war or the assassination of Mubarak is a real possibility. Thus, should the rebel forces win the civil war or Mubarak be assassinated, the odds are that Egypt will eventually become an Islamic state. Should this happen and Egypt become an Islamic state, this would enable Islamic radicals to tighten the circle around Israel. . . .[25]

— — —

The Middle East and North Africa bought nearly half the $40 billion worth of weapons sold abroad, a study published in London said last week [October 1997]. Saudi Arabia led with $9.1 billion, Egypt was second with $2.3 billion, and Israel and Turkey followed with just under $1 billion each, said the International Institute for Strategic Studies, a leading, London-based think tank.[26]

Something to Ponder

Obviously, I do not agree with Edward Tracy's view that the leopard represents China and her allies. I have included his opinion as another differing viewpoint. It is a strange one, but suppose he is right. During the Tribulation the Euphrates River *will* dry up and the kings of the East (China, etc.) *will* move into the Middle East for the Battle of Armageddon (see GWRV, page 236). I do not think, however, this is what Daniel is referring to.

• • •

Every jot and tittle in the Word of God is important. Notice the words *after this* in Daniel 7:6, 7. And notice that they do not appear in Daniel 7:5. Could this suggest a sequence of events; namely, that the third empire cannot come on the scene until after the power and influence of the first two wane; and that the fourth cannot control things until after the third has been organized and given power?

WARNING

It is not difficult to find prophecy experts who say Greece's symbol was the leopard. And it is also not difficult to find experts who say it wasn't. But the four heads in this vision are not what is left of the beast after

Alexander died. They are part and parcel of the beast when it comes to power. Also, Alexander the Great was not given authority. He seized it. The amazing rise and breakup of Greece may foreshadow the life and death of this empire, but we must remember that this will be an End of the Age empire.

> **Daniel 7:7** "After that, in my vision at night I looked, and there before me was a fourth beast—terrifying and frightening and very powerful. It had large iron teeth; it crushed and devoured its victims and trampled underfoot whatever was left. It was different from all the former beasts, and it had ten horns.

The Fourth Beast

We now come to something that most prophecy experts agree on; namely, this fourth beast represents the development of the final Gentile world kingdom. It will be a wicked world kingdom. And here God has given us more information about it than all of the other three kingdoms combined.

After seeing the first two beasts rise to power in the Middle East, and after seeing a third beast being given power there, Daniel saw this fourth beast. He did not find any of the first three beasts terrifying and frightening, but this fourth beast put terror in his courageous heart. It will be a very powerful world <u>kingdom</u> or world government with large iron teeth (larger and stronger than the bear's teeth) that will be used to crush its victims. Then, whatever is left of the victim will be trampled underfoot.

When this beast (world government) comes to power it will be different from any government that has ever existed before. It will begin with ten <u>horns</u> (or ten leaders) that will rule over the ten divisions of the earth.

Grant R. Jeffrey: This tenfold division of the Roman Empire describes the embryonic power base of the Antichrist's world government at the close of "the Times of the Gentiles" and immediately prior to the Second Coming of Christ.[27]

Phyllis Schlafly: The Talbott types [Strobe Talbott, President Clinton's personal foreign policy adviser] in the Clinton Administration know that Americans will never willingly replace sovereignty with "a single global authority," so they instead talk about

☞ **GO TO:**

Daniel 7:23 (kingdom)

Daniel 7:24; 8:22 (horns)

global governance: *world government*

reinvigorated: *stronger*

globalists: *those who put world government above national interests*

incrementally: *one small step at a time*

entities: *groups or organizations*

Lamb: *a name of Jesus*

What Others are Saying:

Fourth Beast /
Fourth Kingdom
(Antichrist)

FINAL GENTILE WORLD
KINGDOM

large iron teeth

ten horns (ten leaders)

Remember
This . . .

☞ **GO TO:**

Daniel 7:24 (king)

II Thessalonians 2:3;
Revelation 13:18
(man)

Revelation 13:5
(mouth)

Revelation 6:2 (bow)

imperialism: one-world
government

What Others
are Saying:

---

global governance, a global village, a global neighborhood, a global commons, a global economy, a **reinvigorated** United Nations, and an expanded NATO. Instead of advocating a "single" global authority, the **globalists** are moving us **incrementally** into a variety of global **entities** with interlacing tentacles of control. They use two principle techniques to increase the power of global organizations at the expense of American freedom to run our own affairs: treaties and international conferences.[28]

We have more information about these ten kings in Revelation. John said, *The ten horns you saw are ten kings who have not yet received a kingdom, but who for one hour will receive authority as kings along with the beast. They have one purpose and will give their power and authority to the beast. They will make war against the Lamb, but the Lamb will overcome them because he is Lord of lords and King of kings—and with him will be his called, chosen, and faithful followers* (Revelation 17:12-14).

> **Daniel 7:8** "While I was thinking about the horns, there before me was another horn, a little one, which came up among them; and three of the first horns were uprooted before it. This horn had eyes like the eyes of a man and a mouth that spoke boastfully.

The Little Horn

While Daniel was thinking about the ten horns (future leaders), he saw another horn (<u>king</u> or future leader). At first, he will be an insignificant leader on the rise to power in a world that already has ten powerful leaders over its ten divisions. But he will quickly become strong enough to oppose and defeat one of the ten leaders, then he will oppose and defeat a second, and then a third. He will have eyes like the eyes of a <u>man</u> and a <u>mouth</u> that boasts great things. Most experts agree that this "little horn" is the Antichrist.

Arnold G. Fruchtenbaum: It is during the ten kingdom stage that the Antichrist will begin his rise to power. Eventually, he will be strong enough to uproot three of the ten kings, and the other seven will simply submit to his authority. Once the other seven submit their authority to the Antichrist, this will begin the fifth and final stage of the Fourth Gentile Empire, the Antichrist stage, which is the stage of absolute **imperialism**. In this sense he is diverse from the other ten.[29]

Grant R. Jeffrey: The prophet Daniel calls him "a little horn" in contrast to the ten horns that represent ten nations arising out of the boundaries of the ancient [Old] Roman Empire. Though endowed by Satan with supernatural powers he will be a man. He will be a great and powerful speaker, impressing people with his brilliant speech.[30]

John Hagee: In Daniel's vision, the "little horn" sprouted among the other ten, which we know are somehow ten divisions of the Old Roman Empire. In his rise to power, the Antichrist will weave his hypnotic spell, first over one nation in the ten-kingdom federation, then over all ten. He will conquer three of the ten nations and then assume primacy over all of them; next he will turn his ravenous eyes toward the Apple of God's eye—Israel.[31]

Gentile Kingdoms	**Ten Divisions**

1 Babylonian (gold)

2 Medo-Persian (silver)

3 Greek (bronze)

4 Old Roman Empire (iron)

5 Revived Roman Empire

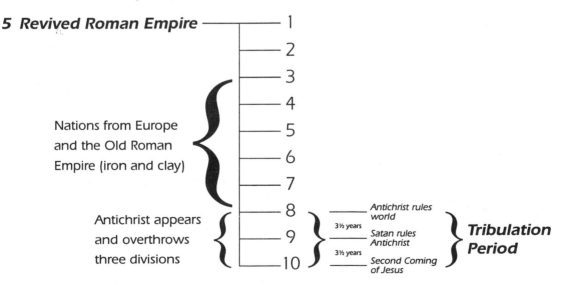

KEY Symbols:

Little Horn

ANTICHRIST

uproots three of the first horns

eyes like the eyes of a man

mouth that speaks boastfully

RELATED CURRENT EVENTS

Remember This . . .

WARNING

Jack Van Impe: Europe is increasingly moving toward unification, and the rest of the world is forming regional military and economic alliances that will make eventual global convergence inevitable (Daniel 7:8, 20, 23, 24).[32]

David Breese: "Why isn't the world better," many people say? It's because this world is not our final dwelling place. God works upon the troubled sea of wicked men in order to cause them to be anxious about their human destiny, and look upward to the Lord, and see his plan, and as a result, receive Christ as personal Saviour.[33]

```
Many people did not take [Adolf] Hitler seri-
ously. But his fiery words and brilliant blue
eyes seemed to hypnotize those who listened to
him. Many Germans believed he was their protector
and friend. His emotional speeches made crowds
cheer "Heil, Hitler!" ("Hail, Hitler!") . . .
Hitler had a clear vision of what he wanted, and
he had the daring to pursue it. But his aims had
no limits, and he overestimated the resources and
abilities of Germany.[34]
```

When the Antichrist makes his first appearance in Revelation he is carrying a bow, but no arrows (see GWRV, pages 88–90). He does not appear with powerful weapons nor does he seem to be Satan's man. He seems to be more like a docile lamb than an indescribable beast.

Some people think the Antichrist will be one of the original ten leaders, But Daniel was thinking about those ten leaders when he saw *another* leader come up. And notice Daniel 7:20: *I also wanted to know about the ten horns on its head and about the other horn that came up . . . Another* and *other* mean the Antichrist will be an "eleventh" leader.

> **Daniel 7:9** "As I looked, "thrones were set in place, and the Ancient of Days took his seat. His clothing was as white as snow; the hair of his head was white like wool. His throne was flaming with fire, and its wheels were all ablaze.

The Vision of God's Throne (Visions of the Four Beasts, Part 2)

Here Daniel's dream shifts from a vision of the Antichrist on earth to a vision of future things in <u>heaven</u>. While the Antichrist is ravaging the earth, several thrones will be set in place including the <u>throne</u> of God. Then the **Ancient of Days** will take his seat. God's <u>clothing</u> and hair will be dazzling white (like the brightness and purity of heaven). God's throne and its <u>wheels</u> (a symbol of mobility) will be burning with <u>fire</u> (a symbol of wrath and <u>judgment</u>).

☞ **GO TO:**

Revelation 4:1-11 (heaven/thrones)

Psalm 45:6; 93:2 (throne)

Micah 5:2 (ancient)

Mark 9:2, 3 (clothing)

Ezekiel 10:1–20 (wheels)

Deuteronomy 4:24 (fire)

II Corinthians (judgment)

David Jeremiah with C.C. Carlson: This is the only place in the Bible where the Ancient of Days is mentioned! It is also the only verse that pictures God in human form. . . . As he sits on his throne, it is with majesty, the sovereign judge of the universe, undergirded with fiery wheels which allow him to bring judgment anywhere in the universe.[35]

John's vision of Jesus reads: *I turned around to see the voice that was speaking to me. And when I turned I saw seven golden lampstands, and among the lampstands was someone "like a son of man," dressed in a robe reaching down to his feet and with a golden sash around his chest. His head and hair were white like wool, as white as snow, and his eyes were like blazing fire. His feet were like bronze glowing in a furnace, and his voice was like the sound of rushing waters. In his right hand he held seven stars, and out of his mouth came a sharp double-edged sword. His face was like the sun shining in all its brilliance* (Revelation 1:12–16).

What Others are Saying:

Ancient of Days: a name for God

Remember This . . .

KEY POINT

There is a righteous God who sits on a throne that can go anywhere, and he judges the activity of people on earth.

☞ **GO TO:**

Revelation 5:11 (thousands)

Romans 14:10,11 (stand)

Exodus 32:33; Revelation 3:4, 5; 20:12; 21:27; 22:19 (books)

Philippians 2:11 (every)

ten thousand times ten thousand: *a Hebrew expression meaning "a great multitude"*

KEY Symbols:

Ancient of Days

GOD

clothing white as snow
hair white like wool
  - brightness and purity of heaven

throne flaming with fire
  - wrath and judgment

wheels all ablaze
  - mobility (God can go anywhere)

Something to Ponder

☞ **GO TO:**

Matthew 25:41–46 (fire)

Revelation 19:20 (Lake of Fire)

> **Daniel 7:10** A river of fire was flowing, coming out from before him. Thousands upon thousands attended him; ten thousand times ten thousand stood before him. The court was seated, and the books were opened.

A Day In Court

Fire symbolizes judgment and a river of fire symbolizes overwhelming and unending judgment. The Antichrist and his wicked followers will provoke a continuous flood of God's wrath. God's throne will be surrounded by thousands upon <u>thousands</u> of angels who minister to him, and **ten thousand times ten thousand** of the saved from the world. In the presence of the angels and the saved, God's court will go into session. As it begins, everyone will <u>stand</u> and be seated before the <u>books</u> will be opened.

These books (plural) are Books of Works or Books of Deeds and books containing the names of the saved. Opening them indicates an evaluation or judgment. This is not the judgment of the saved; it is the judgment of the nations and the lost. We must understand that all people are accountable for their sins.

Today, God is unimportant in the lives of multitudes, but the Bible teaches that the day is coming when every individual will spend some time in God's court. Some may never bow their knee on earth, but <u>every</u> knee will bow in heaven. Think about these judgments mentioned in the Bible:

1) The judgment of the *believer's sin* when Jesus died (John 5:24; Romans 5:9; 8:1; Galatians 3:13).
2) The individual's judgment of *self* (I Corinthians 11:31, 32; Hebrews 12:5–12).
3) The judgment of the *believer's works* (I Corinthians 3:11–15; II Corinthians 5:12).
4) The judgment of the *nations* (Matthew 25:31–46).
5) The judgment of *Israel* (Ezekiel 20:30–38).
6) The believer's judgment of the *angels* (Jude 1:6).
7) The judgment of all *unbelievers* (Revelation 20:11–15).

> **Daniel 7:11** "Then I continued to watch because of the boastful words the horn was speaking. I kept looking until the beast was slain and its body destroyed and thrown into the blazing fire.

Shut Your Big Mouth
(Visions of the Four Beasts, Part 3)

Daniel switched to another vision and kept watching because of the boastful words the little horn (Antichrist) was speaking. He kept watching until the fourth beast (the fourth kingdom) was killed and destroyed in the Lake of (eternal) <u>Fire</u>.

What Others are Saying:

J. Vernon McGee: The emphasis with this kingdom, represented by the last beast, is not on its beginning but on its end. The appearance of "the little horn" is shortly before Christ comes to judge living nations and individuals. This period equates the Great Tribulation Period.[36]

KEY Symbols:

Uriah Smith: The fourth terrible beast continues without change of character, and the little horn continues to utter its blasphemies and hold its millions of votaries in the bonds of a blind superstition till the beast is given to the burning flame; and this is not its conversion, but its destruction.[37]

Fire
judgment

River of Fire
continuous judgment

Books
Book of Works
Book of Deeds

Noah Hutchings: Thus, we see the demise of the last beast, the kingdom of Antichrist. The kings are killed and their armies destroyed, and then the little horn, the Antichrist, and his spiritual adviser, the False Prophet, are taken by the angels and cast into the <u>Lake of Fire</u>.[38]

> **Daniel 7:12** (The other beasts had been stripped of their authority, but were allowed to live for a period of time.)

KEY Symbols:

Little Horn
ANTICHRIST

A Big Power Loss

At the judgment it will be decided that the first three beasts (groups of nations) will lose their right to ever rule again, but they will not suffer the same swift and total destruction as the fourth beast (kingdom of Antichrist). The court will decide to let **fragments** of their kingdoms (some of their territories) and some of their people continue to exist for a period of time beyond the judgment of the fourth kingdom.

Fourth Kingdom
FOURTH BEAST

Final Gentile World Kingdom
REVIVED ROMAN EMPIRE

Wallace Emerson: Prolonged [allowed to live for a period of time] after what, is the question. Obviously, after the destruction of the fourth beast (Daniel 7:11). Therefore, if these four beasts

What Others are Saying:

fragments: *perhaps individual nations, counties, possessions, etc.*

representative: *symbolic*

contemporary: *exist at the same time*

successive: *one does not come after the other*

Millennium: *the 1,000 year reign of Christ on earth*

☞ **GO TO:**

Luke 5:24; 6:5; 7:34; Revelation 1:13 (son of man)

Matthew 24:1–3; Revelation 22:20 (Jesus)

Matthew 24:30; Acts 1:9; Revelation 1:7 (clouds)

☞ **GO TO:**

Isaiah 9:6, 7 (government)

Revelation 20:4 (those)

Luke 1:31–33 (reign)

Revelation 5:9, 10; 11:15 (kingdom)

dominion: *power and permission to rule*

are **representative** of four kingdoms, they are **contemporary** and not **successive**, and they exist and function, presumably at the time of the Revived Roman Empire and survive its destruction.[39]

Noah Hutchings: This part of Daniel's vision extends beyond the destruction of the fourth beast kingdom. This relates to the future and not to the past. In other words, England, Russia, and the Afro-Asian alliance will be stripped of all their power and territories, but they will continue to exist as nations during the **Millennium**.[40]

> **Daniel 7:13** "In my vision at night I looked, and there before me was one like a son of man, coming with the clouds of heaven. He approached the Ancient of Days and was led into his presence.

The Son Of Man (Visions of the Four Beasts, Part 4)

Here Daniel's dream shifts to a vision of *one like a son of man*. We know from other Scriptures that this is a reference to Jesus. Daniel saw Jesus coming with the clouds of heaven, and other Scriptures tell us this is his Second Coming. Jesus will approach the Ancient of Days and be led into his awesome presence.

> **Daniel 7:14** He was given authority, glory, and sovereign power; all peoples, nations, and men of every language worshiped him. His **dominion** is an everlasting dominion that will not pass away, and his kingdom is one that will never be destroyed.

The Real CEO

God's court will give the authority that was stripped from the beasts and all other authority, to the Son of Man. Every government and all power on earth will be turned over to him. The peoples, nations, and men that will worship him are the saved—those who are left after the wicked are destroyed. Jesus will reign over his kingdom forever.

What Others are Saying:

J. Vernon McGee: *An everlasting dominion* seems to contradict the idea of a millennial kingdom of one thousand years. However, at the end of the thousand years, which is a test period with Christ ruling, there will be a brief moment of rebellion against him when Satan is released for a brief season, and then the kingdom will go right on into eternity.[41]

> **Daniel 7:15** "I, Daniel, was troubled in spirit, and the visions that passed through my mind disturbed me.

☞ **GO TO:**

Genesis 41:8 (troubled)

An Anxiety Attack

Daniel had seen a vision of God and one of Jesus, but he did not find his visions something to brag about. He was too upset for that. The other visions <u>troubled</u> him; something in them disturbed and frightened him.

When Nebuchadnezzar dreamed about the awesome statue *his mind was troubled and he could not sleep* (Daniel 2:1). He was so upset he threatened to have all his wise men killed if they did not reveal the dream and its interpretation. When he dreamed about the great tree he said, *the images and visions that passed through my mind terrified me* (Daniel 4:5).

Remember This . . .

> **Daniel 7:16** I approached one of those standing there and asked him the true meaning of all this. "So he told me and gave me the interpretation of these things:

KEY Symbols:

Son of Man
JESUS

Coming With the Clouds of Heaven
SECOND COMIING

Ancient of Days
GOD

I Wanted To Know

There were thousands upon thousands of angels around God's throne and a great multitude of the saved. Daniel did not understand these things but wanted to know what they meant, so he approached one of the heavenly beings, probably an angel, and asked for an explanation. It happened to be a being that could explain things to Daniel.

What Others are Saying:

Charles H. Dyer: We shrink back when we read of multi-metaled statues or beasts that seem to leap from the pages of horror novels. Somehow we imagine Daniel eating a pepperoni pizza before going to bed and recording his nightmares to frustrate the saints throughout history. Daniel's visions may be bizarre, but they are not incomprehensible. After each vision God interpreted the various parts, and his interpretation makes perfect sense when we examine it carefully.[42]

☞ **GO TO:**

Daniel 7:4 (winged lion)

> **Daniel 7:17** 'The four great beasts are four kingdoms that will rise from the earth.

We Are Talking About The Future

In his vision Daniel saw the four beasts come *up out of the sea* (Daniel 7:3). Now the heavenly being tells him *The four great beasts are four kingdoms that will rise from the earth.*

This is important because many experts believe the <u>winged lion</u> is Babylon, a kingdom that had already risen and was at this time near its fall. However, that explanation does not fit because all four of these kingdoms were in Daniel's future.

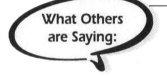
What Others are Saying:

Noah Hutchings: And so the interpreter informed Daniel in verse seventeen that the four great beasts represent four kings, or kingdoms, that would arise in the future. The Word here is emphatic: *These great beasts, which are four, are four kings, **which shall arise*** (KJV). . . . In other words, the lion with eagle's wings could not have been Babylon.[43]

☞ **GO TO:**

Romans 1:7 (Church)

Revelation 13:7 (Tribulation Period)

Matthew 27:52, 53 (believing Israel)

> **Daniel 7:18** But the saints of the Most High will receive the kingdom and will possess it forever—yes, for ever and ever.'

And The Winner Is . . .

The identity of the *saints of the Most High* is a problem because several different groups of people are called saints in the Bible, and it is impossible to say if this is a reference to just one of the groups or all of the groups. One group of saints is called the **Church**, another is called the **Tribulation Saints**, and yet another is called **believing Israel**. However, most experts believe this verse is a reference to believing Israel.

A debate about the identity of the saints, however, is not the point. The heavenly being was making it clear that none of the four beasts would receive God's kingdom. It will go to God's people who will possess it forever; it is repeated to add emphasis—*yes, for ever and ever.*

Church: *people who accept Christ as Savior before the Rapture*

Tribulation Saints: *people who accept Christ as Savior after the Rapture*

believing Israel: *Old and New Testament Jews who believe in the Messiah*

Uriah Smith: The saints; those of all others in low esteem in this world, despised, reproached, persecuted, cast out; those who were considered the least likely of all men ever to realize their hopes; these shall take the kingdom, and possess it forever. The **usurpation** and **misrule** of the wicked shall come to an end.[44]

David Hocking: When his [Christ's] kingdom comes, it doesn't matter how powerful that fourth beast is, or how awesome that confederacy of nations is, or how terrible they treat the people of God. . . . The kingdom of the Messiah will destroy it, and it [the Messiah's kingdom] will be the only kingdom that will last forever and ever. The Bible says that the saints will receive that kingdom.[45]

> **Daniel 7:19** "Then I wanted to know the true meaning of the fourth beast, which was different from all the others and most terrifying, with its iron teeth and bronze claws—the beast that crushed and devoured its victims and trampled underfoot whatever was left.

I Also Wanted To Know

The next thing Daniel wanted the heavenly being to tell him was the meaning of the <u>fourth beast</u>. The thing that seemed to bother him most was the fact that it will be so different from the first three beasts or kingdoms and so much more terrifying with its iron teeth and bronze claws. It will be a ferocious <u>kingdom</u>, crushing and devouring anyone it chooses and trampling underfoot anything left.

```
Keep your eyes on the United Nations for it sees
itself as the best avenue for world peace, world
government, and a new world order which exists in
the world today. Many global leaders are planning
for a new world order and looking to the U.N. to
bring it to pass. The idea that any government or
combination, thereof, can bring to pass a new
world order is a delusion. Nevertheless, under
the leadership of the Antichrist, there will be
an attempt to bring together world government,
world finance, and world religion.[46]
```

What Others are Saying:

usurpation: *seizing of power*

misrule: *bad, poor, or unwise rule*

KEY POINT

All four beasts (kingdoms) would rise in Daniel's future.

☞ GO TO:

Daniel 7:7 (fourth beast)

Daniel 7:17 (kingdom)

RELATED CURRENT EVENTS

KEY POINT

God's people will ultimately be victorious.

KEY Symbols:

Saints of the Most High

CHURCH

TRIBULATION SAIINTS

BELIEVING ISRAEL

imposing: impressive

omniscient: knows everything

Many nations have selected animals to be their symbol. As already noted, I believe the United States is the eagle, England is the lion, Russia is the bear, and the Arab/African coalition is the leopard. In order to depict groups of nations that are very fast, the Holy Spirit puts wings on the animal (Daniel 7:4). In order to depict groups of nations that are very fierce, he puts ribs between the animal's teeth (Daniel 7:5). But there is no animal ferocious enough to depict the Antichrist's kingdom, so it is aptly called a *terrifying and frightening and powerful beast* (verse 7). In order to depict its fierceness it is pictured with large iron teeth and bronze claws. How terrible it must be when there are no animals strange enough, bad enough, or horrible enough to depict this coming kingdom.

> **Daniel 7:20** I also wanted to know about the ten horns on its head and about the other horn that came up, before which three of them fell—the horn that looked more imposing than the others and that had eyes and a mouth that spoke boastfully.

I Also Wanted To Know

Daniel also wanted the heavenly being to explain the ten horns on the head of this fourth kingdom and the other "little horn."

By seeking this information Daniel repeats four things about the other horn (the Antichrist):

1) Three of the first ten will fall before him.
2) He will be more **imposing** than the other ten.
3) He will have eyes.
4) He will speak boastfully.

What Others are Saying:

J. Vernon McGee: At the Time of the End, three of the horns will fall before "the little horn" who is dominant in personality, ability, propaganda, and public appeal. The "little horn" is Antichrist, the Man of Sin (II Thessalonians 2:3–4), and the first beast (Revelation 13:3–6).[47]

Noah Hutchings: It is also related that three of the ten horns will fall before him. There will evidently be a power struggle within the beast kingdom and three of the ten kings will be killed. This may be the same time that the Antichrist himself will be wounded unto death (Revelation 13:3) [see GWRV, page 188].[48]

David Jeremiah with C.C. Carlson: You can combine all the malarkey you have ever heard during political campaigns, all the candidates' promises and solemn vows, and the Antichrist will be master of them all. He'll be able to talk people into anything.[49]

> The transformation of Europe into a massive centralized dictatorship is a key part of the New World Order agenda for centralized control of the planet. The elite who dominate the global financial and political system are seeking to impose a world government, central bank, and currency which would oversee and dictate the policies of three groupings of superstates. These are planned to be the European Union, the American Union (to be evolved out of the North American Free Trade Agreement to include the whole of the Americas), and the Pacific Union (to be evolved out of the Asia-Australia "free trade area" known as APEC). Nation states would be little more than local councils to this vast structure of global control. Indeed, most nation states would be broken up into regions to further diminish the chances of effective resistance.[50]

KEY Symbols:

Antichrist
MAN OF SIN

eyes
mouth that speaks
boastfully

In a vision of Jesus, John said Jesus had seven eyes (see GWRV, page 78). He told us the seven eyes represented the seven spirits of God (Revelation 5:6). In other words, the seven eyes represented the all-seeing **omniscient** vision of the Holy Spirit. Since the eyes of a good man can represent the eyes of a good spirit, what do you think is so important about the eyes of this wicked man (the Antichrist)?

Something to Ponder

We should pay attention to everything mentioned in the Bible, but especially when something is repeated. Here in Daniel 7, the boasting of the Antichrist is mentioned in three different verses (8, 11, and 12). This will surely be one of his dominant characteristics.

Remember This . . .

☞ **GO TO:**

Daniel 7:24 (horn)

Revelation 12:6 (flee)

Revelation 13:5–7 (saints)

> **Daniel 7:21** As I watched, this horn was waging war against the saints and defeating them,

The Coming Battle Between Good And Evil

Daniel is continuing to tell the heavenly being what he saw and what he would like to have explained. He saw a <u>horn</u> (the Antichrist) waging war against the saints and killing them. From studying Revelation, we know that the Antichrist will attack Israel (the woman) and the Jews will <u>flee</u> into the desert (see GWRV, pages 173–174). We also know that he will speak against God and kill all the <u>saints</u> he can during the Tribulation Period. This coming war against the saints is one of the terrible things that attracted Daniel's attention, and the fact that the Antichrist is going to win tells us that it will be a horrible war.

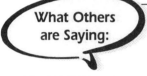
What Others are Saying:

KEY POINT

The Antichrist will persecute and kill Christians and Jews during the Tribulation Period.

David Hocking: I remind you that the world is easily deceived! One example is Joseph Stalin. This nation was deceived by Joseph Stalin. We had treaties and consultations with him and, at the same time, he murdered over thirty million Russians! Christians were deceived many years ago by this man when he came on the scene. We look back and we can see that he was a devil from hell in the garb of human flesh. We know that Stalin, like Hitler, destroyed, murdered, and tortured more people than you can imagine. Don't think that people will know the Antichrist when he comes. The Bible says they are going to be deceived.[51]

☞ **GO TO:**

Daniel 7:10 (court)

Revelation 20:1–4 (judge)

I Corinthians 6:1, 2 (saints)

Matthew 25:31–34 (kingdom)

> **Daniel 7:22** until the Ancient of Days came and pronounced judgment in favor of the saints of the Most High, and the time came when they possessed the kingdom.

Tell Me More

This is more of what Daniel saw and wanted the heavenly being to explain. He is referring back to his <u>vision of God's court</u>, and he wanted information about three things:

1) The Ancient of Days who will come and take a seat in the court.
2) The <u>judgment</u> that will be pronounced in favor of God's <u>saints</u>.
3) The fact that God's saints will possess the <u>kingdom</u>.

> **Daniel 7:23** "He gave me this explanation: 'The fourth beast is a fourth kingdom that will appear on earth. It will be different from all the other kingdoms and will devour the whole earth, trampling it down, and crushing it.

This Is His Answer

Daniel had asked the heavenly being to explain the <u>true meaning</u> of the fourth beast. His answer demands our close attention. Notice four things:

1) The fourth beast is an *earthly kingdom*.
2) The fourth beast will be *different* from all the other kingdoms.
3) The fourth beast will *devour* the **whole earth**.
4) The fourth beast will ***trample and crush*** the earth.

```
The Russian ambassador to Syria is warning that
there could be an explosion of violence in the
Middle East because of the lack of progress in the
Arab-Israeli peace process. "We are passing
through a difficult stage and there is a danger of
an explosion," Victor Goguitidze said at a news
conference in Damascus two days before a regional
tour by Russian Foreign Minister Yevgeny Primakov.
```

> **Daniel 7:24** The ten horns are ten kings who will come from this kingdom. After them another king will arise, different from the earlier ones; he will subdue three kings.

You Asked About Those Horns

In the previous verse we learned that a world kingdom is on the way. The thing to notice in this verse is that ten <u>horns</u> (ten kings or ten divisions) will arise out of that future world kingdom. Then another (an eleventh) king will arise. This reveals a step-by-step development of the "last" Times of the Gentiles empire.

Exactly what the heavenly being meant when he said the Antichrist will be different from the first ten kings is a matter of speculation. But when we add what Daniel gives us to information given in other books of the Bible we develop a picture of an evil man

☞ **GO TO:**

Daniel 7:19 (true meaning)

whole earth: *be a world kingdom*

trample and crush: *be brutal and destructive*

KEY Symbols:

Little Horn

ANTICHRIST

wages war against the saints

defeats (kills) them

RELATED CURRENT EVENTS

☞ **GO TO:**

Daniel 7:20 (horns)

II Thessalonians 2:4 (exalt)

II Thessalonians 2:9 (miracles)

Revelation 17:8 (Abyss)

who will make Adolph Hitler look like a friendly little angel. This eleventh leader (the Antichrist) will have Satanic powers. He will be a polished, brilliant, <u>self-exalting</u>, <u>miracle-working</u> blasphemer who comes straight out of the **Abyss** (see GWRV, page 253) and **subdues** three of the first ten kings.

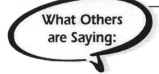

What Others are Saying:

Abyss: the place where God holds the most vicious demonic spirits

subdue: take their power; overthrow or conquer

Club of Rome: an organization of globalists founded in 1968 in Rome to promote world government

KEY Symbols:

Fourth Beast
FOURTH KINGDOM

   devour the whole earth
   trample and crush

What Others are Saying:

Arnold G. Fruchtenbaum: A careful reading of the Daniel passage states that once the fourth empire rules the whole world, then this one-world government will split into ten kingdoms. This requires the ten kingdoms to cover the entire world, not just the territory known as Europe. It would be a mistake to make too much of the European Common Market as being the ten division stage. It would be far more consistent with the text to view it as possibly one of the ten, but not the entire ten. More consistent with Daniel's prophecy is the suggestion of the **Club of Rome** that recommended that the world be divided into ten administrative districts to avoid a world economic class.[52]

Grant R. Jeffrey: The ten regions of the new world government:

Region 1—Canada and the United States of America

Region 2—European Union—Western Europe

Region 3—Japan

Region 4—Australia, New Zealand, South Africa, Israel, and Pacific Islands

Region 5—Eastern Europe

Region 6—Latin America—Mexico, Central and South America

Region 7—North Africa and the Middle East (Moslems)

Region 8—Central Africa

Region 9—South and Southeast Asia

Region 10—Central Asia[53]

Ed Young: There will come along an Antichrist who will at first appear to be a saviour, at first will appear to be very moral and very brilliant, and in the crisis in which the world will find itself at this particular moment in history, the Antichrist will begin to dominate. And three of those ten nations will be destroyed. Then he will become supreme.[54]

The Bible prophesies one-world government and one-world religion for the end-times. We have watched the United Nations become more and more prominent in world governance during the decade of the nineties. The World Community has disciplined Saddam Hussein and the people of Iraq by controlling what Iraq is permitted to buy or sell in the global marketplace. We have witnessed the changing of governments in Rhodesia, South Africa and Haiti through the concerted actions of the U.N. In spite of these "successes," peace on earth still seems as elusive as ever.

Because many armed confrontations are rooted in religious conflicts, insiders at the U.N. are stating that world peace can never be realized unless unity and co-operation can be achieved among the religions of the world. A major step has now been taken toward global cooperation and unity among the world's religions. On June 23-27, 1997, the process for creation of the charter of the United Religions Organization was begun.[55]

RELATED CURRENT EVENTS

KEY Symbols:

Ten Horns
ten kings / divisions
from fourth kingdom

Eleventh King
LITTLE HORN

ANTICHRIST
subdues three kings

> **Daniel 7:25** He will speak against the Most High and oppress his saints and try to change the set times and the laws. The saints will be handed over to him for a time, times, and half a time.

You Asked About The Saints

He will speak against the Most High means he will be anti-God. He will do four specific things against God: 1) blaspheme God; 2) slander the name of God; 3) slander the dwelling place of God (the Church); and 4) slander those who live in heaven. It is safe to predict that the Antichrist will oppose everything connected with God.

Oppress his saints foretells a coming persecution of Christians and Jews. There will be a Satanic philosophy behind his government. He will be anti-Christ and anti-Semitic.

Try to change the set times and the laws probably means he will try to change our calendar and our Judeo-Christian values. The Christian calendar is based upon the year Jesus Christ was born.

☞ **GO TO:**

Revelation 13:6 (four things)

Genesis 1:1 (created)

Revelation 13:5 (forty-two)

Matthew 24:21, 22 (distress)

Revelation 13:16–18 (mark)

Mark of the Beast: *the mark, number or name of the Antichrist*

B.C. is before his birth while A.D. is after his birth. The Jewish calendar is based upon the time God <u>created</u> the heavens and the earth. The Antichrist will not like these things or anything based upon the teachings of God or Jesus Christ. He will probably claim he needs to change them so as not to offend people of other faiths.

Time, times, and half a time is explained in Daniel 4:16. It is three and one-half years or <u>forty-two</u> months. This will be the last three and one-half years (second half) of the Tribulation Period, and the <u>distress</u> upon earth will be terrible.

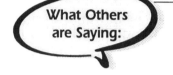

What Others are Saying:

J.R. Church: It is my feeling that this designates the time in which the "**Mark of the Beast**" will be introduced. He will tighten his control on all nations by requiring a personal identification for every citizen. No one will be able to participate in the marketplace without complete government control. . . . During these crucial three-and-a-half years, God will pour out his wrath upon the nations. Earthquakes will be commonplace. Drought and famine will be widespread. Disease will be rampant. All nations will face seeming certain destruction—and the world dictator will be powerless to stop it.[56]

KEY Symbols:

Antichrist

blasphemes God
slanders name of God
slanders dwelling place of God (the Church)
slanders those in heaven

John Hagee: Every single new world order, including the coming Antichrist's, has had one common trait: an attempt to cast God out of the affairs of men. Why? As long as we believe the Word of God and are loyal to the kingdom of God, we represent a government within a government. We are pilgrims and strangers who worship another King and have another citizenship, and as such, we are a hindrance to the New World Order. When our government condones what God condemns, those who have trusted in him become the enemy. And so the Bible-believing Christians of America are labeled dangerous, "intolerant," and enemies of the state.[57]

RELATED CURRENT EVENT

The State Department is becoming increasingly concerned by what is seen as Iran's virtual take-over of Sudan and its stepped-up persecution of the country's 3 million Christians. Senior Mideast intelligence sources say the Khartoum government—aided and abetted by Iran—plans to force the re-settlement of Christians from southern Sudan to the Islamic north, where they will be obliged to send their children to Muslim schools and forbidden to establish new schools of their own. In addition, strict Islamic law will be extended to the south, where authorities recently banned the singing of Christian hymns and the ringing of church bells as "missionary activities offensive to Muslims." The government has also blocked emergency food relief to Christians, which in many cases is distributed only to those agreeing to convert to Islam.[58]

> **Daniel 7:26** " 'But the court will sit, and his power will be taken away and completely destroyed forever.

☞ **GO TO:**

Daniel 7:9, 10 (court)

Daniel 7:11; Revelation 19:19–20 (fire)

It Is The Decision Of This Court . . .

In just one short sentence we have the judgment of the Antichrist. And this brief statement seems almost prophetic itself because it reveals that the Antichrist will come to a quick end. At some point during the Tribulation Period God's <u>court</u> will go into session. Before it is over the decision will be made that the Antichrist should be stripped of his authority and destroyed. Revelation tells us that the Antichrist will be cast into the <u>fiery lake</u> of burning sulfur (the Lake of Fire; see GWRV, page 291).

What Others are Saying:

David Breese: Are we people that should be particularly concerned about the fourth kingdom as well? I think so. I feel so constrained to say, "Keep an eye on history, and when you see the emergence of that empire of the past, which is Rome [the Revived Roman Empire], watch for that to come together, promise peace to the world, and produce the prince that shall come who is the Antichrist. These are days in which we must look up because of the awesome developments of prophetic significance in our time."[59]

Some experts teach that the Church will start a great revival, convert the world, and usher in the kingdom of God on earth. This is known as *Kingdom Theology*. But these visions indicate just the opposite. The last Gentile world power will come close to wiping out God's people.

Something to Ponder

☞ **GO TO:**

Daniel 7:22 (kingdom)

> **Daniel 7:27** Then the sovereignty, power, and greatness of the kingdoms under the whole heaven will be handed over to the saints, the people of the Most High. His kingdom will be an everlasting kingdom, and all rulers will worship and obey him.'

A Fifth And Last Kingdom

When the Antichrist is dethroned the <u>kingdom</u> will be handed over to God's people. This includes the lion kingdom, the bear kingdom, the leopard kingdom, the world kingdom of the Antichrist, and all other kingdoms on earth. God's kingdom is an everlasting kingdom. Every ruler will eventually worship and obey God whether they want to or not.

Something to Ponder

Could the last five verses be a time line or an outline of how events will progress at the End of the (Gentile) Age. Notice the following:

1) A world government will be established (Daniel 7:23).
2) Ten kings or ten divisions will come up from this world government (Daniel 7:24).
3) After the ten kings rise to power over the ten divisions, another king, the Antichrist, will rise to power (Daniel 7:24).
4) After the Antichrist rises to power he will have complete control over God's people for three and one-half years (Daniel 7:25).
5) God will judge the Antichrist and take his power away (Daniel 7:26).
6) The kingdom will be turned over to God's people (Daniel 7:27).

• • •

Notice what these verses say about the saints:

1) *The saints of the Most High will receive the kingdom and will possess it forever* (Daniel 7:18).
2) *This horn was waging war against the saints and defeating them* (Daniel 7:21).
3) *The Ancient of Days came and pronounced judgment in favor of the saints of the Most High, and the time came when they possessed the kingdom* (Daniel 7:22).

4) *He [the Antichrist] will speak against the Most High and oppress his saints* (Daniel 7:25).

5) *The saints will be handed over to him for a time, times, and half a time* [three and one-half years] (Daniel 7:25).

6) *Then the sovereignty, power, and greatness of the kingdoms under the whole heaven will be handed over to the saints* (Daniel 7:27).

> **Daniel 7:28** "This is the end of the matter. I, Daniel, was deeply troubled by my thoughts, and my face turned pale, but I kept the matter to myself."

I Don't Feel So Good

The vision ended when the heavenly being finished saying, *all rulers will worship and obey him.* But that was not the end of the matter for Daniel; he was deeply distressed by the vision and turned pale. However, he <u>wrote</u> it down but did not tell anyone.

Noah Hutchings: No one could be informed about what was coming upon this world at the end of this present age without being troubled. As we behold our world even today, it is no wonder that Daniel was troubled. But the blessed <u>hope</u> as presented in this marvelous chapter of prophecy is the coming of the Son of Man to save the world for both Jew and Gentile.[60]

KEY Symbols:

Antichrist
 cast into the Lake of Fire

☞ **GO TO:**

Daniel 7:1 (wrote)

Titus 2:13 (hope)

What Others are Saying:

KEY Symbols:

God's Statue (Daniel 2)	Gentile Kingdom	Beast (Daniel 7)
Head of gold	Babylonian	First beast (winged lion)
Chest/Arms of silver	Medo-Persian	Second beast (bear with three ribs in mouth)
Belly/Thighs of bronze	Greek	Third beast (a four- winged, four-headed leopard)
Legs of iron	Old Roman Empire	Fourth beast (a terrifying, powerful animal)
Feet of iron and clay	Revived Roman Empire	also Fourth beast

Study Questions

1. Who is the "little horn" and what are some of the things he will do?
2. What titles does Daniel use for God in this chapter? For Jesus?
3. What will cause the defeat of the Antichrist, and when will it happen?
4. Do you think Daniel's vision from God made him proud? Can you name three ways he was affected by it?
5. What do the four beasts symbolize, and why do you think God uses beasts to symbolize them?

CHAPTER WRAP-UP

- Daniel had a vision of four beasts (or kingdoms) rising to power out of the Sea of Humanity: the first like a lion with eagle's wings (perhaps England and the U.S.); the second like a lopsided bear with three ribs in its mouth (perhaps Russia and her allies); the third like a four-winged, four-headed leopard (perhaps an Arab/African coalition); and the fourth terrifying, frightening and powerful (the kingdom of the Antichrist). The fourth had ten horns (kings) and a little horn (the Antichrist); three of the ten horns were overthrown by the little horn. (Daniel 7:1–8)

- Daniel had a vision of God sitting in judgment upon the fourth kingdom and its ruler, the Antichrist. Multitudes of angels and saints surrounded his throne, the books were opened, the Antichrist was judged and punished, and the other beasts were stripped of their authority and allowed to live for a time. (Daniel 7:9–12)

- Daniel saw a heavenly being standing nearby, so he repeated his visions and asked for an interpretation. The heavenly being gave him an explanation. (Daniel 7:15–23)

- The four beasts represent four kingdoms in Daniel's future. The fourth kingdom will establish ten divisions, and the Antichrist will rise and subdue three of these divisions. Then all power on earth will be turned over to him for 3½ years. He will be anti-God and persecute and kill God's saints. (Daniel 7:24–5)

- The end of things will come when Jesus returns. He will destroy the Antichrist, seize his authority, and turn it over to his people. His will be the final kingdom, and it will last forever. (Daniel 7:26–27)

DANIEL 8

CHAPTER HIGHLIGHTS

- Two-Horned Ram
- Shaggy Goat
- Next World Leader
- God Reigns
- Daniel's Reaction

☞ **GO TO:**

Ephesians 1:10 KJV
(dispensation)

dispensation: the way God is running things now, this present order or system

Let's Get Started

So far, our main focus has been on matters concerning the Gentiles. This is about to change, because we are now going to start focusing on how Gentile matters have, and will, affect the Jews and Jerusalem. We can say it like this: we are about to start studying how the Times of the Gentiles will affect Israel in Daniel's future, and especially how it will affect Israel during the Tribulation Period.

Most of this vision, usually called "the Vision of the Ram and the Goat," has already been fulfilled, which makes it past history to us. (Even this fulfilled part is very important since it attests to the fact that Daniel was a true prophet, and his writings were inspired by God.) But Daniel makes it clear that it also has an End of the Age application. Part of it is sealed up so we may not be able to understand all of the details. However, we will learn what we can.

M.R. DeHaan: So we are immediately reminded that, while this Vision of the Ram and . . . Goat had a historic fulfillment in the kingdoms of Greece and of Medo-Persia, nevertheless, it looks beyond all this to the Time of the End, that is the end of this present **dispensation**, the end just before the Son of God will return to set up his kingdom.[1]

What Others are Saying:

☞ **GO TO:**

Daniel 7:1 (first)

Daniel 5:30 (night)

Daniel 5:5 (wrote)

> **Daniel 8:1** In the third year of King Belshazzar's reign, I, Daniel, had a vision, after the one that had already appeared to me.

The Time: Two Years Later
(The Vision Of The Ram And The Goat)

The visions in Chapter 7 were in the <u>first</u> year of Belshazzar's reign (see Time Line #1, Appendix A); but this vision was in the third year of his reign. Two years have passed and the date is about 540-542 B.C. It is about one to three years *before* the <u>night</u> the hand <u>wrote</u> on the wall, signaling Babylon's fall and Belshazzar's death.

It is helpful to understand the situation surrounding this vision. Belshazzar was the last king of Babylon; his Gentile world kingdom would soon fall. The next Gentile world kingdom on God's Statue (the chest and arms of silver—the Medes and Persians) would soon take over (see illustration #5, p. 53). Then they would be followed by another Gentile world kingdom (the belly and thighs of bronze—Greece). This vision provides details about those next two Gentile world kingdoms.

Something to Ponder

Some people say, "I will never believe in a miracle unless I see one." But the reality of miracles is evident throughout the Bible. Jesus performed miracles and multitudes accepted them as a sign that he was God in the flesh. Isn't the fact that daniel foretold events hundreds of years before they happened a miracle? Isn't fulfilled Bible prophecy significant evidence of the existence of the God of the Bible?

What Others are Saying:

Charles H. Dyer: Why the switch in language? In Chapters 2-7 Daniel wrote of events important to all nations, so he wrote in the common commercial language of his day. Beginning in Chapter 8, he focused on events related especially to the people of Israel, so he switched back to the Hebrew.[2]

Remember This . . .

Daniel 1–2:3—Hebrew	For Israel
Daniel 2:4–7:28—Aramaic	For *all* nations
Daniel 8–12—Hebrew	Events important to Israel

☞ **GO TO:**

Isaiah 21:1, 2 (attack)

> **Daniel 8:2** In my vision I saw myself in the citadel of Susa in the province of Elam; in the vision I was beside the Ulai Canal.

The Place: Susa In Elam
Near The Ulai Canal

In this vision Daniel was **transported** to the Babylonian fortress at Susa (see illustration #2, page 19). That was a small city and military base in the province of Elam. Its commander, Abradates, would soon revolt and join the Medes and Persians in their <u>attack</u> on Babylon, so Daniel was taken to this soon-to-be Medo-Persian fortress and found himself beside the Ulai Canal.

transported: moved or carried

nondescript: unimportant

What Others are Saying:

David Jeremiah with C.C. Carlson: In his vision, Daniel was transported to Susa, a small, **nondescript** city in Babylon. He saw himself standing by a canal in front of the palace. What possible difference could it make that God's man in Babylon was somewhere out in the suburbs, on the bank of an unremarkable waterway? This town wouldn't even rate a large red dot on the map. But this place was going to be the very nerve center of the next kingdom. Babylon was a falling star, and the Persian Empire was about to begin.[3]

KEY POINT

Daniel knew Susa would be the capital of the Persian Empire while it was still a small nondescript city.

David Hocking: The truth of the matter is that the opening two verses are powerful. It's dated the third year of Belshazzar, Babylon is in power, Medo-Persia has not come to power yet. Still, Shushan [Susa in NIV], the citadel, was destined to become the capital in the Persian Empire. . . . This is a prediction locating the capitol even before the empire came into power or Shushan [Susa] was in existence as its capital. The river Ulai is a canal which deals with two other rivers which came together at Shushan [Susa], and it was constructed by the Medo-Persians.[4]

☞ **GO TO:**

Daniel 8:20 (kings)

Daniel 5:31 (took over)

Revelation 17:12 (horns)

> **Daniel 8:3** I looked up, and there before me was a ram with two horns, standing beside the canal, and the horns were long. One of the horns was longer than the other but grew up later.

The Ram With Two Horns

In his vision of the future, Daniel saw a ram with two horns. The two horns <u>represent the kings</u> (kingdom) of Media and Persia. We now know them as Darius and Cyrus.

   The two horns, Darius and Cyrus, were very long. But one horn, Cyrus, was longer than the other and came up last. Darius the Mede, the first and shorter horn, <u>took over the kingdom when</u>

<u>Babylon fell</u>. He ruled for about 2 years and died. Then Cyrus the Persian, the second and longer horn, took over the kingdom and ruled for about 20 more years.

What Others are Saying:

David Jeremiah with C.C. Carlson: After the Babylonian kingdom fell, the Medes stepped in first and were joined by the Persians. Soon we don't hear any more about the Medes, for the Persians assimilated the whole Median kingdom, just as the prophecy says.[5]

Uriah Smith: The two horns represented the two nationalities of which the empire consisted. The higher came up last. This represented the Persian element, which, from being at first simply an ally of the Medes, came to be the leading division of the empire.[6]

RELATED CURRENT EVENTS

When the Assyrian Empire broke up, the Medes received the greater part of Iran, Assyria, N. Mesopotamia [in modern Iraq], Armenia, and Cappadocia [in modern Turkey] . . . The Medes dominated the relatively small nation of Persians (c. 600–549 B.C.) until Cyrus II ("the Great"), son of Cambyses I, mastered Media (c. 549 B.C.) and made Pasargadae his capital. Media, however, remained the most important province of Persia, a partner in a dual nation.[7]

— — —

Ancient Persia was a land that included parts of what are now Iran and Afghanistan. Under Cyrus the Great, Darius I, Xerxes, and other leaders it became the home of a great civilization, and the center of a vast empire. The name Persia came from Persis, which was the Greek name for the region. The Persians themselves called the region the land of the Aryans, from which the name Iran comes. The Persians called their language Aryan.[8]

KEY Symbols:

Ram

kingdom of Medo-Persia

- two horns
- shorter horn (Darius the Mede)
- longer horn (Cyrus the Persian)

Remember This . . .

In Bible prophecy <u>horns</u> are symbolic of kings, rulers, and leaders. This is very important and can be confusing since Revelation talks of two beasts with horns (see GWRV, pages 170, 250). In Daniel 8:20 we are told that the two horns represent the king of Media and Persia. So when you see horns mentioned in a symbolic way in the Bible, remember they represent kings, rulers, and teachers.

> **Daniel 8:4** I watched the ram as he charged toward the west and the north and the south. No animal could stand against him, and none could rescue from his power. He did as he pleased and became great.

☞ **GO TO:**

Daniel 2:32, 39 (kingdom of silver)

Charge

As Daniel was watching the ram it charged first to the west, then to the north, and finally to the south. No nation or empire was strong enough to resist it. And no nation or empire was strong enough to rescue those it defeated. The ram did as it pleased and became a great <u>kingdom</u>.

David Hocking: It does not mention eastward. That's exactly what happened in ancient Persia—they never went east. I love the details of the Bible. They may not seem important, but you must understand that everything in God's Word IS GOD'S WORD. It is there for a reason. Even the order of the directions given (west . . . north . . . south) are exactly what happened. The order here is exactly the order that Persia followed in conquering the world. They went west first, then they went north and conquered. Eventually, they went south all the way to Egypt, conquering all of the south and Arabia as well.[9]

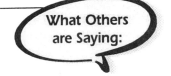

What Others are Saying:

> **Daniel 8:5** As I was thinking about this, suddenly a goat with a prominent horn between his eyes came from the west, crossing the whole earth without touching the ground.

☞ **GO TO:**

Daniel 8:21 (shaggy goat)

Daniel 2:32, 39 (kingdom of bronze)

Revelation 17:1–18 (Mystery Babylon)

Mystery Babylon: the birthplace of false religions

The Shaggy Goat With One Horn

As Daniel's vision of the future continued, he saw a shaggy goat with one large horn between its eyes. This <u>shaggy goat represents the king (kingdom) of Greece</u> and adds that the large horn represents the first king of Greece. *Crossing the whole earth without touching the ground* is like saying it had wings; it flew or moved very fast.

Greece was to the west of Persia. Its first king, after the fall of the Medes and Persians, was Alexander the Great (the large horn on the goat). Alexander came across the earth and crushed everything in front of him. His <u>kingdom</u> of Greece defeated the million man Persian army in a little less than three years.

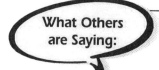
Hal Lindsey: I wondered why God used these two symbols? Why did he use the symbol of a ram for Persia, and the symbol of a goat, a buck goat, for Greece? Then I was shocked as I began to research in history books and found that this was no mystery in the ancient world. The figure of the ram was chosen by the Medo-Persians to depict themselves because it was represented in the astrological zodiac as Aries, Aries the Ram. And so, they all believed in astrology back then. That was part of the Babylonian influence, **Mystery Babylon**. And so they had the ram because they believed that their sign of the zodiac was Aries. And so that is why they were depicted as a ram. Daniel picked that up and used it as a symbol. But amazingly enough Alexander himself later chose as the symbol of his empire, Capricorn, which was another part of the zodiac. Do you know what Capricorn is? A buck goat.[10]

KEY Symbols:

Shaggy Goat
kingdom of Greece

Large Horn
*first king of Greece
(Alexander the Great)*

**Without Touching the
Ground**
moving very fast

David Jeremiah with C.C. Carlson: In twelve brief years, the Greeks conquered the entire civilized world without losing a battle. Greece became the dominant force in the world faster than any other kingdom before it, and God had said that was how it was going to happen some two hundred years before.[11]

Noah Hutchings: Inasmuch as these two nations are so clearly identified by their national emblems, we should also expect the beasts of Chapter 7 to relate to nations with similar emblems—namely, England, the United States, Russia, the Afro-Asian bloc, and the Revived Roman Empire.[12]

> **Daniel 8:6** He came toward the two-horned ram I had seen standing beside the canal and charged at him in great rage.

A Furious Attack

The shaggy goat with one horn (Greece under Alexander the Great) charged the ram with two horns (the kingdom of the Medes and Persians) with a furious rage.

David Hocking: That's like a summary statement of what you read in history of the tactics of Alexander the Great, he was so vicious and so furious that it stunned the Persian armies. They couldn't believe it! He devastated them. It wasn't a matter of get-

ting the victory and then negotiating the win, Alexander just destroyed them until there was no hope. The fear of Alexander the Great spread over the empire. There were many units which just laid down in front of him, begging for mercy when they heard he was coming.[13]

> **Daniel 8:7** I saw him attack the ram furiously, striking the ram and shattering his two horns. The ram was powerless to stand against him; the goat knocked him to the ground and trampled on him, and none could rescue the ram from his power.

The Ram Goes Down

In his vision of the future, Daniel saw the following:

1) The goat butted the ram furiously (the Greeks attacked the Medes and Persians without mercy).
2) The ram's horns were broken (the Greeks inflicted terrible losses on the Medes and Persians).
3) The ram was powerless (the Greeks defeated the Medo-Persian military).
4) The ram was knocked to the ground (the Medo-Persian people were subdued and humbled).
5) The ram was trampled upon (the Medo-Persian people were crushed).
6) The ram could not be rescued (no one could stop the Greeks).

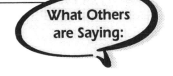

What Others are Saying:

Oliver B. Greene: This monstrosity of Daniel's vision was in the form of a goat, and it had a horn—but it points to a man, not an animal. The ram is down, the he-goat is now in power.[14]

Uriah Smith: The two horns were broken, and the ram was cast to the ground and stamped upon. Persia was subdued, the country ravaged, its armies cut to pieces and scattered, its cities plundered, and the royal city of Persepolis (see Illustration #2, page 19) . . . sacked and burned.[15]

World Book Encyclopedia: Susa, also called Shush, was once the capital of the ancient Kingdom of Elam and the Persian Empire. . . .Darius I built palaces in the city in the late 500's B.C., and made it a capital of the Persian Empire. Susa declined after Alexander the Great conquered it in the late 300's B.C. Persepolis, was also a capital of ancient Persia. King Darius I of Persia founded Persepolis about 518 B.C. in a mountain region of what is now southwest Iran. Darius and his successors built large stone and mud-brick palaces in the capital, which became the royal ceremonial center for the religious holiday of the New Year. Every year at this festival, the king would renew his divine right as king, and representatives of all the peoples within the Persian Empire would bring him gifts. In 330 B.C., Alexander the Great seized Persepolis.[16]

☞ **GO TO:**

Daniel 8:22 (four horns)

Daniel 7:2 (four winds of heaven)

KEY Symbols:

The Broken Horn
death of Alexander the Great

Four Horns
Alexander's four top generals

Four Winds of Heaven
north / south / east / west

What Others are Saying:

> **Daniel 8:8** The goat became very great, but at the height of his power his large horn was broken off, and in its place four prominent horns grew up toward the four winds of heaven.

The Broken Horn

In his vision of the future, Daniel learned that the goat (the Greek empire) would become very great after it defeated the ram (the Medes and Persians). But what about the large horn (Alexander the Great)? At the height of his power he would be broken off (die). Four other horns (leaders) would take his place and grow toward the *four winds of heaven* (north, south, east, and west).

This is exactly what happened. History and tradition tells us that Alexander the Great expanded the Greek empire until he sat down and wept because he had no more worlds to conquer. Then, at the height of his power and prime of his life (just under 33 years old), he suddenly died.

What happened to the Greek empire upon Alexander's death? The Greek empire was divided into four parts and Alexander the Great was replaced by four prominent horns which history identifies as his four top generals.

David Jeremiah with C.C. Carlson: As Alexander was sweeping over the civilized earth, he thought he was doing his own work. He believed that all of his achievements were products of his own genius, but he was just filling out the outline of prophecy that God had given.[17]

Uriah Smith: Human foresight and speculation would have said, When he becomes weak, his kingdom racked by rebellion, or paralyzed by luxury, then the horn will be broken, and the kingdom shattered. But Daniel saw it broken in the very prime of its strength and the height of its power, when every beholder would have exclaimed, Surely, the kingdom is established, and nothing can overthrow it. Thus it is often with the wicked. The horn of their strength is broken when they think they stand most firm.[18]

J.G. Hall: His four generals seized upon different parts of the kingdom and divided it among themselves as follows: Cassander took Greece and Macedon; Lysimachus took Asia Minor, now Turkey and Thrace; Seleucus took Syria and Babylonia; Ptolemy took Egypt and Palestine.[19]

Gentile Kingdoms

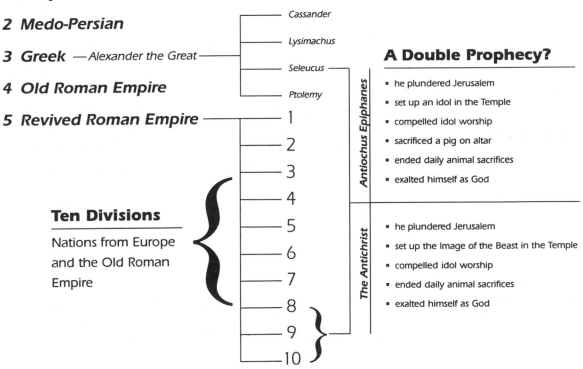

1 Babylonian

2 Medo-Persian

3 Greek —Alexander the Great

4 Old Roman Empire

5 Revived Roman Empire

Cassander
Lysimachus
Seleucus
Ptolemy

1
2
3
4
5
6
7
8
9
10

Ten Divisions

Nations from Europe and the Old Roman Empire

Antiochus Epiphanes

The Antichrist

A Double Prophecy?

- he plundered Jerusalem
- set up an idol in the Temple
- compelled idol worship
- sacrificed a pig on altar
- ended daily animal sacrifices
- exalted himself as God

- he plundered Jerusalem
- set up the Image of the Beast in the Temple
- compelled idol worship
- ended daily animal sacrifices
- exalted himself as God

☞ **GO TO:**

Daniel 7:26 (distant future)

Daniel 7:8 (little horn)

Beautiful Land: Israel

sealed up: hidden until a certain time

What Others are Saying:

Something to Ponder

KEY Symbols:

Horn Out of the Four Horns

no one knows
some believe the Antichrist

WARNING

> **Daniel 8:9** Out of one of them came another horn, which started small but grew in power to the south and to the east and toward the Beautiful Land.

Will The Real Horn Please Stand Up?

Out of one of them means out of one of the four parts of the divided Greek empire. *Came another horn* means there would arise another leader. He would start small and then grow in power in three directions: 1) toward the south, 2) toward the east, and 3) toward the **Beautiful Land**.

Noah Hutchings: Martin Luther said: "This chapter in Daniel refers to both Antiochus and Antichrist." The majority seem to concur with Luther's opinion—the prophecy was fulfilled in type in Antiochus, but the real little horn will be the Antichrist.[20]

A Double Prophecy?

Here we run into a big problem. Many prophecy experts believe this leader (another horn) turned out to be Antiochus Epiphanes, a descendant of Seleucus who took over Syria and Babylonia when Alexander the Great died. But many other, equally good, experts believe this leader was not Antiochus Epiphanes. The Bible itself says this prophecy is **sealed up** and concerns the <u>distant future</u>. The friendly disagreement and lack of certainty is fueled by the fact that Antiochus Epiphanes fulfilled *many* of the requirements of this prophecy but definitely not all. What is the most likely answer? As bad as he was, Antiochus Epiphanes was only an incomplete imitation of the *real <u>little horn</u>* (the Antichrist). God may have let him exist to reveal many things about the real horn, but the world will not know the real horn until the Tribulation Period arrives.

Because Antiochus Epiphanes was a Syrian some experts suggest that the Antichrist will be a Syrian, but that is just speculation. He may be a Syrian, but it is impossible to know for sure. Do not forget that the Antichrist will not be revealed until after the Rapture, and his nationality will not be nearly as important as his evil deeds. The emphasis in this chapter is on his inconspicuous beginning, the great power he attains, and his great wickedness.

> **Daniel 8:10** It grew until it reached the host of the heavens, and it threw some of the starry host down to the earth and trampled on them.

He Will Grow And Grow And Grow . . .

One thing to notice here is the phenomenal growth of the Antichrist. We learned that he will start out <u>small</u> and grow in <u>power</u>, and we learned that he will start out as a "<u>little horn</u>" and grow until he takes over the whole world. Here we are told that he will grow until he reaches the *host of the heavens*. This is a Biblical phrase referring to the residents of heaven. The point here is that the Antichrist will become exceedingly powerful.

Another thing to notice is this matter of throwing some of the starry host down to the earth and <u>trampling</u> on them. In the Bible stars symbolize two things: 1) <u>angels</u>, and 2) the <u>Jews</u>. Since this chapter is dealing with Daniel's prophecies about the Jews, this probably means the Antichrist will cause the fall and destruction of many Jews. Those who think this is a reference to Antiochus Epiphanes can point to history and show that he forceded many Jews to blaspheme God and worship idols. He even killed approximately 100,000 Jews and sold another 40,000 into slavery.

J. Vernon McGee: This statement is admittedly difficult to interpret. I think that the natural interpretation is that Antiochus challenged God and was permitted to capture Jerusalem and the Temple. This warfare included the spiritual realm where angels and demons were involved. Some of the feats attributed to Antiochus are astounding; if they are true, demonic power was exhibited.[21]

Here is a small sample of the crimes of Antiochus:

1) He plundered Jerusalem.
2) He outlawed the Jewish religion and replaced it with Greek worship.
3) He outlawed the observance of the Sabbath.
4) He outlawed circumcision.
5) He outlawed the reading of the Scriptures.
6) He burned whatever Scriptures he could find.
7) He sacrificed a pig on the altar at the Temple.
8) He set up an idol in the Temple.
9) He compelled idol worship.
10) He claimed he was God manifest in the flesh.

☞ **GO TO:**

Daniel 8:9 (small)

Revelation 13:2 (power)

Daniel 7:8 (little horn)

Daniel 7:7, 23 (trampling)

Revelation 1:20 (stars/angels)

Genesis 15:5; 26:4; 37:9-11; Revelation 12:1 (stars/Jews)

What Others are Saying:

KEY Symbols:

Host of the Heavens
residents of heaven
the saved, angels, etc.

Stars
angels, Jews

Antichrist
starts out small and grows in power
starts out as a little horn and grows until he takes over the world

> **Daniel 8:12** Because of rebellion, the host of the saints and the daily sacrifice were given over to it. It prospered in everything it did, and truth was thrown to the ground.

☞ **GO TO:**

Revelation 13:7 (Saints)

Daniel 7:21, 25 (saints)

Matthew 27:22–26 (Christ)

Proverbs 12:17 (truth)

Matthew 24:5, 11, 24; II Thessalonians 2:9–12 (deceit)

Numbers 28:1-8 KJV (sacrifices)

The High Cost Of Low Living

Because of **rebellion** by those on earth, and most especially the Jews, all those who accept Christ during the Tribulation Period, all the Tribulation <u>Saints</u> (see GWRV, page 191), and all the <u>Jews</u> (believing Israel) will be given over to the power of the Antichrist. This will be the high cost of low living. Because the sacrifice of <u>Christ</u> upon the cross was rejected by the Jews the daily sacrifice of animals at the rebuilt Jewish Temple will be rejected by God. Those sacrifices will be sinful, so authority over them will be handed to the Antichrist. He will be permitted to stop the sacrifices, and he will prosper in all his endeavors. <u>Truth</u> will be ignored in favor of <u>deceit</u> and lies.

In the Old Testament God told the Jews to <u>sacrifice animals for their sins</u>. Their animal sacrifices pictured or illustrated the sacrifice of Jesus on the cross for the sins of those who believe in Jesus. When Jesus was crucified God stopped accepting the animal sacrifices. But the Jews continued to offer them until their nation and Temple were destroyed. Now that their nation has been re-established they want to rebuild the Temple and start offering animal sacrifices again. The problem is that God will not accept their offerings. The Jews have rejected the sacrifice of God's Son, so he will reject the sacrifice of their animals.

Remember This . . .

rebellion: *ignoring or disobeying God*

> **Daniel 8:13** Then I heard a holy one speaking, and another holy one said to him, "How long will it take for the vision to be fulfilled—the vision concerning the daily sacrifice, the rebellion that causes desolation, and the surrender of the sanctuary and of the host that will be trampled underfoot?"

☞ **GO TO:**

Daniel 4:13, 17, 23 KJV (holy one)

Daniel 9:27 (desolate)

What An Angel Wanted To Know

Have you ever gone through a terrible time and asked, "How long? How long will God let this go on?" In his vision Daniel heard two <u>holy ones</u> discussing the situation. These holy ones were angels, and one was asking the other several questions:

sanctuary: *the Temple*

1) How long will it take for this vision of the Antichrist to be fulfilled?
2) How long will God let the Antichrist have authority over the animal sacrifices at the Temple?
3) How long will God let the Temple be <u>desolate</u> because of the rebellion?
4) How long will God let the **sanctuary** be under the Antichrist's control?
5) How long will God let his people be under the Antichrist's power?

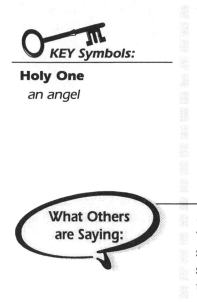
Billy Graham: Our certainty that angels right now witness how we are walking through life should mightily influence the decisions we make. God is watching, and his angels are interested spectators too. The Amplified Bible expresses I Corinthians 4:9 this way: *God has made an exhibit of us . . . a show in the world's amphitheatre—with both men and angels* (as spectators).[24]

> **Daniel 8:14** He said to me, "It will take 2,300 evenings and mornings; then the sanctuary will be **reconsecrated**."

2,300 Days (Daniel's Seventy Weeks)

This is a very difficult passage; it may be that the interpretation is still hidden, but we do have some ideas. 2,300 days is almost 6 years and 5 months. But we know from other Scriptures that Jerusalem will be trodden down for 3½ years, or <u>42 months</u>, or 1,260 days (see GWRV, pages 155, 190). So what is the answer?

Perhaps there is a clue in the actions of Antiochus Epiphanes. It can be shown that exactly 2,300 days passed between the time he first began his persecution of the Jews and the time it ended. It can also be shown that he captured Jerusalem and started the persecutions almost three years (probably 1,040 days) before he stopped the Jewish sacrifices. If this is correct, it means the Antichrist will start persecuting the Jews about 7 months after the Tribulation Period begins (6 years and 5 months plus 7 months = 7 years), but the most severe persecution and **defilement** of the Temple will not begin until the Tribulation Period mid-point.

Joseph Chambers: This quote put the Antichrist's unclean activities in the Jewish Temple almost seven years. Could this suggest that the one-world government is allowed to actually help build the Temple as part of a covenant agreement? If so, it would explain why the area is trodden underfoot by unclean powers for almost the whole Tribulation Period. Daniel is clear that the actual **Abomination of Desolation** (see GWRV, pages 196–198) does not occur until the middle of this period.[25]

William E. Biederwolf: Antiochus Epiphanes took Jerusalem in B.C. 170. Three years later, B.C. 167, in June he sent Appolonius against the city who at that time caused all sacrifices to cease. On December of this same year Appolonius set up the heathen altar in the Temple and on December 25 the heathen sacrifices began. Three years later on this date, December 25, B.C. 164, Judas Maccabeus restored the true sacrifice. The three-and-a-half years dating from June, B.C. 167 was a period of severe oppression and sacrilege against the Temple.[26]

WARNING

There have been several unusual interpretations of this 2,300 day period. One well-known group (Seventh-Day Adventists) said it meant 2,300 years. Based on that, many Seventh Day Adventists unwisely predicted the date of the Second Coming to be in 1843. Others have said it means 1,150 evenings and 1,150 mornings, but there are many problems with that including the fact that it does not fit anything else in the Bible. It is best to take the 2,300 days literally.

Many people have tried to predict the date of the Second Coming, but everyone who has tried has failed. Date-setting is inconsistent with Bible teaching and a good sign of a lack of spiritual matyrity.

Remember This . . .

> **Daniel 8:15** While I, Daniel, was watching the vision and trying to understand it, there before me stood one who looked like a man.

I Was Confused

While Daniel was watching the vision someone suddenly appeared in front of him. He looked like a man, but he was actually the angel Gabriel.

KEY Symbols:

One Who Looked Like a Man
Gabriel
- hero of God

☞ **GO TO:**

Daniel 8:2 (Ulai)

Daniel 9:21; Luke 1:19, 26 (Gabriel)

Daniel 10:21; Jude 1:9; Revelation 12:7 (Michael)

Remember This . . .

☞ **GO TO:**

Ezekiel 2:1, 3, 6, 8; Matthew 8:20; 9:6 (son of man)

son of man: *son of Adam*

Time of the End: *End of the Times of the Gentiles*

chasten: *persecute*

KEY POINT

Only two angels are named in the Bible—Gabriel and Michael.

☞ **GO TO:**

Matthew 17:1-9 (face)

> **Daniel 8:16** And I heard a man's voice from the Ulai calling, "Gabriel, tell this man the meaning of the vision."

Gabriel, Explain The Vision

Daniel was standing beside the <u>Ulai</u> canal when he had this vision (the Vision of the Ram and the Goat). After seeing many things, someone who looked like a man suddenly appeared in front of him. Then there came a voice that said, *"Gabriel, tell this man the meaning of the vision."*

This is the first time an angel is identified by name in the Bible. Only two angels are identified by name, both are identified in the Book of Daniel, and both are also identified in the New Testament. The two angels are <u>Gabriel</u> and <u>Michael</u>.

> **Daniel 8:17** As he came near the place where I was standing, I was terrified and fell prostrate. "Son of man," he said to me, "understand that the vision concerns the time of the end."

An Important Point

As Gabriel came near where Daniel was standing, Daniel was overwhelmed with fear and fell on his face. Gabriel called Daniel "**son of man**" and told him the vision concerns the **Time of the End**. Notice, he said, *time of the end* and not the "end of time." The *time of the end* refers to the End of the Times of the Gentiles not the end of the world.

The point of Gabriel's message is this: the fulfillment of the vision is set for some future date. The time when God will let the Antichrist take authority over the sacrifices, make the Temple desolate, and **chasten** his people is set for the End of the Times of the Gentiles.

> **Daniel 8:18** While he was speaking to me, I was in a deep sleep, with my face to the ground. Then he touched me and raised me to my feet.

I Couldn't Take It

The stress was too much for Daniel. While Gabriel was speaking Daniel fainted—fell into a trance. It was a deep sleep, and he fell with his <u>face</u> to the ground. Gabriel had to revive him before continuing.

> **Daniel 8:19** He said: "I am going to tell you what will happen later in the time of wrath, because the vision concerns the appointed time of the end.

☞ **GO TO:**

Zephaniah 1:14–16 (wrath)

I Have News For You

Gabriel informed Daniel that he was going to tell him what will happen in the **Time of <u>Wrath</u>**. Again he emphasized that the vision concerns the Time of the End which means at the End of the Times of the Gentiles. No one can deny that there were many similarities during the reign of Antiochus Epiphanes, but that definitely was not the Tribulation Period. The terrible things in this vision are still future.

Messengers from On High

One of the main tasks of an angel is that of being a messenger. God used the following angels:

1) Angels urged Lot to leave Sodom and Gomorrah, (Genesis 19:1–26)
2) An angel revealed prophecies to Zechariah. (Zechariah 1:9; 2:3; 4:1, 5; 5:5; 6:4, 5)
3) An Angel told the women at the tomb that Jesus had been raised from the dead. (Matthew 28:1–7)
4) An angel announced the birth of John the Baptist to Zechariah. (Luke 1:11–20)
5) An angel revealed the birth of Jesus to Joseph. (Luke 1:26–38; Matthew 1:20–21)
6) Angels announced the birth of Jesus to shepherds. (Luke 2:8–20)
7) An angel told Peter to wake up, put on his clothes, and follow him. (Acts 12:1–11)
8) An angel told Paul he would stand trial before Caesar. (Acts 27:21–26)

Something to Ponder

Time of Wrath: another name for the Tribulation Period

> **Daniel 8:20** The two-horned ram that you saw represents the kings of Media and Persia.

The Two-Horned Ram Explained

Without this interpretation from God there is no telling what kind of strange explanations people would come up with. However, Gabriel clearly identified the <u>ram</u> with the two horns as representing the combined kingdom of the Medes and Persians.

☞ **GO TO:**

Daniel 8:3–7 (ram)

KEY Symbols:

Ram
kingdom of Medo-Persia

Two Horns
Darius and Cyrus

☞ **GO TO:**

Daniel 8:5–8 (goat)

KEY Symbols:

Shaggy Goat
Kingdom of Greece

Large Horn
Alexander the Great

☞ **GO TO:**

Daniel 8:8 (four horns)

KEY Symbols:

Four Horns
four kingdoms from Greece (Alexander's four generals)

☞ **GO TO:**

Daniel 8:9 (horn)

stern-faced: a striking appearance with fierce features

intrigue: Satanic deceit and treachery

G-8: the world's seven richest nations plus Russia

> **Daniel 8:21** The shaggy goat is the king of Greece, and the large horn between his eyes is the first king.

The Shaggy Goat Explained

Gabriel's next revelation was the identity of the shaggy <u>goat</u>. After learning what the two-horned ram symbolized we could probably figure this one out, but we do not have to. The shaggy goat represents the kingdom of Greece. The large horn represents its first king. History has revealed him to be Alexander the Great.

> **Daniel 8:22** The four horns that replaced the one that was broken off represent four kingdoms that will emerge from his nation but will not have the same power.

The Four Horns Explained

Here Gabriel explained the meaning of the *four horns*. They represent the four kingdoms that would emerge from the kingdom of the horn that was broken off (emerge from the kingdom of Greece). These were the four generals who divided up the Greek empire following the death of Alexander the Great (see Flow Chart, page 215): Cassander, Lysemachus, Seleucus, and Ptolemy. The strongest of the four eventually turned out to be Seleucus. It was his empire that produced Antiochus Epiphanes, but none of these four, even at their greatest strength, ever approached the power of Alexander the Great.

> **Daniel 8:23** "In the latter part of their reign, when rebels have become completely wicked, a stern-faced king, a master of intrigue, will arise.

The Next World Leader

This is the small <u>horn</u>. He will appear at the Time of the End. What he does will take place in the Time of Wrath. It will be near the end of the reign of the empires that emerged from the Greek empire. The wickedness on earth, and most especially the wickedness in Israel, will be great. This sinful era will provoke the terrible wrath of God. He will permit a **stern-faced** king to arise; a man who is bold, determined, and reckless. He will be a master

---

of **intrigue**, a man (the Antichrist) with supernatural occultic powers.

David Jeremiah with C.C. Carlson: His [the Antichrist's] destructiveness will be so universal that the world will reel under his power. Antiochus did the same, but his cruelty was child's play compared to the Antichrist. Everything I know about Antiochus Epiphanes causes me to shudder, but when I think about what the Antichrist is going to be, I can't imagine the magnitude of this depravity.[27]

> **Daniel 8:24** He will become very strong, but not by his own power. He will cause astounding devastation and will succeed in whatever he does. He will destroy the mighty men and the holy people.

More About The Next World Leader

He will become very strong is shown in other Scriptures to mean that he will have <u>power and authority</u> over the <u>whole earth</u>. *But not by his power* is usually thought to be a reference to his <u>Satanic</u> power. *He will cause astounding devastation* could be a reference to his amazing hi-tech weapons (nuclear bombs, smart bombs, laser-guided missiles, biological and chemical weapons) or it could refer to the great devastation these weapons will cause during the Tribulation Period. *He will destroy the mighty men and the holy people* refers to all those who oppose him but especially to those who accept Christ after the Rapture and, of course, the Jews (believing Israel), God's chosen people.

KEY Symbols:

Antichrist
LITTLE HORN
stern-faced king
master of intrigue

RELATED CURRENT EVENTS

☞ **GO TO:**

Revelation 13:5–8 (power and authority)

Daniel 7:23–24 (whole earth)

II Thessalonians 2:9; Revelation 13:2, 4 (Satan)

KEY Symbols:

Antichrist
power and authority
causes devastation
destroys mighty men and holy people

RELATED CURRENT EVENTS

I challenge you to convince the people of Iraq that they are not affected by world government right now! They are being told, right now, how much oil they can sell each month and what they are permitted to do with the money. They are regularly audited to insure compliance with U.N. mandates, and their military installations face periodic inspections. Furthermore, they nave no veto power over these actions by the world government which we call the United Nations. They must comply or else.

The fifty-second session of the U.N. General Assembly, just convened in October, has been dedicated to reform the United Nations. The new Secretary, General Kofi Annan, has presented to the nations of the world his proposals for the reformation process. The proposed reforms are many and far-reaching. However, two of these reforms should be understood by every person on earth. They are 1) the establishment of a World Criminal Court, and 2) the abolishment of the veto power presently enjoyed on the Security Council by the "big five" (United States, Great Britain, France, Russia, Red China). If implemented, these two reforms will propel us into world government—the world government prophesied in the Bible over which the Antichrist will soon rule.[29]

☞ **GO TO:**

Revelation 17:8 (Abyss)

Matthew 24:4; II John 1:7 (deceive)

II Thessalonians 2:4 (exalt himself)

Daniel; 9:27 (covenants)

Zechariah 13:8 (perish)

Revelation 19:19 (war)

Revelation 19:20 (lake)

Revelation 19:16–21 (King)

> **Daniel 8:25** He will cause deceit to prosper, and he will consider himself superior. When they feel secure, he will destroy many and take his stand against the Prince of princes. Yet he will be destroyed, but not by human power.

The Rise And Fall Of A World Leader

This is more of Gabriel's revelation about the Antichrist. Satan's man will come out of the Abyss and quickly rise to power over the whole world. Notice the following:

1) *He will cause deceit to prosper* speaks of his corruption and treachery. More often than not he will use deceit to achieve his goals.

2) *He will consider himself superior* refers to his self-exaltation and his views of others. He will magnify himself and think what he does is right because he is better than others.

3) *When they feel secure* refers to another one of his favorite tools. He will make <u>covenants</u> and treaties to lull people into a false sense of security. Then he will break them.

4) *He will destroy many* describes the result of his treachery and false covenants. Multitudes of betrayed people will be struck down and <u>perish</u>.

5) *He will take his stand against the Prince of princes* (Jesus) means he will be against the Christ. He will even take an army and try to make <u>war</u> against Jesus.

6) *He will be destroyed* refers to the fact that he will be cast alive into the <u>fiery lake</u> of burning sulfur (the Lake of Fire).

7) There will be no human power strong enough to destroy him, but Jesus, the *King of kings and Lord of lords* will.

RELATED CURRENT EVENTS

Daniel 8:26 "The vision of the evenings and mornings that has been given you is true, but seal up the vision, for it concerns the distant future."

☞ **GO TO:**

Daniel 8:14 (evenings)

It Is Hard To Believe

Daniel must have been appalled at the fact that the Temple will be desecrated for 2,300 <u>evenings</u> and mornings. Most would think that people would have more respect or that God would put a stop to it sooner, but Gabriel assured Daniel that it will end. Then he told Daniel to seal up the vision which is generally understood as "do not reveal the interpretation (keep it a secret)." This vision will be fulfilled during the Tribulation Period.

KEY POINT

God told Daniel to keep the meaning of the vision secret.

RELATED CURRENT EVENTS

Congressman Ron Paul (R-TX) has introduced H.R. 1146, The American Sovereignty Restoration Act, to withdraw the United States immediately from the United Nations. "Our Constitution does not give Congress the authority to cede our national sovereignty to an international body," said Paul. "In recent years, U.N. influence has crept into our national policy, education system, science, culture, and environment."[30]

☞ **GO TO:**

Luke 21:26 (coming)

Daniel 9:22 (understand)

> **Daniel 8:27** I, Daniel, was exhausted and lay ill for several days. Then I got up and went about the king's business. I was appalled by the vision; it was beyond understanding.

It Was Sickening

The stress from Daniel's experience and the knowledge of those things <u>coming</u> on the world was almost too much for him. He was tired and became sick with an illness that lasted for several days. Afterwards, he got up and went back to work. But he was devastated by the vision and there was still much that he did not <u>understand</u>. It may be that Gabriel did not tell him more because Daniel could not handle it all at once. We will see in Chapter 9 that Daniel was told more at a later time.

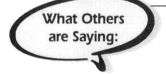

What Others are Saying:

David Jeremiah with C.C. Carlson: When we read about the coming man of sin [the Antichrist], the one who is going to rule this world and destroy those who have been left behind, it should compel us to look at those around us and tell them about the accurate prophecies in God's Word. The prophetic Word of God ought to motivate us to see our planet as a world that is lost. That lost world is falling into the lap of Satan, person by person, because Christian people don't care. If we really believed what Daniel has to tell us, it would change our lives.[31]

🔑 KEY Symbols:

God's Statue (Daniel 2)	Gentile Kingdom	Beast (Daniel 7)	Vision of Ram/Goat
Chest/Arms of silver	Medo-Persian	Second beast	Ram
Belly/Thighs of bronze	Greek	Third beast	Goat

Study Questions

1. Why would a loving God permit an evil man like the Antichrist to rise to power and do these terrible things?
2. Who or what should people rely on to interpret Bible prophecy?
3. What is the relationship between Bible prophecy and history?
4. When the world gets a one-world government will it have freedom of religion, peace, and safety?
5. Where will the Antichrist get his power? How much will he have and what will be his final end?

CHAPTER WRAP-UP

- Daniel had a vision in the third year of King Belshazzar. First, he saw a two-horned ram with one horn longer than the other. The ram (Medo-Persia) was powerful and became great. Its two horns represented the kings of Media and Persia. The short horn represented Darius and the long horn represented Cyrus. Their kingdom defeated Babylon and became the next great Gentile kingdom (Daniel 8:1–4, 21).

- Next Daniel saw a shaggy goat (Greece) with one large horn moving swiftly across the whole earth. The goat attacked the ram with great rage and defeated it. At the peak of the goat's power the large horn broke off and four weaker horns grew up in its place. The shaggy goat represents Greece, and its large horn represents Alexander the Great. The goat defeated the two-horned ram of Medo-Persia, but died shortly thereafter. The four weaker horns represent Alexander's four generals who took his place (Daniel 8:5–8, 21–23).

- Then Daniel saw another horn. It was very small at first, but it grew to the heavens, opposed Jesus, stopped the Jewish sacrifices, desecrated the Temple, and made war on God's people. It was successful in everything it did. This horn represents the Antichrist. He will begin as a little horn but will grow until he rules the world. He will be deceitful and corrupt, cause great destruction on earth, kill most of God's people, and be anti-God and anti-Christ (Daniel 8:9–13, 23–25).

- The Antichrist will be very powerful, but God is greater. This future world leader will be destroyed (Daniel 8:25).

- These things were almost too much for Daniel to handle. In his vision, the angel Gabriel appeared to him and terrified him to the point he fell on his face and went into a deep sleep. Afterwards he was exhausted and sick for several days, and found the whole event appalling and beyond his understanding (Daniel 8:17–18, 27).

DANIEL 9

CHAPTER HIGHLIGHTS

- Daniel's Discovery
- Daniel's Confession
- Daniel's Plea for Forgiveness
- Gabriel Appears
- Seventy Sevens

Let's Get Started

In order to fully understand Daniel's prayer found in Chapter 9 we need to begin with some background on the covenant God made with Israel. God had promised Abraham, Isaac, and Jacob many descendants, prosperity, and land. When Jacob had an encounter with God his name was changed to Israel, his children became known as the children of Israel, and his country became known as the land of Israel. During a great famine the children of Israel migrated to the land of Egypt where they eventually became slaves. They remained slaves until Moses led them out of Egypt 430 years later. He took them to Mt. Sinai where God swore to keep the promises he made to their forefathers. He made a special covenant with them and gave them specific instructions about keeping it. A major provision concerned the land: they agreed to let the land rest every seventh year. If they kept their part of the covenant, God promised to bless them. If they did not, God said he would chastise them. If the chastisement didn't work, he said he would destroy their nation and scatter the people among the nations. For hundreds of years, Israel went through cycles of rebellion and chastisement that kept them in line. But eventually the nation of Israel split into a Northern Kingdom called Israel and a Southern Kingdom called Judah (see Illustration #4, page 36). At first, the Northern Kingdom of Israel was the most rebellious. It would not listen and was taken captive by the Assyrians. Then things worsened in the Southern Kingdom and God began to deal with it through the prophet Jeremiah. He had Jeremiah warn the people of Judah that they should repent or he would

☞ **GO TO:**

Genesis 11:31–12:7 (Abraham)

Genesis 26:1–5 (Isaac)

Genesis 28:1–22 (Jacob)

Genesis 32:22–32 (name)

Exodus 12:31–42 (Moses)

Deuteronomy 7:6–8 (forefathers)

Leviticus 25; 26 (land)

Leviticus 26:30–34 (scatter)

Jeremiah 25:1–13 (Jeremiah)

Psalm 132:17–18; Luke 1:68–79 (horn)

destroy their nation and turn them over to the Babylonians for seventy years. Of course they didn't listen, and that's why we find them in Babylonian hands in the Book of Daniel.

Now, with this background information covered we can turn our attention to Chapter 9. This chapter can be divided into two parts: 1) Daniel's famous prayer, and 2) God's answer to his prayer. The prayer is unquestionably one of the greatest prayers in the Bible, and God's answer is unquestionably one of the greatest prophetic revelations in the Bible. We have in these two things an excellent example of how to pray, and a compact and comprehensive outline of the End of the (Gentile) Age.

What Others are Saying:

Noah Hutchings: Chapter 8 tells about a little horn, the Antichrist, who will rise up in the last days to challenge the Christ of God. This little horn will magnify himself and command millions to be killed for failing to worship him as God. He will rule over a ten-nation kingdom, and gain control of the whole earth. The prophecy about the little horn began in Chapter 7 where his kingdom is described and its chronological appearance is given. Chapter 8 describes his evil nature and his great power. Chapter 9 tells about his deceitful dealings with the nation of Israel. Chapter 9 also tells us about a greater horn than the little horn. This great <u>horn</u> will not be from the horn of the Syrian dynasty, but from the horn of David, the royal house of Israel.[1]

☞ **GO TO:**

Daniel 5:31 (Darius)

> **Daniel 9:1** In the first year of Darius son of Xerxes (a Mede by descent), who was made ruler over the Babylonian kingdom—

The Time

We have shown that Babylon fell around 539 B.C. (see Time Line #1, Appendix A) and <u>Darius</u> the Mede took over the kingdom. Historians tell us he died about 2 years later. Since our present verse took place during the first year of his reign, the time of this event is established at around 538-537 B.C. which is probably the same year as Chapter 6 when Daniel was thrown into the lions' den. Also, since Chapter 1 opens around the year 605 B.C. when Daniel was about 13 or 14 years old, we can calculate that Daniel and all Israel had been in captivity about 69 years, and Daniel was now a little more than 80 years old.

> **Daniel 9:2** in the first year of his reign, I, Daniel, understood from the Scriptures, according to the word of the LORD given to Jeremiah the prophet, that the desolation of Jerusalem would last seventy years.

☞ **GO TO:**

Daniel 6:10 (prayed)

Jeremiah 25:1-13; 29:10; II Chronicles 36:15–21 (seventy years)

Daniel's Discovery

We know that it was a time of upheaval in Daniel's life. Babylon had just fallen, a new empire had taken over, and a sick king was on the throne. We also know that Daniel regularly <u>prayed</u> three times a day. It is not unreasonable to assume that he also read the Scriptures when he prayed.

While reading the Book of Jeremiah, which Daniel considered to be the Word of God, Daniel made an interesting discovery. He read that Jerusalem would be desolate for <u>*seventy years*</u>. He was probably concerned about his people, and even though he was a prophet, he wanted to know what the other prophets had to say about the future of the Jews. So he read prophecy. Isn't is fascinating that we still have that same prophecy 2500 years later?

What Others are Saying:

Uriah Smith: Although Daniel, as prime minister of the foremost kingdom [Babylon] on the face of the earth, was cumbered with cares and burdens, he did not let this deprive him of the privilege of studying into things of higher moment, even the purposes of God as revealed to his prophets.[2]

David Jeremiah with C.C. Carlson: As he read that prophecy, it must have grabbed his heart, because he realized that the time for the return of his people to Jerusalem was drawing near. He probably wasn't sure whether the seventy years was calculated from the first deportation or the second or the third (see Remember This, page 20). Daniel and his friends were taken in the first phase, so as he was praying, he was trying to think when those seventy years would be accomplished. But one thing he knew. It was getting close! It was almost time for God to take the Jews back into their land [Israel].[3]

> **KEY POINT**
>
> Through the study of Scripture and constant prayer, a person can determine God's will.

David Breese: Please learn something from that! A lot of people say, "We can't know dates and we can't know details and its all very vague." Daniel said, "I read the prophetic writings of Jeremiah and I found out from Jeremiah's writings how long the captivity of Israel will be in the land of Babylon."[4]

☞ **GO TO:**

Jonah 2:1–10 (prayed)

Matthew 4:2 (fasting)

Genesis 37:34
(sackcloth)

Jonah 3:6; Job 2:8
(ashes)

petition: *a specific pleading*

sackcloth: *a very coarse material similar to burlap*

What Others are Saying:

KEY Symbols:

Sackcloth and Ashes
symbol of humiliation, grief, or sorrow

Remember This . . .

> **Daniel 9:3** So I turned to the Lord God and pleaded with him in prayer and petition, in fasting, and in sackcloth and ashes.

Daniel's Response

After discovering in the Word of God the fact that Jerusalem would be desolate for seventy years Daniel began to fast (see Something to Ponder, pages 161–162) and pray. Aside from the fact that he was obviously praying for God's will, notice these things:

1) The God he turned to was the Lord God.
2) He pleaded with God in <u>prayer</u>.
3) He pleaded with God in **petition**.
4) He pleaded with God by denying himself through <u>fasting</u>.
5) He pleaded with God by wearing drab and uncomfortable **sackcloth**.
6) He pleaded with God by dirtying himself with <u>ashes</u> (sitting in them and/or putting them on his face or head).

David Hocking: It was a sign of remorse, a sign of humbling, a sign that he was nothing. That is so foreign to us. That isn't the way we think at all! Then we wonder why God doesn't answer prayer. *Humble thyself in the sight of the Lord, and he shall lift you up* (James 4:10), the Bible says.[5]

Noah Hutchings: Sackcloth and ashes indicated extreme self-abasement and need for God's mercy. After Daniel had emptied himself of all self-glory and self-righteousness, he sought the face of the Lord God by prayer. He ran after the Lord in prayer; he pursued the Lord to get his attention.[6]

God has asked his people to approach him in prayer. This is an important way Christians show their faith and dependence upon him. But prayer is more than talking to God. It is more than an outward show of humility. True prayer is deliberate, humble, and sincere. On occasion, God's people endeavor to show this by making sacrifices, chastening themselves, and demonstrating their grief. When done for the right reason the goal is to get God's attention and not the attention of human beings.

It does no good to fast, wear sackcloth, or sit in ashes if it is done for show or not done sincerely. Also understand that for health reasons some people should not fast without consulting a doctor first.

WARNING

> **Daniel 9:4** I prayed to the LORD my God and confessed: "O Lord, the great and awesome God, who keeps his covenant of love with all who love him and obey his commands,

He Is My God

Daniel addressed his <u>prayer</u> to *the Lord my God. My God* shows humility, submission, and a personal relationship. He followed that up with praise and respect by calling God *the great and awesome God.* This recognizes God's amazing ability to do mighty things. Daniel continued his praise by acknowledging that God is a God who *keeps his* covenant *of love with all who love him and obey his commands.* This is an acknowledgment that Judah's problems were not because of a lack of faithfulness on God's part, but rather, Judah's problems were because the nation did not keep its part of the covenant.

God makes <u>covenants</u> because he loves people, and he absolutely *will not go back* on his covenants when people love and obey him.

What is Confession?

We need to know because *it is written: " 'As surely as I live,' says the Lord, 'every knee will bow before me; every tongue will* <u>confess</u> *to God.' " So then, each of us will give an account of himself to God.* Webster's dictionary says confession means "to admit one's guilt" or "to acknowledge one's sins." That is good, but not good enough. A better definition says confession means "to say the same thing." We have to say the same thing that is in our heart and the same thing that God says about our sin. We have to be sincere because there is nothing that we do and nothing in our heart that God does not know. We have to say the same thing because we cannot fool God.

☞ **GO TO:**

I Thessalonians 5:17, 18 (pray)

Genesis 17:1–22 (covenant)

Romans 14:11–12 (confess)

KEY POINT

True prayer is deliberate, humble, and sincere.

Remember This . . .

KEY POINT

When we confess sin, what we say in our heart has to match what God says about our sin.

Something to Ponder

☞ **GO TO:**

I Corinthians 12:22–27 (body)

emasculated: *made eunuchs*

fornication: *forbidden sexual sins*

> **Daniel 9:5** we have sinned and done wrong. We have been wicked and have rebelled; we have turned away from your commands and laws.

We Are Guilty

This is true confession and the word "we" is prominent in this prayer. Notice three things:

1) We have *sinned* and done *wrong*.
2) We have been *wicked* and *rebelled*.
3) We have *turned away* from your commands and laws.

Why were Judah, Jerusalem, and the Temple destroyed? Why were hundreds of thousands of people killed, **emasculated**, and raped? Why were so many people made slaves? The answers to these questions—sin, rebellion, and breaking God's commands and laws. Who did Daniel blame? Did he blame the leaders of Judah? Did he blame the wicked people in his nation? No. He identified himself with his people by saying *we* are at fault.

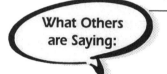

What Others are Saying:

David Jeremiah with C.C. Carlson: In the New Testament, especially in I Corinthians, we learn that as Christians we are one body. When one hurts, we all hurt. When one rejoices, we all rejoice. This may be a rather radical idea in our era of pointing fingers and condemning the sins of others, but I wonder what would happen if we pastors would stand in the pulpit on Sunday when there was known sin in the church and pray, "O God, we have committed adultery. O God, we have committed **fornication**. O God, we have been dishonest." Wouldn't that be a shocker?[7]

☞ **GO TO:**

Jeremiah 25:2–11 (not listened)

Daniel 9:4; Ephesians 2:4; I John 4:8 (love)

sins of commission: *wrongdoing, all thoughts and acts contrary to God's will and laws*

> **Daniel 9:6** We have not listened to your servants the prophets, who spoke in your name to our kings, our princes, and our fathers, and to all the people of the land.

We Have **Not** Listened

Daniel confessed that he and the people of Judah were not only guilty of **sins of commission** but were guilty of **sins of omission** as well. More specifically, he confessed that everyone refused to <u>listen</u> to the prophets of God who tried to warn them about the impending danger.

David Hocking: We hear the Word of God through God's instruments—just simple people who preach and teach the Word of God. We hear what God says, but a lot of us let it go in one ear and out the other. We don't want to concentrate on it. We don't want to listen to it unless it's really entertaining. . . . We wonder why he isn't working in our lives. One reason is that we haven't been really listening to his servants teach the Word.[8]

David Breese: It's time, dear friends, for personal spiritual **revival**. It's time for revival to move out from us personally into a land (America) that's in desperate spiritual condition today. Let me tell you something. If that doesn't happen, zero will be the possibilities of this nation.[9]

David Jeremiah with C.C. Carlson: There are a lot of folks who go to prayer, not to ascertain the will of God, but to ask him to do what they want. Prayer is not getting God to adjust his program to what we want, it is adjusting our lives to the revealed will of God. When we pray, it isn't God who changes, it's us. Maybe we've been looking for change at the wrong end of the cycle.[10]

Daniel 9:4 mentions the <u>love</u> of God, and we know that the Bible teaches that God is love. We can be thankful for that. But should preachers then preach nothing but that? Should preachers just stick to sugar-coated messages about the love of God, Fatherhood of God, and brotherhood of man? Should society brand as fanatics those preachers who say our nation and the church is sick, and unless there is repentance we will all come under the judgment of God? Would we be wise to do like Judah and not listen to the call for repentance?

> **Daniel 9:7** "Lord, you are righteous, but this day we are covered with shame—the men of Judah and people of Jerusalem and all Israel, both near and far, in all the countries where you have scattered us because of our unfaithfulness to you.

Unfaithfulness Has A Price

Here Daniel made a comparison between God and all the people of Israel and Judah. He noted that God is **righteous**, but all the

---

What Others are Saying:

sins of omission: *not doing God's will or keeping his laws*

revival: *renewed zeal to obey God*

KEY POINT

Prayer is not getting God to adjust *his* program, it's getting us to adjust *our* program.

Something to Ponder

☞ GO TO:

Isaiah 5:16 (righteousness)

Proverbs 3:33–35; 13:18 (shame)

Ezekiel 37:15–22 (kingdom)

---

people were covered with <u>shame</u>. Because of their unfaithfulness to God, wherever they went they would carry their shame. God was right, they were wrong, and it was a disgrace.

David Hocking: Do we feel that way? "God we're embarrassed in front of you because of what we've been doing. We've neglected your Word. We haven't been paying attention to your prophets. We're into all kinds of corruption—idolatry, immorality. This man [Daniel] humbled himself before God.[11]

righteous: sinless, God always does the right thing

repentance: turning away from wrong and toward God

Ed Young: Let me tell you something ladies and gentlemen. I don't believe any of us can really be forgiven for sin unless we truly confess and repent of our sin. And there has to be in that the element of shame; shame that we have disappointed God, we have disappointed ourselves, we have disappointed others. Shame is a part of confession and **repentance**.[12]

WARNING

Some experts teach that the ten tribes that made up the Northern <u>Kingdom</u> called Israel were lost or extinct by this time. But Daniel did not believe this. It is true that the nation had been destroyed and taken captive by Assyria, but pay close attention to the fact that Daniel mentions *all Israel, both near and far.* In his opinion the ten tribes of Israel were scattered with those that were close to him and those that were far away in other countries.

☞ **GO TO:**

Romans 3:23; I John 1:8, 10 (sinned)

> **Daniel 9:8** O LORD, we and our kings, our princes, and our fathers are covered with shame because we have sinned against you.

Shame! Shame!

Daniel was earnestly humbling himself. He was also acting as a priest confessing sin on behalf of the entire nation. He was admitting guilt on behalf of everyone; that everyone was literally covered with shame. Why? Because everyone had <u>sinned</u> against God.

Consider these seven Biblical reasons why your prayer may not be answered:

Something to Ponder

1) unbelief or doubting God (James 1:5; Hebrews 11:6)
2) asking for the wrong reason (James 4:3)
3) sin in your life (Isaiah 59:2; John 9:31; I Peter 3:7)

4) neglecting the needs of others (Proverbs 21:13)

5) failure to forgive others (Mark 11:25)

6) it is not God's will (Luke 22:42)

7) self-exaltation (Luke 18:9–14)

> **Daniel 9:9** The Lord our God is merciful and forgiving, even though we have rebelled against him;

The Character Of God

Daniel was simply reminding God of his **mercy** and **forgiveness**. He knew that God could not abandon his people even though the people had rebelled.

If you were God, would you <u>forgive</u> the Jews? They were guilty. They rebelled. They broke the covenant. They ignored and killed the prophets. They lied. They committed adultery. They worshipped idols. If you were God, would you show <u>mercy</u> and take them back? Obviously you are just a human being, but the Lord is <u>slow to anger</u>, abounding in <u>love</u>, and forgiving of sin and <u>rebellion</u>.

> **Daniel 9:10** we have not obeyed the LORD our God or kept the laws he gave us through his servants the prophets.

We Have Been Unfaithful

Israel and Judah had the Scriptures and prided themselves on following God, but Daniel confesses that they did not obey God. They also prided themselves on following <u>Moses</u>, but again we hear Daniel confess that they did not keep the **Law of Moses**. Actually, they did not keep any of the other laws given through God's servants the <u>prophets</u> either.

Consider this Bible prayer list:

1) for those in authority over us (I Timothy 2:2)

2) for people to do God's work (Matthew 9:38)

3) for those who persecute us (Matthew 5:44)

☞ **GO TO:**

Nehemiah 9:17;
Matthew 6:14, 15;
Mark 11:25; I John
1:9 (forgive)

Deuteronomy 4:31;
Matthew 5:7 (mercy)

Exodus 34:6, 7 (anger)

Romans 5:8 (love)

Numbers 14:18
(rebellion)

**Something
to Ponder**

mercy: *showing pity, love and forgiveness*

forgive: *acting as though it never happened*

☞ **GO TO:**

Exodus 2:1–10 (Moses)

Exodus 24:12-18;
Deuteronomy 5:1–21
(Law of Moses)

Matthew 23:29–32;
Luke 11:47–48;
I Thessalonians
2:14–15 (prophets)

**Something
to Ponder**

Law of Moses: all the rules God gave to Moses

4) for God's kingdom to come, his will to be done, food, forgiveness, and deliverance from temptation (Matthew 6:9–13)

5) for the peace of Jerusalem (Psalm 122:6)

6) for others (Ephesians 6:18; 3:14–19)

7) for wisdom (James 1:5)

> **Daniel 9:11** All Israel has transgressed your law and turned away, refusing to obey you. "Therefore the curses and sworn judgments written in the Law of Moses, the servant of God, have been poured out on us, because we have sinned against you.

We Chose To Be Cursed

Daniel confessed that everyone had broken the **law** and everyone had <u>turned</u> away from God. It wasn't a matter of ignorance or misunderstanding. It was a deliberate refusal to obey God.

Notice the terrible result. They were under the **curses** and judgments of God written in the Law of Moses. These were clearly spelled out, but many people simply could not accept the fact that God would put anyone under a curse. The problem was they were blaming God instead of themselves. The reason Israel came under the curses was *because we have sinned against you.*

☞ **GO TO:**

Leviticus 26:14–17 (laws)

Isaiah 53:6 (turned away)

Deuteronomy 28:15–68 (curses)

Daniel 9:7 (righteous)

law: the Law of Moses

curses: the predictions of harm that would befall them

Daniel had already confessed that God is <u>righteous</u>. God never does wrong. Take the time to study Deuteronomy 28 and notice that God's covenant with Israel was conditional. If Israel kept the covenant he would bless the nation in many ways. If Israel broke the covenant, kept breaking it, and refused to repent, many curses would come upon the nation. This was Israel's choice:

1) obedience with blessings, or

2) disobedience with curses.

Israel eventually chose the wrong thing.

Remember This . . .

☞ **GO TO:**

Exodus 24:8 (covenant)

Matthew 10:28–33; Mark 9:42–49; Luke 16:19–31 (hell)

> **Daniel 9:12** You have fulfilled the words spoken against us and against our rulers by bringing upon us great disaster. Under the whole heaven nothing has ever been done like what has been done to Jerusalem.

You Have Fulfilled Your Words

Daniel acknowledged that God simply did what he promised if Israel refused to keep the <u>covenant</u>. And it was terrible. No city had ever been attacked, plundered, and destroyed like Jerusalem. No temple had ever been desecrated and destroyed like the Temple at Jerusalem. Nebuchadnezzar struck Jerusalem with a vengeance unlike anything known before.

Something to Ponder

According to several polls most Americans and most church members believe in a place called hell. But for many seminary professors, theologians, and liberal pastors the idea of a place called hell is repulsive and unbelievable. They say God is too loving and compassionate to cast people into hell. The idea of hell is a relic of pagan thinking, and those who believe in hell believe in a God who is cruel, vindictive, and capable of doing evil. It is up to each person to choose what they want to believe, but there is no escaping the fact that the Bible plainly teaches the existence of <u>hell</u> and the fact that God fulfills his words. Please read all of Deuteronomy 28 again and then re-read this verse. What do you think?

> **Daniel 9:13** Just as it is written in the Law of Moses, all this disaster has come upon us, yet we have not sought the favor of the LORD our God by turning from our sins and giving attention to your truth.

We Refused To Change

Daniel is confessing that the disasters had come upon him and his people in exactly the same way it was written in the Law of Moses. God did not deviate from what was written. Even though the disasters had struck the people, they still refused to <u>seek</u> the Lord. They still refused to repent of their sins, and they still refused to <u>listen</u> to the truths in the <u>Word</u> of God.

John J. Davis: Taking the teachings of Jesus on future judgment and eternal punishment at face value should bring a new sense of urgency to our evangelistic efforts. When Jesus looked at the people in Jerusalem nearly 2,000 years ago, he wept because of their rebellion and what it would ultimately mean. So deeply passionate was the Apostle <u>Paul</u> over the lost condition of his people Israel that he de-

☞ **GO TO:**

II Chronicles 7:14 (seek)

Leviticus 26:14–46 (listen)

Matthew 24:35 (words)

Romans 1:1 (Paul)

Romans 9:2–4 (cursed)

What Others are Saying:

clared, *I have great sorrow and unceasing anguish in my heart. For I could wish that I myself were <u>cursed</u> and cut off from Christ for the sake of my brothers, those of my own race, the people of Israel.* Paul understood well the awesome implications of God's future judgment. For him the eternal misery of the lost was not a mere theological speculation. It was a reality that affected his entire ministry, and Paul did everything he could to point people to Jesus Christ: the only one who could save them from hell.[13]

☞ **GO TO:**

Psalm 96:11–13 (righteous)

Genesis 6–8 (flood)

KEY POINT

God is patient, but he does not hesitate to enforce his Word.

> **Daniel 9:14** The LORD did not hesitate to bring the disaster upon us, for the LORD our God is righteous in everything he does; yet we have not obeyed him.

God Is Righteous

Some complain about the slow pace and lack of justice in the United States. It is no secret that some cases drag through the courts for years and some criminals get light sentences because judges hesitate to enforce the penalties of the law. It is different with God. He is patient, but he does not hesitate to enforce his Word. He did not hesitate to bring disaster upon the Jews, and he will not hesitate to send a Tribulation Period to punish others.

Here Daniel repeats the fact that God is <u>righteous</u>. God never mistreats people. His character will not allow him to do that. Nevertheless, he will not allow sin to go unpunished. The Jews knew that, and still disobeyed him.

Something to Ponder

When Noah was alive the earth was corrupt and filled with violence. The wickedness of man was great, and his thoughts were constantly on evil. So God told Noah he intended to destroy the earth with a <u>flood</u>, and he had Noah warn the wicked. No one listened, yet God did not hesitate to send the flood.

Today we have a large amount of historical and scientific evidence to show that the flood did happen. In our modern society multitudes are disobeying God. But according to the Bible he is still righteous and disobedience will bring his wrath. This is something the Church should be concerned about too. Many church members are asking for prayer in schools when they never have prayer in their homes. Many others cry out for character in our government leaders, but they never cry out for character in their church. What does a righteous God think of all this?

> **Daniel 9:15** "Now, O Lord our God, who brought your people out of Egypt with a mighty hand and who made for yourself a name that endures to this day, we have sinned, we have done wrong.

☞ **GO TO:**

Jeremiah 32:17–25 (mighty hand)

Exodus 7:14–12:30 (plagues)

James 4:8 (near)

God's Name Is Great

Here Daniel was remembering that God delivered the children of Israel out of the land of Egypt. *With a <u>mighty hand</u>* refers to the ten <u>plagues</u> or ten great miracles God performed to convince Pharoah to let them go. Daniel called attention to the fact that God's great acts gained God great fame. Then Daniel repeated something he had already said in several ways: the people of Israel and Judah had sinned. It was not God who had done wrong. It was the Jews.

Richard L. Pratt Jr.: As I have evaluated my own prayers and listened to the prayers of others, I have found that we frequently neglect God. In an average ten minute prayer, most of us spend fewer than 30 seconds talking to God about God. How must God feel when we talk to him about everything but him? James wrote, *Come <u>near</u> to God and he will come near to you.* God will bless us with his special presence when we draw near to him. One reason that prayer often becomes an empty ritual instead of a rich spiritual experience is that we ignore God when we pray.[14]

What Others are Saying:

KEY POINT

We know Israel's God is the true God because he works through them and refuses to let their nation be destroyed.

John White: I need to believe two things when I pray: first, that God exists; and, second, that he rewards those who earnestly seek him. I found it easy enough to believe that God exists, but I have had great difficulty in believing that he would answer me. I sought him earnestly enough, but I felt neither good enough nor spiritual enough to deserve answers. I know that this is nonsense, but my feelings interfered with my faith and, in my case, it became a serious problem. Then one day it was as though God said, "Don't you trust me?" Light began to break around me, and my heart melted. Even now that question brings tears to my eyes. Not trust him? How could I do anything but trust him after all his goodness to me? I need to have confidence in the person whom I know and love.[15]

Is God's name Jehovah, Allah, Diana, Gaia, Ishtar, Mother Earth, or what? His name is very important. The world cannot know who to worship unless it knows God's name. What is God's name, and who do we worship? That is one reason

Something to Ponder

why Jehovah works through Israel and refuses to let the tiny nation be wiped out. He is showing the world that Israel's God, the Lord God Jehovah, is God.

> **Daniel 9:16** O Lord, in keeping with all your righteous acts, turn away your anger and your wrath from Jerusalem, your city, your **holy** hill. Our sins and the **iniquities** of our fathers have made Jerusalem and your people an object of scorn to all those around us.

Jerusalem Is God's City

Does God get angry? Would God pour out his <u>wrath</u> on anyone or anything? The person who says no either does not know or does not believe what's in the Bible. God does get angry, and he did use wicked nations to vent his wrath on Israel and Judah.

But let's notice something. Daniel said, *I, Daniel, understood from the Scriptures, according to the word of the LORD given to Jeremiah the prophet, that the desolation of Jerusalem would last seventy years* (Daniel 9:2). He also said, *God is righteous in everything he does* (Daniel 9:14). And we know *righteous* means God always does the right thing. In this verse, Daniel 9:16, Daniel is appealing to God's righteousness to turn away his anger and wrath from Jerusalem because the <u>seventy years</u> is almost up. A righteous God would not allow that time to be exceeded.

Who owns Jerusalem? God. Does Jerusalem have a special status? Yes. God has kept it and plans to use it for his own purposes. Anyone who tries to do anything with it other than what God wants is going against his will. What has caused Jerusalem to be such a problem for the world? Sin on behalf of the Jews.

In the German Christian magazine, *ethos*, No. 3/1996, page 27, the following was written: "Long before the actual negotiations over the status of Jerusalem between Israel and the PLO begin, an apparently insoluble conflict smolders. At the beginning of December 1995, the General Assembly of the U.N. declared with a great majority that Israel's claim to control over Jerusalem is illegal. A corresponding resolution was accepted with 133 votes. Only Israel voted against it. The U.S.A. and twelve other countries withheld their vote."[16]

☞ **GO TO:**

Psalm 2:6 (holy hill)

Psalm 7:11 (wrath)

Jeremiah 25:1–13; 29:10 (seventy years)

holy: *God declares it is different or separate from any other city*

iniquities: *a general term referring to all kinds of wickedness*

KEY Symbols:

Jerusalem
God's city
his holy hill

RELATED CURRENT EVENTS

> **Daniel 9:17** "Now, our God, hear the prayers and petitions of your servant. For your sake, O Lord, look with favor on your desolate sanctuary.

evince: to show clearly

For Your Glory

God does not have to listen to our prayers and petitions. Daniel was well aware of that, so he asked God to hear him. The thoughts of his mind were focusing upon the Temple which was God's house, God's own dwelling place on earth when the nation was faithful. Daniel pleaded with God to look upon his requests favorably and restore the Temple.

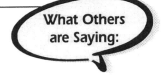

What Others are Saying:

Uriah Smith: [It is] not that God is moved with motives of ambition and vain glory; but when his people are jealous for the honor of his name, when they **evince** their love for him by pleading with him to work, not for their own personal benefit, but for his own glory, that his name may not be reproached and blasphemed among the heathen, this is acceptable with him.[17]

David Hocking: So often, we have our own agenda when we pray. Have you noticed that? We have our little list. Are the concerns on our list, God's concerns? We would see far more answers if we prayed about God's concerns.[18]

> **Daniel 9:18** Give ear, O God, and hear; open your eyes and see the desolation of the city that bears your Name. We do not make requests of you because we are righteous, but because of your great mercy.

We Ask For Mercy

In Daniel 9:17, Daniel asked God to look with favor on the desolate sanctuary. In this verse he asked God to notice the desolation of his <u>city</u> Jerusalem. Daniel based his request not on the righteousness of the Jews but on the great mercy of God.

Consider the situation. Daniel had been fasting. He was wearing sackcloth and sitting in ashes. He was earnestly pleading with God to hear his request, see the desolation of Jerusalem, and respond with mercy on the Jews.

☞ **GO TO:**

Daniel 9:16 (city)

Luke 2:38, 21:28; Ephesians 1:7 (redemption)

Divine Presence: presence of God

Redemption: when Israel's sins are forgiven and the nation is delivered from Gentile control

KEY Symbols:

Jerusalem
City of God

Jews
people of God

☞ **GO TO:**

Psalm 87:2, 3 (city of God)

Exodus 3:7; 5:1 (people of God)

In the present political climate, Moslems and Christians are also singing Jerusalem's praises, claiming it for themselves. But whereas the Bible mentions Jerusalem by name over 500 times, the Koran does not mention it even once. And Christian theology denigrates the importance of the earthly Jerusalem, favoring the heavenly Jerusalem, City of God. . . . Jerusalem is saturated with the **Divine Presence**, and will continue as the Jewish capital until the coming of the **Redemption**.[19]

> **Daniel 9:19** O Lord, listen! O Lord, forgive! O Lord, hear and act! For your sake, O my God, do not delay, because your city and your people bear your Name."

A Final Request

These are the last words of Daniel's prayer. Israel and Judah had not listened to God, but Daniel asked God to listen to him. He pled for forgiveness for his people. He wanted God to hear him, act on his prayer, and not delay because the seventy years was almost up and because God's name was at stake. He was concerned about God's name and glory. And he did something noteworthy: he linked the city of Jerusalem to the Jews. Both bear the name of God: Jerusalem is the City of God and the Jews are the people of God.

What Others are Saying:

Wallace Emerson: If ever a prayer showed full appreciation of a sinning people, of a merciful God, of a spiritual, and moral cause and effect, and if ever a prayer acknowledged the majesty, the righteousness, and the power of Jehovah, it is this prayer. This prayer, even as the prayer of Moses, calls upon God for his own sake to forgive and to restore, not because of the righteousness of Israel or Daniel's own righteousness but for "thy own great mercies" . . . "for thy own sake."[20]

☞ **GO TO:**

Romans 3:23 (sinned)

Daniel 6:4, 5 (administrators)

> **Daniel 9:20** While I was speaking and praying, confessing my sin and the sin of my people Israel and making my request to the LORD my God for his holy hill—

Before My Prayer Ended

While Daniel was talking to God and confessing his sin and the sin of his people Israel, and while he was talking to God about the Temple, something happened. We will find out what in Daniel 9:21, but for the moment let us focus on the fact that Daniel was confessing *his* sin. He may have been the best man on earth, but he still <u>sinned</u>. Two of his fellow <u>administrators</u> and 120 satraps diligently tried to find something to accuse him of, but they could not find anything. Still, Daniel was a sinner. And so is everyone else.

> **Daniel 9:21** while I was still in prayer, Gabriel, the man I had seen in the earlier vision, came to me in swift flight about the time of the evening sacrifice.

Daniel 9:19 (delay)

Daniel 8:16 (Gabriel)

A Heavenly Visitor

Daniel had asked God not to <u>delay</u>; he didn't. Daniel didn't even get to say, "Amen" before the angel Gabriel appeared. This is the same <u>Gabriel</u> Daniel had seen in the Vision of the Ram and the Goat. He came in swift flight at about three in the afternoon (the time the evening sacrifice was offered before the Temple was destroyed).

M.R. DeHaan: The sacrifices in Jerusalem had been discontinued, but Daniel, even though there was no actual sacrificing going on, still observed the time that God has instituted, the time of day when the sacrifice was to be offered. During that time he was upon his face before Almighty God, still continuing his regular habit of prayer and still spiritually sacrificing unto the Lord God, and it was at this time that the angel Gabriel came.[21]

What Others are Saying:

> **Daniel 9:22** He instructed me and said to me, "Daniel, I have now come to give you insight and understanding.

Daniel 8:27 (vision)

I Have More Information For You

At the close of Chapter 8, we learned that Daniel's <u>vision</u> of the Antichrist (the Vision of the Ram and the Goat) had left him appalled, exhausted, and ill for several days. We also learned that

DANIEL 9   **247**

KEY Symbols:

Antichrist
stern-faced king

God's People
holy people

Jesus
prince of princes

☞ **GO TO:**

Daniel 8:23 (stern-faced king)

Daniel 8:24 (holy people)

Daniel 8:25 (Prince of princes)

I Corinthians 12:7–11 (interpretation)

esteemed: *held in high regard*

Holy Spirit: *the third person of the Trinity, the invisible presence of God*

What Others are Saying:

Gabriel had explained many things to Daniel, but there was much more that he did not understand. In this verse we learn that Gabriel returned while Daniel was praying to provide more insight and understanding. Thus we see that what we are about to learn is more about the Antichrist of Chapter 8. To be more specific, Daniel has been praying about Jerusalem, the Temple, and his people, so we are going to be told what will happen to the city, the Temple, and the people starting with Daniel's lifetime and working toward the End of the (Gentile) Age (the Time of the End).

> **Daniel 9:23** As soon as you began to pray, an answer was given, which I have come to tell you, for you are highly esteemed. Therefore, consider the message and understand the vision:

I Am Here To Help You

As soon as Daniel started praying, Gabriel was given an answer to this prayer and authorized to take it to Daniel. He appeared to Daniel and told Daniel what he was authorized to do and why: he was authorized to help Daniel understand the Vision of the Ram and the Goat because Daniel was highly **esteemed** in heaven. When we refer back to the vision it is important to notice that it concerned the <u>stern-faced king</u> (the Antichrist), the <u>holy people</u> (all of God's people, but particularly the Jews), and the <u>Prince of princes</u> (Jesus). It is a great honor that God would give this revelation to Daniel.

The swiftness of this answer is interesting. A close reading of this verse indicates that Daniel had already started praying when the answer was given to Gabriel. Thus we see that Gabriel left heaven, located Daniel, and appeared to Daniel almost instantaneously. This lets us know that when there is no hindrance from Satan or his evil forces it is possible for our prayers to be answered in the blink of an eye.

Uriah Smith: Think of celestial beings, the highest in the universe—the Father, the Son, the holy angels—having such regard and esteem for a mortal man here upon earth as to authorize an angel to bear the message to him that he is greatly beloved! This is one of the highest pinnacles of glory to which mortals can attain.[22]

Ed Young: God sent an angel to give Daniel an answer to his prayer. Has anybody had an angel come and answer your prayer? No! God doesn't operate like that today. Why? Because we have the **Holy Spirit** as believers in our lives. The Holy Spirit <u>gives interpretation</u>. The Holy Spirit gives meaning.[23]

> **Daniel 9:24** "Seventy 'sevens' are decreed for your people and your holy city to finish transgression, to put an end to sin, to atone for wickedness, to bring in everlasting righteousness, to seal up vision and prophecy, and to anoint the most holy.

490 Years Are Decreed To Do Six Things

Gabriel told Daniel a decree had been issued. Since Gabriel came from heaven we can believe the decree was issued in heaven by God himself. Gabriel told Daniel *seventy sevens* (see Time Line #3, Appendix A) will pass upon your people and your holy city. Three questions answer this: 1) How long is *seventy sevens*, 2) Who does *your people* refer to, and 3) What does *your city* refer to?

First, *seventy sevens* is seventy times seven (70 X 7 = 490) or 490 of something. It could be 490 minutes, 490 days, or 490 of anything. However, because Daniel was reading <u>Jeremiah's</u> prophecy about Judah spending seventy <u>years</u> of captivity in Babylon when he started praying—a prophecy about **years**—most prophecy experts agree that this time period is 490 years. Also, this has been verified by history as you will see later in this chapter. Second, *your <u>people</u>* refers to Daniel's people, the Jews. Third, *your city* refers to Daniel's home city, Jerusalem. So Gabriel's first words were that God had decreed that 490 years would pass upon Israel and Jerusalem for the purpose of doing these six things:

1) *To finish transgression*—God has decreed that he will finish (shut up or arrest) all **transgression**.

2) *To put an end to sin*—God has decreed that he will put an end to all **sin**.

3) *To atone for wickedness*—God has decreed that he will make an **atonement** for **wickedness**. (Note: Christians believe this occurred when Jesus died on the cross, but the Jews, as a nation, have had their hearts <u>hardened</u> and will not accept it until after these 490 years have passed.)

KEY POINT

The Holy Spirit gives interpretation (meaning).

☞ **GO TO:**

Daniel 9:2 (Jeremiah)

Jeremiah 25:1–13; 29:10 (years)

Daniel 9:16 (people)

Daniel 9:16 (city)

Romans 11:25–27 (hardened)

KEY POINT

When there is no hindrance from Satan or his evil forces it is possible for our prayers to be answered in the blink of an eye.

years: *a Jewish year is 360 days*

transgression: *rebellion against God*

sin: *missing the mark, wrongdoing*

atonement: *provide a covering, pardon, blot out*

wickedness: *all sin*

4) *To bring in everlasting righteousness*—God has decreed that he will bring in a **Kingdom of Everlasting Righteousness**. (It will begin with the Millennium.)

5) *To seal up vision and prophecy*—God has decreed that he will fulfill everything he has promised in visions and prophecies.

6) *To anoint the most holy*—God has decreed that he will anoint the most holy. (Some experts say this means anoint a new Temple; others say it means anoint Jesus as the Messiah. It probably means both.)

Daniel had been praying about his people, the Temple, and the city of Jerusalem. There seems to be little doubt here that Gabriel was telling Daniel that God has a plan involving 490 years. The 490 year plan is a decree of God and will be carried out. When all 490 years have passed rebellion will cease, sin will stop, atonement will have been accomplished, righteousness will prevail, all visions and prophecies will be fulfilled, and a new Temple/Messiah will be anointed.

What Others are Saying:

KEY Symbols:

Seventy Sevens
490 years

Something to Ponder

William S. McBirnie: Now these 490 years are to bring about these six things. And what's true of Israel, is also true of the Gentiles. These 490 years will bring in for the Gentiles, an end of rebellion against the Messiah, an end to the sins of the Gentiles, a complete reconciliation for iniquity, an everlasting righteousness for the Gentiles. And among the Gentiles, when the 490 years are ended, there'll be no need for the Bible, and visions, and preaching. Because every tongue will be confessing, every knee will be bowing, and they too, with Israel, will meet in this holy, anointed tabernacle in Jerusalem.[24]

Let's pause and recognize an important point here. There are many people who do not believe in a Tribulation Period. They teach that the Church will succeed in converting the world and bringing in the kingdom of everlasting righteousness (Kingdom Theology) without the world going through a terrible ordeal like the Tribulation. But here we see it plainly stated that Israel must go through all 490 years (the last seven are the Tribulation Period) before the Kingdom of Everlasting Righteousness can begin.

> **Daniel 9:25** "Know and understand this: From the issuing of the decree to restore and rebuild Jerusalem until the Anointed One, the ruler, comes, there will be seven 'sevens,' and sixty-two 'sevens.' It will be rebuilt with streets and a trench, but in times of trouble.

☞ **GO TO:**

II Chronicles 36; Ezra 1:1–4 (Cyrus)

Ezra 6:1–12 (Darius)

Ezra 7:11–26 (Artaxerxes)

Nehemiah 2:1–8; 17, 18 (Jerusalem)

Nehemiah 2:17–3:32 (rebuilding)

Luke 4:18; Acts 10:38–43 (Anointed One)

Nehemiah 4 (opposed building)

Matthew 21:1–11 (triumphal entry)

When God's Clock Will Start

Here Gabriel revealed the fact that God would start keeping time on the seventy sevens (490 years) when a certain decree was issued. Pay attention to this starting point because it means that God's 490-year clock was not running when Gabriel met with Daniel. His clock was not ticking at that time but when it did start, it would not tick continuously through to the 490 years. God was going to use this clock like a stop watch; he would turn it on and off as he wished (see Time Line #3, Appendix A).

So we learn that God planned to start his 490 year clock when a certain decree was issued. Again we need to pay close attention to every word here because over the next few years there would be several decrees concerning the Jews going back to Israel and rebuilding the Temple and Jerusalem, but there would be only one decree that would fulfill all the words in this passage.

Cyrus issued a decree in 538 B.C. to release the Jews, but it did not fit this prophecy because it made no mention of rebuilding Jerusalem. Darius issued a decree in 519 B.C., but all it did was repeat the decree of Cyrus with the exception that it allowed the Jews to rebuild the Temple. Artaxerxes issued a decree in 458 B.C., but it did not fit because it made no mention of rebuilding Jerusalem. But he issued a second decree in 445 B.C. that fulfills the words of this prophecy, and that is when the rebuilding of Jerusalem began. So the commencement date or the starting of God's clock on the seventy sevens (490 years) would turn out to be a decree *in the month of Nisan in the twentieth year of King Artaxerxes.*

But there is more. This verse mentions two very important events: the rebuilding of Jerusalem and the Anointed One. And it gives two time periods: seven sevens (7 X 7 = 49 years) and sixty-two sevens (62 X 7 = 434 years). The first time period (49 years) relates to the rebuilding of Jerusalem; the second time period (434 years) relates to the coming of the Anointed One.

Concerning the rebuilding of Jerusalem, it took 49 years to accomplish that. The Bible and secular historians record many things about it. The Ammonites, Moabites, and Samaritans all opposed the rebuilding of Jerusalem. They laughed at the Jews, ridiculed them, plotted to kill Nehemiah, and threatened war. They caused so much trouble the Jews stationed guards with weapons and trumpets at 500 foot intervals around the wall; the Jews wore swords while they worked and kept shields within a few feet of every man.

Concerning the Anointed One (Jesus the Messiah), Gabriel said the decree would be issued, seven sevens (49 years) would pass, sixty-two sevens (434 years) would pass, and then he would come. This is a reference to the first coming of Jesus, and we learn that he would appear 483 years (49 years + 434 years = 483 years) after the proper decree. But let's be careful here. This is a reference to his <u>Triumphal Entry</u>, not his birth. Notice these words spoken during his Triumphal Entry about his coming, *As he approached Jerusalem and saw the city, he wept over it and said, "If you, even you, had only known on this day what would bring you peace—but now it is hidden from your eyes. The days will come upon you when your enemies will build an embankment against you and encircle you and hem you in on every side. They will dash you to the ground, you and the children within your walls. They will not leave one stone on another, because you did not recognize the time of God's coming to you."* (Luke 19:41–44)

This is what we have: 1) the starting date which is the date Artaxerxes issued his second decree, and 2) the ending date which is the date Jesus made his Triumphal Entry into Jerusalem. We only need to determine if that spans the required 483 years. And the answer is, yes, right to the very day.

Sir Robert Anderson, a highly respected English lawyer and former head of Scotland Yard, figured it out. He multiplied 483 years times the Jewish prophetic year of 360 days per year and found that 483 Jewish years equals 173,880 days. Then he took the date of the decree (March 14, 445 B.C.) and calculated the number of days to the Triumphal Entry (April 6, 32 A.D.), taking into account leap year and the fact that there was only one year between 1 B.C. and 1 A.D. (no year numbered 0), and the total was 173,880 days. So we see that exactly 483 years passed between the decree and the first coming (Triumphal Entry) of Jesus.

KEY Symbols:

The Anointed One
JESUS THE MESSIAH

KEY Symbols:

God's Clock
490+ YEARS

first time period
- 49 years

second time period
- 434 years

What Others are Saying:

Grant R. Jeffrey: According to the Talmud (a collection of ancient Jewish religious writings and law), "The first day of the month of Nisan is the New Year for the computation of the reign of kings and for festivals." In other words, when no other date is given, we assume the event occurred on the first day of Nisan. The Royal

Observatory in Greenwich, U.K., has calculated that the first of Nisan in the twentieth year of the reign of King Artaxerxes occurred on March 14, 445 B.C.[25]

Peter and Paul Lalonde: 483 years later, to the day, was Sunday, April 6, 32 A.D. On that day, which we commemorate as Palm Sunday, Jesus rode into Jerusalem on a donkey and revealed himself as Israel's Messiah.[26]

God's clock is like a stop watch that can be started and stopped at will. He would start it when the decree was issued. He would allow two time periods to tick off: 49 years and 434 years. Then he would stop it. And he would not restart it for a long time.

> **Daniel 9:26** After the sixty-two 'sevens,' the Anointed One will be cut off and will have nothing. The people of the ruler who will come will destroy the city and the sanctuary. The end will come like a flood: War will continue until the end, and desolations have been decreed.

After The Sixty-Two Sevens (434 Years)

Gabriel was telling Daniel that after the second time period of sixty-two sevens (434 years) Jesus would be cut off (crucified). He would have nothing; no earthly possessions, home, throne, or kingdom. In fact, he would not have put an end to sin, finished transgression, or fulfilled all the visions and prophecies either. Jesus would die before doing everything that God decreed for him to do. This was done at the cross in 32 A.D.

And there was more bad news. Following the death of Jesus, Jerusalem and the rebuilt Temple would be destroyed again. This was done by a Roman General named Titus in 70 A.D. He sacked and burned Jerusalem, killed 5 million Jews, and tore the Temple apart stone by stone.

But there was another important point. Gabriel mentioned a *ruler who will come.* This is a reference to the coming Antichrist, and it is important because it identifies the group of nations he will come out of. We just pointed out that the Romans destroyed Jerusalem and the Temple in 70 A.D., so the Romans are *the people of the ruler who will come.* This tells us that when the Antichrist comes he will come out of the nations that made up the Old Roman Empire during the earthly life of Jesus.

Remember This . . .

☞ **GO TO:**

Matthew 24:6–7 (wars)

Revelation 16:16 (Armageddon)

Church Age: the period of time the Church (followers of Jesus Christ) are on earth

KEY Symbols:

God's Clock
*stops after 483 years for an indefinite period of time known as the **Church Age** (see GWRV, page 13) third time period*
- *seven years*
- *the Tribulation Period*

This brings us to a final point. We have looked at the first two time periods: seven sevens (49 years) and sixty-two sevens (434 years). This is a total of sixty-nine sevens or 483 years. But God decreed seventy sevens or 490 years would pass before everything was fulfilled. This means he must start his clock again so the last 7 years can tick off. We have also noticed four things that would happen after the period of sixty-two sevens (434 years): 1) Jesus would be killed (32 A.D.), 2) Jerusalem would be destroyed (70 A.D.), 3) the Temple would be destroyed (70 A.D.), and 4) Jerusalem and the Temple would be desolate until the Time of the End. These four things had to happen before God would restart his clock. His clock is stopped right now. It has been stopped for over 1,900 years, and we do not know when he will restart it. However, most prophetic experts think it will be soon because Jerusalem is no longer desolate and many of the Jews are seeking to rebuild the Temple.

How will the seventy sevens (490 years) end? They will end with a flood of destruction. Nations will rise against nations and there will be <u>wars</u> and rumors of wars all through history until the last and greatest war called the Battle of <u>Armageddon</u> (see GWRV, pages 239–240). The Jews themselves would suffer many things and Jerusalem would be desolate until the Time of the End.

KEY Symbols:

Old Roman Empire
the people of the ruler who will come

Antichrist
the ruler who will come

RELATED CURRENT EVENTS

Speaking as the mid-point of his five-year term [as president of the European Commission] approaches, [Jaques] Santer sought to reassure people that Europe has within its grasp two historic opportunities. The first is completion of the single market, now given a highly symbolic deadline of 1 January 1999, the date when monetary union is due to come into existence. The second is the E.U.'s opportunity early in the next decade to embrace the east and central European states dominated by the Soviet Union during the Cold War. . . . Asked what his message for the new millennium would be, Santer said: "Simply that we should build a very strong Europe which is both an international and economic power but which can also play a part in world affairs."[29]

Remember This . . .

The failure to accomplish everything God wanted was not on the part of Jesus but on the part of the Jews. Jesus prepared to make his Triumphal Entry by sending two disciples after a donkey and her colt. He said, *If anyone says anything to you, tell him that the Lord needs them.* . . . The Bible says, *This took place to fulfill what was spoken through the prophet: Say to the Daughter of Zion, "See, your king comes to you, gentle and riding on a donkey, on a colt, the foal of a donkey"* (Matthew 21:1–5; Zechariah 9:9). Referring to himself as "Lord" in fulfillment of Bible prophecy amounted to a public declaration of his Messiahship. He approached Jerusalem as the Messiah weeping over the city. He said, *If you, even you, had only known on this day what would bring you peace—but now it is hidden from your eyes* (Luke 19:41–42). If the Jews had realized this was the prophesied day that their Messiah would arrive, that accepting him would bring them peace, and if they would have done that, he would have fulfilled everything and established his kingdom right away. But they failed to recognize the day and to accept him as the Messiah. Jesus knew that would happen. He knew that his crucifixion was near and would soon be *cut off*. Because of the Jewish failure their nation was spiritually separated from God, the Church was brought in to take their place, and the last seven years of Gabriel's message (the Tribulation Period) remains to be fulfilled. This will happen before the Second Coming of Jesus.

• • •

The Antichrist will come out of a group of nations called the Revived Roman Empire. Most experts believe this group of nations has now come on the scene and is called by the modern, non-Biblical name of the European Community. Following the Rapture (see GWRV, page 63–67), a popular leader will arise unlike anyone the world has ever seen. He will gain strength in Europe and then take over the world government.

The last seven years of the Gentile age will be terrible. Most people will not survive. If a person does not die before it comes then there is only one way to avoid it—go in the Rapture by genuinely accepting Jesus as the Messiah.

 **WARNING**

> **Daniel 9:27** He will confirm a covenant with many for one 'seven.' In the middle of the 'seven' he will put an end to sacrifice and offering. And on a wing of the temple he will set up an abomination that causes desolation, until the end that is decreed is poured out on him."

confirm: *he will cause the signing of an agreement*

covenant: *a comprehensive Middle East peace agreement*

many: *representatives of many nations and groups of nations*

Temple Mount: *area in Jerusalem where all the Jewish Temples have been located*

Levitical priests: *members of the tribe of Levi who assisted the High Priest with services*

The Final Seven Years (The Seventieth-Week of Daniel)

The final seven years of the 490 did not occur before the Triumphal Entry in 32 A.D. because that ended the 434 year period. They also did not take place between 32 A.D. and 70 A.D. because Jerusalem and the Temple had to be destroyed before they could begin. They also have not taken place since 70 A.D. because they cannot occur without the Temple. This means everything in this verse is still future.

Prophecy experts call these final seven years the Tribulation Period. *He* refers to the Antichrist. He will come from the <u>same people</u> who destroyed Jerusalem and the Temple in 70 A.D. (the Romans). This verse tells us he will **confirm** a **covenant** with **many** for *one seven* (seven years). The world does not know who the Antichrist is today, but this will be a sure sign of his identity. Gabriel does not spell out the conditions of this covenant, but other verses indicate that Israel will think it has <u>peace</u> and safety; most experts think this is what will allow the Jews to rebuild the Temple. Gabriel also does not spell out who the *many* refers to, but it will probably be groups like the United Nations, European Community, United States of America, Palestinian Liberation Organization, and, of course, Israel.

In the middle of the seven divides the seven-year Tribulation Period into two equal segments of three and one-half years each (see GWRV, Timeline #2, Appendix A). And the Tribulation Period mid-point is significant because *he* (the Antichrist) *will put an end to sacrifice and offering*. He will declare the highly touted covenant with many signatures invalid. It is even likely that he will send a so-called "peace-keeping" force into Jerusalem to prevent sacrifices and offerings from being made.

He will put an end to sacrifice and offering also implies the rebuilding of the Temple. Offerings and sacrifices have to start before they can be stopped, and they have always been made at the Temple. This lets us know that the Temple will be rebuilt between now and the middle of the Tribulation Period. It also signifies that, at least for a short time, Israel will have some sort of limited sovereignty over East Jerusalem and the **Temple Mount**.

Also, at the middle of the Tribulation Period, the Antichrist will set up *an abomination that causes desolation* (Abomination of Desolation). This will be something that desecrates or contaminates the <u>Temple</u>. Gabriel does specify but there is good reason to believe that it is an <u>image</u> of the Antichrist. Whatever it is, the Jews should <u>flee</u> into the mountains when it happens because tribulation and death will be their lot in Jerusalem. But we also see that the Temple will be defiled *until the end that is decreed is poured out on him* which means this will continue until the Antichrist is captured and cast into the lake of burning <u>sulfur</u> (the Lake of Fire).

What Others are Saying:

David Ingraham: The word "confirm" might also be rendered "enforce." A third party mediating between Muslim and Israeli interests, and arbitrating "peace and safety" likely will be required to "enforce" the covenant of peace.[28]

Peter and Paul Lalonde: Despite the fact that the Jews do not have a temple today, many religious Jewish organizations have been making preparations for this future Temple. One group has prepared a model and blueprints. Another group, using the instructions found in the Bible, is fashioning the precise instruments that will be needed for Temple rituals. Still another has been training **Levitical** <u>**priests**</u>. While the Temple is not yet in place, there are many groups ready to pounce on the opportunity the moment it arises.[29]

John Hagee: The last time I was in Israel, I was amazed to discover that a Temple society there has already made all of the implements necessary for Temple worship to be reinstated exactly as in the days of Moses. Every detail in every instrument and every fabric has been replicated as they prepare to make daily sacrifices in the Temple again.[30]

RELATED CURRENT EVENTS

Yasser Arafat [PLO leader] announced he was terminating the U.S. role in the peace process. The Israeli Middle East *Globes* quoted him saying: "The Americans now have no standing. In fact, they have no position on the peace process, and what is going on now is a conspiracy against the peace process. Israel must understand that our position is that Jerusalem is the capital of the Palestinian people, and will remain forever an Arab capital, Islamic and Christian." Notice no mention of it being a 'shared' capital with the Jews.[33]

— — —

Senior British officials . . . set Europe and Israel on a collision course when they said London will exert intense pressure on Israel to be more forthcoming in the peace process after Britain assumes the presidency of the European Union on January 1 [1998]. They signalled that, despite Israeli objections, Europe now intends to translate its formidable economic power into political clout and become a major player in the peace process.[32]

Study Questions

1. What evidence do we have that Daniel knew the Scriptures?
2. What does this chapter teach about forgiveness?
3. What characteristics of God are identified by Daniel?
4. What is the object of Daniel's prayer?
5. What are some of the things associated with the Tribulation Period?

CHAPTER WRAP-UP

- Daniel was reading the Book of Jeremiah when he discovered that Jerusalem would be desolate for 70 years. He knew that period was almost over and wanted God to cause the city and the Temple to be rebuilt. (Daniel 9:1–3)

- He confessed that he and his people had sinned, done wrong, been wicked, rebelled, broke God's laws, ignored the prophets, been unfaithful, disobeyed God, and transgressed God's law. (Daniel 9:3–15)

- Daniel asked God to turn away his anger and wrath, to hear his prayer and petitions, to look with favor on the desolate Temple, to have mercy, to consider his (God's) name, to forgive, and to act without delay. (Daniel 9:16–19)

- Gabriel appeared with a message for Daniel. He said he had come to give Daniel insight and to help him understand the vision. (Daniel 9:20–23)

- Gabriel said God had decreed 490 more years of dealing with his people. A decree would be issued, and it would take 49 years to rebuild Jerusalem. Then 434 more years and Jesus would come. Jesus would be killed and Jerusalem and the Temple would be destroyed. The last 7 years would begin with a covenant, but it would be broken after 3 1/2 years. The animal sacrifices would cease and the Temple would be defiled and made desolate. (Daniel 24–27)

DANIEL 10

CHAPTER HIGHLIGHTS

- Fasting and Praying
- Vision of the Anointed One
- Effect on Daniel
- A Heavenly Being
- Strength and Assurance

Let's Get Started

Chapters 10–12 of Daniel are all one vision, the "Vision of the Anointed One." This is the last and longest of Daniel's visions. Chapter 10 can be considered an introduction to the vision, Chapter 11 the vision itself, and Chapter 12 an epilogue or postscript to the vision.

Many of the verses in these three chapters concern the unseen **spirit world**. This may be an eerie thought for some, but the Bible plainly <u>teaches</u> that **fallen angels** and **demonic spirits** are real and must be faced. How else can we account for all of the evil in the world? How else can we explain World War I, the Holocaust, Satan worship, witchcraft, and other horrors? Biblically speaking, <u>Satan</u> and his followers are ultimately responsible for all of these things.

William L. Owens: For approximately two centuries the Church has not openly discussed the subject of demonic powers. This hesitancy is probably due to the emerging Age of Reason. It almost seems that the church has been afraid to admit that demons are real. Social pressure in an enlightened era has probably accounted for the reluctance on the part of the Church to acknowledge this subject. In this writer's opinion, Satan has been the personality behind the Church's silence. The devil does not want to be exposed, and he will exert his entire force in active resistance against exposure.[1]

☞ **GO TO:**

Luke 7:21; 8:2; Acts 19:12, 13; Jude 1:6 (teaches)

Revelation 12:7–9 (Satan)

spirit world: *personalities in the invisible, non-physical realm*

fallen angels: *angels that sinned by rebelling against God*

What Others are Saying:

demonic spirits: *spirits that bring or cause evil to human beings*

☞ **GO TO:**

Daniel 5:30 (king of Babylon)

> **Daniel 10:1** In the third year of Cyrus king of Persia, a revelation was given to Daniel (who was called Belteshazzar). Its message was true and it concerned a great war. The understanding of the message came to him in a vision.

The Time And The Subject

The third year of Cyrus king of Persia establishes the time (see Time Line #1, Appendix A). Belshazzar, the <u>king of Babylon</u> was killed around 539 B.C. Darius the Mede took over the kingdom, and ruled for about two years before he died. Cyrus the Persian became king, and in the third year of his reign Daniel received this vision. So the time is around 534 B.C., roughly 5 years after the fall of Babylon, and Daniel would be in his mid-80's.

We shall soon be studying this vision that God revealed to Daniel. Since it is from God we know it is true. It concerned a great war, but not the typical kind of war. It concerned a war in the spirit world, a war among the supernatural. Along with this vision Daniel received understanding of it.

What Others are Saying:

David Jeremiah with C.C. Carlson: One part of the *great war* was the turmoil in Daniel's heart. Although they had been freed, there were still many Jews left in Babylon. Surprising as it may seem, fewer than fifty thousand people volunteered to return to Israel. There were many Jews who were still living as aliens in a land of idols.[2]

> **Daniel 10:2** At that time I, Daniel, mourned for three weeks.

21 Days

Daniel does not say why he was mourning. Some experts think it was because so few of his people had returned home. Others think it was because those who did return were having a hard time. We are not sure what it was, but we do know it was breaking this godly man's heart because he grieved for 21 days.

> **Daniel 10:3** I ate no choice food; no meat or wine touched my lips; and I used no lotions at all until the three weeks were over.

☞ **GO TO:**

Nehemiah 9:1–3; Esther 4:1–4 (fast)

A Partial Fast

This was not a total <u>fast</u>, but it was certainly a partial fast. Daniel ate no choice foods; he ate no meat and refused wine. He used no lotions, did not anoint his body with oil, and did not use any perfumes. He chose to do these things as a sign to God showing that he was sincere about his grief; he continued this for 21 days.

What Others are Saying:

David Jeremiah with C.C. Carlson: When Daniel was burdened he didn't go to a counselor, complain to his friends, or gripe to his neighbors. Daniel went right to the source. He prayed.[3]

> **Daniel 10:4** On the twenty-fourth day of the first month, as I was standing on the bank of the great river, the Tigris,

KEY Symbols:

Nisan
first Jewish month

The Date And Place (The Vision Of The Anointed One)

It was the twenty-fourth day of the first month, and Daniel was standing on the bank of the great Tigris River (see Illustration #2, page 19). On the Jewish calendar it is the month of Nisan. On our calendar it would be April 24, 534 B.C.

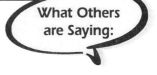

What Others are Saying:

J. Vernon McGee: The time was the twenty-fourth of Nisan, April 24. Daniel is dealing with exact dates. This makes it difficult for the critics to wrestle with, because the one who wrote this [Daniel] was dealing with specific dates, and he was not giving a late date for the Book of Daniel![4]

> **Daniel 10:5** I looked up and there before me was a man dressed in linen, with a belt of the finest gold around his waist.

☞ **GO TO:**

Leviticus 8:6–9 (sash)

Hebrews 4:14–16 (High Priest)

Revelation 1:13 (golden)

Could It Be Jesus?

Daniel looked up and saw a man in front of him. He did not say who the man was so we will try to identify him by his dress and features. The man was dressed in linen and had a belt of fine gold around his waist.

This brings to mind two events in the Bible. When Aaron was **ordained** to be the **High Priest** (see GWRV, Illustration #2, page 21) of Israel Moses tied a <u>sash</u> around his waist. And when Jesus,

ordained: *officially appointed to be a priest*

High Priest: *spiritual head of Old Testament Israel*

preincarnation: before he
was born in the flesh

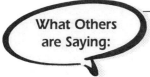

**What Others
are Saying:**

postincarnate: after he
lived in the flesh

☞ **GO TO:**

Matthew 17:2 (face)

Micah 4:13 (bronze)

Genesis 1:1–13
(created)

I Thessalonians 4:13–
18 (raise the dead)

our High Priest, appeared to John on the Isle of Patmos (see GWRV, Illustration #1, page 20) he was wearing a golden sash around his chest. Not all experts agree, but Daniel probably saw Jesus.

J. Vernon McGee: Now that is a vision of Christ, and I believe Daniel saw Christ—not in his **preincarnation**, but he saw him as the **postincarnate** Christ, in his office as priestly **Intercessor** and Judge and the great Shepherd of the sheep.[5]

> **Daniel 10:6** His body was like chrysolite, his face like lightning, his eyes like flaming torches, his arms and legs like the gleam of burnished bronze, and his voice like the sound of a multitude.

His Features

Although Daniel did not call this man by name his features were similar to those of the resurrected Christ in Revelation 1:13-16:
His face like lightening reminds us of the shekinah glory of God.

Daniel 10	Revelation 1 (see GWRV, pages 20–22)
dressed in linen	a robe reaching down to his feet
a belt of fine gold around his waist	a golden sash around his chest
face like lightening	face like the sun
eyes like flaming torches	eyes like blazing fire
arms and legs like gleam of burnished bronze	feet like bronze glowing in a furnace
voice like sound of a multitude	voice like sound of rushing waters

Intercessor: someone who
pleads for others

His eyes like flaming torches speak of his great insight and ability to see everything. *His arms and legs like the gleam of burnished bronze* are symbols of judgment. *His voice like the sound of a multitude* reminds us of the voice that created everything, the voice of the one who will raise the dead in the Rapture.

**What Others
are Saying:**

Noah Hutchings: If one were to give a description of the man Daniel saw to an artist, and gave the description of the man John saw to another artist, they would come up with similar drawings. The man whom John saw was the Lord Jesus Christ as he will appear when he returns to the earth.[6]

> **Daniel 10:7** I, Daniel, was the only one who saw the vision; the men with me did not see it, but such terror overwhelmed them that they fled and hid

My Companions Were Terrified

Daniel does not say who was with him, but he does mention that none of them saw the vision. The Apostle Paul had a similar experience while traveling on the road to Damascus. There Paul had a vision of Jesus, but none of his companions saw anything.

Although Daniel's companions did not see anything something happened to scare them terribly. They were so affected by this event that they ran and hid. They may not have realized it, but they were dealing with the supernatural.

> **Daniel 10:8** So I was left alone, gazing at this great vision; I had no strength left, my face turned deathly pale and I was helpless.

I Was Overwhelmed

Daniel's companions abandoned him forcing Daniel to stare at this great vision alone. If he was as scared as they were he couldn't do anything about it because his strength abandoned him leaving him too weak to run. He found himself standing there alone, <u>pale</u> and helpless.

> **Daniel 10:9** Then I heard him speaking, and as I listened to him, I fell into a deep sleep, my face to the ground.

The Lights Went Out

We are not told that Daniel <u>fell</u> to the ground, but it seems that way. He was pale and weak, heard a voice, and listened, but something happened to him. He may have fainted or passed out because he says he fell into a deep <u>sleep</u> with his face to the ground. We can't be sure what happened, but it would appear that some change came over him to prepare him to receive this vision.

> **Daniel 10:10** A hand touched me and set me trembling on my hands and knees.

☞ **GO TO:**

Acts 9:1–9 (Jesus)

 *KEY Symbols:*

The Anointed One
eyes like flaming torches
  - great insight and ability to see everything

☞ **GO TO:**

Daniel 7:28 (pale)

arms and legs like the gleam of burnished bronze
  - judgment
voice like sound of a multitude
  - voice that created everything and will raise the dead in the Rapture

☞ **GO TO:**

Matthew 17:7; Revelation 1:17 (fell)

Daniel 8:18 (sleep)

Someone Touched Me

latter days: the last days of the Times of the Gentiles

Daniel was on the ground, in a deep sleep, and too weak to move when a hand touched him. We don't know who it was, but we do know it was someone from the supernatural realm, probably an angel. The purpose of the touch was to strengthen Daniel, but when the hand touched him, he started trembling. He was terrified, and the hand pulled him up to his hands and knees.

What Others are Saying:

M.R. DeHaan: Then after a period of great amazement on the part of Daniel, with his face toward the ground, the heavenly messenger touched him and strengthened him and gave him the message which he was to put down for these **latter days** for our instruction.[7]

☞ **GO TO:**

Daniel 9:23 (highly esteemed)

Daniel 10:5 (man)

Daniel 8:18 (feet)

> **Daniel 10:11** He said, "Daniel, you who are highly esteemed, consider carefully the words I am about to speak to you, and stand up, for I have now been sent to you." And when he said this to me, I stood up trembling.

I Want Your Undivided Attention

The angel's first words mention that Daniel was <u>highly esteemed</u>. This was a repeat of what the angel Gabriel said in Chapter 9.

The angel urged Daniel to make a special effort to understand what he was about to reveal. He told Daniel to stand up. He explained that the reason he appeared was because he had been sent. It is not said who sent him, but it was probably the <u>man</u> (Jesus) who Daniel had just seen. Daniel obeyed and stood on his <u>feet</u>, even though he was still shaking.

What Others are Saying:

Billy Graham: Time after time Jesus has assured us that he and the angels would be victorious. *When the Son of man shall come in his glory, and all the holy angels with him, then shall he sit upon the throne of his glory* (Matthew 25:31 KJV). The Apostle Paul wrote, *The Lord Jesus shall be revealed from heaven with his mighty angels, in flaming fire . . .* (II Thessalonians 1:7, 8 KJV).[8]

☞ **GO TO:**

Daniel 10:2, 3 (three weeks)

Daniel 7:15; 8:15; 9:23 (visions)

> **Daniel 10:12** Then he continued, "Do not be afraid, Daniel. Since the first day that you set your mind to gain understanding and to humble yourself before your God, your words were heard, and I have come in response to them.

God Heard You

The angel could tell that Daniel was afraid, so he tried to calm Daniel down before beginning.

Daniel had been fasting and praying for <u>three weeks</u>, and the angel knew it. He informed Daniel that his prayers were heard the first day Daniel started praying. Daniel was asking for understanding concerning the <u>visions</u> of Chapters 7, 8, and 9, and the angel said that providing understanding was the purpose behind his visit.

William L. Owens: One cannot understand the purpose of evil spirits or the reason for evil unless the person of Satan is considered. The Bible presents Satan as the **personification** of evil and the archenemy of the eternal God. The Scriptures are not clear about the origin of demons; however, it is probable that demons fell from heaven with the <u>fall of Satan</u> (see GWRV, pages 175–176). Evil spirits are so closely related in nature and character to Satan that it is difficult to imagine them apart from him. Therefore, one may conclude through deduction, that demons are created beings, like unto Satan, who followed him in his rebellion.[9]

Billy Graham: Lucifer [another name for Satan], our archenemy, controls one of the most powerful and well-oiled war machines in the universe. He controls principalities, powers, and dominions. Every nation, city, village, and individual has felt the hot breath of his evil power. He is already gathering the nations of the world for the last great battle in the war against Christ—Armageddon.[10]

> **Daniel 10:13** But the prince of the Persian kingdom resisted me twenty-one days. Then Michael, one of the chief princes, came to help me, because I was detained there with the king of Persia.

A War In The Heavenlies

Here the angel pulled back a curtain so-to-speak to show Daniel a cosmic struggle in the <u>heavenly realm</u>. He revealed that more is going on in the world than most people realize. Behind the scenes is an unseen war between God and Satan, the angels of God and the demons of Satan, the Spirit of Christ and the <u>spirit</u> of Antichrist.

The angel told Daniel that the prince of the Persian kingdom (a

☞ **GO TO:**

Isaiah 14:12–17 (fallen)

personification: the creature or source of evil

What Others are Saying:

KEY Symbols:

Satan
LUCIFER

☞ **GO TO:**

Ephesians 6:11, 12 (heavenly realm)

I John 4:1–3 (spirit)

Ephesians 2:2 (ruler)

II Corinthians 4:4 (this age)

fallen angel or evil spirit) had prevented him from getting through with an answer to his prayer. The evil spirit was so powerful he managed to hold off this good angel for 21 days—the same length of time Daniel had been fasting and praying. Furthermore, the only way the good angel finally got through to Daniel was for Michael, one of the chief angels, to render assistance.

What Others are Saying:

KEY Symbols:

An Unseen War Between

God and Satan
angels and demons
Spirit of Christ and spirit of AntiChrist

William L. Owens: The war's first skirmish was recorded in the dawn of man's history (Genesis 3:1-19). It was in this skirmish that one of Satan's most powerful weapons was revealed, the weapon of temptation. Scripture reports that man fell before this mighty weapon of Satan and that he became subject unto the world's king. This was the recorded beginning of the great conflict.[11]

Ed Young: We don't understand all of it, but I think it's safe to say that Satan and all of his fallen angels have some kind of hierarchy, some kind of government, in which they are in charge of certain jurisdictions, certain countries in this world. Certainly there would be fallen angels, demons, over the United States, over Russia, over China, etc., etc., etc.[12]

Noah Hutchings: To help us identify the prince of Persia, let us consider verse twenty-one [Daniel 10:21]. The Man [angel] told Daniel that Michael was his prince, meaning that Michael was the national guardian angel of Israel. Therefore, the prince of Persia would be an angelic being over the nation of Persia. Inasmuch as this creature resisted Christ, he would be an agent of Satan.[13]

RELATED CURRENT EVENTS

KEY Symbols:

Prince of the Persian Kingdom

a fallen angel or evil spirit

Michael

one of God's chief angels
the prince of Israel

Two days before Christmas, 1993, I was stuck working late. My coworker Frances and I were at our computers, our backs to each other, when I heard my name called. I went over to Frances to see what she wanted. She looked puzzled. Before either of us could speak, we heard a horrible cracking sound. The huge metal cabinet bolted above my desk tore completely out of the wall. It smashed my chair in half, and partially embedded itself in the wall beside my desk.

   Three maintenance men carried it away the next morning. "Whoever sits here is lucky to be alive," one remarked. I don't consider it luck at all. It wasn't Frances who had spoken at that one critical moment. God had sent an angel to call my name.[14]

The Bible teaches that this present world is evil and there is a <u>ruler</u> called the *Ruler of the Kingdom of the Air* influencing people to sin. He is also called *the* <u>God of this Age</u> (Satan) who is blinding those who refuse to accept Christ. So we see that there is a wicked personality operating behind the scenes to cause sin and unbelief.

Remember This . . .

> **Daniel 10:14** Now I have come to explain to you what will happen to your people in the future, for the vision concerns a time yet to come."

type: *an example or a symbol*

antitype: *the opposite of a type, the real thing*

The Target

This may well be the key verse in this chapter. From it we learn that what follows in Chapters 10–12 concerns two things:

1) *your people* means Daniel's people, the nation of Israel, and
2) the future.

What Others are Saying:

David Hocking By the way, in the end-time when the Battle of Armageddon occurs, there will be unclean spirits that will influence the kings of the earth to gather against the people of Israel. The devil is focusing on Israel. The devil's plan is to hurt Israel and the Messiah. That's clear in the Old Testament as well as in Revelation. Some of us don't understand that in international affairs, there are demons assigned to the political leaders of all of the countries influencing them to turn their backs on Israel. That's the primary attack of history.[15]

KEY Symbols:

Your People
Daniel's people (the Jews)
Israel

Wallace Emerson: The occurrences listed are to be concerned with the latter days. While background material will be introduced, the focus of the chapters is the end-time. . . . But even though we recognize this, it is sometimes difficult to distinguish between the **type** and the **antitype**, between the background data and the main thrust of the passage especially when we have them mingled in the same verse or verses. This seems to be especially true in Daniel 11:21–35.[16]

☞ **GO TO:**

Luke 1:20, 64 (speak)

> **Daniel 10:15** While he was saying this to me, I bowed with my face toward the ground and was speechless.

I Couldn't Talk

While the angel was revealing these things to Daniel, he simply looked down and said nothing. The next verse indicates that it was not that Daniel did not know what to say but because something happened to him stopping him from <u>speaking</u>.

☞ **GO TO:**

Isaiah 6:6, 7 (lips)

Isaiah 6:1–8 (seraph)

Hebrews 1:14 (ministering)

> **Daniel 10:16** Then one who looked like a man touched my lips, and I opened my mouth and began to speak. I said to the one standing before me, "I am overcome with anguish because of the vision, my lord, and I am helpless.

seraphim, cherubim: creatures that guard the throne of God

Someone Else Touched Me

We are dealing with the spirit world here and do not know how many beings are involved. At times we do not even know if we are dealing with Jesus, angels, **seraphim**, **cherubim**, (see GWRV, page 70) who or what. Here, someone who looked like a man touched Daniel on his <u>lips</u>. This was done to enable Daniel to speak. After it happened, Daniel addressed the being by saying that he was overcome with grief and helpless.

What Others are Saying:

M.R. DeHaan: It is well for us to remember that round about us in the atmosphere, observing our behavior and conduct and standing ready to help those who belong to the Lord Jesus Christ, are great **myriads** of angelic beings. It is our ignorance of their existence that causes us untold trouble and loss of much joy and happiness. If we could understand better the teaching of the Scripture concerning the ministry of angels in our own personal and individual life, it would bring us untold comfort.[17]

myriads: large numbers, too many to count

KEY POINT

We are dealing with the spirit world in Chapter 10 and we do not know how many heavenly beings are involved.

[handwritten annotation]: ?? no capital in hebrew — translator made that decision!

Oliver B. Greene: Daniel addresses the angelic visitor as <u>lord</u>; but the word is not capitalized, and therefore we know that this is not Jesus, the Lord of Glory. This could be the same <u>seraph</u> [angel] who visited Isaiah when he saw the Lord, high and lifted up. Paul tells us in the first chapter of Hebrews that the angels are <u>ministering spirits</u> to the heirs of salvation." The angels are the servants of the sons of God—not just when we reach heaven, but while we are here on earth.[18]

> **Daniel 10:17** How can I, your servant, talk with you, my lord? My strength is gone and I can hardly breathe."

☞ **GO TO:**

Daniel 10:8 (strength)

I Am Weak And Out Of Breath

Daniel respectfully addressed the being about his own physical condition. His vision and this experience was having such a tremendous effect upon him that his <u>strength</u> was gone and breathing was difficult.

Oliver B. Greene: Think of that! Daniel had spent the night with lions, he had faced Nebuchadnezzar, Belshazzar, and all the others without fear and trembling; but now the vision he had seen struck him dumb and took away all of his strength.[19]

What Others are Saying:

> **Daniel 10:18** Again the one who looked like a man touched me and gave me strength.

☞ **GO TO:**

Daniel 10:10, 16 (touched)

Touched A Third Time

As Daniel stood there physically shaken and weak, this being <u>touched</u> him again. The first touch strengthened Daniel a little and left him trembling on his hands and knees. The second touch enabled him to speak. This third touch energized him with even more strength.

Daniel was Touched Three Times:

1) The first touch strengthened Daniel but left him trembling.
2) The second touch enabled him to speak.
3) The third touch trengthened him even more.

Remember This . . .

> **Daniel 10:19** "Do not be afraid, O man highly esteemed," he said. "Peace! Be strong now; be strong." When he spoke to me, I was strengthened and said, "Speak, my lord, since you have given me strength."

☞ **GO TO:**

Daniel 10:16 (anguish)

John 14:27 (peace)

Ephesians 6:10 (strong)

God Loves You

The being comforted Daniel and again tried to settle him down. He reminded Daniel that Daniel was highly esteemed in heaven which is similar to saying, "God loves you."

Daniel had experienced <u>anguish</u> over this vision so the being wished him, _peace_ and told Daniel to _be **strong**_. After this encouragement Daniel was immediately strengthened and felt better, so he asked the being to continue with the message.

The Pulpit Commentary: Even to hold converse [conversation] with angelic beings, entailed expenditure of vital energy. The overpowering sense of the spiritual has to be resisted, at least so far, in order that mental action may go on. Had strength not been imparted, the revelations bestowed would not have produced any permanent impression on the mind.[20]

☞ GO TO:

Daniel 10:14 (explain)

Daniel 10:13 (prince)

Acts 19:13–16 (evil)

Revelation 16:13, 14 (kings)

Daniel 5:30, 31 (Medes)

Daniel 10:1 (Persia)

Daniel 8:3, 20 (long horn)

Daniel 8:5–7, 21 (shaggy goat)

> **Daniel 10:20** So he said, "Do you know why I have come to you? Soon I will return to fight against the prince of Persia, and when I go, the prince of Greece will come;

A Time Yet To Come

The heavenly being asked Daniel a question but did not wait for an answer. He had already given the answer: he came to <u>explain</u> what will happen to the Jews in the future.

The heavenly being then told Daniel, _Soon I will return to fight against the prince of Persia._ In other words, he had appeared to Daniel for the express purpose of delivering a message, but he needed to return to the heavenlies because there was a spiritual war going on that required his involvement. The <u>prince</u> of Persia (evil spirit in charge of Persia) needed to be opposed, but when he went back to oppose the prince of Persia, the prince of Greece (evil spirit in charge of Greece) would move in and take over.

Something to Ponder

Remember This . . .

The Bible not only teaches that there are evil spirits in charge of the nations on earth, it also teaches that <u>evil spirits</u> can possess people. It is easy to believe this is what happened to Adolph Hitler, Joseph Stalin, and others. This is what will happen to the Antichrist, what will give him power to take over the world government, and what will summon the <u>kings</u> of the earth to the Battle of Armageddon.

The <u>Medes</u> and Persians defeated Babylon. Darius the Mede, the short horn on the ram with two horns, took over and was followed by Cyrus, king of <u>Persia</u>, the <u>long horn</u>, two years later. But Alexander the Great of Greece, the <u>shaggy goat</u>, replaced him. These events have already happened.

> **Daniel 10:21** but first I will tell you what is written in the Book of Truth. (No one supports me against them except Michael, your prince.

☞ **GO TO:**

Daniel 11:13 (Michael)

It Is Written

The heavenly being informed Daniel that he would tell Daniel what has already been recorded about the future in God's heavenly Scriptures. That revelation will come in Chapters 11 and 12, but first this messenger wanted Daniel to know that no one was helping him fight the princes of Persia or Greece except Michael. *Your prince* is Daniel's prince and it identifies Michael as the angel or prince that God has placed in charge of Israel. This is the same <u>Michael</u> who helped the heavenly being get through with the answer to Daniel's prayer.

The Bible is a Book of Truth and the greatest book ever written. It has been published in more than 600 different languages and dialects, has probably more than 100 billion copies in print, and has weathered attacks in every generation and on every continent. It is time now for people to understand that the Bible has a heavenly origin and a heavenly or supernatural protection.

KEY Symbols:

Book of Truth
names of the saved
deeds of men

David Hocking: Michael is the prince of Israel. The devil has his demonic forces assigned to the nations of the world, but Michael, the Archangel, is the prince of Israel and he can call legions of angels to help him any time he wants.[21]

What Others are Saying:

Oliver B. Greene: God's Word will never fail nor be destroyed. All hell cannot discredit the Word of God, regardless of what the modernists, liberals, atheists, free-thinkers, or anyone else may say about the Word of God, regardless of what they write about it, regardless of what they do to it. God has *the Scripture of truth* [KJV] reserved and protected in heaven, and it cannot be destroyed or discredited.[22]

KEY Symbols:

Michael
Daniel's prince
in charge of Israel

Study Questions

1. Should we believe the things in this vision? Why?
2. What does this chapter tell us about prayer?
3. Was Daniel's meeting with angels a glorious experience? What happened to him?
4. What does this chapter teach us about angels?
5. What does this chapter tell us about evil spirits?

KEY POINT

The angel came to Daniel to explain what will happen to the Jews in the future.

- During the third year of the reign of Cyrus king of Persia, Daniel was fasting and praying when he received a message. (He had gone without choice food, meat, wine, and lotions for twent-one days.) (Daniel 10:1–4)

- While standing by the Tigris River, Daniel looked up and saw a vision of someone believed to be Jesus (the Anointed One). Daniel's companions did not see the vision, but something scared them into running and hiding. (Daniel 10:5-7)

- Daniel became weak, turned pale, was helpless, and fell to the ground in a deep sleep. (Daniel 10:8, 9)

- The hand of a heavenly being touched Daniel, putting him on his hands and knees, and causing him to tremble. A voice told Daniel to stand up and listen. The voice assured Daniel that God heard his prayers and sent an answer, but the prince (evil spirit) in charge of the kingdom of Persia detained him. The Archangel Michael helped the heavenly being get past the evil spirit. (Daniel 10:10–14)

- Daniel couldn't talk until someone touched his lips. Then he told the heavenly being he was in anguish, helpless, and having trouble breathing. The heavenly being assured him that he was highly esteemed, wished him peace, and strengthened him. (Daniel 10:15–21)

DANIEL 11

CHAPTER HIGHLIGHTS

- Persia and Greece
- North Versus South
- Antiochus Epiphanes
- The Antichrist
- Time of the End

Let's Get Started

As previously noted, Chapters 10–12 deals with one vision (the Vision of the Anointed One). Chapter 10 is the prologue, Chapter 12 is the epilogue, and Daniel 11 is the vision itself.

This remarkable chapter is 45 verses long with each verse being in Daniel's future. However, from our point in time, much of it has been fulfilled, and it would be easy for us to divide it into two convenient sections:

- 35 verses of historical background
- 10 verses of future prophecy

This chapter could be divided that way but not without making it a little misleading. The first 35 verses are historical events that also foreshadow future events. They predict historical struggles that, to us, have already happened, but those historical struggles are also examples of future things that will happen at the End of the Age. Someone has said, "history repeats itself." These historical events illustrate things that will be repeated in the future.

It might help us to grasp this concept if we recall that Babylon was defeated by the <u>Medes and Persians</u>. The Medes and Persians were defeated by Alexander the Great of <u>Greece</u>. When he died his kingdom was divided and given to four <u>horns</u> (see Flow Chart, page 215), his four generals: Cassander took Greece and Macedon, Lysimachus took Asia Minor (now Turkey and Thrace), Seleucus took Syria and Babylonia, and Ptolemy took Egypt and Palestine. For the next 200–300 years these empires fought each other in a continuous struggle for supremacy. Israel was often caught in the

☞ **GO TO:**

Daniel 5:28–31 (Medes and Persians)

Daniel 8:5–8; 20, 21 (Greece)

Daniel 8:8 (horns)

Daniel 12:4 (seal)

South: *the power to the south of Israel (in this case, Egypt)*

North: *the power to the north of Israel (in this case, Syria)*

KEY POINT

The 35 historical verses hold examples of future things that will happen at the End of the Age.

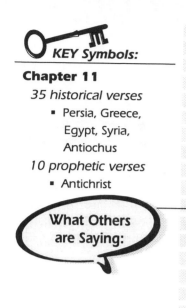

KEY Symbols:

Chapter 11

35 historical verses
- Persia, Greece, Egypt, Syria, Antiochus

10 prophetic verses
- Antichrist

What Others are Saying:

middle and greatly harmed by their constant fighting. In this chapter the angel accurately predicted some of their battles and their effect upon Israel. But God also revealed their battles because they are excellent examples of the turmoil that will exist in the Middle East at the End of the Age.

One final point; understanding these verses is not easy. It may even be that some of them are <u>sealed</u> so that good interpretations are not possible until a future time of God's choosing. That may be why so many experts skip over the hard verses. But God gave them, and we will explain what we can.

David Hocking: Whenever the **South** [southern Greek kingdom] went to invade the **North** [northern Greek kingdom], or the North went down to invade the South, they were all walking through Israel. Israel suffered every time. It was a time of indignation and persecution for Israel, and Daniel said that would continue until the Tribulation Period. You could explain to the Jewish people from Daniel's vision why they have suffered so much. They are always the brunt of attack. There are always those who want to harm them.[1]

> **Daniel 11:1** And in the first year of Darius the Mede, I took my stand to support and protect him.)

Who Took A Stand?

The facts in this chapter are so accurate the critics claim it couldn't possibly have been written by Daniel. They emphatically declare that it would be humanly impossible for him to predict these things before they happened. This is a big reason behind their argument that Daniel was written 200–300 years later than it claims, and a good reason why we need to identify the speaker in this verse.

Forget the chapter and verse divisions because they were not in the original writings. This verse follows the last verse of Chapter 10 where the speaker is a heavenly being. He is the same one speaking here. We have not been told his name, but it seems likely that he is the angel Gabriel. And Daniel is the secretary recording this vision.

Keep in mind two facts from previous chapters: 1) <u>Darius</u> the Mede ruled over the combined kingdom of the Medes and Persians, and 2) Satan had placed an evil spirit called the <u>prince</u> of the Persian Kingdom in charge of Persia. When Darius came to power Satan had an evil spirit in charge of Persia, so this good

☞ **GO TO:**

Daniel 5:31 (Darius)

Daniel 10:13 (prince)

Ezra 6:1–12; Daniel 9:25 (decree)

Daniel 10:1 (Cyrus)

KEY Symbols:

Satan

prince of the Persian Kingdom
- Persians

God

Gabriel
- Medes

angel took a stand to support and protect Darius. We are not sure why but it might be because Darius was kind to the Jews. He even issued a <u>decree</u> to let them rebuild their Temple in Jerusalem.

Notice that Daniel received this vision in the third year of <u>Cyrus</u> (see Time Line #1, Appendix A). Now notice in this verse that the angel is talking about something that happened in the first year of Darius. In other words, the angel is looking back and telling Daniel that he supported and protected Darius a few years earlier.

What Others are Saying:

Billy Graham: The Bible teaches that the demons are dedicated to controlling this planet for their master, Satan. Even Jesus called him *the prince of this world* (John 12:31). He is the master-organizer and strategist. Many times throughout Biblical history, and possibly even today, angels and demons engage in warfare. Many of the events of our times may very well be involved in this unseen struggle.[2]

Something to Ponder

America has experienced an explosion of interest in Satanic activity in recent years. There have been several cases of young people killing parents, teachers, and classmates. Many have gone from believing in aliens, ghosts, and UFO's to believing in the occult and trying to make contact with Satan or his fallen angels. Is it possible that a struggle is going on in the spirit world for control over people in this world? The Bible says, "Yes."

☞ **GO TO:**

Daniel 2:39 (kingdom)

Daniel 10:1 (Cyrus)

> **Daniel 11:2** "Now then, I tell you the truth: Three more kings will appear in Persia, and then a fourth, who will be far richer than all the others. When he has gained power by his wealth, he will stir up everyone against the kingdom of Greece.

Persia's Future

Keep in mind the time of this vision. Persia was the ruling world <u>kingdom</u>, and it was the *third year of <u>Cyrus</u> king of Persia*. The angel was telling Daniel the fact that this vision was a truth about Persia's future. Following Cyrus, four more kings would reign in Persia. The fourth king, a man by the name of Xerxes, would be richer than all the others. He would use his great wealth to gain power, build a great army, and stir up his people against the Greeks. Xerxes attacked the Greeks, had some initial successes, took some slaves, and did a lot of damage, but he eventually suffered a terrible defeat.

David Hocking: Daniel told us that three more kings would arise in Medo-Persia. They did. They were called Cambyses, Pseudo-Smerdis, and Darius Hystaspis. The fourth king, who was to be far richer and more powerful, was Xerxes. . . . Xerxes took four years to gather an army of hundreds of thousands, perhaps a million soldiers. He launched a disastrous campaign against Greece in 480 B.C.[3]

GO TO:

Daniel 11:36 (pleases)

Daniel 8:3–8; 19–21 (Greece)

Daniel 2:39 (kingdom)

> **Daniel 11:3** Then a mighty king will appear, who will rule with great power and do as he pleases.

Greece's Future

This is what the angel told Daniel about the rise of Greece. A mighty king will appear; he will rule with great power and do as he <u>pleases</u>.

What happened? The Persian king Xerxes did have some success against the Greek Empire, but he never gained the upper hand. What he did do was stir up a lot of <u>Greek</u> hatred against Persia, and cause the Greeks to look forward to an opportune time for revenge. That happened when a mighty king named Alexander the Great came on the scene. No one could resist Alexander. He quickly conquered Persia and assumed authority over the entire <u>kingdom</u>.

KEY Symbols:

Alexander the Great
did as he pleased

Antichrist
will also do as he pleases

Remember This . . .

The mighty king was Alexander the Great. History tells us he was unquestionably the most successful military man on earth in his day. He extended the Greek kingdom until there were no other kingdoms to conquer. He had an insatiable desire for war and no one could stop him. The Bible says there will be another king who will do as he <u>pleases</u>. We call that power hungry man the Antichrist. It is hard to believe the world will turn complete control over to one man, and especially when that one man belongs to Satan. The world will obviously not be like the world we live in today.

GO TO:

Daniel 8:5–8; 21–22 (four)

> **Daniel 11:4** After he has appeared, his empire will be broken up and parceled out toward the four winds of heaven. It will not go to his descendants, nor will it have the power he exercised, because his empire will be uprooted and given to others.

Greece Will Be Divided

Here the angel predicted the future of Greece. The empire would break up and be parceled out in <u>four</u> directions. It would not go to a descendant of the mighty king. It would be weakened and divided among others.

History records that Alexander the Great died as a young man. He was about 33 years old, an alcoholic, suffering from malaria, and fighting depression because there were no more kingdoms to conquer. Historians say that he was asked who he wanted to take over the kingdom and he replied, "Give it to the strong." The result of that was a power struggle, the murder of his entire family, and the eventual division of the empire into four parts.

What Others are Saying:

David Jeremiah with C.C. Carlson: Alexander didn't have any heirs. He had an illegitimate son and a legitimate son, the latter of whom was born after Alexander's death. His brother was mentally retarded. Shortly after Alexander died, all three of these people were murdered.[4]

Uriah Smith: Within fifteen years after his death, all his posterity had fallen victims to the jealousy and ambition of his leading generals. Not one of the race of Alexander was left to breath upon the earth. So short is the transit [transition] from the highest pinnacle of earthly glory to the lowest depths of oblivion and death. The kingdom was rent into four divisions, and taken possession of by Alexander's four ablest, or perhaps most ambitious and unprincipled generals—Cassander, Lysimachus, Seleucus, and Ptolemy.[5]

> **Daniel 11:5** "The king of the South will become strong, but one of his commanders will become even stronger than he and will rule his own kingdom with great power.

Egypt: The King Of The South

The angel narrowed his prophecy down to two of the four kingdoms that would come into existence following the division of the Greek Empire. The kingdom to the south of Israel would become strong. A commander from that kingdom would become even stronger, and he would rule his own kingdom.

History records that one of the four generals under Alexander the Great was a man named Ptolemy. He acquired Egypt and Pal-

dynasties: a long line of kings

KEY Symbols:

South (Egypt)
south of Israel
king of the South

North (Syria)
north of Israel
king of the North

estine when the kingdom was divided. Egypt soon rose to prominence, and Ptolemy became rich and powerful.

One of the other three generals, Seleucus, acquired Syria, but he had problems ruling and once had to flee for his life. He went to Egypt where his old friend Ptolemy ruled. Ptolemy took him in, gave him a high position in Egypt and provided money and assistance so that Seleucus was soon able to go back and retake the Syrian kingdom. This time he was so successful that he soon became stronger than Ptolemy.

When the Bible mentions a direction such as north or south, that direction is always in relation to the land of Israel. The *king of the North* will always refer to a power north of Israel and the *king of the South* will always refer to a power south of Israel.

• • •

Ptolemy and Seleucus were generals who took over two parts of Alexander's empire. As the first rulers in their new empires they established **dynasties** that would rule for years to come. There were several kings named Ptolemy who ruled in Egypt over the next 300 years and several kings named Seleucus who ruled in Syria over the next 250 years. The discussion in this verse refers to Ptolemy I and Seleucus I.

> **Daniel 11:6** After some years, they will become allies. The daughter of the king of the South will go to the king of the North to make an alliance, but she will not retain her power, and he and his power will not last. In those days she will be handed over, together with her royal escort and her father and the one who supported her.

handed over: *made powerless*

concubine: *a least-favored wife*

Sometimes Everything Goes Wrong

The angel now skips over several years to a new generation of kings. He tells Daniel that the *king of the South* and the *king of the North* (Egypt and Syria) would become allies. He predicted that the daughter of the *king of the South* would go to the *king of the North* to seal the alliance. He also predicted that the idea would not work, that the daughter would lose her power, and then the king would lose his power. Furthermore, the angel predicted that she would be **handed over** together with everyone who had anything to do with her.

By this time 50 or more years had passed. The *king of the South* was an Egyptian king named Ptolemy Philadelphus. The *king of the North* was a Seleucid who called himself Antiochus Theos (Antiochus the God). The two kingdoms were having trouble getting along and these two kings wanted to change things. They thought it would be wise to forge an alliance, so Ptolemy Philadelphus offered to let his daughter, Bernice, marry Antiochus Theos. There was just one problem—Antiochus Theos was already married, so Antiochus Theos divorced his wife, Laodice, and disowned their children. He quickly married Bernice, and the alliance was sealed. But it wasn't long until Ptolemy Philadelphus died. Antiochus then changed the status of Bernice to **concubine** and remarried Laodice. Although Laodice married him, she wanted revenge, so she poisoned Antiochus, had Bernice murdered, and named one of her sons king. Thus, the attempt to forge an alliance was a total failure.

> **Daniel 11:7** "One from her family line will arise to take her place. He will attack the forces of the king of the North and enter his fortress; he will fight against them and be victorious.

War Between The South And The North

As the angel continued the prophecy he told Daniel that one from the daughter's (Bernice) family would arise to take her place. He said this relative would attack the *king of the North*, enter into his stronghold, and win the battle.

When Ptolemy Philadelphus died, his son Ptolemy Euergetes assumed the throne in Egypt. He was the brother of Bernice and was angry over what happened to his sister. Revenge was one of his first acts. He gathered a large army and attacked the fortress of Seleucia where Laodice was. He won the battle, captured Laodice, and put her to death.

God tells us to <u>love</u> our enemies, but <u>revenge</u> is just the opposite. It is something God hates and has even been known to make him angry. Some say revenge is sweet, but it is unlikely that Laodice would say that. Before taking revenge one should ponder the fact that it is a terrible thing to come under the <u>judgment of God</u>.

☞ **GO TO:**

Matthew 5:44 (love)

Ezekiel 25:15–17 (revenge)

II Corinthians 5:10, 11 (judgment)

Something to Ponder

☞ **GO TO:**

Psalm 115:4–8 (idols)

Jerome: a famous Bible expert who translated ancient writings into Latin

talent: about 450 pounds

> **Daniel 11:8** He will also seize their gods, their metal images, and their valuable articles of silver and gold and carry them off to Egypt. For some years he will leave the king of the North alone.

Helpless Gods

The angel focused his prophecy on the gods and riches of Syria. Ptolemy Euergetes (Bernice's brother) would seize the Syrian gods, images, and valuables and take them back to Egypt. And it would be a long time before the two kingdoms fought each other again.

Historians say Ptolemy Euergetes was on the verge of capturing all of Syria when he received word of an insurrection back home in Egypt. He quickly grabbed up all the valuables he could find and returned to Egypt. According to **Jerome** he took 4,000 **talents** of gold, 40,000 talents of silver, and 2,500 Syrian idols.

Remember This . . .

Listen to what the Bible says about <u>idols</u>: *But their idols are silver and gold, made by the hands of men. They have mouths, but cannot speak, eyes, but they cannot see; they have ears, but cannot hear, noses, but they cannot smell; they have hands, but cannot feel, feet, but they cannot walk; nor can they utter a sound with their throats. Those who make them will be like them, and so will all who trust in them.* Worshiping idols is a waste of time, but multitudes will worship the image of the Antichrist during the Tribulation Period.

> **Daniel 11:9** Then the king of the North will invade the realm of the king of the South but will retreat to his own country.

The North Strikes Back

The next angelic prediction was that Syria would invade Egypt. However, Syria would not be successful and would have to retreat to their own country.

The Syrian king Callinicus directed an attack on Egypt but lost the battle and had to return home empty-handed.

> **Daniel 11:10** His sons will prepare for war and assemble a great army, which will sweep on like an irresistible flood and carry the battle as far as his fortress.

☞ **GO TO:**

Daniel 11:42 (Egypt)

Gaza: a narrow strip of land between Egypt and Israel

Back And Forth

The next angelic prediction was that the sons of Callinicus would prepare for war, organize an army, and quickly move against one of the main Egyptian fortresses.

Callinicus had two sons. History reveals that the oldest became king first. He prepared to attack Egypt but was a poor and unpopular leader, so two of his generals poisoned him. Then the youngest son, Antiochus the Great, assumed the throne. He continued the war preparations, was a better leader, and launched an attack. He won a big victory against the Egyptians at **Gaza** (see Illustration #2, page 19) and considered trying to conquer the entire nation.

David Hocking: Seleucus Callinicus had two sons—Seleucus Ceraunus and Antiochus the Great. They stirred war. After Ceraunus was killed, Antiochus the Great moved south into Egyptian territory and captured the Egyptian fortress at Gaza. Ptolemy Philopator offered no serious resistance at this time.[6]

What Others are Saying:

Remember This . . .

The Antichrist will move into the Middle East. He will then take an army and move south through Gaza and take <u>Egypt</u>. Several other nations will also fall at that time.

> **Daniel 11:11** "Then the king of the South will march out in a rage and fight against the king of the North, who will raise a large army, but it will be defeated.

☞ **GO TO:**

Psalm 33:16 (army)

Seesaw

The angel told Daniel that Egypt would be angered and go out to fight Syria. Syria would have a great army, but it would be defeated.

Ptolemy Philopater replaced his father, Euergetes, as king of Egypt. He had a terrible temper and was greatly angered by Syria's victory at Gaza. He finally struck back and defeated Syria's great <u>army</u>.

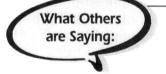
Noah Hutchings: History records that the Egyptian fortress at Gaza delayed the Syrian army long enough for Philopater to marshal his entire army. The two forces met at Raphia near Gaza. The surprise effect which the Syrian hoped for was gone, and the Egyptian army, being fresher and better supplied, soundly defeated the invaders.[7]

☞ **GO TO:**

Proverbs 16:18 (pride)

Daniel 11:45 (end)

blitzkrieg: sudden and violent war

> **Daniel 11:12** When the army is carried off, the king of the South will be filled with pride and will slaughter many thousands, yet he will not remain triumphant.

Pride Goes Before Destruction

Here the angel told Daniel that the victory of Ptolemy Philopater over Antiochus the Great would cause Philopater to be filled with <u>pride</u>. He would slaughter many thousands, but his victory would not turn out to be a great triumph.

When Ptolemy Philopater defeated Antiochus the Great at Raphia he killed 10,000 Syrians and took several thousand prisoners, but he was overcome with pride and did not follow up on his great victory. Instead of continuing on into Syria to capture the whole kingdom he signed a foolish peace treaty with Antiochus the Great and returned home to receive glory and have a good time.

**What Others
are Saying:**

Oliver B. Greene: Because of this tremendous victory, Ptolemy's heart "was lifted up," and had he been a man of character he might have followed up this victory by fighting Antiochus and seizing his kingdom; but he was too anxious to return to his drinking and sensual pleasures, and thereby lost the opportunity to drive on to complete victory and become a world ruler. Therefore, he was "not strengthened" by his great victory over Antiochus. He defeated the king—but he did not take the kingdom.[8]

**RELATED
CURRENT
EVENTS**

On August 2, 1990, Iraq invaded Kuwait and set off the Persian Gulf Crisis. One day later the U.N. Security Council condemned Iraq. Four days later it imposed sanctions. On November 29, 1990, it authorized the use of force against Iraq if it did not abandon its occupation of Kuwait by January 15, 1991. When Iraq failed to comply a coalition of nations attacked Iraq and had it on the brink of total defeat in just 100 hours. But the coalition stopped short and did not complete the job. Now Iraq has returned as a threat to the world again.

The Antichrist will be filled with pride and will defeat many nations. His move through the Middle East will be a **blitzkrieg**, but his triumphs will come to an <u>end</u>, and he will have no one to help him.

> **Daniel 11:13** For the king of the North will muster another army, larger than the first; and after several years, he will advance with a huge army fully equipped.

A Broken Peace Treaty

This time the angel prophesied that Syria would muster a larger and better equipped army. And after several years he would advance on Egypt once again.

The peace treaty that Ptolemy Philopater signed with Antiochus the Great let the Syrian king take his army and return home. Upon his return, Antiochus started a program to rebuild his military. Over the next 14 years he built a powerful force, suppressed all his enemies, enriched his nation, and began to reach out and take whatever he wanted. Soon he received word that the Egyptian king Ptolemy Philopater had died and his five-year-old son Ptolemy Epiphanes had succeeded him. Antiochus the Great looked at the situation and decided it would be a good time to attack Egypt, so he broke his covenant and struck Egypt thinking he would have an easy victory.

KEY POINT

Some <u>covenants</u> are just tools to buy time or gain an advantage.

> **Daniel 11:14** "In those times many will rise against the king of the South. The violent men among your own people will rebel in fulfillment of the vision, but without success.

Who Wants A Five-Year-Old King?

The angel predicted rebellion against Egypt. *Your own people* refers to Daniel's people, the Jews. The angel predicted that wicked Jews would join the rebellion against Egypt but without success.

Many of Egypt's most influential citizens were greatly disappointed when Ptolemy Epiphanes was crowned king. Some of them banded together and rebelled against his leadership killing several of the king's most faithful subjects. There were also Jews within Egypt and back in Israel who joined in the rebellion. All these rebels believed that Antiochus the Great would defeat Egypt, so they wanted to be on the right side. What they did not count on

☞ **GO TO:**

Daniel 9:26 (people)

Daniel 9:27 (covenant)

Anointed One: Jesus

 **KEY Symbols:**

Your Own People
Daniel's people, the Jews

There will be wicked
Jews during the
Tribulation Period who
will join forces with
the Antichrist. Many
Jews will oppose the
covenant with Anti-
christ, but some
wicked Jews will
betray their people
and sign it.

was Egypt signing a mutual aid treaty with Rome. That powerful nation entered the picture and changed everything.

In fulfillment of the vision is an interesting phrase. It reminds us of the Vision of the Ram and the Goat in Chapter 9. That vision reveals that *the people of the ruler who will come* (the Romans) would destroy Jerusalem and the Temple after the **Anointed One** was killed. We know the Romans did this in 70 A.D., but this present verse has them moving into the Middle East *in fulfillment of the vision*. In other words, it was the providence of God that Rome went to Egypt's aid. That put them in position to fulfill the Vision of the Ram and the Goat.

> **Daniel 11:15** Then the king of the North will come and build up siege ramps and will capture a fortified city. The forces of the South will be powerless to resist; even their best troops will not have the strength to stand.

A Northern Victory

This is more detail from the angel concerning the previous verse. He predicted that Syria would capture an Egyptian fortified city. He added that Egypt's forces would be powerless to stop him and that even the best Egyptian troops would not be strong enough to stop Syria.

The rebellion resulting from crowning a five-year-old boy as king of Egypt and the insurrection of the Jews greatly weakened Egypt. This was just what Antiochus wanted, so he set out to attack Egypt. Unfortunately for Antiochus, the Romans had entered the picture, and they had one of their experienced ministers serving as guardian and assistant to the young king. He called on a famous Egyptian general named Scopas to help. Scopas quickly organized an army and went out to meet Antiochus the Great. But he wasn't strong enough, and Antiochus the Great defeated his army. After defeat, Scopas and a few of his troops fled to the fortress city of Sidon, but Antiochus the Great pursued them and laid seige to the city. Egypt got word and sent troops to help, but they were not strong enough to defeat Antiochus either. He defeated them, starved out the besieged Egyptians, captured the fortress city of Sidon, and sent the surviving troops away stark naked. Everything the angel said was accomplished.

> **Daniel 11:16** The invader will do as he pleases; no one will be able to stand against him. He will establish himself in the Beautiful Land and will have the power to destroy it.

☞ **GO TO:**

Daniel 11:41 (Beautiful Land)

Daniel 11:45 (mountain)

Poor Israel

The angel is providing all this information about Syria and Egypt because their struggles greatly affected Israel. Every time one country attacked the other the invading army had to pass through Israel. It didn't happen every time, but the Jews often took a beating. The angel revealed these things for Daniel's understanding, and although we are receiving a lot of information about Syria and Egypt, this is really a message about Daniel's people Israel.

Here the angel predicted that Antiochus the Great would do as he pleased. No one would be strong enough to stop him. He would settle down in the <u>Beautiful Land</u> and be strong enough to destroy it.

The Egyptians were weak and knew it. They had signed a mutual aid treaty with Rome, so they asked Rome for help. The Romans were rapidly becoming a great power, so they warned Antiochus the Great not to invade Egypt. So Antiochus held back and settled down in Israel while he pondered his options. He had the power to destroy Israel, but did not because of the Jews who had rebelled and supported him in Egypt.

Noah Hutchings: In order to reach Egypt, Antiochus the Great had to first conquer Israel, which was at that time under the protection of Egypt and guarded by an Egyptian army. Antiochus was successful in overrunning the Egyptian garrison stationed in Israel, and in Israel he was able to do according to his will because the Jews, relying upon the protection of Egypt, had no army to resist him.[9]

During the Tribulation Period the Antichrist will invade the Beautiful Land and use it as a base to attack other nations. He will locate his headquarters at the beautiful holy <u>mountain</u>, and that is where he will be when he is captured.

KEY POINT

These wars greatly affected Israel.

KEY Symbols:

Beautiful Land
ISRAEL

What Others are Saying:

Remember This . . .

☞ **GO TO:**

Daniel 11:6 (alliance)

Jeremiah 6:14 (peace)

Revelation 6:2 (man)

Daniel 9:27 (break treaty)

Revelation 12:13–17 (destroy Jews)

Saladin: a Muslim leader who broke a peace treaty

KEY Symbols:

True Peace
  peace between America and Canada

False Peace
  the peace of Saladin peace that can be broken

> **Daniel 11:17** He will determine to come with the might of his entire kingdom and will make an alliance with the king of the South. And he will give him a daughter in marriage in order to overthrow the kingdom, but his plans will not succeed or help him.

Try Diplomacy: A False Peace Treaty

The angel told Daniel that Antiochus would be determined in his desire to capture Egypt. In order to do that he would enter into an <u>alliance with Egypt</u>. He would give one of his daughters in marriage to the king of Egypt in order to overthrow the Egyptian kingdom, but it would not work.

Fear of drawing the Romans into the conflict on the side of Egypt and having to fight both nations at the same time caused Antiochus the Great to occupy the land of Israel while he waited and strengthened his forces. But his fear did not deter him from wanting to conquer Egypt. It just caused him to change his tactics.

By this time Ptolemy Epiphanes, the child king of Egypt, was about seven years old and Antiochus the Great had a daughter who was a little older, perhaps as much as 5 or 6 years older. Her name was Cleopatra. Antiochus the Great suggested that Syria and Egypt stop fighting and sign a <u>peace</u> treaty. He suggested that Ptolemy and Cleopatra marry to seal the treaty. Antiochus the Great thought his daughter would be loyal to him, dominate the young Egyptian king, and help bring about Syria's acquisition of Egypt, but Cleopatra did not cooperate. She was loyal to her husband and sided with the Egyptians against her own father. The false treaty did not work.

What Others are Saying:

David Jeremiah with C.C. Carlson: He [Antiochus] was determined to unite Syria and Egypt, so what did he do? Of course, he decided to give the king of Egypt his daughter. His daughter was a very desirable woman. The king had hoped to put a spy in the palace, somebody on his side. The plan was thwarted, however, because the daughter fell in love with the Egyptian king and forgot all about Daddy.[10]

Something to Ponder

Today the Arabs and PLO are suggesting that Israel should swap "land for peace." But there are two definitions of peace in the Arab language. The first definition is the true peace we Americans think of. It is the kind of peace that exists between the United States and Canada. The second definition is the "peace of **Saladin**." That is a truce that can be broken at a convenient time. When Yasser Arafat speaks to his Arab brothers he makes it plain that "land for peace" means the "peace of Saladin."

• • •

The Anichrist will be a *wolf in sheep's clothing*. This means he will actually be a war-monger, but he will come on the scene as a <u>man of peace</u>. He will sign a peace treaty to protect Israel, but he will <u>break it three-and-a-half years later</u>. Then he will try to <u>destroy the Jews</u>. His sweet sounding words will be a charade and his written agreements will be worthless pieces of paper.

This is not the same Cleopatra who was famous for her relationship with the great Roman leaders Julius Caesar and Mark Antony. That Cleopatra reigned between 69–30 B.C., but this Syrian Cleopatra reigned more than 100 years earlier. There were seven Egyptian queens named Cleopatra.

Remember This . . .

> **Daniel 11:18** Then he will turn his attention to the coastlands and will take many of them, but a commander will put an end to his insolence and will turn his insolence back upon him.

In Come The Romans

The next thing the angel prophesied was that Antiochus would abandon his plans to take Egypt and go after the coastlands. He would be successful at first, but a commander would end his rampage, and Antiochus would <u>reap</u> what he sowed.

Antiochus the Great was furious over Rome's protection of Egypt and his daughter's betrayal. He assembled a 300 ship navy and started seizing the cities and islands along the coasts of the Mediterranean Sea. However, most of these coastal cities were under Roman control and Rome was not about to let Antiochus the Great take their territory. To prevent this, the Romans commissioned a young naval commander named Scipio to take a fleet of Roman warships and go after the Syrian vessels. Scipio found and sank most of the Syrian navy thereby turning Antiochus the Great's insolence back upon himself.

☞ **GO TO:**

Galatians 6:7 (reap)

Daniel 9:26 (people)

Daniel 11:40 (ships)

**Remember
This . . .**

The Romans would be in control of Israel when the Anointed One (Jesus) came. They are the <u>people</u> who would destroy Jerusalem and the Temple. This verse points to their arrival on the scene in the Middle East. They (the Old Roman Empire) would be there for the First Coming, and they (the Revived Roman Empire) will be back for the Second Coming of Jesus. In fact, the *king of the North* will attack them with many <u>ships</u> during the Tribulation Period, but he will be defeated.

> **Daniel 11:19** After this, he will turn back toward the fortresses of his own country but will stumble and fall, to be seen no more.

The Tax Man Cometh

The angel continued revealing the vision to Daniel. He predicted that Antiochus would return to his own country following his defeat along the coastlands. But things would not go well in his homeland. He would stumble and be seen no more.

Antiochus the Great returned home with one eye over his shoulder. He expected the Roman army to be right on his heels. As soon as he got home he sent messengers to Rome seeking peace. The Romans had the upper hand and were in no mood to be generous. They offered peace, but at a very high price. Antiochus the Great had to give them all the territory he controlled in Europe, a big chunk of what he controlled in Asia, all but ten of his warships, an enormous tribute, and heavy taxes every year for the next 12 years. He agreed to their terms but had trouble coming up with the money and was killed while trying to seize it a few months later.

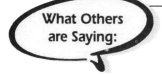

**What Others
are Saying:**

Noah Hutchings: The peace terms laid down by the Romans were harsh. He had to relinquish all his holdings in Europe and much of Western Turkey. He also had to pay twenty-three hundred [and] thirty talents to Rome at the signing of the peace treaty, and one thousand talents a year for the next twelve years. A few months later, when robbing the temples in his own provinces for money to pay the war obligation, he was killed in the temple of Bel in Elymais.[11]

> **Daniel 11:20** "His successor will send out a tax collector to maintain the royal splendor. In a few years, however, he will be destroyed, yet not in anger or in battle.

No Tax Cuts Under This Administration

Here the angel prophesied the future of the successor to Antiochus the Great. He would send out the tax collector to keep payments going, but shortly thereafter would be destroyed. He would not die, however, in a rage or in battle.

Antiochus the Great was succeeded by his oldest son Seleucus Philopater. Seleucus inherited the large debt his father agreed to pay in order to obtain peace with Rome. He raised taxes to meet the agreement, but his nation was so impoverished he had trouble collecting them. By the time he neared the last year of the 12 year taxation clause he was in a financial crisis. He desperately instructed his treasurer to go to Jerusalem and confiscate the gold and silver vessels that were being used at the Temple. A short time later someone poisoned him.

Oliver B. Greene: In each instance concerning the battles, the victories, and the defeats of these kings of the North and of the South, we see over and over again that the <u>wages of sin is death</u>, and God is not mocked. . . . Whether we are king or peasant, if God is <u>for us</u>, who can be against us? But by the same token, whether we are king or peasant, if God is against us we are defeated.[12]

The Antichrist will not die in battle. He will be captured by Jesus at the Second Coming and thrown alive into the fiery <u>lake</u> of burning sulfur (Lake of Fire).

> **Daniel 11:21** "He will be succeeded by a contemptible person who has not been given the honor of royalty. He will invade the kingdom (Israel) when its people feel secure, and he will seize it through intrigue.

The Contemptible Person

The angel told Daniel the next king to rule would be a wicked person. Although he would be the king, he would not be the true heir to the throne. He would invade the kingdom (Israel) during a time of peace and seize it through <u>intrigue</u>.

☞ **GO TO:**

Romans 6:23 (wages)

Romans 8:31 (for us)

Revelation 19:20 (lake)

KEY POINT

The wages of sin is death. God is not mocked.

 *KEY Symbols:*

Sin
death

Flesh
corruption

 **What Others are Saying:**

 **Remember This . . .**

☞ **GO TO:**

Daniel 8:23 (intrigue)

Daniel 8:9 (horn)

Matthew 24:5; II Timothy 3:13 (deceive)

Daniel 7:24; Revelation 13:1; 17:12 (ten kingdoms)

Antiochus Epiphanes
was not the true heir
to the throne.

precursor: a living example

After Seleucus Philopater tried to confiscate the Temple vessels he was poisoned. He had two sons—Demetrius, the oldest, was in position to be crowned king, but Seleucus Philopater had a younger brother, Antiochus, who was an extraordinarily good manipulator. Like his father Antiochus the Great, Antiochus was wicked and cunning, and like his sister Cleopatra, who was married off to Ptolemy Epiphanes of Egypt, he was deceitful and treacherous. He used his manipulative skills, treachery, and deceit to acquire the crown over his nephew Demetrius, the rightful heir. Antiochus later became known as Antiochus Epiphanes (see Flow Chart, p.215). He is widely recognized by prophecy experts as a **precursor** or forerunner of the <u>horn</u> in Chapter 8. What the angel has to say about this man exemplifies what the Antichrist will do at the End of the Age.

Antiochus Epiphanes picked up where his father Antiochus the Great left off. He was another *king of the North* (Syria) who attacked the *king of the South* (Egypt). Before he did that he convinced everyone he was just moving a small number of troops to the Egyptian border. He actually moved a large army, but he had to move it into Israel before getting to the Egyptian border.

**What Others
are Saying:**

J. Vernon McGee: He came to the throne with a program of peace. (The Antichrist will come to power in the same way. He will introduce the Great Tribulation with three and one-half years of peace, and the people of the world will think they are entering the Millennium when they are really entering the Great Tribulation Period. Antiochus was a deceiver and a flatterer. My friend, beware of that type of person. You can find them even in the ministry.[13]

**Something
to Ponder**

<u>Deceit</u> can only prosper where there is ignorance. When the Rapture occurs the only true leaders and religious people left on earth will be lost. The Antichrist will rise to power in a world of Biblical ignorance. His deceitful ways and sweet-sounding words of peace and prosperity will meet no resistance because people will not recognize him for what he is.

**Remember
This . . .**

Our national leaders are diligently working to establish a world government. That government will divide into <u>ten kingdoms</u>. The Antichrist will not be given the honor of being king over one of those kingdoms, but with Satan's help he will seize the world government through intrigue.

But mark this: There will be terrible times in the last days. (II Timothy 3:1)

> **Daniel 11:22** Then an overwhelming army will be swept away before him; both it and a prince of the covenant will be destroyed.

A Powerful Military Leader With His Own High Priest

This angelic prophecy states that the contemptible king would destroy a great army. It also predicted a *prince of the covenant* would be destroyed.

Antiochus Epiphanes attacked Egypt and the Egyptians struck back with a large army. The casualties on both sides were high, but Antiochus Epiphanes won the battle and captured the Egyptian king Ptolemy Philometer, the son of Cleopatra (Antiochus' sister).

Antiochus Epiphanes broke so many agreements and betrayed so many people it is difficult to say who the *prince of the <u>covenant</u>* was. One could pick from several examples. The best guess, however, seems to be the Jewish High Priest Onias III. Antiochus Epiphanes had him deposed and murdered. Then he appointed the brother of Onias III, a man named Jason, to be the High Priest of Israel. With the approval of Antiochus Epiphanes, Jason persuaded many Jews to abandon their faith.

David Hocking: According to history, Antiochus routed the forces of Egypt in a battle between Pelusium and the Casian Mountains. The *prince of the covenant* is a reference to Onias III who was the High Priest. He was deposed by Antiochus and replaced by his brother, Jason. Jason wanted Greek culture to be established in Israel and Antiochus encouraged this.[14]

> **Daniel 11:23** After coming to an agreement with him, he will act deceitfully, and with only a few people he will rise to power.

Deceit And More Deceit

Here the angel was prophesying the fact that the contemptible person (Antiochus Epiphanes) would make an agreement with his captive (Ptolemy Philometer), but Antiochus Epiphanes would be deceiving him. With only a few people he would rise to power.

☞ **GO TO:**

Daniel 11:28, 29 (covenant)

Revelation 16:13 (False Prophet)

KEY POINT

The Antichrist will be a powerful military leader, and he will have his own religious spokeman called the <u>False Prophet</u>, who will cause multitudes to follow his anti-Christian beliefs.

What Others are Saying:

☞ **GO TO:**

Daniel 8:12 (truth)

Daniel 8:9 (power)

II Thessalonians 2:10; Matthew 24:11, 24 (deceit)

Matthew 24:24 (elect)

KEY Symbols:

**Prince of the
Covenant**
*the Jewish High Priest
Onias III*

*Remember
This . . .*

☞ **GO TO:**

John 8:44 (liar)

Daniel 11:39 (attack)

After Antiochus Epiphanes defeated Egypt's army and captured Ptolemy Philometer, the Egyptians quickly crowned Philometer's brother, Ptolemy Euergetes, king. Antiochus Epiphanes wanted to march against him, but he had lost too many troops when he defeated Ptolemy Philometer. He saw the crowning of Ptolemy Euergetes as an opportunity to divide the remaining Egyptian forces, to take more spoils, and perhaps to have himself crowned king of Egypt. He made an agreement to help his captured nephew Ptolemy Philometer regain the crown in exchange for Philometer's help and support against Ptolemy Euergetes. It worked. <u>Truth</u> was thrown to the ground. Ptolemy Philometer helped Antiochus Epiphanes and his support strengthened the Syrian king. But what Philometer didn't know until later was the fact that Antiochus Epiphanes was just tricking him. It was a deceitful tactic on the part of Antiochus Epiphanes to make himself more <u>powerful</u>.

<u>Deceit</u> will be a way of life during the Tribulation Period. The Antichrist will perform Satanic miracles and deceive many. Jesus said, *many false prophets will appear and deceive many people.* He said, *false Christs and false prophets will appear and perform great signs and miracles to deceive even the <u>elect</u>—if it were possible.*

• • •

Antiochus Epiphanes was a living example of the Antichrist, the wicked man who will gain control of the whole world during the Tribulation Period. Here are a just a few of the Antichrist's titles:

• *Master of Intrigue*—Daniel 8:24
• *Man of Lawlessness*—II Thessalonians 2:3
• *Lawless One*—II Thessalonians 2:8
• *Beast that comes up from the Abyss*—Revelation 11:7

> **Daniel 11:24** When the richest provinces feel secure, he will invade them and will achieve what neither his fathers nor his forefathers did. He will distribute plunder, loot, and wealth among his followers. He will plot the overthrow of fortresses—but only for a time.

A Wicked Robin Hood

This angelic prophecy states that Antiochus Epiphanes would invade the richest provinces of Egypt at a time when they feel secure. He would take plunder, loot, and wealth but not keep it. He would give it to his followers, and for a time, he would plot the overthrow of Egyptian strongholds.

The covenant Antiochus Epiphanes made with Ptolemy Philometer put many of the Egyptians at ease. It did not occur to them that they were dealing with a thief and a <u>liar</u>. At a time when they felt secure, Antiochus Epiphanes raided some of the richest provinces of Egypt. He took wealth and territory that none of his ancestors were able to take. Then, like the head of a gang of thieves, he distributed the loot among his followers. That bought the loyalty of even more men, so he planned to attack more places. But things eventually changed.

David Jeremiah with C.C. Carlson: He moved into the richest provinces and robbed them of all the valuables he could find. With the loot he bought the allegiance of the renegades he needed to perpetrate his crimes. He had an army of mercenaries to march against the king of the South.[15]

During the Tribulation Period the Antichrist will <u>attack</u> and conquer many nations. He will use his booty and conquered territory to reward those wicked people who support him.

> **Daniel 11:25** "With a large army he will stir up his strength and courage against the king of the South. The king of the South will wage war with a large and very powerful army, but he will not be able to stand because of the plots devised against him.

Treason In The South

Here the angel predicted Antiochus Epiphanes would build up his forces and muster the courage to mount a great attack on Egypt. He predicted that Egypt would fight back with a powerful army, but Egypt would lose due to plots devised against it.

Antiochus Epiphanes attacked Egypt. This time the *king of the South* was another brother of Ptolemy Philometer named Ptolemy Physcon. He pulled together a large army and fought back, but some of his men committed treason, deserted him, and joined Antiochus Epiphanes. Their unfaithfulness caused Egypt's defeat.

What Others are Saying:

Remember This . . .

☞ **GO TO:**

Daniel 11:39 (South)

Remember This . . .

☞ **GO TO:**

Daniel 7:24; Revelation 12:3; 13:1; 17:12, 13 (ten)

John 13:1 (Feast of Passover)

The *king of the South* and his four-nation alliance will wage war against the Antichrist, but he will not be able to stand, and the Antichrist will defeat him and his army.

• • •

Daniel received this vision (the Vision of the Anointed One) 200 years before any of these battles occurred.

> **Daniel 11:26** Those who eat from the king's provisions will try to destroy him; his army will be swept away, and many will fall in battle.

Do Not Bite The Hand That Feeds You

This angelic prediction identifies some of those who would be involved in the treason as *those who eat from the king's provisions.* In other words, the *king of the South* would be betrayed by members of his own court. That betrayal would lead to a military defeat and many casualties.

Information is scarce, but it seems that most of the members of the court were related to both Ptolemy Physcon (the reigning king) and Ptolemy Philometer (the captured king). Some were more loyal to Ptolemy Philometer and believed Antiochus Epiphanes was just helping him recover his throne, so they betrayed Physcon, Egypt was defeated, and many Egyptians were killed.

Something to Ponder

Remember This . . .

It is difficult to imagine people being gullible enough to do some of these things, but history has identified many leaders who made terrible mistakes. Consider the coming world government. It will be divided into ten divisions. Each division will have its own king or leader. Then the Antichrist will appear. He will subdue three of the kings, and the others will be gullible enough to turn their power over to him.

Jesus celebrated the Feast of Passover with his disciples in the Upper Room. After they finished eating, he humbly washed their feet, but was troubled in his spirit because he knew one of those he ate with would betray him. Out of friendship and love he gave Judas Iscariot a piece of bread. Judas took a bite, quickly left, and turned his back on the one who loved him more than anyone else.

> **Daniel 11:27** The two kings, with their hearts bent on evil, will sit at the same table and lie to each other, but to no avail, because an end will still come at the appointed time.

☞ **GO TO:**

Revelation 6:2 (white horse)

Daniel 8:25 KJV (peace)

Daniel 9:27 (covenant)

Daniel 7:8; Revelation 13:5 (mouth)

Lies, Lies, and More Lies

The angel told Daniel the *king of the North* (Syria) and the *king of the South* (Egypt) would sit at the same table. They would have evil in their hearts and lie to each other. But the lies would not aid either one because the end would still come at the time of God's choosing.

Antiochus Epiphanes and Ptolemy Philometer sat down to discuss the situation. They were supposedly going to settle their differences, but all they did was lie to one another.

Remember This . . .

⬅ **WARNING**

Revelation pictures the Antichrist arriving on the scene riding a <u>white horse</u>. He will use <u>peace</u> to destroy many and a <u>covenant</u> to dupe Israel. His actions will make Antiochus Epiphanes look like an amateur, and the gullibility of Ptolemy will be exceeded only by the gullibility of our future government leaders.

The Antichrist will come forth with a <u>mouth</u> that boasts great things and utters proud words. He will be an eloquent speaker and a tremendous negotiator.

> **Daniel 11:28** The king of the North will return to his own country with great wealth, but his heart will be set against the holy covenant. He will take action against it and then return to his own country.

☞ **GO TO:**

Exodus 19:5; Leviticus 24:8; 26:9 (covenant)

Revelation 13:3, 12, 14 (fatal)

He Opposed God's Covenant

Here the angel prophesied that Antiochus would leave Egypt with a large amount of wealth and return to his own land, but he would oppose the <u>covenant</u> God had with Israel. He would violate that covenant before returning home.

It appeared that Antiochus Epiphanes and Ptolemy Philometer had settled their differences around the conference table. A large amount of Egypt's wealth was handed over to Antiochus Epiphanes, and he headed back to Syria with his army. The route home took him through Israel.

KEY Symbols:

Holy Covenant
God's covenant with Israel

Things had changed in Israel since Antiochus Epiphanes had passed through on his way to Egypt. A rumor had circulated that Antiochus Epiphanes was dead which caused many Jews to rejoice. Some of them had revolted and driven the Syrians out of Jerusalem. Antiochus Epiphanes learned of this as he neared Jerusalem and decided to make the Jews pay. God's covenant with Israel was not something he believed anyway, so he attacked and plundered the city, killed approximately 40,000 Jews, sold thousands more into slavery, looted the Temple, and let his troops rape the women.

What Others are Saying:

David Hocking: We read that after his [Antiochus'] victory in Egypt, his heart will be moved against *the holy covenant*—God's covenant with Israel. God gave the land to Israel, and the Antichrist will move against the land and do damage before he returns to his own land. Historically, Antiochus Epiphanes returned from Egypt with a lot of plunder and he marched through Judea only to discover that an insurrection had occurred. . . . He put down the insurrection and took that opportunity to plunder the Temple. The abomination had started. Antiochus plundered the treasures of the Temple.[16]

Remember This . . .

When the Antichrist comes on the scene and history approaches the Tribulation Period mid-point (see GWRV, Time Line #2, Appendix A) the Antichrist will appear to be killed by a <u>fatal</u> wound to the head. It will be a sword wound and it will be healed to the amazement of the whole world. Multitudes will follow him, and yet, he will be worse than Antiochus Epiphanes ever thought of being.

> **Daniel 11:29** "At the appointed time he will invade the South again, but this time the outcome will be different from what it was before.

A Worthless Agreement

The angel told Daniel Antiochus Epiphanes would invade Egypt one more time, but things would be different this time.

Antiochus Epiphanes was determined to conquer Egypt, so he tried again. His two nephews, Ptolemy Philometer and Ptolemy Physcon, had settled their differences and were sharing the throne. They opposed Antiochus Epiphanes and appealed to Rome for help.

David Jeremiah with C.C. Carlson: Every peace treaty that has been made since the world began has been broken. This one was just like the rest.[17]

```
The Munich Agreement at first seemed to avoid
war. Chamberlain [Neville Chamberlain, Prime
Minister of Great Britain] reported to cheering
crowds in England "peace with honor" and "peace
in our time." A few months after the conference,
Hitler broke his promise and had German troops
take control of Czechoslovakia. . . . The Munich
Agreement became a classic example of an
ill-advised policy of appeasement (concession).
After Munich, agreements with an aggressive na-
tion were thought to invite war rather than pre-
vent it. Such agreements are still sometimes
referred to as "another Munich."[18]
```

> **Daniel 11:30** Ships of the western coastlands will oppose him, and he will lose heart. Then he will turn back and vent his fury against the holy covenant. He will return and show favor to those who forsake the holy covenant.

They're Back

The angel predicted that Antiochus Epiphanes would be opposed by *ships of the western coastlands*. They would cause him to change his mind about invading Egypt again. He would turn around and vent his fury on the covenant of God one more time. But he would deal kindly with those who abandoned the covenant.

When the two Egyptian kings appealed to Rome for help the Romans responded by sending their navy. Rome's naval commander met Antiochus Epiphanes at **Alexandria** and told him to get out of Egypt and leave the nation alone. The order was by decree of the Roman Senate and if Antiochus did not obey he would be attacked by Rome. Then the commander drew a circle on the ground around the feet of Antiochus and demanded that he not step out of it until he stated his intentions. Antiochus decided to leave Egypt.

Antiochus Epiphanes headed home through Israel, but he was even more furious than before. His entire army was aware that he was afraid and running, so when he got to Jerusalem he vented his anger and plundered the city again, killing thousands of Jews

What Others are Saying:

RELATED CURRENT EVENTS

☞ **GO TO:**

Revelation 12:9–13 (Satan)

Alexandria: *an Egyptian port city on the Mediterranean Sea built by Alexander the Great*

Sabbath: *the seventh day of the week, Saturday*

and selling thousands more into slavery. He outlawed the Jewish religion and replaced it with Greek worship. He outlawed circumcision, the reading of the Scriptures, and the observance of the **Sabbath**. Those who abandoned the Jewish faith were spared, but those who did not were killed.

At the Tribulation Period mid-point <u>Satan</u> and his angels will be hurled down to the earth out of heaven. Satan will know his time is short, and he will be filled with fury. He will vent his fury on God's people and destroy whatever he can before the Second Coming of Christ.

☞ **GO TO:**

Daniel 9:27; 12:11; Matthew 24:15, 21 (abomination)

Revelation 13:15 (power)

Revelation 13:13–15 (image)

Revelation 14:9–10 (wrath)

> **Daniel 11:31** "His armed forces will rise up to desecrate the temple fortress and will abolish the daily sacrifice. Then they will set up the abomination that causes desolation.

More Contemptible Acts

The angel revealed that the army of Antiochus Epiphanes would desecrate the Temple (see Illustration #17, page 299). They would abolish the daily sacrifice and set up the <u>abomination</u> that would make the Temple desolate.

Antiochus Epiphanes posted some of his troops to guard the Temple with reserve troops nearby. The Sabbath came and thousands of Jews gathered at the Temple to offer sacrifices and worship God. They were ignoring Antiochus Epiphanes, so he counted them among his enemies and had his army kill them. Then he built an altar to one of his Greek gods, brought in Jews, and compelled them to sacrifice pigs on it to his heathen gods. Those who refused were killed.

What Others are Saying:

Holy Place: the innermost sanctuary of the Temple

Great Tribulation: the last 3½ years of the Tribulation Period

Randall Price: The expression [abomination that causes desolation] . . . describe[s] the act of setting up an idolatrous image in the **Holy Place**, thus defiling or "making desolate" the Temple, and ending the offering of all sacrifices. This was done in the past by Antiochus Epiphanes (Daniel 11:31), whose act reflects the future defilement by the Antichrist (Daniel 9:27). Both Daniel and Jesus indicated that this future act would signal the start of the **Great Tribulation** (Daniel 12:11; Matthew 24:15; Mark 13:14).[19]

Peter and Paul Lalonde: The False Prophet, we are told, will have the <u>power to give life</u> unto the image of the beast, that the image of the beast should both speak, and cause that as many as would not

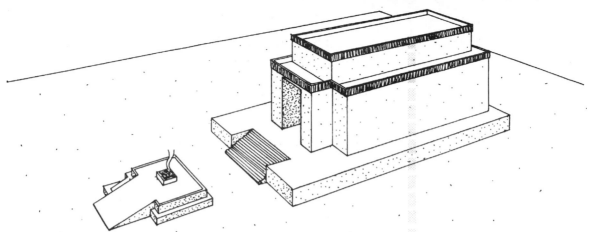

worship the image of the beast should be killed. Imagine a first century prophet trying to describe an image that comes to life. It would have made no sense to him. Yet he wrote it down. Today, we are just beginning to discover the incredible wonder of holograms. A hologram is simply a three-dimensional image, made only of light, that can be made to look so much like a real object that you actually think you can reach out to touch it—but alas, there's nothing there. Even more amazing is the fact that these holographic objects can easily be manipulated to make them appear to be moving, or even speaking.[20]

During the Tribulation Period the False Prophet will set up an <u>image</u> of the Antichrist (the Image of the Beast) and compel the inhabitants of the earth to worship it. Those who refuse will be killed. Those who worship the image will be spared for a while, but eventually, they will fall under the <u>wrath</u> of God.

> **Daniel 11:32** With flattery he will corrupt those who have violated the covenant, but the people who know their God will firmly resist him.

Flattery From Hell

Daniel was informed by the angel that Antiochus Epiphanes would corrupt some of the unfaithful Jews with flattering words, but the faithful Jews would firmly resist him.

The Jews had their share of traitors and lukewarm believers. Some, such as the new High Priest Alcimus, were even leaders in the Jewish religion. Antiochus Epiphanes courted them with flattering words in order to corrupt them to his false religion and use them against the faithful. Many who questioned the Word of God were <u>deceived</u>, but a group of strong believers revolted.

Illustration #17

The Temple in Jerusalem— The abomination that causes desolation will be set up on a wing of the Temple. Sacrifices made on the outside altar will be stopped.

Remember This . . .

☞ **GO TO:**

II Thessalonians 2:9–12 (deception)

Revelation 3:15, 16 (lukewarm)

Something to Ponder

☞ **GO TO:**

Matthew 24:9
(persecute)

Revelation 13:7, 15
(power)

KEY Symbols:

Maccabees

THE HAMMER

revolted against
blasphemy

Hassideans: an orthodox
religious sect of Jews

Remember This . . .

Jesus placed church members in one of three states: cold, lukewarm, or hot. The cold are pretenders who lack true spiritual life. The lukewarm are indifferent or straddling the fence. The hot are passionate about their love for him. This last group is the only one Jesus finds acceptable.

> **Daniel 11:33** "Those who are wise will instruct many, though for a time they will fall by the sword or be burned or captured or plundered.

The Maccabean Period

Here the angel predicted that a group of wise people would teach many, but for a while they would be persecuted in four ways:

1) some would be killed by the sword,
2) some would be killed by fire,
3) some would be captured, and
4) some would be robbed.

A large number of Jews recognized the corruption, treachery, and false teachings of Antiochus Epiphanes. They wisely tried to remain faithful to God and teach others. Some, who were called the **Hassideans**, revolted and fled into the mountains. They joined the Maccabees family and fought against Antiochus Epiphanes and the rulers who followed him. They carried on their struggle for independence for more than 100 years. Many died in war, some were tortured and burned, while others were captured. Most had their villages and camps plundered and destroyed.

A Jewish priest named Mattathais who wanted the Jews to remain faithful to God, killed an unfaithful Jew who was about to offer a heathen sacrifice at the Temple. Fearing for his life, Mattathais took his five sons, one of which was named Judas Maccabaeus, and fled into the hills. The family became known as the Maccabees because of their subsequent revolt against Antiochus. They were very successful in their struggle against him, and so upset him that he could no longer eat, and he eventually died in his own land of malnutrition.

❖ ❖ ❖

For a time (the seven-year Tribulation Period) the Antichrist will be given power to make war against God's people and conquer them. The False Prophet will set up an image and kill those who refuse to worship it. Many of God's people will fall.

> **Daniel 11:34** When they fall, they will receive a little help, and many who are not sincere will join them.

Lukewarm

The angel predicted the fall of the wise (Maccabees). They would also receive a little help and have many insincere people join them.

The courageous struggle of the Maccabees cost the family and their followers many lives. They eventually lost the struggle, but not before they won several major battles. Some of their victories were so impressive that many Jews thought the Maccabees might win. That caused a dilemma for the fence-sitting Jews. They feared the wrath of Antiochus Epiphanes if he won, but they also feared the wrath of their countrymen if the Maccabees won. They wanted to be on the winning side, so every Maccabean victory was accompanied by more Jews joining the cause. However, many of them were not true believers; they just did not want to be accused of treason if their people won.

At the end of the **Church Age** (see GWRV, Time Line #1, Appendix A) there will be many fence-sitters or lukewarm church members. Their lack of sincere commitment will not be acceptable to Christ, so they will miss the Rapture and live during the Tribulation Period. Their lukewarm attitude will be a terrible mistake.

> **Daniel 11:35** Some of the wise will stumble, so that they may be refined, purified, and made spotless until the time of the end, for it will still come at the appointed time.

The Time Of The End

This angelic prophecy starts with the wise (the faithful) during the struggle of the Maccabees and skips forward to the End of the Age. The angel predicted that some of the wise would stumble, but their misfortune would continue as a test of their zeal and faith until the End of the Age.

The Jews moved from being under the control of the Syrians to being under the control of the Romans. In 70 A.D. Jerusalem and the Temple were destroyed. Those who weren't killed were scattered throughout the world. Some of the faithful have been robbed, persecuted, and killed ever since. Multitudes were burned to death

Church Age: the time the true church is on earth before the Rapture

KEY POINT

Those who are lukewarm will miss the Rapture.

☞ GO TO:

Zechariah 12:2 (reeling)

 **KEY Symbols:**

Cold
   pretenders who lack true spiritual life

Lukewarm
   indifferent or straddling the fence

Hot
   passionate about their love for Jesus

in Hitler's ovens. Today, they have their nation back, but they are a cup of <u>reeling</u> (see GWRV, page 151) for the entire world. This will continue until the Second Coming of Christ at the end of the Tribulation Period.

What Others are Saying:

David Hocking: The Antichrist is going to do all those things that Antiochus Epiphanes did. He will be crafty, and he will move into a position of great power. He is a counterfeit Christ all the way! He will break his treaty with the people of Israel and will desecrate the rebuilt Temple.[21]

☞ **GO TO:**

Daniel 7:8, 20 (boastfully)

II Thessalonians 2:3, 4 (God)

Revelation 13:1, 5, 6 (blasphemy)

Revelation 13:8 (earth)

Revelation 19:20 (fiery)

Isaiah 14:14 (like Most)

> **Daniel 11:36** "The king will do as he pleases. He will exalt and magnify himself above every god and will say unheard-of things against the God of gods. He will be successful until the time of wrath is completed, for what has been determined must take place.

The Coming Antichrist

This angelic revelation lists several characteristics of the coming Antichrist:

1) *The king will do as he pleases* speaks of his absolute authority in the world. He will be a dictator with a massive military and worldwide support. Whatever he says will be carried out.

2) *He will exalt and magnify himself above every god* speaks of his <u>boasting</u>. His heart will be filled with pride. He will boast of his abilities, achievements, and greatness.

3) *He will say unheard-of things against the <u>God</u> of gods* means he will be a <u>blasphemer</u>. His speeches will be filled with anti-God, anti-Christ, anti-Bible, anti-Christian, and anti-church rhetoric. Christians will be persecuted and killed.

4) *He will be successful until the* time of wrath *is completed* speaks of his rapid rise to power over the <u>earth</u>, and his terrible end in the <u>fiery lake</u> of burning sulfur (Lake of Fire).

5) *What has been determined must take place* means God will give him a free reign until all the prophecies are fulfilled.

Prince of Darkness: the Antichrist

KEY POINT

The Antichrist *will say unheard-of things against the God of gods.*

Grant R. Jeffrey: In total contrast to Jesus who came to "do his Father's will" the Antichrist will "do according to his own will." The coming **Prince of Darkness** will be a true child of this age of assertiveness, self-promotion, and self-will. He will exalt his own sinful desires against all opposition until he is defeated by Christ.[22]

David Hocking: It is Satan who said, "I will be <u>like the Most High</u> God." This lawless man has the same problem of setting his will against God. . . . Nobody will stand in his way. He will be honored and worshiped because of it. Self-deification is certainly the religion of our culture. . . . This lawless one is going to speak against God. . . . This will continue until God's wrath will finish him off at the end of the Tribulation Period.[23]

> **Daniel 11:37** He will show no regard for the gods of his fathers or for the one desired by women, nor will he regard any god, but will exalt himself above them all.

More About The Antichrist

Here are four more things the angel revealed to Daniel about the coming Antichrist. These are gods he will not honor:

1) *He will show no regard for the gods of his fathers* is an indication that the Antichrist will come from a pagan family. Christians and Jews believe in one God. The family of the Antichrist will believe in many gods, but their religion will be meaningless to him.

2) He will show no desire *for the one desired by women* is most often interpreted to mean no desire for the Messiah. It is well-known that the desire of all Jewish women was to be the mother of the Messiah. The Antichrist will not care anything about the Messiah. He will be anti-Christ not pro-Christ.

3) *Nor will he regard any god* means he will not worship anyone's god because *he* will sit in the Temple and declare that *he* is <u>God</u>.

4) *He will exalt himself above them all* reveals his ultimate goal—to have everyone <u>worship</u> him.

KEY Symbols:

Antichrist
absolute authority
boaster
blasphemer
rapid rise to power
will have free reign

☞ **GO TO:**

II Thessalonians 2:4 (God)

Revelation 13:4 (worship)

I Timothy 4:1–3; II Timothy 3:1–7 (prophecies)

Genesis 18:20; 19:1–13 (Sodom)

KEY Symbols:

Jesus
came to do his Father's will

Antichrist
will do according to his own will

ecumenical: *unity among religions*

KEY Symbols:

Antichrist

- *will come from a pagan family*
- *will not care about Jesus*
- *will declare that he is God*
- *will make everyone worship him*

Something to Ponder

WARNING

☞ **GO TO:**

Revelation 13:2 (power)

King James Version: *English translation of the Bible that appeared in 1611 at the authorization of King James*

J. Vernon McGee: . . . [He] will oppose all religions and worship, except worship of himself. He is not only a believer in the **ecumenical** movement, he promotes it; in fact, he is it. One religion for one world will be his motto, and he is that religion.[24]

Noah Hutchings: There is another possible explanation of this scripture. We are told in several prophecies that in the last days there would be a great increase in homosexuality. Jesus said that it would be as it was at Sodom. We are seeing this alarming rise in sexual perversion to the extent that marriages between members of the same sex are becoming quite common. The laws against homosexuality have been removed in almost every country in the world. By the time Antichrist appears, homosexuals may be considered more normal than heterosexuals. Therefore, the prophecy that the Antichrist will not regard the desire of women could simply mean that he will be a sexual pervert.[25]

The **King James Version (KJV)** of the Bible reads: *Neither shall he regard the God of his fathers.* Based on that wording a large number of people contend that the Antichrist will be a Jew. They say he will not regard the God of his father Abraham, his father Isaac, or his father Jacob. But most experts agree that the correct translation reads *the gods of his fathers* and not *the God of his fathers.* The plural word "gods" is a reference to heathen or pagan gods. The Antichrist will be a non-Christian Gentile.

The Antichrist will be involved in New Age teaching at its very worst. He will blaspheme the God of heaven and then tell people that he is God. Multitudes who will absolutely refuse to worship the Lord God Almighty will gladly worship this demon-possessed man as their god.

> **Daniel 11:38** Instead of them, he will honor a god of fortresses; a god unknown to his fathers he will honor with gold and silver, with precious stones and costly gifts.

His Chief Love

Daniel 11:37 discussed gods the Antichrist will not honor. This verse identifies what god he will honor: the god of fortresses. Fortresses are a symbol of power. The Antichrist will sell his soul for power. He will spend great wealth to acquire it and will use it to honor his god. And who is his true god? Satan.

David Hocking: *To honor a god of fortresses* means that he will place his confidence in military power. Military budgets around the world have gotten out of control. This man will not change that but justify it by the need for world domination and control. There has been discussion of a multi-national force that could dominate the world because of the sophistication of the weapons. Our whole world is being set up for this final day. We seem to think it would be wonderful to have the whole world controlled by one force with enough power to dominate the entire globe! That's the god of the Antichrist, and he will spend all kinds of treasure and "pleasant things" to bring about this power.[26]

Grant R. Jeffrey: The closing days of this age will witness an unparalleled revival of idol worship and satanic rituals involving demons. Only two decades ago such a statement would have seemed absurd. However, the rise of open worship of Satan and a growing fascination with the occult characterize our generation.[27]

Charles H. Dyer: The Antichrist will spend his money on weapons of war. His strength will come from fortresses, not from faith in God. World events will seem to vindicate this leader's faith in bombs and bullets. Daniel describes a series of coalitions that rise against the Antichrist during the seven-year period [the Tribulation Period]. But these other alliances are no match for the power of the end-time ruler.[28]

```
A teenager accused of fatally stabbing his mother
and gunning down two classmates testified . . .
that he was driven by demons who told him he
would be "nothing" if he didn't kill. A sobbing
Luke Woodham, 17, said he remembered getting a
butcher knife and seeing his mother's bloody
body—all the while his head ringing with instruc-
tions from his satanic mentor, fellow teenager
Grant Boyette. Investigators say the 19-year-old
Boyette led a cultlike group of teenagers who
plotted to kill students at Pearl High School
[Mississippi]. Several members of the group,
including Boyette, face conspiracy charges. "I
remember I woke up that morning and I'd seen
demons that I always saw when Grant told me to do
something," Woodham said.[29]
```

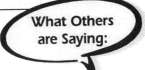

What Others are Saying:

KEY Symbols:

Fortresses
power

Antichrist
will worship the god of fortresses

RELATED CURRENT EVENTS

☞ **GO TO:**

Revelation 13:2, 4, 5, 14, 15 (given)

Daniel 11:38 (god)

II Corinthians 4:4 (world)

Daniel 11:32 (flattery)

foreign: *not the God of Israel*

> **Daniel 11:39** He will attack the mightiest fortresses with the help of a foreign god and will greatly honor those who acknowledge him. He will make them rulers over many people and will distribute the land at a price.

Satanic Power

The Antichrist will rise to power as a man of peace, but he will really be a man of war. He will seek, and be <u>given</u>, great power and authority. Then he will immediately use it to let the world know he is in control. He will quickly attack some of the strongest powers on earth with the help of a **foreign** <u>god</u> called the god of fortresses. That god is the god of the <u>world</u>—Satan.

The Antichrist will use <u>flattery</u> and bribes to procure and honor followers. He will appoint those who follow him to positions of authority over large numbers of people, and he will divide his conquered territories among those who make commitments to him.

What Others are Saying:

Balfour Declaration: *a document signed in 1917 by British Prime Minister Arthur James Balfour declaring British support for creating a Jewish homeland*

KEY Symbols:

Satan

GOD OF FORTRESSES

GOD OF THIS WORLD

Arnold G. Fruchtenbaum: The passage states that he will honor a god that his ancestors on his mother's side never honored: the god of fortresses, who is Satan. His policy will be that "might makes right." Furthermore, with the help of this foreign god, Satan, he will be able to take over the strongest defenses in the world, and he will appear totally invincible. Those who submit to his authority and deity will be increased and given positions of status and authority in his kingdom. He will divide territory he has conquered among those who will be loyal to him and confess him to be god.[30]

Grant R. Jeffrey: In his ingenious plans to reform the world's economy the Antichrist will win great popularity with his plans to redistribute the wealth of society. Early in this century the communists won initial popularity in their promises to divide the land of the rich to distribute it to the peasants. The rise of democratic socialism in Europe has prepared the masses for the promises of the coming world dictator to "divide the land for gain." A growing sense of entitlement in the citizens of the West is setting the stage for the economic system of the Antichrist.[31]

David Hocking: The Middle East was divided years ago according to the **Balfour Declaration**. It bothers me that people are now talking about dividing up the Middle East with different boundaries. The reasons are understandable—we've set up "demilitarized zones" which are vast in scope and there are troubled areas like the problem of the Kurds and Iraq. Sometimes our own government falls into the pattern of the coming Antichrist. . . . We talk in global terms as though we can influence the whole world.[32]

> **Daniel 11:40** "At the time of the end the king of the South will engage him in battle, and the king of the North will storm out against him with chariots and cavalry and a great fleet of ships. He will invade many countries and sweep through them like a flood.

The Time Of The End

At the time of the end refers to the End of the Times of the Gentiles not the end of the world. These three things will take place:

1) Up to this point the *king of the South* has always referred to Egypt. But starting with this verse it is probably referring to a four-nation Arab coalition led by Egypt. The third <u>beast</u> in Chapter 7 is such a <u>kingdom</u>. This coalition will engage the Antichrist in Battle.

2) Up to this point the *king of the North* has always referred to Syria. But starting with this verse the *king of the North* is probably a coalition of northern nations including Russia, Syria, and others. This attack on the Antichrist will probably be Russia's second attempt to take control of the Middle East by force. Almost all prophetic experts expect Russia (<u>Gog</u>, of the land of Magog) to lead a coalition of nations against Israel in the latter days of this age. But a few prophetic experts including myself expect two different Russian led invasions. The *king of the North* will use **chariots**, **cavalry**, and a large naval force.

3) The Antichrist will strike back with a great force and Satanic power. He will defeat the *kings of the North and South*, invade several Middle Eastern countries, and overwhelm them.

Jesus said, "Watch," and here are three things to watch for:
1) A coalition of nations stationing troops in the Middle East.
2) A coalition of nations in Africa.
3) A coalition of nations north of Israel.

☞ **GO TO:**

Daniel 11:35 (end)

Daniel 7:6 (beast)

Daniel 7:17 (kingdom)

Ezekiel 38:2 (Gog)

chariots: *possibly tanks*

cavalry: *possibly troops on horseback*

hegemony: *a united Arab force with one leader*

KEY Symbols:

King of the South
four-nation Arab coalition led by Egypt
possibly third beast

King of the North
coalition of northern nation including Russia, Syria, and others
possibly second beast

Remember This . . .

David Hocking: The problem is with the South and the North. When they make trouble with Israel, the Lawless One will immediately react because he has made a covenant with Israel. He will enter those countries and overwhelm them and pass through. . . . Syria and Egypt are going to go back on their promise and they are going to attack Israel.[33]

David Jeremiah with C.C. Carlson: The second player involved in the end-times battles is the *king of the North*, who includes those major powers north of Israel: Syria, Turkey, and, of course, the vast area of Russia. All evangelical conservative Bible scholars [experts] believe that the *king of the North* refers to Russia and its allies.[34]

Wallace Emerson: Again, the *king of the South* on the present chess board would seemingly have to be someone who has finally consolidated the Arab countries (possibly part of Arabic Africa) into a **hegemony** of four heads discussed in Chapter 7. This might be inferred from the mention of Egypt, Libya, and Ethiopia with other Arab countries (possibly Arabia and other North African states). . . . Who, of the possible opponents [kings of North and South], has a substantial navy? There are many small navies in the world, a few of second rank (England, France, etc.) but only two great naval powers, America and Russia. If the *kings of the North and the South* are Arab countries, they do not at present have significant navies or any in prospect, but Russia does, and Russia has identified herself closely with the Arab world.[35]

John Hagee: This is not the first time we have seen the kings of the North and the South. This time, as before, they represent a resurgent Russian Empire conspiring with a Pan-Islamic Confederation to cleanse Jerusalem and seize control of the oil of the Middle East. Though savaged in battle when they attack Israel, these kings will draw on their vast resources of men and material to field a viable fighting force once again.[36]

RELATED CURRENT EVENTS

The United States is suggesting the creation of an African Crisis Force [AFC]. This African army would be empowered to intervene in humanitarian situations throughout Africa. In support of troops from African nations, President Clinton has offered to commit as many as 10,000 American troops and to fund as much as $40 million of the AFC's annual expenses.

A multitude of experts teach that there will be a future Russian invasion of Israel. Some merge the Scriptures in Daniel 11:40–45 with those in Ezekiel 38 and 39 and teach that there will be just one invasion. Others point to several differences between the two passages and say that it will take two invasions to resolve the problems. The first invasion would be the one described in Ezekiel 38 and 39 in which Russia's army and air force would suffer a terrible defeat. The second invasion would be the one described here in Daniel 11 in which Russia's navy would be defeated. This would explain why the nations of Persia, Gomer, and Togarmah are mentioned in Ezekiel but not in Daniel and why the Antichrist is mentioned in Daniel but not in Ezekiel. The first invasion could be to plunder and loot, while the second invasion could be to oppose the Antichrist.

Something to Ponder

> **Daniel 11:41** He will also invade the Beautiful Land. Many countries will fall, but Edom, Moab, and the leaders of Ammon will be delivered from his hand.

Center Stage

The whole world will suffer at the hands of the Antichrist, but the Middle East will be the major hot spot. The Arabs will want to destroy the nation of Israel because of their ancient hatred, and because they will want to retake the Temple Mount. The Antichrist will want to occupy Israel so he can maintain a foothold in the Middle East to protect his oil supplies and be worshipped in the Temple. Other nations will want to take Israel, so they can drive the Antichrist out and seize the oil for themselves. This area will see a lot of action during the Tribulation Period.

Three things we learn in this verse:

1) *He will invade the Beautiful Land* means the Antichrist will move his military into Israel. This is consistent with Chapter 9 where we learn that he will <u>confirm</u> a <u>covenant</u> with many for seven years regarding Israel and then break it 3½ years later.

2) <u>*Many countries*</u> *will fall* signifies the defeat of several nations. This includes the *king of the North*, the *king of the*

☞ **GO TO:**

Daniel 9:27 (confirm)

Isaiah 28:14–22 (covenant)

Daniel 11:40 (many countries)

Matthew 24:16 (flee)

Jordan
a safe haven
will be delivered
- Edom
- Moab
- Ammon

South, and all their allies. They will try to drive the Antichrist out of the Middle East, but he will be too powerful for them.

3) *Edom, Moab, and the leaders of Ammon* is a reference to three areas located in the nation we call Jordan (see Illustration #2, page 19) today. The capital of Jordan is Amman, a name derived from Ammon. This area will be spared during the Tribulation Period. The ancient city of Petra is located in southern Jordan and that seems to be the place where many Jews will <u>flee</u> to during the last half of the Tribulation Period, so this may explain why these three areas are spared.

What Others are Saying:

Charles H. Dyer: I believe the invasion of *the Beautiful Land* in Daniel 11:41 is parallel to the gathering of the armies at Armageddon. The Antichrist summons an "International Task Force" to eliminate the final pockets of resistance to his domination of the world. They gather at Armageddon and move south toward Egypt and Africa.[37]

Arnold G. Fruchtenbaum: The passage states that while the Antichrist will conquer the whole world, three nations will escape his domination: Edom, Moab, and Ammon. All three of these ancient nations currently comprise the single modern state of Jordan. The city of Bozrah in Mount Seir is located in ancient Edom or southern Jordan. Since this area will escape the domination of the Antichrist, it is logical for the Jews to flee to this place.[38]

Wallace Emerson: In verse 41, Edom and Moab and the chief of Ammon will escape (i.e., the present kingdom of Transjordan which, so far at least, has been less anti-Israel than the others and, hence, might reasonably be expected to escape the consequences visited upon the others.)[39]

Something to Ponder

When the Antichrist gains control of the one-world government he will be praised, at first, as a savior, but things will turn sour. He will have to use force to hold his government together. Consider this example: At first the Moslems will like his world religion because he will tolerate everything except Christianity and Judaism. However, what do you think will happen when he demands they worship him instead of Allah? In conclusion, the Antichrist will gain control, be all-powerful, and do as he pleases, but the time will come when he does have some opposition. The only problem is that his opposition won't be strong enough to stop him.

> **Daniel 11:42** He will extend his power over many countries; Egypt will not escape.

☞ **GO TO:**

Ezekiel 29:1–16 (Egypt)

Egypt's Terrible Fate

After establishing a military presence in the land of Israel, the Antichrist will extend his power over many countries. How many countries is not said, but this is the third time we have been told this. And it is plain that God intends for Egypt to be one of the nations dominated by the Antichrist.

Today, Egypt is a target for some of the most dangerous terrorists in the world. Muslim fanatics are desperately trying to take over the government and turn Egypt into a staging ground for attacks on Israel. If they succeed, something will have to be done to protect Israel. This is not a good sign, but it is interesting to watch Bible prophecy be fulfilled.

What Others are Saying:

Arnold G. Fruchtenbaum: Ezekiel is commanded to prophesy against Egypt (verses 1–2) and predict the coming dispersion of the Egyptians from their land (verses 3–5) because of their long history of mistreatment of Israel (verses 6–7). The land of Egypt will suffer a period of total desolation (verses 8–10), which will last for forty years (verses 11–12a), and the Egyptians will be scattered all over the world like Israel was before her (verse 12b). But after the end of the period of forty years, the Egyptians will be regathered (verse 13) and brought back into their land (verse 14). Though Egypt will become a kingdom again, it will never be a powerful one (verse 15). Nor will Israel ever again be guilty of placing her confidence in Egypt (verse 16), but will trust in the Lord their God.[40]

Noah Hutchings: It is prophesied that in the last days a judgment will be visited upon Egypt and the land would be desolate and polluted for forty years. If even a dog walks over the land it will die. This has never happened to this day, and it would appear that it will occur when the Antichrist puts his hand upon Egypt. This judgment will probably be in the form of nuclear contamination from atomic bombs.[41]

☞ **GO TO:**

Exodus 20:17 (covet)

> **Daniel 11:43** He will gain control of the treasures of gold and silver and all the riches of Egypt, with the Libyans and Nubians in submission.

Riches And Power

KEY Symbols:

Antichrist
covetous
greedy
military genius

When Egypt falls the Antichrist will plunder the nation. It seems like a poor nation by the world's standards, but some of their ancient treasures are among the most valuable in the world. Articles of gold and silver have been displayed in many places around the world and, by anyone's standards, are priceless. The Antichrist will covet these articles.

However, he will not only be <u>covetous</u> and greedy but will be a military genius as well. He will want to secure his southern flank in the Middle East, so after he conquers Egypt he will move against the Libyans and Nubians (Sudan, Ethiopia, and possibly Djibouti). They will quickly surrender.

One might wonder why a loving God would allow this to happen, but there is a lot of wickedness in this area of the world and God often uses one wicked group to punish another, e.g. Libya has killed many of its own people, forced the Muslim religion on others, and tried to export revolution to other nations.

What Others are Saying:

sarcophagi: decorated stone coffins, many were used in human form with facial features

David Hocking: Some of the poorest people in the world are in Egypt; however, Egypt has enormous wealth. . . . I've seen their treasures—furniture overlaid with gold. I've seen seven **sarcophagi** filled with precious stones and gold. Some people have said that the gold of Egypt is equal to or greater than anything that has ever come out of Fort Knox, or ever will! There's so much wealth in Egypt that, since Israel nearly took them over, they buried it in the Tombs of the Bulls. That is a well-known fact. They intend to protect it at all costs! The Lawless One [the Antichrist] knows it's there, and he will have power over these treasures.[42]

Grant R. Jeffrey: The economic prosperity produced by the Satanic cunning of the Antichrist will be short-lived. In the end, everything will turn to dust in his hands. James 5:1–3 [NKJV] elaborates on this prophecy: *Come now, you rich, weep and howl for your miseries that are coming upon you! Your riches are corrupted, and your garments are moth-eaten. Your gold and silver are corroded, and their corrosion will be a witness against you and will eat your flesh like fire. You have heaped up treasure in the last days.*[43]

> **Daniel 11:44** But reports from the east and the north will alarm him, and he will set out in a great rage to destroy and annihilate many.

☞ **GO TO:**

Revelation 16:12–16 (East)

Revelation 9:14–16 (200 million)

Revelation 16:14 (world)

Revelation 19:17–21 (people)

Revelation 9:15 (one-third)

Armageddon

The Antichrist will have very little time to celebrate his impressive victories in Africa. Rumors will soon reach him that a great army is massing in the East and another is gathering in the North. Identifying the army from the East is no problem. The majority of prophecy experts agree that this is a reference to the *kings of the East* mentioned in Revelation. According to that prophecy, the Euphrates River will dry up and a <u>200 million</u> man army (China and her allies) will march into the Middle East. Identifying the *king of the North* is a problem. Russia and her allies will have suffered major defeats by this time, so we have no strong explanation other than to say this northern army will probably come from many nations around the <u>world</u> including remnants from Russia, Turkey, Syria, and Lebanon.

These armies will pose a major threat to the Antichrist. His anger will burn and he will go forth with plans to destroy these great armies. Can you imagine how many <u>people</u> will die in this battle when just one of these armies will have 200 million troops?

Grant R. Jeffrey: The eastern armies will fight as they march across Asia, <u>killing one-third</u> of humanity in their path. The final battle will center on the Valley of Jezreel [also called the Plain of Esdralon] "to a place called in Hebrew, Armageddon(see GWRV, pages 239–240)."[44]

Noah Hutchings: Today China is rapidly becoming a nation to be reckoned with. For the past thousand years, China has been a weak and impoverished nation, but here at the End of the Age it has risen up with the other nations to take its place in the pavilion of prophecy.[45]

There are some today, Yasser Arafat and the PLO, who are calling for the United Nations and/or the United States to send troops to Israel to serve as a buffer between the Israelis and their neighbors. We should be leery of any power stationing troops in that area. That is what the Antichrist will do, and it will ultimately lead to the Battle of Armageddon.

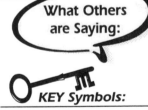

What Others are Saying:

KEY Symbols:

Kings of the East
China and her allies
200 million man army

Kings of the North
remnants of Russia and other nations

WARNING

☞ **GO TO:**

I Chronicles 11:5–8 (Jerusalem)

Revelation 19:11–16 (armies)

Revelation 19:20 (fiery lake)

> **Daniel 11:45** He will pitch his royal tents between the seas at the beautiful holy mountain. Yet he will come to his end, and no one will help him.

No More Antichrist

This identifies the place where the Antichrist will locate his military headquarters near the end of the Tribulation Period. *Between the seas* means between the Mediterranean Sea and the Dead Sea. *At the beautiful mountain* means at Jerusalem (also called Mt. Zion). *He will come to his end* is a reference to the Second Coming of Jesus with the armies (see GWRV, page 288) of heaven, the capture of the Antichrist, and the Antichrist being *thrown alive into the fiery lake of burning sulfur.*

Today there are a lot of people who have high hopes for a New World Order. They are working day and night to organize the United nations into a world government that can impose its will on every nation. They have charted an international criminal court to try national leaders and others who do not cooperate, have founded command-and-control centers for an international army to support their world government, and are looking for a great leader who can pull off all this together. They will find one, but their world government will eventually come crashing down.

What Others are Saying:

David Hocking: When Jesus comes, all these multi-national forces will be entrenched in the Middle East. The Lord Jesus will personally take them on and wipe them out![46]

David Jeremiah with C.C. Carlson: When the nations that are gathered together against Jerusalem see the Lord's armies in heaven coming after them, they will forget about the fact that they are at war with each other. They will all get together and decide that they are going to fight against the Lord. All the armies with their military leaders and advanced technology won't have a chance. After the Antichrist is captured, and the False Prophet too, the two of them will be thrown alive into the Lake of Fire.[47]

KEY Symbols:

Jerusalem
MOUNT ZION

the beautiful mountain

Wallace Emerson: The final phrase *he shall come to his end and none shall help him* [KJV] dismisses Antichrist without fanfare and almost with the wave of God's hand. He is not even given a lengthy obituary.[48]

Study Questions

1. What does this chapter teach us about the permanence of Gentile world kingdoms?
2. What do we learn about the ambition of some leaders from the constant struggles between the *kings of the North* and the *kings of the South*?
3. Contrast the beginning of the career of the Antichrist with the end of his career.
4. Where will the Antichrist get his power, and what will it take to overcome him?
5. Will the Antichrist be a man of peace or a man of war?

CHAPTER WRAP-UP

- During the reign of King Cyrus of Persia, a heavenly being appeared to Daniel and revealed that he had given Darius the Mede supernatural help when he came to power. He predicted that Cyrus would be followed by four more kings in Persia and the fourth would stir up the Persians against the Greeks. Then a Greek king (Alexander the Great) would rise to power and defeat Persia. At the height of the Greek king's power he would die, and his kingdom would be divided into four parts and given to those who were not his heirs. (Daniel 11:1–4)

- One of Alexander's generals acquired the territory north of Israel and another acquired the territory south of Israel. The Bible calls the northern power the *king of the North* and it calls the southern power the *king of the South*. These two groups fought with each other for many years. When the armies campaigned against one another they passed through Israel and the Jewish people often suffered. These two nations worshiped idols, deceived each other, made and broke several peace treaties, drew other armies into their struggles, persecuted the Jews, and often imposed their beliefs on the Jews. (Daniel 11:5–20)

- One *king of the North* was Antiochus Epiphanes, and the Bible calls him a contemptible person. He was not the rightful heir to the throne in Syria, but through deceit and cunning he managed to crown himself king. He deposed the Jewish High Priest in Israel and appointed one of his own choosing, persuaded many Jews to abandon their faith, captured most of Egypt, made and broke several peace treaties, plundered Jerusalem and the Temple, enslaved and killed thousands of Jews, outlawed the Jewish religion, and desecrated the Temple. He is a forerunner of the Antichrist because that wicked man (the Antichrist) will do many of these same things but to a greater extent. (Daniel 11:21–34)

- The vision in this chapter skips forward more than 2,000 years to a description of the coming Antichrist at the Time of the End (the End of the Age not end of the world). He will have absolute authority over his empire, be filled with pride and boasting, blaspheme God, declare that he is God, defile the Temple, honor Satan, fight many wars, conquer many people, and appoint his wicked supporters to positions of power. (Daniel 11:35–39)

- This vision describes some of the wars the Antichrist will be involved in at the End of the Age. He will send troops to the Middle East. An army from the south and another from the north will try to drive him out, but he will defeat them both. He will occupy and plunder many countries including Egypt, Ethiopia, and Sudan, but not Jordan. Two other great armies will be organized to attack him: an unidentified army from the north and a great army from the east (China and her allies). Jesus will come to stop them from destroying the whole earth, and when he does they will settle their differences, join forces, and attack Jesus at the Battle of Armageddon. In the end the Antichrist will be captured and destroyed. (Daniel 11:40–45)

GOD'S WORD FOR THE BIBLICALLY-INEPT

DANIEL 12

CHAPTER HIGHLIGHTS

- Time of the End
- Some Good News
- Seal the Words
- Extra Days
- Go Your Way

Let's Get Started

This book begins with the fall of <u>Jerusalem</u> and Israel, and ends with the restoration of Israel and the beginning of the Millennium. The entire book spans the time between the beginning of the Times of the Gentiles and the End of the Times of the Gentiles (see Time Line #2, Appendix A). Israel is God's clock that signals the Time of the End. The Jews have suffered many things and will suffer more things in the future, but their return to the land is an indication that the end of their problems is in sight.

Chapter 12 concludes the Vision of the Anointed One that began in Chapter 10. It is a vision about what will happen to the nation of Israel. It concerns a time *in the future* which we know is the *Time of the End* or the End of the Times of the Gentiles, not the end of the world.

☞ **GO TO:**

Daniel 1:1 (Jerusalem)

Daniel 10:14 (future)

Daniel 11:40 (End)

Isaiah 66:8 (nation)

David Hocking: In 586 B.C., the Babylonians destroyed Jerusalem. . . . They took a lot of people captive and things haven't looked good for them since. The Jews have been crying for that land for a long time. In 1948, hope came into the Jewish breast as David Ben Gurion announced that a <u>nation</u> called Israel had been born. . . . The Jews started returning in larger numbers than they had throughout history at the turn of this century under the leadership of Theodore Hertzl. The Balfour Declaration which Britain gave in 1914 encouraged the Jews, but it wasn't until 1948 that Israel became a nation. The Time of the End requires that Israel be in the land.[1]

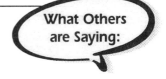

What Others are Saying:

☞ **GO TO:**

Daniel 11:35, 45 (End)

Daniel 10:13, 21 (Michael)

Jude 1:9 (archangel)

Daniel 10:13 (Persia)

Revelation 6–16 (judgments)

Zechariah 13:8 (one-third)

Exodus 32:33; Revelation 3:4, 5; 20:12–15; 21:27 (book)

Jeremiah 30:7 KJV (Jacob's Trouble)

Michael: *who is like unto God*

Lamb's Book of Life: *contains the names of everyone who truly accepts Jesus as their Savior*

Auschwitz: *a famous WW II German concentration camp*

> **Daniel 12:1** "At that time Michael, the great prince who protects your people, will arise. There will be a time of distress such as has not happened from the beginning of nations until then. But at that time your people—everyone whose name is found written in the book—will be delivered.

The Time Of The End

This verse makes several points:

1) *At that time* identifies the time we are dealing with. It takes us back to the events in the closing verses of Chapter 11 where we were studying *the Time of the End*.

2) *Michael the great prince* is **Michael** the archangel. He is the powerful angel who helped Gabriel overcome the prince of Persia and who will help cast Satan out of heaven (see GWRV, pages 175–176). His name means "who is like unto God." He may be the most powerful angel in heaven.

3) *Who protects your people* identifies Michael's main responsibility. It is to protect Daniel's people (the nation of Israel). There have been many attempts to eliminate them but it is Michael's responsibility to prevent that.

4) *Will arise* means Michael will intercede on behalf of Israel and exercise his protective powers over the nation. He will act like a sentry and make sure nothing destroys the people of Israel. Those who do attack Israel will be challenging one of the most powerful spiritual forces in heaven.

5) *A time of distress* is another name for the Tribulation Period. Jesus was talking about that time when he said, *there will be great distress, unequaled from the beginning of the world until now—and never to be equaled again. If those days had not been cut short, no one would survive, but for the sake of the elect those days will be shortened* (Matthew 24:21,22) The distress will include all the seal, trumpet and bowl judgments (see GWRV, Time Line #2, Appendix A) prophesied in Revelation.

6) *Delivered* refers to a specific group of people who will survive the Tribulation Period. In the whole land of Israel two-thirds of the Jews will perish, but one-third will be delivered.

7) *The book*, called the **Lamb's Book of Life** (see GWRV,

pages 48, 302–303), contains the names of those Jews who are faithful to God. Everyone whose name is on this list will survive the Trbulation Period.

Oliver B. Greene: It seems that the work of Michael is to deliver God's people—particularly the children of Israel—from the power of the archenemy, the devil. In the battle which he finally leads against the devil and his angels in the heavenlies, Michael will be victorious and will cast the devil down to earth.[2]

What Others are Saying:

Wallace Emerson: This is the Time of Jacob's Trouble. But we ask ourselves, how, with all that Jacob has already gone through, could there be any greater trouble? How could anything exceed the extermination camps of **Auschwitz**? Still, this is the greater tribulation that shall come upon all the earth and equally upon Israel.[3]

KEY Symbols:

Tribulation Period
a time of distress

David Hocking: Many years ago, I was in private conversation with Prime Minister Menachem Begin [of Israel], and we were discussing prophecy. He asked me if I believed the evangelical argument about the Tribulation Period. I said I did (and do), and then he asked if I believed that Israel was going to be persecuted. Then, he asked how I could believe that when 6 million of their people had been killed under Hitler. I expressed my sorrow about it, but I said that I did not believe that the Holocaust was a fulfillment of that prophecy. Then I asked what he believed. He said, "I hope you're not right, but more and more, I think you are."[4]

KEY Symbols:

Michael (archangel)
protects Israel
overcame the prince of Persia
will help cast Satan out of heaven

The names of the Tribulation Period reveal clues about the terrible events to come.

Remember This . . .

Isaiah 34:8	A day of vengeance
Jeremiah 30:7	A time of trouble for Jacob (Israel)
Daniel 9:24–27	The seventieth-week
Zephaniah 1:14–16	The great day of the Lord
	A day of wrath
	A day of distress and anguish
	A day of trouble and ruin
	A day of darkness and gloom
	A day of clouds and blackness
	A day of trumpet and battle cry

☞ **GO TO:**

Revelation 20:4–6
(thousand)

Matthew 27:52, 53
(Saints)

Matthew 27:32–50
(Crucifixion)

Revelation 11:3–12
(Two Witnesses)

Matthew 27:52, 53
(raised)

Revelation 20:11–15
(Great White Throne)

KEY Symbols:

First Resurrection
Resurrection of Life
(believers in 4 phases)

Second Resurrection
Resurrection of
Damnation
(unbelievers in 1 phase)

Old Testament Saints: *true*
believers in God who lived
before the death of Christ

Crucifixion: *the execution*
of Jesus Christ on the cross

Two Witnesses: *two*
powerful men of God who
will preach during the
Tribulation Period

everlasting life: *eternal or*
unending life

> **Daniel 12:2** Multitudes who sleep in the dust of the earth will awake: some to everlasting life, others to shame and everlasting contempt.

Some Good News

Most of what we have read about the Time of the End has been bad news, but there is also a lot of good news. One promising event will be the resurrection of the dead. A study of the subject reveals that there will be two resurrections (see Time Line #4, Appendix A). Jesus said, *Do not be amazed at this, for a time is coming when all who are in the graves will hear his voice and come out—those who have done good will rise to live, and those who have done evil will rise to be condemned* (John 5:28,29). The first resurrection is called the Resurrection of Life; the second is called the Resurrection of Damnation. The first is a Resurrection of *believers*; the second is a resurrection of *unbelievers*. Revelation teaches that the Millennium, a thousand year period, will be between the two. Also, Scripture reveals that the first resurrection will have four phases while the second resurrection will have just one.

First Resurrection (Resurrection of Life)

Phase 1—Resurrection of Jesus and some **Old Testament Saints** three days after the **Crucifixion**

Phase 2—Resurrection of the Church at the Rapture before the Tribulation Period

Phase 3—Resurrection of the **Two Witnesses** near the Tribulation Period mid-point

Phase 4—Resurrection of the Tribulation Saints and the remainder of the Old Testament Saints at the end of the Tribulation Period

Second Resurrection (Resurrection of Damnation)

Phase 1—Resurrection of all unbelievers at the end of the Millennium

In this verse the angel is discussing the resurrection of the Jews. The resurrection of the Gentiles is not being considered. A few of the Jewish believers were **raised to everlasting life** when Jesus was raised. The other Jewish believers will be raised to everlasting life when the Tribulation Period is over. All unbelieving Jews will be raised a thousand years later in the Second Resurrection.

Others to shame and everlasting contempt is a reference to the **Great White Throne Judgment** (see GWRV, pages 301–304). The names of the unbelievers (those who did not accepted Jesus as the Messiah) have not been placed in the Lamb's Book of Life. When they are raised they will stand before the **judgment seat** of God and be cast into the Lake of Fire where they will suffer everlasting punishment.

Will the Jews be resurrected?

Messianic Jews (those who accept Christ) are Christians that will be resurrected in Phase 2. The Old Testament Saints are believing Israel in the Old Testament and some were resurrected in Phase 1 along with Christ. Other Old Testament Saints will be resurrected with the Tribulation Saints—both Jews and Gentiles who accept Christ after the Rapture. Some believing Jews will flee to Petra during the Tribulation Period and will not be killed, but instead will live on earth into the Millenium.

J. Vernon McGee: When the Church is raptured out of the world, the Old Testament Saints will not yet be raised. Why? Because the time to enter the kingdom is at the end of the Great Tribulation Period when Christ comes to establish his kingdom here on the earth. Then the Old Testament Saints will be raised.[5]

Noah Hutchings: The resurrection of the Church is not in view here because the Rapture of the Church will have already occurred. There is no evidence that the Church will go through the Tribulation. Every saved person of the **dispensation of grace** will be resurrected before the Tribulation begins. Daniel was not concerned about the Gentiles; he was concerned only about his people. The resurrection described by the Lord in this scripture relates only to Israel.[6]

> **Daniel 12:3** Those who are wise will shine like the brightness of the heavens, and those who lead many to righteousness, like the stars for ever and ever.

A Promise To Soul Winners

Wisdom comes from God. Fools despise it, but the wise seek it. *Those who are wise* in this verse are those who lead people to Christ during the Time of the End. This is true for the Church today, but it will be especially true of those who witness during the difficult days of the Tribulation Period. During the Tribulation, many believers will be put to death because of the Word of God and the testimony they

Great White Throne Judgment: the judgment of the unsaved

judgment seat: the throne God will sit on when he judges unbelievers

Remember This . . .

What Others are Saying:

dispensation of grace: the time the true Church is on earth before the Rapture (the Church Age)

☞ **GO TO:**

James 1:5 (wisdom)

Proverbs 1:7 (despise)

Matthew 24:9 (death)

Revelation 6:9 (testimony)

Ephesians 2:8–10 (saved)

Matthew 25:31–40 (those in need)

maintain. They will accept Christ, be <u>saved</u>, and lead others to Christ. They will help <u>those in need</u> at the cost of their lives.

These wise believers are going to shine with a brightness *like the brightness of the heavens*, and the believers who lead others to Christ will shine *like the stars*.

What Others are Saying:

David Jeremiah with C.C. Carlson: God says that during that time of awful trouble on the Jewish nation, he is going to raise up some who are going to be teachers of righteousness. Can you imagine what it will cost a person to stand up in the Tribulation Period with a Bible in hand and declare the righteousness of God? Those people know that when they teach the truth of God, their heads could roll at any moment. There is a special place in God's kingdom for those who accurately teach God's Holy Book.[7]

☞ **GO TO: 12:4**

Matthew 5:18 (disappear)

expositions: explanations

> **Daniel 12:4** But you, Daniel, close up and seal the words of the scroll until the time of the end. Many will go here and there to increase knowledge."

Seal The Book Until . . .

Daniel was told to close and seal the Book of Daniel until the Time of the End which probably means to preserve the book and its prophecies until the End of the Age. And since Daniel couldn't do that himself it means this book's messages are divinely protected by God. Not one word will <u>disappear</u> until everything is fulfilled. It also means that some of these things cannot be understood until then, but the word *until* implies that the time will come when these things can be understood.

Some experts say *go here and there* refers to rapid travel, and *increase knowledge* refers to an explosion of knowledge. They cite how man has progressed from traveling 30 mph by horse in Daniel's day to traveling several hundred mph by airplane today. And how it took about 1,700 years for knowledge to double after the death of Christ, but now with computers, the internet, etc., it doubles in under two years. But while knowledge and speed of travel have increased many people still will be perplexed by what is happening at the Time of the End, and they will be searching for answers. Fortunately, many will search in the Word of God and knowledge of Bible prophecy will greatly increase.

What Others are Saying:

Jack Van Impe: Isn't it strange that **expositions** of this book were not attempted until recent times? No expositor made any published attempt to explain Daniel, verse by verse, until the twentieth century.[8]

Charles H. Dyer: As the "Time of the End" draws closer, we should expect to see our understanding of Bible prophecy increase. World events will finally begin to line up more precisely with events predicted in the Bible. When the morning newspaper and the evening news start sounding more like the words of Daniel, Jesus, or the Apostle John, our "prophetic blinders" will be removed. God does predict the future, and his prophecies will all begin to make sense to us when world events parallel the predictions found in the Bible.[9]

David Jeremiah with C.C. Carlson: I am convinced that in the Great Tribulation the Book of Daniel will be the most important reading matter for many people. Imagine some innocent person who doesn't know a great deal about the Word of God, cast into the midst of hell on earth. He says, "Can somebody tell me what's going on?" Someone says, "Let me give you this book. It's the writing of an old sage by the name of Daniel."[10]

> **Daniel 12:5** Then I, Daniel, looked, and there before me stood two others, one on this bank of the river and one on the opposite bank.

Two Heavenly Beings

At the beginning of this vision we learned that Daniel was standing on the bank of the <u>Tigris</u> River (see Illustration #2, page 19). Now we learn that he saw two "heavenly beings"—one on each side of the river. It is not said, but in all likelihood they were angels.

> **Daniel 12:6** One of them said to the man clothed in linen, who was above the waters of the river, "How long will it be before these astonishing things are fulfilled?"

A Question For Jesus

When this vision began we learned that Daniel saw someone dressed in <u>linen</u>. From Daniel's description and other Scriptures we concluded that Daniel saw Jesus. Then <u>two</u> heavenly beings appeared and asked

☞ **GO TO: 12:5**

Daniel 10:4 (Tigris)

KEY Symbols:

Two Heavenly Beings
  angels
Man Clothed in Linen
  Jesus

☞ **GO TO: 12:6**

Daniel 10:5 (linen)

Daniel 12:5 (two)

fulfilled: *take place or happen*

Jesus a question that many want answered: *How long will it be before these astonishing things are **fulfilled**?*

Care must be taken to fully understand what exactly was asked. The question is not "How long will it be until the Time of the End" but "how long will it take for these things to be fulfilled at the Time of the End?"

Noah Hutchings: They [the angels] asked the Lord in the vision given to Daniel how long it would take for the prophecies concerning the time of trouble [the Tribulation Period] referred to in verse one of the twelfth chapter to be fulfilled.[11]

David Jeremiah with C.C. Carlson: Daniel was still by the bank of the Tigris, receiving his last vision from the angel, when he looked up and saw two angels, one on each side of the river. He must have blinked his eyes and looked again, because hovering over the river was a man clothed in linen. I personally believe this was the Son of God. The angels began to ask questions that Daniel probably wanted to ask. One said, "How long will it be before these astonishing things are fulfilled?"[12]

KEY POINT

Israel will not be delivered until they decide to stop trusting in themselves and start trusting in their Messiah, the Lord Jesus Christ.

☞ **GO TO: 12:7**

Revelation 10:5, 6 (forever)

Daniel 7:25 (time)

Revelation 13:5 (42 months)

Zechariah 14:2, 3 (Jerusalem)

> **Daniel 12:7** The man clothed in linen, who was above the waters of the river, lifted his right hand and his left hand toward heaven, and I heard him swear by him who lives forever, saying, "It will be for a time, times, and half a time. When the power of the holy people has been finally broken, all these things will be completed."

Jesus Takes An Oath

A person usually raises one hand to take an oath, but Jesus raised both hands. Raising one hand in a court of law symbolizes the veracity and significance of a witness's words, but here Jesus raised both hands as if to say, "my answer is *doubly* significant." It was a way of stressing the certainty of his words. He then took an oath and, because he could swear by none higher, swore by God who lives <u>forever</u>.

His answer, *a <u>time</u>, times, and a half a time*, is explained in Daniel 4:16 to be three and one-half years. Specifically, it is the *last* three and one-half years (<u>42 months</u> or 1,260 days) of the Tribulation Period. During that time <u>Jerusalem</u> will be turned over to the Antichrist, the Temple will be desolate, the Jewish people will turn to Jesus as their Messiah, and all of the prophecies will be fulfilled.

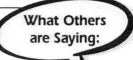
Grant R. Jeffrey: The Hebrew phrase *a time, times, and half a time* indicates 1,260 days [see Time Line #3, Appendix A] because a *time* equals a year of 360 days, *times* equals two years, and *half a time* equals half a year of 180 days. Daniel therefore describes a *time, times, and half a time,* as a period of precisely 1,260 days for the duration of Antichrist's power over the Tribulation Saints of God. This period of 1,260 days is the last three and one-half years of the seven-year treaty period (Daniel's Seventieth-Week of years).[13]

David Hocking: The Israeli air force is well-prepared. All of their armaments and their capability is phenomenal. Their dedication is greater than ours because it is an issue of survival. Still, they are no match for the global strategy that is now gathering against them. They are no match at all. What's going to happen? "The power of the holy people is going to be shattered." I don't want to say that to Israel, but we have to be faithful to the Word of God. Their confidence must be in the Lord.[14]

> **Daniel 12:8** I heard, but I did not understand. So I asked, "My lord, what will the outcome of all this be?"

☞ **GO TO: 12:8**

Daniel 9:2 (Scriptures)

I Just Don't Get It

Daniel was a highly educated man who studied the <u>Scriptures</u>. He even admitted that he heard what Jesus said. But he confessed that he did not understand it, so he asked Jesus to tell him more.

> **Daniel 12:9** He replied, "Go your way, Daniel, because the words are closed up and sealed until the time of the end.

☞ **GO TO: 12:9**

Daniel 12:4 (sealed)

Divinity: *the Divine nature of the message (that it came from God)*

Don't Worry About It

Daniel asked for more information, but Jesus did not provide it. Jesus could have explained the vision but gently told Daniel to go about his business because the words of the vision are *closed up and <u>sealed</u>.* People may understand some of it as the Time of the End approaches, but not everything will be fully understood until the last three and one-half years of the Tribulation Period arrive.

Oliver B. Greene: In other words, "Daniel, you have seen, you have heard, and you have obeyed. You have penned down the words. Now close the book, seal it up—and do not worry or fret about it. This vision is for the Time of the End.[15]

David Jeremiah with C.C. Carlson: God told Daniel that he was not going to give him any more information. He said, "Look, Daniel there's no time for idle preoccupation in the prophetic realm." How that word is needed today! There are many who are making megabucks in the prophetic world, saying that the Rapture will happen at a certain time, or before the year 2,000. The truth is, we don't know. Many people are led astray by all the craziness of date setting. We don't want to get caught in that trap.[16]

The Pulpit Commentary: This is a refusal to grant Daniel's prayer, but in the refusal no condemnation of Daniel is implied. The oracles were sealed until circumstance broke the seal. The purpose of prophecy was not to enable men to write history beforehand. It is to be a sign that, recognized in its fulfillment, may afford evidence of the **Divinity** of the message or person to whom it referred.[17]

☞ **GO TO: 12:10**

Zechariah 13:8, 9 (refined)

Revelation 6:9–11 (Word)

Revelation 7:4–14 (144,000)

Revelation 11:3 (Two)

Revelation 14:6 (angel)

II Timothy 3:13 (bad)

II Thessalonians 2:9, 10 (deceive)

II Corinthians 4:4 (blind)

Matthew 24:24 (possible)

> **Daniel 12:10** Many will be purified, made spotless and refined, but the wicked will continue to be wicked. None of the wicked will understand, but those who are wise will understand.

A Great Separation

Jesus told Daniel that many will be **saved** and **refined** at the Time of the End. One-third of the Jews and multitudes of Gentiles will believe the Word of God and accept Jesus as their Messiah. The world can expect some great revivals during the Tribulation Period; the 144,000 Jewish **evangelists** (see GWRV, pages 108–111, 205–209), the Two Witnesses, and God's angel will reach multitudes for Christ.

However, the wicked will continue in their sin. The Apostle Paul even said they will go from bad to worse. This verse indicates a great separation with multitudes being saved and living holy lives, while the remainder of society becomes more immoral and violent. Satan will deceive the wicked, so that none of them will understand what is going on. They will be blind to the realization that it is the Time of the End. But it will not be possible to deceive the wise. They will understand and put their faith in Jesus.

Oliver B. Greene: Those whose "eyes of understanding" have been opened by the Holy Spirit see the End of this Age approaching; but the wicked who are blinded by "the God of this Age" [Satan] see nothing about which to be alarmed. They live as though they plan to stay here forever. They have no time for God, and no desire to prepare to meet him. Things will continually grow worse as the end approaches.[18]

M.R. DeHaan: What it really means is that the wicked shall do more wicked[ness], because they do not understand. They do not know the program, they do not know what God is doing, they do not believe that the end is near; somehow they feel that they are going to pull themselves up by their bootstraps, that everything is going to come out all right, that finally man will learn his lesson and bring in the man-made **Utopian millennium** of peace. They are deluded by Satan who has blinded their eyes. . . .[19]

> **Daniel 12:11** "From the time that the daily sacrifice is abolished and the abomination that causes desolation is set up, there will be 1,290 days.

An Extra 30 Days

We recall that Jesus lifted his hands and took an oath that the last half of the Tribulation Period would last three and one-half years or 1,260 days. We also remember that the angel Gabriel told Daniel that the last half of the Tribulation Period would begin when the Abomination of Desolation is set up on the wing of the Temple. From this we can calculate that there will be 1,260 days from the Tribulation Period mid-point to the Second Coming of Jesus. The Antichrist will rule during those years and then be cast into the Lake of Fire. But the Abomination of Desolation (Image of the Beast) will remain for an extra 30 days (1,260 days + 30 days = 1,290) before being destroyed. Why it will be permitted to exist for those 30 days is not said. It seems to be one of those sealed things, but here are three possibilities:

1) It will take time to rid the earth of the Antichrist's impact.
2) It will take time to gather the **elect** and assemble them in Israel.
3) There will be a period of grace before judgment (see next verse).

What Others are Saying:

saved: *to receive eternal life and the forgiveness of sins*

refined: *their ways will be made perfect*

evangelist: *one who declares the true Word of God*

Utopian millennium: *perfect society for 1,000 years*

☞ **GO TO: 12:11**

Daniel 12:7 (lifted)

Daniel 9:27 (Abomination)

Revelation 19:20 (Lake)

Daniel 12:4, 9 (seal)

Mark 13:26, 27 (elect)

elect: *Jews who follow God; his chosen people*

What Others are Saying:

J. Vernon McGee: For 1,290 days the idol of the Beast remains in the Temple. Actually, this is thirty days beyond the three and one-half years. The last half of the Great Tribulation is 1,260 days, and for some unexplained reason the image of Antichrist will be permitted to remain 30 days after Antichrist himself has been cast into the Lake of Fire.[20]

Noah Hutchings: From the time Antichrist stands in the Temple and declares himself to be God, to the restoration of Israel to the land would be twelve hundred ninety days—an extra month, or thirty days. Although we do not know for sure, we assume an extra thirty days will be required to regather the Jews. The angels are to go into all the nations of the world and bring back all the twelve tribes to Palestine. There will not be an Israelite left in any Gentile nation.[21]

☞ **GO TO: 12:12**

Matthew 25:31–46 (nations)

Daniel 12:8 (heard)

> **Daniel 12:12** Blessed is the one who waits for and reaches the end of the 1,335 days.

45 More Days

Here a period of 45 days is mentioned and again Jesus did not explain. Most experts realize that the reason is sealed, but a few speculate on the matter because people want to know. Just remember that any answer is conjecture.

However, the verse does add to what we know. Something will happen at the end of the 45 days that will be a blessing to everyone who reaches the end of it. This implies that not everyone will make it. It is my opinion that this 45 day period is when Jesus will judge the nations. Some will be blessed with the privilege of entering the Millennium, while others will be cursed and sent to eternal punishment.

interlude: an interval or period of time

Messianic Kingdom: the Millennial kingdom when Christ will reign on earth

What Others are Saying:

Noah Hutchings: The extra forty-five days will be required for the judgment of Israel and the giving of rewards to the righteous and redeemed.[22]

Marriage Supper of the Lamb: a feast on earth attended by Jesus

Arnold G. Fruchtenbaum: Those who manage to make it to the 1,335th day are promised a unique blessing which could hardly be anything else but the Millennium. That many will not make it to this day is clear from other Scriptures, since they are killed in the **interlude**.[23]

Oliver B. Greene: If God had wanted us to know the full meaning of the 1,290 days and the 1,335 days, he would have made it known—either here, or in some other place in the Bible. These days have nothing to do with the Rapture of the Church, nor with the saints who make up the Church; and at the appointed time, God will reveal to wise men exactly the meaning of these days.[24]

David Hocking: This may be the setting up of the **Messianic Kingdom** with Jesus Christ ruling in Jerusalem. There are many topographical changes that will take place. A Millennial Temple will be established even though it won't take the Lord any time at all to build it. The Dead Sea will be changed so that fish will live in it. . . . Revelation 19 talks about the "**Marriage Supper of the Lamb**" (see GWRV, pages 283–284) also. It's possible that the blessing "on he who waits" is the Marriage Supper of the Lamb which could easily last 45 days or longer.[25]

David Jeremiah with C.C. Carlson: I have some sanctified guesses, but I do not believe it's wise scholarship to theorize. It's not hard for me to understand why Daniel said, *I heard, but I did not understand.*[26]

☞ **GO TO: 12:13**

Daniel 12:9 (Go your way)

Hebrews 9:27 (die)

Daniel 12:2 (awake)

> **Daniel 12:13** "As for you, go your way till the end. You will rest, and then at the end of the days you will rise to receive your allotted inheritance."

Some Final Advice For Daniel

Jesus ended the vision without answering Daniel's question, but these closing remarks are very important. Here are 5 points:

1) *Go your way* means continue on with your life. Don't worry about these things; trust Jesus and be faithful.

2) *You will rest* probably refers to Daniel's death. Unless a person leaves in the Rapture that person is destined to <u>die</u>.

3) *At the end of the days* can mean several things: at the end of the Tribulation Period, at the end of the 1,290 days, or at the end of the 1,335 days. It probably means the 1,335 days.

4) *You will arise* refers to the time when multitudes will <u>awake</u> or arise from the dead. This multitude here in-

cludes the Old Testament Saints and the Tribulation Saints (Resurrection of Life).

5) *To receive your allotted inheritance* means to take possession of your rewards. Daniel, no doubt, will receive many rewards.

resurrection morning: *when Christians are raised from the dead*

Redeemer and King: *other names for Jesus*

David Hocking: One other possibility about the promise of blessing is that the resurrection doesn't take place until the end of 1,335 days. When we read those last two verses, we read Daniel will "arise to his inheritance" at the end of the 1,335 days. So, perhaps the resurrection of Old Testament Saints comes at that time.[27]

David Jeremiah with C.C. Carlson: Daniel's long, strange, wonderful journey was about to end. No more would he be the target for cruel, jealous office seekers. He had seen the last of the den of hungry lions. His righteous soul would cease to be plagued by the sins of Jew or Gentile. Daniel would rest and await the resurrection morning, when he will be richly rewarded by his wonderful Redeemer and King.[28]

Study Questions

1) What are some of the good things that will happen at the Time of the End?
2) What are some of the bad things that will happen at the Time of the End?
3) What indication do we have that heaven and hell actually exist?
4) What are the three time periods mentioned in this chapter? When will the Tribulation Period end and when will the Millennium begin?
5) What did Jesus say would happen to Daniel?

CHAPTER WRAP-UP

- Chapter 12 concerns what will happen to Israel at the Time of the End or the End of the Times of the Gentiles, not the end of the world. Michael the archangel is assigned to protect Israel and he will be careful to intercede for Israel against her enemies. The Tribulation Period will be a time of great trouble; a time worse than anything that has happened before, but the saved of Israel will be delivered. (Daniel 12:1)

- Much of the Tribulation Period is bad news, but there is also good news. One good thing is the resurrection of the Jewish believers. The unbelievers, however, will be raised to shame and everlasting contempt in the Resurrection of Damnation, while the believers will be raised to everlasting life in the fourth phase of the Resurrection of Life. Those who led others to Christ during the Tribulation Period will shine with the brightness or glory of Christ. (Daniel 12:2, 3)

- Daniel was twice told to close up and seal the words of this prophecy until the Time of the End. These prophecies will be divinely preserved and protected until then, and some prophecies will not be understood until then. When the Time of the End arrives two things will take place: a) people will be perplexed by world events, and b) many will study Bible prophecy causing an explosion in prophetic knowledge. (Daniel 12:4, 9)

- Jesus appeared and took an oath that the last half of the Tribulation Period would last for three and one-half years or 1,260 days. During that terrible time the wicked will be confused and grow worse, but multitudes will understand the Tribulation events and be saved. After the Tribulation Period there will be two brief periods of time, one of 30 days and another of 45 days. The purpose is not revealed, but it probably concerns the judgment of the nations and preparations for the Millennium. (Daniel 12:5–7; 10–12)

- Daniel was told to go his way twice in this chapter which was a way of telling him to be at peace, trust Christ, and continue his course. He was also told he would die but would be raised to receive an inheritance at the Time of the End. (Daniel 12:9, 13)

APPENDIX A — TIME LINES

Time Line #1

THE LIFE OF DANIEL

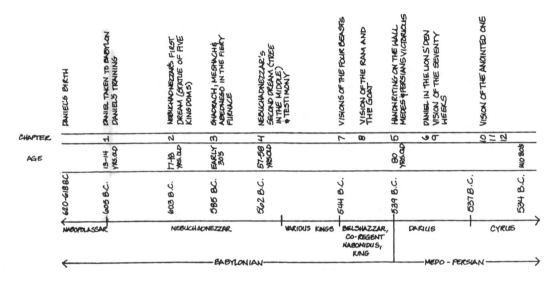

Time Line #2

THE TIMES OF THE GENTILES *

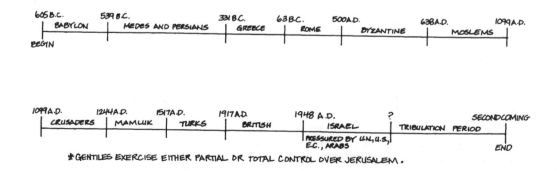

* GENTILES EXERCISE EITHER PARTIAL OR TOTAL CONTROL OVER JERUSALEM.

Time Line #3

DANIEL'S SEVENTY WEEKS / SEVENTY SEVENS

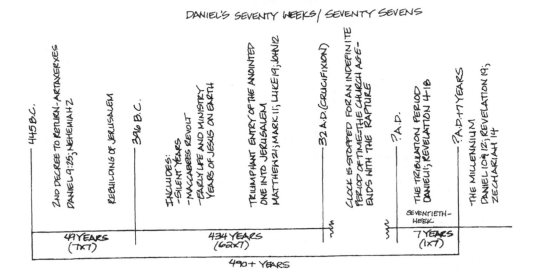

445 B.C.

2ND DECREE TO RETURN - ARTAXERXES
DANIEL 9:25; NEHEMIAH 2

REBUILDING OF JERUSALEM

396 B.C.

INCLUDES:
-SILENT YEARS
-MACCABEES REVOLT
-EARLY LIFE AND MINISTRY
 YEARS OF JESUS ON EARTH

TRIUMPHANT ENTRY OF THE ANOINTED
ONE INTO JERUSALEM
MATTHEW 21; MARK 11; LUKE 19; JOHN 12

32 A.D. (CRUCIFIXION)

CLOCK IS STOPPED FOR AN INDEFINITE
PERIOD OF TIME - THE CHURCH AGE-
ENDS WITH THE RAPTURE

? A.D.

THE TRIBULATION PERIOD
DANIEL 9; REVELATION 4-18

SEVENTIETH-WEEK

? A.D.+7 YEARS

THE MILLENNIUM
DANIEL 10 & 12; REVELATION 19;
ZECHARIAH 14

| 49 YEARS (7X7) | 434 YEARS (62X7) | | 7 YEARS (1X7) | |

490+ YEARS

Time Line #4

THE TWO RESURRECTIONS
1st-RESURRECTION OF LIFE / 2nd-RESURRECTION OF DAMNATION
(BELIEVERS & UNBELIEVERS - JOHN 5:28-29)

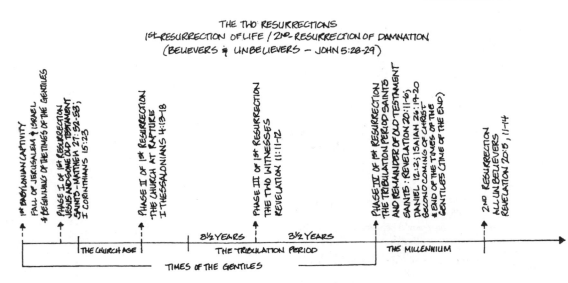

1ST BABYLONIAN CAPTIVITY

FALL OF JERUSALEM & ISRAEL
& BEGINNING OF THE TIMES OF THE GENTILES

PHASE I OF 1ST RESURRECTION
JESUS AND SOME OLD TESTAMENT
SAINTS - MATTHEW 27:52-53;
I CORINTHIANS 15:23

PHASE II OF 1ST RESURRECTION
THE CHURCH AT RAPTURE
I THESSALONIANS 4:13-18

PHASE III OF 1ST RESURRECTION
THE TWO WITNESSES
REVELATION 11:11-12

PHASE IV OF 1ST RESURRECTION
THE TRIBULATION PERIOD SAINTS
AND REMAINDER OF OLD TESTAMENT
SAINTS: REVELATION 20:11-6;
DANIEL 12:1-3; ISAIAH 26:19-20
SECOND COMING OF CHRIST
& END OF THE TIMES OF THE
GENTILES (TIME OF THE END)

2ND RESURRECTION
ALL UNBELIEVERS
REVELATION 20:5, 11-14

THE CHURCH AGE

3½ YEARS   3½ YEARS

THE TRIBULATION PERIOD

THE MILLENNIUM

TIMES OF THE GENTILES

APPENDIX B — THE ANSWERS

CHAPTER ONE

1. God delivered Jerusalem into the hands of her enemy. He used a pagan king, Nebuchadnezzar, to defeat the Jews. (Daniel 1:1, 2)
2. He changed Daniel's country, name, status, residence, language, and school, but he could not change Daniel's allegiance to his God. (Daniel 1:8)
3. Ashpenaz was afraid of Nebuchadnezzar, so he thought the king might kill him for disobedience if Daniel was unhealthy. (Daniel 1:10)
4. His request for a ten day test shows that he was willing to trust the outcome to God. (Daniel 1:12)
5. They were healthier, better nourished, wiser, and more intelligent than anyone else in Babylon. (Daniel 1:15, 20)

CHAPTER TWO

1. He suspected they were guilty of conspiracy and lying. (Daniel 2:9)
2. Instead of depending upon God, they were depending on man's ability to get messages from the stars, moon, and spirits which, of course, failed them. (Daniel 2:10)
3. The six steps were to ask for permission to speak, request for time, tell his friends, ask them to pray with him, pray, and praise God. (Daniel 2:16–19)
4. The God of heaven. He is the God of gods and the Lord of kings. (Daniel 2:44, 47)
5. Each person will have to decide. But most commentators say "no" because he called Daniel's God "your God" not "my God." (Daniel 2:47)

CHAPTER THREE

1. Probably anti-Semitism. It is bad because people should not be persecuted for refusing the religion of those in power. We should oppose those who want to force people to worship their way. (Daniel 3:8, 12)
2. He said to worship the image or be cast into a blazing furnace. Multitudes will have to make this choice during the Tribulation Period. Revelation teaches that those who do not worship the image will be killed and those who do will be cast into the Lake of Fire. (Daniel 3:11)
3. No. They were not sure they would be rescued. But just like Daniel did earlier, they had resolved not to defile themselves. Our commitments to God should be kept no matter what. (Daniel 3:18)
4. He saw four men walking around in the fire. They were unharmed. One of them appeared out of nowhere and was like a *son of the gods*. He asked the three Jews to come out. (Daniel 3:25, 26)
5. No one could say anything against the God of Shadrach, Meshach, and Abednego. If they did they would be cut to pieces and their houses would be destroyed. Free speech and freedom of worship were not allowed by this one-world leader. (Daniel 3:29)

CHAPTER FOUR

1. Daniel had the spirit of God in him. (Daniel 4:9, also see Daniel 1:17, 20)
2. A messenger who was one of the holy ones, probably angels, from heaven. Mercifully, he left the stump, preserved it, and limited Nebuchadnezzar's affliction to seven years. (Daniel 4:14–16)
3. That the Most High is sovereign over the kingdoms of men, gives kingdoms to anyone he wishes, and sets over them the lowliest of men. Those who do not know this do not know God. (Daniel 4:17)
4. No. When Nebuchadnezzar did not repent he was driven from his beautiful palace and stricken with a mental illness. (Daniel 4:29–33)
5. He is able to humble the proud. No—everything he does is right, and all his ways are just. Humbling Nebuchadnezzar was an important factor in his repentance. (Daniel 4:37)

CHAPTER FIVE

1. He would be clothed in purple, have a gold chain placed around his neck, and made the third highest ruler in Babylon. He responded, *keep your gifts and give your rewards to someone else*. The king gave him the rewards anyway. (Daniel 5:16, 17, 29)
2. No. He refused the king's gifts and rewards, and he issued a scathing reprimand to the king for his sin. (Daniel 5:18–23)
3. No. The walls, guards, weapons, and troops did not keep the hand of God out or stop him from causing the fall of Babylon. (Daniel 5:5, 30)
4. Yes. Because of sin God judged Belshazzar and Babylon. He decreed their fall. (Daniel 5:26-28)
5. He turned pale, was very scared, his knees knocked, and his legs gave way. But he did not repent. (Daniel 5:6)

CHAPTER SIX

1. He was an honest government official. (Daniel 6:4, 5)
2. Those in charge may try to force everyone to worship someone other than the true God. (Daniel 6:7, 12)
3. Both are important, but man's laws are sometimes wrong and they can change. God's law is always right and is eternal. (Daniel 6:9, 14, 26)
4. He was innocent in God's sight and trusted God. (Daniel 6:21, 23)
5. Yes. And Darius told the whole world. (Daniel 6:27)

CHAPTER SEVEN

1. The Antichrist. He will boast, overthrow three of the ten kings, take over the fourth kingdom (the one-world government), wage war on the saints, and change times and laws. (Daniel 7:8, 20, 21, 24, 25)
2. God: the Ancient of Days and the Most High; Jesus: Son of Man. (Daniel 7:9, 13, 18, 22, 24, 25)
3. God will take his power away. It will happen at the Second Coming of Jesus. (Daniel 7:13, 14, 26)
4. No. He was troubled in his spirit (his thoughts disturbed him), he turned pale, and he kept quiet about it. (Daniel 7:15 and 28)
5. The four beasts symbolize four kingdoms or groups of nations. From a moral perspective nations act more like beasts than God. The history of nations is mostly unchristian and vicious. (Daniel 7:17)

CHAPTER EIGHT

1. Because of rebellion. Rebellion causes people to reject Christ and disobey God. Some of the forms of rebellion include these acts: establishing a world religion and world government, promoting things contrary to the will of God like abortion and homosexuality, the killing of Christians and Jews, trading land for peace in Israel, trying to rebuild the Temple to restart animal sacrifice, and because of rebellion, God will permit the Antichrist to rise to power. But no matter what we do, we are accountable to God for our actions. (Daniel 8:12)
2. The only reliable source is the Bible itself. Without Gabriel's explanations we could not understand this vision. (Daniel 8:19–26)
3. Bible prophecy is history written before it happens. Daniel's prophetic Vision of the Ram and the Goat was literally fulfilled by history. (Daniel 8:20, 21)
4. No. It will have deceit, corruption, devastation, and violent religious persecution. (Daniel 8:24, 25)
5. His power will be Satanic. He will rule the world, but God will destroy him. (Daniel 8:24, 25)

CHAPTER NINE

1. He was reading the Book of Jeremiah, knew God keeps his covenants, knew what was in the Law of Moses, and knew God brought Israel out of Egypt. (Daniel 9:2, 4, 11, 13, 15)
2. Forgiveness requires humility, sincere prayer, and confession. Daniel fasted, prayed, wore sackcloth, and sat in ashes. He confessed his sins over and over again. (Daniel 9:3–16)
3. He is righteous, merciful, forgiving, mighty, and can be angered. (Daniel 9:7, 9, 15, 16)

4. To obtain forgiveness for Israel and Judah, to turn away God's anger, to show concern for God's name, and to enlist God's help. (Daniel 9:16-19)
5. It will begin when a world leader signs a seven-year covenant. He will break the covenant, stop the animal sacrifices, and desecrate the Temple. (Daniel 9:27)

CHAPTER TEN

1. Yes. Daniel said the message is true and the heavenly being said it is written in the Book of Truth. (Daniel 10:1, 21)
2. God hears prayer. Evil spirits can hinder answers to prayer, and the answer may have a dramatic effect on us. (Daniel 10:2, 8-10, 13, 15–17)
3. No. He became sick, was helpless and afraid, went into a deep sleep, couldn't talk, and had trouble breathing. Daniel 10:8-10; 15–17
4. Some are good and others are bad; some serve God while others serve Satan. Angels deliver messages, fight wars, and assist God's people. (Daniel 10:10-13, 18, 19)
5. They are real, powerful, can hinder prayer, rule over nations, and oppose the angels of God. (Daniel 10:13)

CHAPTER ELEVEN

1. All of them will fall. Persia was defeated by Greece. Greece was divided into four kingdoms. The Antichrist's kingdom will also fall. (Daniel 11:3, 4, 45)
2. Some leaders are never satisfied with the glory, power, and wealth they have. They covet what others have and are willing to seize it by force. (Daniel 11:8, 18, 21, 24, 28, 39, 42, 43)
3. When he begins he will do as he pleases, exalt himself, and attack mighty fortresses. When he comes to his end no one will help him. (Daniel 11:36-45)
4. He will get his power from the god of fortresses (Satan), and he will not be overcome until Jesus returns to capture him. (Daniel 11:38, 45)
5. He will present himself as a man of peace, but his short career will be marred by several wars. (Daniel 11:39, 40, 41, 43-45)

CHAPTER TWELVE

1. Israel will be delivered. The Old Testament and Tribulation Saints will be raised, and multitudes will be saved. (Daniel 12:1, 2, 10)
2. It will be a time of great trouble. The wicked will continue in their sin and not understand what is going on. They will be destined for everlasting shame and contempt. (Daniel 12:1, 2, 10)
3. Multitudes who sleep in the dust of the earth will awake: some to everlasting life, others to shame and everlasting contempt. (Daniel 12:2)
4. 1,260 days, 1,290 days, and 1,335 days. The Tribulation Period will end 1,260 days after the Abomination of Desolation is set up. The Millennium will begin 75 days after the Tribulation Period ends. (Daniel 12:7, 11)
5. He would die, be raised from the dead, and receive a reward. (Daniel 12:13)

APPENDIX C — THE EXPERTS

Irvin Baxter, Jr.—Pentecostal minister, editor of *Endtime Magazine*, and author of several books. (Endtime, P.O. Box 2066, Richmond, IN 47375-2066)

Steve Beard—Editor of *Good News Magazine*. (Good News, P.O. Box 150, Wilmore, KY 40390)

Richard Booker—Bible teacher and author of several best-selling Christian books. (Destiny Image, P.O. Box 351, Shippensburg, PA 17257)

David Breese—President of World Prophetic Ministry, and Bible teacher on *The King Is Coming* television program. (World Prophetic Ministry, P.O. Box 907, Colton, California 92324)

Ron Carlson and Ed Decker—Ron Carlson is President of *Christian Ministries International* and author. (Christian Ministries International, 7601 Superior Terrace, Eden Prairie, MN 55344). Ed Decker is President of *Saints Alive* and author of several books. (Saints Alive Ministries, P.O. Box 1076, Issaquah, WA 98027)

Joseph Chambers—Senior Editor of *The End-Times And Victorious Living*, pastor, and author of several books. (Paw Creek Ministries, Inc., 5110 Tuckaseegee Road, Charlotte, NC 28208)

J.R. Church—Host of the nationwide television program *Prophecy in the News*. (Prophecy Publications, P.O. Box 7000, Oklahoma City, Ok 73153)

M.R. DeHaan—Former pastor, author of more than 20 books, and host of the *Radio Bible Class*.

Charles H. Dyer—Professor of Bible exposition at Dallas Theological Seminary in Dallas, Texas and author of several books. He lives in Garland, Texas.

Wallace Emerson—Former college professor and dean. He celebrated his 100th birthday in 1987 just before going home to be with the Lord.

Arno Froese—Editor of *Midnight Call* and *News From Israel*. (Midnight Call, Inc., 4694 Platt Springs Road, West Columbia, South Carolina 29170; News From Israel, P.O. Box 4389, West Columbia, SC 29171-4389)

Arnold G. Fruchtenbaum—Founder of *Bible Institute* in Israel and *Ariel Ministries* in the United States with fellowships ministering to Jews in several major cities. (San Antonio, TX)

Billy Graham—World famous evangelist and author of several books. (Billy Graham Evangelistic Association, 1300 Harmon Place, P.O. Box 779, Minneapolis, MN 55440-0779)

Oliver B. Greene—Author, radio show host, and former Director of The Gospel Hour, Inc.

John Hagee—Founder and pastor of Cornerstone Church and president of Global Evangelism Television.

Charles Halff—Executive Director of The Christian Jew Foundation, radio host for *The Christian Jew Hour*, and featured writer for *Message of the Christian Jew*. (The Christian Jew Foundation, P.O. Box 345, San Antonio, TX 78292)

J.G. Hall—Former pastor, author, and lecturer under the Staley Distinguished Scholar Lecture Series at Bethany Bible College.

Jack W. Hayford—Pastor of The Church On The Way, teacher, composer, author of more than 20 books and Senior Editor of the *Spirit-Filled Life Bible*.

Ed Hindson—Minister of Biblical Studies at Rehoboth Baptist Church in Atlanta, Georgia, Vice President of *There's Hope*, adjunct professor at Liberty University in Virginia, and an executive board member of the Pre-Trib Research Center in Washington, D.C.

David Hocking—Pastor, radio host, and Director of Hope For Today Ministries. (P.O. Box 3927, Tustin, CA 92781-3927)

Noah Hutchings—President of The Southwest Radio Church, one of the oldest and best-known prophetic ministries in the world. (P.O. Box 1144, Oklahoma City, OK 73101)

David Icke—No information on him. I quoted from an article he wrote that appeared in the Spotlight newspaper.

David Ingraham—Writes for *Bible In the News*, a publication of Southwest Radio Church. (P.O. Box 1144, Oklahoma City, Ok 73101)

Grant R. Jeffrey—Best-selling author of six books. (Frontier Research Publications Inc., Box 129, Station "U," Toronto, Ontario, Canada M8Z5M4)

David Jeremiah and C. C. Carlson—David Jeremiah is President of Christian Heritage College and Senior Pastor of Scott Memorial Baptist Church in El Cajon, California, and host of a popular radio program called *Turning Point*. Carole Carlson has authored/co-authored a total of nineteen books, the most famous being *The Late Great Planet Earth* with Hal Lindsey.

Rick Joyner—His books are available through Whitaker Distributors. (Whitaker Distributors, 30 Hunt Valley Circle, New Kensington, PA 15068)

Kevin R. Kemper—Writer for the Prophetic Observer, a publication of Southwest Radio Church. (P.O. Box 1144, Oklahoma City, Ok 73101)

Peter and Paul Lalonde—Founders and co-hosts of *This Week in Bible Prophecy*. (This Week In Bible Prophecy at P.O. Box 1440, Niagara Falls, NY 14302-1440)

Hal Lindsey—Many call him the father of the modern day prophecy movement. He is President of Hal Lindsey Ministries and author of more than a dozen books with a combined worldwide sales that exceeds 35 million copies. (P.O. Box 4000, Palos Verdes, CA 90274)

Marlin Maddoux—Host of *Point of View Radio Talk Show* (International Christian Media, P.O. Box 30, Dallas, TX 75221).

Jan Markell—All I know is she is a journalist who wrote an article published in *The Messianic Times*. (That publication can be contacted at P.O. Box 1857, Hagerstown, MD 21742)

Faith McDonnell—Religious Liberty Associate at the Institute on Religion and Democracy. (Institute on Religion and Democracy, 1521 16th Street NW, Suite 300, Washington, D.C. 20036)

J. Vernon McGee—Former host of the popular *Thru the Bible* radio program (Thru The Bible Radio, Box 100, Pasadena, CA 91109).

Arieh O'Sullivan—Journalist for the *Jerusalem Post International Edition*. (This publication can be reached at P.O. Box 81, Jerusalem 91000 Israel.)

William L. Owens—Pastor, Bible teacher, author, and evangelist.

Randall Price—President of World of the Bible Ministries, Inc., and author. (World of the Bible Ministries, Inc., 110 Easy Street, San Marcos, TX 78666-7336)

The Pulpit Commentary—This 23 volume series is a classic Bible commentary and is one of the most used reference books for this author. It is published by the William B. Eerdmans Publishing Company and edited by H.D.M. Spence and Joseph S. Exell.

Shlomo Riskin—Journalist for the *Jerusalem Post International Edition*. (This publication can be reached at P.O. Box 81, Jerusalem 91000 Israel)

Carol Rushton—Former journalist for the *Jerusalem Post International Edition*, speaker on the Southwest Radio Church, daughter of Dr. Noah Hutchings. (Southwest Radio Church, P.O. Box 1144, Oklahoma City, OK 73101)

Phyllis Schlafly—Radio and television talk show host, editor of *The Phyllis Schlafly Report*, and head of Eagle Forum. (Eagle Forum, P.O. Box 618, Alton, IL 62002)

Richard H. Schneider—Senior Staff Editor of *Guideposts Magazine*. (Guideposts, 16 East 34 Street, New York, NY 10016)

Jay Alan Sekulow—Chief Counsel for The American Center For Law And Justice, author, and television speaker. (ACLJ, P.O. Box 64429, Virginia Beach, VA 23467-4429)

Brett Selby—Journalist for *Bible In the News*, a Southwest Radio Church publication. (P.O. Box 1144, Oklahoma City, OK 73101)

Uriah Smith—Former pastor and author of several books.

Edward Tracy—Pastor, author, and teacher. (Convale Publications, P.O. Box 136, Pine Grove, CA 95665)

James P. Tucker, Jr.—Correspondent for *The Spotlight* newspaper, a publication of Liberty Lobby, Inc. (300 Independence Ave. SE, Washington, D.C. 20003)

Union Gospel Press—*The Bible Expositor and Illuminator* is unquestionably one of the best quarterly Sunday School books available today. The information it contains is Biblically solid, easy to follow, and covered in-depth.

Jack Van Impe—Co-host, along with his wife Rexella, of a worldwide television ministry that analyzes the news in light of Bible prophecy. (Jack Van Impe Ministries International, P.O. Box 7004, Troy, MI 48007)

Joan Veon—Businesswoman, international freelance journalist, talk show host, and author. (The Women's Group, Inc., P.O. Box 1323, Olney, MD 20831)

Dave Weber—Editor of *Dave Weber Reports*, and author. (Dave Weber Reports, P.O. Box 280008, Columbia, SC 29228-0008)

World Book Encyclopedia—This encyclopedia provides accurate and authoritative source material in an easy-to-use and easy-to-understand format. It is designed and written to meet the reference and study needs of students.

Ed Young—Pastor, author, and radio and television preacher. (Winning Walk, P.O. Box 1414, Houston, TX 77251-1414)

To the best of our knowledge, all of the above information is correct. We were unable to obtain information for those experts that are missing.

—THE STARBURST EDITORS

ENDNOTES

Daniel 1

1. Hayford, Jack W., *UNTIL THE END OF TIME*, p. 22.
2. Smith, Uriah, *DANIEL AND THE REVELATION*, p. 24.
3. Young, Ed, *DARE TO BE A DANIEL*, Taped Message # A1066.
4. Smith, Uriah, *DANIEL AND THE REVELATION*, p. 27.
5. Lindsey, Hal, *DANIEL*, Taped Message # 352.
6. Lalonde, Peter and Paul, *301 STARTLING PROOFS AND PROPHECIES*, p. 204.
7. Young, Ed, *DARE TO BE A DANIEL*, Taped Message # A1066.
8. Jeremiah, David with C.C. Carlson, *THE HANDWRITING ON THE WALL*, p. 29.
9. *THE WORLD BOOK ENCYCLOPEDIA*, 1990, Volume H, p. 254.
10. Schlafly, Phyllis, *THE PHYLLIS SCHLAFLY REPORT*, August 1997, p. 2.
11. Jeremiah, David with C.C. Carlson, *THE HANDWRITING ON THE WALL*, pp. 30–31.
12. Jeffrey, Grant R., *FINAL WARNING*, p. 19.
13. Van Impe, Jack, *2001: ON THE EDGE OF ETERNITY*, p. 168.
14. Hagee, John, *DAY OF DECEPTION*, p. 214.
15. Sekulow, Jay, *CASENOTES*, Volume 7, Number 2, The American Center For Law and Justice.
16. McGee, J. Vernon, *THRU THE BIBLE WITH J. VERNON MCGEE*, p. 529.
17. Hutchings, Noah, *EXPLORING THE BOOK OF DANIEL*, p. 16.
18. DeHaan, M.R., *DANIEL AND THE PROPHET*, p. 24.
19. Sekulow, Jay, *CASENOTES*, Volume 2, Number 5, The American Center for Law and Justice.
20. Greene, Oliver B., *DANIEL*, p. 35.
21. Jeremiah, David with C.C. Carlson, *THE HANDWRITING ON THE WALL*, p. 33.
22. *MIDNIGHT CALL*, September 1997, p. 30.
23. Young, Ed, *DARE TO BE A DANIEL*, Taped Message # A1066.
24. DeHaan, M.R., *DANIEL AND THE PROPHET*, pp. 38–39.
25. Greene, Oliver B., *DANIEL*, p. 14.
26. Hocking, David, *DARE TO BE A DANIEL*, p. 39.
27. Ibid., p. 15.
28. Halff, Charles, *SIGNIFICANCE OF BIBLE NUMBERS*, p. 6.
29. Hocking, David, *DARE TO BE A DANIEL*, pp. 14–15.
30. Hutchings, Noah, *EXPLORING THE BOOK OF DANIEL*, p. 21.
31. Joyner, Rick, *THE FINAL QUEST*, p. 10.
32. Greene, Oliver B., *DANIEL*, p. 47.
33. Jeremiah, David with C.C. Carlson, *THE HANDWRITING ON THE WALL*, p. 44.

Daniel 2

1. Hayford, Jack W., *UNTIL THE END OF TIME*, p. 30.
2. Emerson, Wallace, *UNLOCKING THE MYSTERIES OF DANIEL*, p. 23.
3. Hocking, David, *DARE TO BE A DANIEL*, Vol I, p. 19.
4. Lalonde, Peter and Paul, *301 STARTLING PROOFS AND PROPHECIES*, p. 260.
5. Hagee, John, *DAY OF DECEPTION*, p. 163.
6. Lindsey, Hal, *DANIEL*, Taped Message # T353.
7. Hutchings, Noah, *EXPLORING THE BOOK OF DANIEL*, p. 28.
8. Jeremiah, David with C.C. Carlson, *THE HANDWRITING ON THE WALL*, pp. 48–49.
9. Selby, Brett, *BIBLE IN THE NEWS*, January 1996, p. 1.
10. *THE PULPIT COMMENTARY, DANIEL, HOSEA AND JOEL, DANIEL*, p. 45.
11. Selby, Brett, *BIBLE IN THE NEWS*, January 1996, p. 1.
12. Emerson, Wallace, *UNLOCKING THE MYSTERIES OF DANIEL*, p. 24.
13. *THE PULPIT COMMENTARY, DANIEL, HOSEA AND JOEL, DANIEL*, p. 50.
14. Rainey, Jim, *THE JACKSON SUN NEWSPAPER*, February 25, 1996, p. 1B.
15. *THE PULPIT COMMENTARY, DANIEL, HOSEA AND JOEL, DANIEL*, p. 51.
16. Smith, Uriah, *DANIEL AND THE REVELATION*, p. 36.
17. Breese, David, *THE BOOK OF DANIEL*, Part I, p. 5.
18. Greene, Oliver B., *DANIEL*, pp. 64–65.
19. Ibid., p. 64.
20. Jeremiah, David with C.C. Carlson, *THE HANDWRITING ON THE WALL*, p. 53.
21. Breese, David, *THE BOOK OF DANIEL*, Part I, p. 5.
22. Young, Ed, *DARE TO BE A DANIEL*, Taped Messge # A0167.
23. Ibid., A1067.
24. Hocking, David, *DARE TO BE A DANIEL*, p. 26.
25. Greene, Oliver B., *DANIEL*, p. 69.
26. Young, Ed, *DARE TO BE A DANIEL*, Taped Message # A1067.
27. Hutchings, Noah, *EXPLORING THE BOOK OF DANIEL*, p. 35.
28. Hocking, David, *DARE TO BE A DANIEL*, p. 29.
29. Greene, Oliver B., *DANIEL*, p. 75.
30. McGee, J. Vernon, *THRU THE BIBLE WITH J. VERNON MCGEE*, p. 537.
31. Hutchings, Noah, *EXPLORING THE BOOK OF DANIEL*, p. 37.
32. Jeremiah, David with C.C. Carlson, *THE HANDWRITING ON THE WALL*, p. 55.
33. Smith, Uriah, *DANIEL AND THE REVELATION*, pp. 43–44.
34. McGee, J. Vernon, *THRU THE BIBLE WITH J. VERNON MCGEE*, p. 538.
35. Greene, Oliver B., *DANIEL*, p. 79.
36. Jeffrey, Grant R., *FINAL WARNING*, p. 31.
37. Hagee, John, *BEGINNING OF THE END*, p. 37.
38. Baxter, Irvin, Jr., *ENDTIME*, March/April 1998, p. 21
39. Hutchings, Noah, *EXPLORING THE BOOK OF DANIEL*, p. 39.
40. Hagee, John, *BEGINNING OF THE END*, p.36.
41. Young, Ed, *DARE TO BE A DANIEL*, Taped Message # A1068.
42. Jeremiah, David with C.C. Carlson, *THE HANDWRITING ON THE WALL*, pp. 57–58.
43. Jeffrey, Grant R., *FINAL WARNING*, p. 33.

44. Jeremiah, David with C.C. Carlson, *THE HANDWRITING ON THE WALL*, p. 59.
45. Dyer, Charles H., *WORLD NEWS AND BIBLE PROPHECY*, p. 197.
46. Hocking, Daivd, *DARE TO BE A DANIEL*, p. 37.
47. Breese, David, *RAGING INTO APOCALYPSE*, p. 91.
48. Hutchings, Noah, *EXPLORING THE BOOK OF DANIEL*, p. 50.
49. Lalonde, Peter and Paul, *301 STARTLING PROOFS AND ROPHECIES*, p. 243.
50. Harper, James, *THE SPOTLIGHT*, October 6, 1997, p. 1.
51. *THE SPOTLIGHT*, May 11, 1998, p. 1
52. Dyer, Charles H., *WORLD NEWS AND BIBLE PROPHECY*, p. 205.
53. Van Impe, Jack, *2001: ON THE EDGE OF ETERNITY*, p. 89.
54. *THE SPOTLIGHT*, September 8, 1997, p. 8.
55. Jeffrey, Grant R., *PRINCE OF DARKNESS*, pp. 73–74.
56. Tucker, Jr., James P., *THE SPOTLIGHT*, p. 18.
57. Jeffrey, Grant R., *PRINCE OF DARKNESS*, p. 81.
58. Booker, Richard, *BLOW THE TRUMPET IN ZION*, p. 113.
59. McGee, J. Vernon, *THRU THE BIBLE WITH J. VERNON MCGEE, DANIEL*, p. 542.
60. Greene, Oliver B., *DANIEL*, p. 106.

Daniel 3

1. DeHaan, M.R., *DANIEL THE PROPHET*, p. 73.
2. Lindsey, Hal, *DANIEL*, Taped Message # 355.
3. DeHaan, M.R. *DANIEL THE PROPHET*, pp. 74, 83.
4. McGee, J. Vernon, *THRU THE BIBLE WITH J. VERNON MCGEE*, p. 543.
5. Jeremiah, David with C.C. Carlson, *THE HANDWRITING ON THE WALL*, pp. 73–74.
6. McGee, J. Vernon, *THRU THE BIBLE WITH J. VERNON MCGEE*, p. 544.
7. *CPWR NEWSLETTER*, Volume 1, Issue 1, September 1997, p. 5.
8. Greene, Oliver B., *DANIEL*, p. 122.
9. Hocking, David, *DARE TO BE A DANIEL*, p. 125.
10. *PULPIT COMMENTARY, THE BOOK OF DANIEL*, p. 125.
11. Hocking, David, *DARE TO BE A DANIEL*, p. 46.
12. Jeremiah, David with C.C. Carlson, *THE HANDWRITING ON THE WALL*, p. 75.
13. Breese, David, *DESTINY BULLETIN*, October 1997, p. 4.
14. *THE WORLD BOOK ENCYCLOPEDIA*, 1990, Volume A, p. 896.
15. Hutchings, Noah, *EXPLORING THE BOOK OF DANIEL*, p. 65.
16. Coral Ridge Ministries, *IMPACT*, October 1997, p. 3.
17 Lindsey, Hal, *DANIEL*, Taped Message # 355.
18. Coral Ridge Ministries, *IMPACT*, October 1997, p. 3.
19. *PULPIT COMMENTARY, THE BOOK OF DANIEL*, p. 100.
20. Hocking, David, *DARE TO BE A DANIEL*, p. 48.
21. Church, J.R., *PROPHECY IN THE NEWS*, November 1997, p. 16.
22. Jeremiah, David with C.C. Carlson, *THE HANDWRITING ON THE WALL*, p. 76.
23. *THE COMMERCIAL APPEAL, NEWS IN BRIEF*, October 24, 1997, p. A2.
24. Baxter, Irvin, Jr., *ENDTIME*, July/August 1997, p. 8.
25. Hutchings, Noah, *EXPLORING THE BOOK OF DANIEL*, pp. 69–70.
26. Jeremiah, David with C.C. Carlson, *THE HANDWRITING ON THE WALL*, pp. 77–78.
27. DeHaan, M.R., *DANIEL AND THE PROPHET*, pp. 77–78.
28. Kemper, Kevin R., *THE PROPHET OBSERVER*, July 1994, p. 1.
29. Hutchings, Noah, *EXPLORING THE BOOK OF DANIEL*, p. 70.
30. Jeremiah, David with C. C. Carlson, *THE HANDWRITING ON THE WALL*, p. 78.

31. Lindsey, Hal, *DANIEL*, Taped Message # T355.
32. Young, Ed, *DARE TO BE A DANIEL*, Taped Message # A1069.
33. Schneider, Richard H., *GUIDEPOSTS, DYING FOR THEIR FAITH*, November 1997, p. 4.
34. Emerson, Wallace, *UNLOCKING THE MYSTERIES OF DAVID*, p. 52.
35. Hutchings, Noah, *EXPLORING THE BOOK OF DANIEL*, p. 72.
36. Hocking, David, *DARE TO BE A DANIEL*, p. 56.
37. Breese, David, *THE BOOK OF DANIEL*, Taped Message # DB98.
38. Young, Ed, *DARE TO BE A DANIEL*, Taped Message # A1069.
39. Miller, Kenneth, *LIFE MAGAZINE*, June 1998, p. 89.
40. Young, Ed, *DARE TO BE A DANIEL*, Taped Message # A1069.
41. Lindsey, Hal, *DANIEL*, Taped Message # T355.
42. Breese, David, *THE BOOK OF DANIEL*, Taped Message # DB98.
43. Ibid.
44. Hutchings, Noah, *EXPLORING THE BOOK OF DANIEL*, p. 77.

Daniel 4

1. Jeremiah, David with C.C. Carlson, *THE HANDWRITING ON THE WALL*, p. 88.
2. Hutchings, Noah, *EXPLORING THE BOOK OF DANIEL*, p. 81.
3. Hocking, David, *DARE TO BE A DANIEL*, p. 69.
4. Smith, Uriah, *DANIEL AND THE REVELATION*, p. 105.
5. Joyner, Rick, *THE FINAL QUEST*, p. 11.
6. Hocking, David, *DARE TO BE A DANIEL*, p. 71.
7. Carlson, Ron and Ed Decker, *FAST FACTS ON FALSE TEACHINGS*, p. 185.
8. Ibid., p. 183.
9. Ibid., p. 184.
10. Smith, Uriah, *DANIEL AND THE REVELATION*, p. 106.
11. Jeremiah, David with C.C. Carlson, *THE HAND WRITING ON THE WALL*, p. 91.
12. Smith, Uriah, *DANIEL AND THE REVELATION*, p. 91.
13. *DAVE WEBER REPORTS*, June 1996, p. 6.
14. Breese, David, *THE BOOK OF DANIEL*, Taped Message # DB98.
15. Greene, Oliver B., *DANIEL*, p. 167.
16. Smith, Uriah, *DANIEL AND THE REVELATION*, p. 106.
17. Hocking, Daivd, *DARE TO BE A DANIEL*, p. 75.
18. Graham, Billy, *ANGELS*, p. 10.
19. McGee, J. Vernon, *THRU THE BIBLE WITH J. VERNON MCGEE*, p. 552.
20. Emerson, Wallace, *UNLOCKING THE MYSTERIES OF DANIEL*, p. 62.
21. DeHann, M.R., *DANIEL THE PROPHET*, p. 132.
22. Ibid., pp. 133–134.
23. Graham, Billy, *ANGELS*, p. 47.
24. DeHaan, M.R., *DANIEL THE PROPHET*, p. 135.
25. Graham, Billy, *ANGELS*, p. 31.
26. Emerson, Wallace, *UNLOCKING THE MYSTERIES OF DANIEL*, p. 63.
27. Greene, Oliver B., *DANIEL*, p. 172.
28. Hutchings, Noah, *EXPLORING THE BOOK OF DANIEL*, p. 94.
29. DeHaan, M.R., *DANIEL THE PROPHET*, p. 138.
30. Lindsey, Hal, *DANIEL*, Taped Message # T356.
31. DeHann, M.R., *DANIEL THE PROPHET*, pp. 138–139.
32. Emerson, Wallace, *UNLOCKING THE MYSTERIES OF DANIEL*, p. 68.
33. Greene, Oliver B., *DANIEL*, p. 175.
34. DeHaan, M.R., *DANIEL THE PROPHET*, p. 140.
35. Jeremiah, David with C.C. Carlson, *THE HANDWRITTING ON THE WALL*, p. 96.
36. Hutchings, Noah, *EXPLORING THE BOOK OF DANIEL*, p. 65.

Daniel 5

1. McGee, J. Vernon, *THRU THE BIBLE WITH J. VERNON MCGEE*, p. 557.
2. Young, Ed, *DARE TO BE A DANIEL*, Taped Message # A1072.
3. Union Gospel Press Publication, *BIBLE EXPOSITOR AND ILLUMINATOR*, October 19, 1997, p. 90.
4. DeHaan, M.R., *DANIEL THE PROPHET*, pp. 148–149.
5. Greene, Oliver B., *DANIEL*, p. 191.
6. Jeremiah, David with C.C. Carlson, *THE HANDWRITING ON THE WALL*, p. 101.
7. Breese, David, Taped Message # DB99.
8. Hocking, David, *DARE TO BE A DANIEL*, p. 94.
9. McGee, J. Vernon, *THRU THE BIBLE WITH J. VERNON MCGEE*, p. 558.
10. Young, Ed, *DARE TO BE A DANIEL*, Taped Message # A1072.
11. Hutchings, Noah, *EXPLORING THE BOOK OF DANIEL*, p. 108.
12. Union Gospel Press Publication, *BIBLE EXPOSITOR AND ILLUMINATOR*, October 19, 1997, p. 92.
13. Jeremiah, David with C.C. Carlson, *THE HANDWRITING ON THE WALL*, pp. 103–104.
14. Greene, Oliver B., *DANIEL*, p. 195.
15. Hocking, David, *DARE TO BE A DANIEL*, p. 98.
16. Ibid., p. 99.
17. Jeremiah, David with C.C. Carlson, *THE HANDWRITING ON THE WALL*, pp. 103–104.
18. Young, Ed, *DARE TO BE A DANIEL*, Taped Message # A1072.
19. Lindsey, Hal, *DANIEL*, Taped Message # T357.
20. Greene, Oliver B., *DANIEL*, p. 200.
21. Union Gospel Press Publication, *BIBLE EXPOSITOR AND ILLUMINATOR*, p. 93.
22. Hutchings, Noah, *EXPLORING THE BOOK OF DANIEL*, p. 118.
23. Hocking, David, *DARE TO BE A DANIEL*, p. 102.
24. Lindsey, Hal, *DANIEL*, Taped Message # T357.
25. Hutchings, Noah, *EXPLORING THE BOOK OF DANIEL*, p. 119.
26. Young, Ed, *DARE TO BE A DANIEL*, Taped Message # A1072.
27. Jeremiah, David with C.C. Carlson, *THE HANDWRITING ON THE WALL*, p. 112.
28. Hall, J.G., *PROPHECY MARCHES ON*, p. 34.
29. Lindsey, Hal, *DANIEL*, Taped Message # T357.

Daniel 6

1. Hutchings, Noah, *EXPLORING THE BOOK OF DANIEL*, p. 123.
2. Lindsey, Hal, *DANIEL*, Taped Message # T358.
3. Hutchings, Noah, *EXPLORING THE BOOK OF DANIEL*, p. 124.
4. Union Gospel Press Publication, *BIBLE EXPOSITOR AND ILLUMINATOR*, January 1978, p. 104.
5. Lindsey, Hal, *DANIEL*, Taped Message # T358.
6. Hutchings, Noah, *EXPLORING THE BOOK OF DANIEL*, p. 128.
7. Lindsey, Hal, *DANIEL*, Taped Message # T358.
8. Rushton, Carol, *PROPHETIC OBSERVER*, March 1995, p. 4.
9. Maddoux, Marlen, *POINT OF VIEW RADIO*, Newsletter, November 26, 1997, p. 1.
10. Jeremiah, David with C.C. Carlson, *THE HANDWRITING ON THE WALL*, p. 117.
11. Greene, Oliver B., *DANIEL*, p. 216.
12. Lindsey, Hal, *DANIEL*, Taped Message # T358.
13. Smith, Uriah, *DANIEL AND THE REVELATION*, p. 133.
14. Breese, David, *DESTINY BULLETIN*, November 1997, p. 3.
15. Schneider, Richard H., *GUIDEPOST, DYING FOR THEIR FAITH*, November 1997, p. 4.

16. McDonnell, Faith and Steve Beard, *FAITH UNDER FIRE*, Good News, November/December 1997, p. 12.
17. *MIDNIGHT CALL MAGAZINE*, August 1997, p. 28.
18. Greene, Oliver B., *DANIEL*, p. 227.
19. McDonnell, Faith, and Steve Beard, *FAITH UNDER FIRE*, Good News, November/December 1997, p. 12.
20. Schneider, Richard H., *GUIDEPOST, DYING FOR THEIR FAITH*, November 1997, p. 5.
21. McDonnell, Faith, and Steve Beard, *FAITH UNDER FIRE*, Good News, November/December 1997, p. 12.
22. Hutchings, Noah, *EXPLORING THE BOOK OF DANIEL*, p. 132.
23. Greene, Oliver B., *DANIEL*, p. 229.
24. Graham, Billy, *ANGELS*, p. 24.
25. Breese, Dave, *THE BOOK OF DANIEL*, Taped Message # DB99.
26. Greene, Oliver B., *DANIEL*, p. 235.
27. Hocking, David, *DARE TO BE A DANIEL*, p. 125.
28. Emerson, Wallace, *UNLOCKING THE MYSTERIES OF DANIEL*, pp. 97–98.
29. Smith, Uriah, *DANIEL AND THE REVELATION*, p. 135.
30. Hocking, David, *DARE TO BE A DANIEL*, p. 127.
31. Breese, David, *THE BOOK OF DANIEL*, Taped Message # DB99.
32. Greene, Oliver B., *DANIEL*, p. 237.

Daniel 7

1. Hocking, David, *DARE TO BE A DANIEL*, Volume II, p. 9.
2. Tracy, Edward, *THE COVENANT OF DEATH*, p. 26.
3. Emerson, Wallace, *UNLOCKING THE MYSTERIES OF DANIEL*, p. 25.
4. Hutchings, Noah, *EXPLORING THE BOOK OF DANIEL*, p. 150.
5. Breese, David, *THE BOOK OF DANIEL*, Taped Message # DB99.
6. Emerson, Wallace, *UNLOCKING THE MYSTERIES OF DANIEL*, p. 117.
7. McGee, J. Vernon, *THRU THE BIBLE WITH J. VERNON MCGEE*, p. 568.
8. Lindsey, Hal, *DANIEL*, Taped Message # T359.
9. Markell, Jan, *THE MESSIANIC TIMES*, Spring 1997, p. 7.
10. Tracy, Edward, *THE COVENANT OF DEATH*, p. 30.
11. Emerson, Wallace, *UNLOCKING THE MYSTERIES OF DANIEL*, p. 123.
12. Tracy, Edward, *THE COVENANT OF DEATH*, p. 32.
13. Hutchings, Noah, *EXPLORING THE BOOK OF DANIEL*, pp. 151–152.
14. Hocking, David, *DARE TO BE A DANIEL*, Volume II, p. 6.
15. Burns, Robert, *THE ASSOCIATED PRESS, THE JACKSON SUN*, November 21, 1997, p. 2A.
16. Emerson, Wallace, *UNLOCKING THE MYSTERIES OF DANIEL*, pp. 127–128.
17. Tracy, Edward, *THE COVENANT OF DEATH*, p. 35.
18. Hocking, David, *DARE TO BE A DANIEL*, Volume II, pp. 7–8.
19. Lindsey, Hal, *DANIEL*, Taped Message # T359.
20. *MIDNIGHT CALL*, Russia, January 1998, pp. 34–35.
21. Emerson, Wallace, *UNLOCKING THE MYSTERIES OF DANIEL*, pp. 129.
22. Tracy, Edward, *THE COVENANT OF DEATH*, p 37.
23. Hutchings, Noah, *EXPLORING THE BOOK OF DANIEL*, pp. 157–158.
24. Hocking, David, *DARE TO BE A DANIEL*, Volume II, pp. 10–11.
25. *INTERNATIONAL INTELLIGENCE BRIEFING*, November 1996, p. 4.

26. O'Sullivan, Arieh, *THE JERUSALEM POST*, October 25, 1997, p. 6.
27. Jeffrey, Grant R., *FINAL WARNING*, p. 51.
28. Schlafly, Phyllis, *THE PHYLLIS SCHLAFLY REPORT*, October 1997, p. 1.
29. Fruchtenbaum, Arnold G., *THE FOOTSTEPS OF THE MESSIAH*, pp. 27–28.
30. Jeffrey, Grant R., *PRINCE OF DARKNESS*, p. 30.
31. Hagee, John, *BEGINNING OF THE END*, pp. 117–118.
32. Van Impe, Jack, *2001: ON THE EDGE OF ETERNITY*, p. 70.
33. Breese, David, *THE BOOK OF DANIEL*, Taped Message # DB99.
34. *THE WORLD BOOK ENCYCLOPEDIA*, 1990, Vol. H, p. 254.
35. Jeremiah, David with C.C. Carlson, *THE HANDWRITING ON THE WALL*, pp. 140–141.
36. McGee, J. Vernon, *THRU THE BIBLE WITH J. VERNON MCGEE*, p. 572.
37. Smith, Uriah, *DANIEL AND THE REVELATION*, p. 155.
38. Hutchings, Noah, *EXPLORING THE BOOK OF DANIEL*, p. 171.
39. Emerson, Wallace, *UNLOCKING THE MYSTERIES OF DANIEL*, p. 126.
40. Hutchings, Noah, *EXPLORING THE BOOK OF DANIEL*, pp. 171–172.
41. McGee, J. Vernon, *THRU THE BIBLE WITH J. VERNON MCGEE*, p. 573.
42. Dyer, Charles, *WORLD NEWS AND BIBLE PROPHECY*, p. 194.
43. Hutchings, Noah, *EXPLORING THE BOOK OF DANIEL*, p. 174.
44. Smith, Uriah, *DANIEL AND THE REVELATION*, pp. 17–18.
45. Hocking, David, *DARE TO BE A DANIEL*, pp. 17–18.
46. Breese, David, *DESTINY NEWSLETTER*, October 1997, p. 3.
47. McGee, J. Vernon, *THRU THE BIBLE WITH J. VERNON MCGEE*, p. 575.
48. Hutchings, Noah, *EXPLORING THE BOOK OF DANIEL*, p. 176.
49. Jeremiah, David with C. C. Carlson, *THE HANDWRITING ON THE WALL*, p. 149.
50. Icke, David, *SPOTLIGHT*, May 12, 1997, p. 16.
51. Hocking, David, *DARE TO BE A DANIEL*, Volume II, pp. 24–25.
52. Fruchtenbaum, Arnold G., *THE FOOTSTEPS OF THE MESSIAH*, p. 27.
53. Jeffrey, Grant R., *FINAL WARNING*, p. 86.
54. Young, Ed, *DARE TO BE A DANIEL*, Taped Message # A1075.
55. Baxter, Irvin, Jr., *ENDTIME*, July/August 1997, p. 7.
56. Church, J.R., *RAGING INTO APOCALYPSE*, pp. 198–199.
57. Hagee, John, *BEGINNING OF THE END*, pp. 123–124.
58. Fenyvesi, Charles, *U.S. NEWS AND WORLD REPORT*, August 2, 1993, p. 17.
59. Breese, David, *THE BOOK OF DANIEL*, Taped Message # DB99.
60. Hutchings, Noah, *EXPLORING THE BOOK OF DANIEL*, p. 178.

Daniel 8

1. DeHaan, M.R., *DANIEL THE PROPHET*, p. 219.
2. Dyer, Charles H., *WORLD NEWS AND BIBLE PROPHECY*, p. 191.
3. Jeremiah, David with C.C. Carlson, *THE HANDWRITING ON THE WALL*, pp. 158–159.
4. Hocking, David, *DARE TO BE A DANIEL*, Volume II, p. 40.
5. Jeremiah, David, with C.C. Carlson, *THE HANDWRITING ON THE WALL*, p. 159.

6. Smith, Uriah, *DANIEL AND THE REVELATION*, p. 191.
7. *HARPER'S BIBLE DICTIONARY*, 1973, pp. 431–432.
8. *THE WORLD BOOK ENCYCLOPEDIA*, 1990, Volume P, p. 297.
9. Hocking, David, *DARE TO BE A DANIEL*, Volume II, p. 41.
10. Lindsey, Hal, *DANIEL*, Taped Message # T361.
11. Jeremiah, David with C.C. Carlson, *THE HANDWRITING ON THE WALL*, p. 160.
12. Hutchings, Noah, *EXPLORING THE BOOK OF DANIEL*, p. 185.
13. Hocking, David, *DARE TO BE A DANIEL*, Volume II, pp. 44–45.
14. Greene, Oliver B., *DANIEL*, p. 299.
15. Smith, Uriah, *DANIEL AND THE REVELATION*, p. 196.
16. *THE WORLD BOOK ENCYCLOPEDIA*, 1990, Volume SO–SZ, p. 1011.
17. Jeremiah, David with C.C. Carlson, *THE HANDWRITING ON THE WALL*, p. 162.
18. Smith, Uriah, *DANIEL AND THE REVELATION*, pp. 196–197.
19. Hall, J. G., *PROPHECY MARCHES ON*, pp. 43–44.
20. Hutchings, Noah, *EXPLORING THE BOOK OF DANIEL*, p. 189.
21. McGee, J. Vernon, *THRU THE BIBLE WITH J. VERNON MCGEE*, p. 580.
22. Hocking, David, *DARE TO BE A DANIEL*, Volume II, pp. 47–48.
23. Greene, Oliver B., *DANIEL*, p. 304.
24. Graham, Billy, *ANGELS*, pp. 121–122.
25. Chambers, Joseph, *A PLACE FOR THE ANTICHRIST*, p. 248.
26. Biederwolf, William E., *THE PROPHECY HANDBOOK*, p. 215.
27. Jeremiah, David with C.C. Carlson, *THE HANDWRITING ON THE WALL*, p. 169.
28. Veon, Joan, *ENDTIME*, July/August 1997, pp 22–23.
29. Breese, David, *DESTINY NEWSLETTER*, October 1997, p. 3.
30. Lindsey, Hal, *INTERNATIONAL INTELLIGENCE BRIEFING*, October 1997, p. 5.
31. Jeremiah, David with C.C. Carlson, *THE HANDWRITING ON THE WALL*, p. 170.

Daniel 9

1. Hutchings, Noah, *EXPLORING THE BOOK OF DANIEL*, p. 199.
2. Smith, Uriah, *DANIEL AND THE REVELATION*, p. 233.
3. Jeremiah, David with C.C. Carlson, *THE HANDWRITING ON THE WALL*, p. 173.
4. Breese, David, *THE BOOK OF DANIEL*, Taped Message # DB100.
5. Hocking, David, *DARE TO BE A DANIEL*, Volume II, p. 66.
6. Hutchings, Noah, *EXPLORING THE BOOK OF DANIEL*, p. 202.
7. Jeremiah, David, *THE HANDWRITING ON THE WALL*, p. 179.
8. Hocking, David, *DARE TO BE A DANIEL*, Volume II, pp. 67–68.
9. Breese, David, *THE BOOK OF DANIEL*, Taped Message # DB100.
10. Jeremiah, David, *THE HANDWRITING ON THE WALL*, p. 175.
11. Hocking, David, *DARE TO BE A DANIEL*, Volume II, p. 68.
12. Young, Ed, *DARE TO BE A DANIEL*, Taped Message # A1079.
13. Davis, John J., *DECISION MAGAZINE*, March 1994, p. 14.
14. Pratt, Richard L. Jr., *DECISION MAGAZINE*, February 1996, p. 13.
15. White, John, *DECISION MAGAZINE*, October 1994, p. 14.
16. *NEWS OF ISRAEL*, Novemeber 1996, p. 8.
17. Smith, Uriah, *DANIEL AND THE REVELATION*, p. 236.

18. Hocking, David, *DARE TO BE A DANIEL,* Volume II, p. 73.
19. Riskin, Shlomo, *THE JERUSALEM POST,* August 5, 1995, p. 31.
20. Emerson, Wallace, *UNLOCKING THE MYSTERIES OF DANIEL,* p. 159.
21. DeHaan, M.R., *DANIEL THE PROPHET,* p. 250.
22. Smith, Uriah, *DANIEL AND THE REVELATION,* p. 242.
23. Young, Ed, *DARE TO BE A DANIEL,* Taped Message # A1079.
24. McBirnie, William S., *FIFTY MESSAGES ON SECOND COMING,* p. 110.
25. Jeffrey, Grant R., *FINAL WARNING,* p. 65.
26. Lalonde, Peter and Paul, *301 STARTLING PROOFS,* p. 280.
27. Smart, Victor, *THE EUROPEAN,* February 19, 1997, p. 1.
28. Ingraham, David, *BIBLE IN THE NEWS,* July 1995, p. 11.
29. Lalonde, Peter and Paul, *301 STARTLING PROOFS,* p. 209.
30. Hagee, John, *BEGINNING OF THE END,* p. 128.
31. Lindsey, Hal, *INTERNATIONAL INTELLIGENCE BRIEFING,* July 1997, p. 1.
32. Davis, Douglas, *THE JERUSALEM POST,* December 27, 1997, p. 3.

Daniel 10

1. Owens, William L., *THE REALITY OF EVIL SPIRITS,* p. 107.
2. Jeremiah, David with C.C. Carlson, *THE HANDWRITING ON THE WALL,* p. 205.
3. Ibid., pp. 205–206.
4. McGee, J. Vernon, *THRU THE BIBLE WITH J. VERNON MCGEE,* p. 591.
5. Ibid.
6. Hutchings, Noah, *EXPLORING THE BOOK OF DANIEL,* pp. 236–237.
7. DeHaan, M.R., *DANIEL THE PROPHET,* p. 264.
8. Graham, Billy, *ANGELS,* p. 110.
9. Owens, William L., *THE REALITY OF EVIL SPIRITS,* p. 106.
10. Graham, Billy, *ANGELS,* p. 124.
11. Owens, William L., *THE REALITY OF EVIL SPIRITS,* p. 17.
12. Young, Ed, *DARE TO BE A DANIEL,* Taped Message # A1080.
13. Hutchings, Noah, *EXPLORING THE BOOK OF DANIEL,* pp. 242–243.
14. Wynn, Linda M., *ANGELS ON EARTH,* November/December 1996, p. 2.
15. Hocking, David, *DARE TO BE A DANIEL,* Volume II, p. 130.
16. Emerson, Wallace, *UNLOCKING THE MYSTERIES OF DANIEL,* p. 174.
17. DeHaan, M.R., *DANIELD OF THE PROPHET,* pp. 271–272.
18. Greene, Oliver B., *DANIEL,* pp. 406–407.
19. Ibid., p. 407.
20. *PULPIT COMMENTARY, THE BOOK OF DANIEL,* p. 296.
21. Hocking, David, *DARE TO BE A DANIEL,* Volume II, p. 137.
22. Greene, Oliver B., *DANIEL,* pp. 408–409.

Daniel 11

1. Hocking, David, *DARE TO BE A DANIEL,* Volume II, p. 163.
2. Graham, Billy, *ANGELS,* p. 110.
3. Hocking, David, *DARE TO BE A DANIEL,* Volume II, p. 144.
4. Jeremiah, David with C.C. Carlson, *THE HANDWRITING ON THE WALL,* p. 218.
5. Smith, Uriah, *DANIEL AND THE REVELATION,* p. 283.
6. Hocking, David, *DARE TO BE A DANIEL,* Volume II, pp. 148–149.
7. Hutchings, Noah, *EXPLORING THE BOOK OF DANIEL,* pp. 256–257.
8. Greene, Oliver B., *DANIEL,* pp. 421–422.

9. Hutchings, Noah, *DARE TO BE A DANIEL,* p. 259.
10. Jeremiah, David with C.C. Carlson, *THE HANDWRITING ON THE WALL,* p. 220.
11. Hutchings, Noah, *EXPLORING THE BOOK OF DANIEL,* p. 261.
12. Greene, Oliver B., *DANIEL,* p. 426.
13. McGee, J. Vernon, *THRU THE BIBLE WITH J. VERNON MCGEE,* p. 598.
14. Hocking, David, *DARE TO BE A DANIEL,* Volume II, pp. 165–166.
15. Jeremiah, David with C.C. Carlson, *THE HANDWRITING ON THE WALL,* p. 221.
16. Hocking, David, *DARE TO BE A DANIEL,* Volume II, pp. 165–166.
17. Jeremiah, David with C.C. Carlson, *THE HANDWRITING ON THE WALL,* p. 222.
18. *THE WORLD BOOK ENCYCLOPEDIA,* 1990, Volume M, p. 927.
19. Price, Randall, *IN SEARCH OF TEMPLE TREASURES,* p. 343.
20. Lalonde, Peter & Paul, *301 STARTLING PROOFS AND PROPHECIES,* p. 231.
21. Hocking, David, *DARE TO BE A DANIEL,* Volume II, pp. 171–172.
22. Jeffrey, Grant R., *PRINCE OF DARKNESS,* p. 31.
23. Hocking, David, *DARE TO BE A DANIEL,* Volume II, pp. 176–177.
24. McGee, J. Vernon, *THRU THE BIBLE WITH J. VERNON MCGEE,* p. 600.
25. Hutchings, Noah, *EXPLORING THE BOOK OF DANIEL,* p. 274.
26. Hocking, David, *DARE TO BE A DANIEL,* Volume II, p. 180.
27. Jeffrey, Grant R., *PRINCE OF DARKNESS,* p. 288.
28. Dyer, Charles H., *WORLD NEWS AND BIBLE PROPHECY,* p. 215.
29. The Associated Press, *THE JACKSON SUN,* June 5, 1998, p. A1.
30. Fruchtenbaum, Arnold G., *THE FOOTSTEPS OF THE MESSIAH,* p. 146.
31. Jeffrey, Grant R., *PRINCE OF DARKNESS,* p. 234.
32. Hocking, David, *DARE TO BE A DANIEL,* Volume II, p. 182.
33. Ibid.
34. Jeremiah, David with C.C. Carlson, *THE HANDWRITING ON THE WALL,* p. 229.
35. Emerson, Wallace, *UNLOCKING THE MYSTERIES OF DANIEL,* pp. 188–189.
36. Hagee, John, *BEGINNING OF THE END,* p. 175.
37. Dyer, Charles, *WORLD NEWS AND BIBLE PROPHECY,* p. 233.
38. Fruchtenbaum, Arnold G., *THE FOOTSTEPS OF THE MESSIAH,* p. 204.
39. Emerson, Wallace, *UNLOCKING THE MYSTERIES OF DANIEL,* p. 190.
40. Fruchtenbaum, Arnold G., *THE FOOTSTEPS OF THE MESSIAH,* pp. 351–352.
41. Hutchings, Noah, *EXPLORING THE BOOK OF DANIEL,* p. 277.
42. Hocking, David, *DARE TO BE A DANIEL,* Volume II, pp. 183–184.
43. Jeffrey, Grant R., *PRINCE OF DARKNESS,* p. 235.
44. Ibid., p. 257.
45. Hutchings, Noah, *EXPLORING THE BOOK OF DANIEL,* p. 278.
46. Hocking, David, *DARE TO BE A DANIEL,* Volume II, p. 188.
47. Jeremiah, David with C.C. Carlson, *THE HANDWRITING ON THE WALL,* pp. 232–233.
48. Emerson, Wallace, *UNLOCKING THE MYSTERIES OF DANIEL,* p. 191.

Daniel 12

1. Hocking, David, *DARE TO BE A DANIEL*, Volume II, pp. 192–193.
2. Greene, Oliver B., *DANIEL*, pp. 459–460.
3. Emerson, Wallace, *UNLOCKING THE MYSTERIES OF DANIEL*, p. 211.
4. Hocking, David, *DARE TO BE A DANIEL*, Volume II, pp. 195–196.
5. McGee, J. Vernon, *THRU THE BIBLE WITH J. VERNON MCGEE*, p. 604.
6. Hutchings, Noah, *EXPLORING THE BOOK OF DANIEL*, pp. 285–286.
7. Jeremiah, David with C.C. Carlson, *THE HANDWRITING ON THE WALL*, p. 240.
8. Van Impe, Jack, *2001: ON THE EDGE OF ETERNITY*, p. 116.
9. Dyer, Charles H., *WORLD NEWS AND BIBLE PROPHECY*, p. 267.
10. Jeremiah, David with C.C. Carlson, *THE HANDWRITING ON THE WALL*, p. 242.
11. Hutchings, Noah, *EXPLORING THE BOOK OF DANIEL*, p. 292.
12. Jeremiah, David with C.C. Carlson, *THE HANDWRITING ON THE WALL*, pp. 242–243.
13. Jeffrey, Grant R., *PRINCE OF DARKNESS*, p. 139.
14. Hocking, David, *DARE TO BE A DANIEL*, Volume II, p. 203.
15. Greene, Oliver B., *DANIEL*, p. 483.
16. Jeremiah, David with C.C. Carlson, *THE HANDWRITING ON THE WALL*, pp. 243–244.
17. *THE PULPIT COMMENTARY, DANIEL, HOSEA, AND JOEL, DANIEL*, p. 339.
18. Greene, Oliver B., *DANIEL*, p. 484.
19. DeHaan, M.R., *DANIEL THE PROPHET*, pp. 313–314.
20. McGee, J. Vernon, *THRU THE BIBLE WITH J. VERNON MCGEE*, pp. 605–606.
21. Hutchings, Noah, *EXPLORING THE BOOK OF DANIEL*, p. 295.
22. Ibid., p. 296.
23. Fruchtenbaum, Arnold G., *THE FOOTSTEPS OF THE MESSIAH*, p. 79.
24. Greene, Oliver B., *DANIEL*, p. 485.
25. Hocking, David, *DARE TO BE A DANIEL*, Volume II, pp. 206-207.
26. Jeremiah, David with C.C. Carlson, *THE HANDWRITING ON THE WALL*, pp. 244–245.
27. Hocking, David, *DARE TO BE A DANIEL*, Volume II, p. 208.
28. Jeremiah, David with C.C. Carlson, *THE HANDWRITING ON THE WALL*, p. 245.

INDEX

Boldface numbers indicate specially defined (What?) terms and phrases as they appear both in the text *and* the sidebar.

Books by Starburst Publishers

(Partial listing—full list available on request)

Revelation—God's Word for the Biblically-Inept ™

Daymond R. Duck

Revelation—God's Word for the Biblically-Inept ™ is the first in a new series designed to make understanding and learning the Bible as easy and fun as learning your ABC's. Reading the Bible is one thing, understanding it is another! This book breaks down the barrier of difficulty and helps take the Bible off the pedestal and into your hands.

(trade paper)   ISBN 0914984985 $16.95

Daniel—God's Word for the Biblically-Inept ™

Daymond R. Duck

A Revolutionary Commentary™ that includes every verse of the book of Daniel. Icons, sidebars and bullets combined with comments from leading experts.

(trade paper)   ISBN 0914984489 $16.95

The Bible—God's Word for the Biblically-Inept ™

Larry Richards　　　　　　　　Available October '98

A Bible overview that makes the Bible easy to understand. Each chapter contains select verses from books of the Bible along with illustrations, definitions, and references to related Bible passages.

(trade paper)   ISBN 0914984551 $16.95

Health and Nutrition—God's Word for the Biblically-Inept ™

Kathleen O'Bannon Baldinger　　Available February '99

Gives scientific evidence that proves that the diet and health principles outlined in the Bible is the best diet for total health. Experts include: Pamela Smith, Julian Whitaker, Kenneth Cooper, and TD Jakes.

(trade paper)   ISBN 0914984055 $16.95

Women of the Bible—God's Word for the Biblically-Inept ™

Kathy Collard Miller　　　　　　Available March '99

Shows that although the Bible was written many years ago, it is till relevant for today. Gain valuable insight from the successes and struggles of such women as Eve, Esther, Mary, Sarah, and Rebekah. Comments from leading experts will make learning about God's Word easy to understand and incorporate into your daily life.

(trade paper)   ISBN 0914984063 $16.95

On The Brink

Daymond R. Duck

Subtitled: Easy-to-Understand End-Time Bible Prophecy. Also by the author of *Revelation* and *Daniel— God's Word for the Biblically-Inept*, *On TheBrink* is organized in Biblical sequence and written with simplicity so that any reader will easily understand end-

time prophecy. Ideal for use as a handy-reference book.

(trade paper)   ISBN 0914984586 $10.95

The World's Oldest Health Plan

Kathleen O'Bannon Baldinger

Subtitled: Health, Nutrition and Healing from the Bible. Offers a complete health plan for body, mind and spirit, just as Jesus did. It includes programs for diet, exercise and mental health. Contains foods and recipes to lower cholesterol and blood pressure, improve the immune system and other bodily functions, reduce stress, reduce or cure constipation, eliminate insomnia, reduce forgetfulness, confusion and anger, increase circulation and thinking ability, eliminate "yeast" problems, improve digestion, and much more."

(trade paper)   ISBN 0914984578 $14.95

God's Abundance

Edited by Kathy Collard Miller

Subtitled: 365 Days to a More Meaningful Life. This day-by-day inspirational is a collection of thoughts by leading Christian writers such as, Patsy Clairmont, Jill Briscoe, Liz Curtis Higgs, and Naomi Rhode. *God's Abundance* is based on God's Word for a simpler, yet more abundant life. Most people think more about the future while the present passes through their hands. Learn to make all aspects of your life—personal, business, financial, relationships, even housework—a "spiritual abundance of simplicity."

(hardcover)   ISBN 0914984977 $19.95

Promises of God's Abundance

Kathy Collard Miller

Subtitled: *For a More Meaningful Life.* The second addition to our best-selling *God's Abundance* series. This perfect gift book filled with Scripture, questions for growth and a Simple Thought for the Day will guide you to an abundant and more meaningful life.

(trade paper)   ISBN 0914984098 $9.95

God's Unexpected Blessings

Edited by Kathy Collard Miller

Witness God at work and learn to see the *unexpected blessings* in life through essays by such Christians writers as Billy Graham and Barbara Johnson.

(hardcover)   ISBN 0914984071 $18.95

Conversations with God the Father

Mark R. Littleton

Subtitled: *Encounters with the One True God.* Contemplate the nature of God with fictional answers to questions as God might answer them.

(hardcover)   ISBN 0914984195 $17.95

God Is!
Mark R. Littleton

"Heart-Tugging" inspirational stories, quotes, & illustrations that will leave a powerful mental and emotional impact on the reader. Short and easy-to-read sketches, embracing the attributes of God, will inspire your spirit and brighten your day. Topics include: God Is Love, God Is Good, God Is Wise, and more.
(hardcover)   ISBN 0914984926 $14.95

If I Only Knew . . . What Would Jesus Do?
Joan Hake Robie

Finally, a WWJD? for adults. This book looks at everyday problems through the lens of the fundamental teachings of Jesus.
(trade paper)   ISBN 091498439X $9.95

God's Vitamin "C" for the Spirit
Kathy Collard Miller & D. Larry Miller

Subtitled: "Tug-at-the-Heart" Stories to Fortify and Enrich Your Life. Includes inspiring stories and anecdotes that emphasize Christian ideals and values by Barbara Johnson, Billy Graham, Nancy L. Dorner, Dave Dravecky, Patsy Clairmont, Charles Swindoll, and many other well-known Christian speakers and writers. Topics include: Love, Family Life, Faith and Trust, Prayer, and God's Guidance.
(trade paper)   ISBN 0914984837 $12.95

God's Vitamin "C" for the Spirit of WOMEN
Kathy Collard Miller

Subtitled: "Tug-at-the-Heart" stories to Inspire and Delight Your Spirit. A beautiful treasury of timeless stories, quotes, and poetry designed by and for women. Well-known Christian women like Liz Curtis Higgs, Patsy Clairmont, Naomi Rhode, and Elisabeth Elliott share from their hearts on subjects like Marriage, Motherhood, Christian Living, Faith, and Friendship.
(trade paper)   ISBN 0914984934 $12.95

God's Vitamin "C" for the Spirit of MEN
D. Larry Miller

Subtitled: "Tug-at-the-Heart" Stories to Encourage and Strengthen Your Spirit. Compiled in the format of bestselling *God's Vitamin "C" for the Spirit*, this book is filled with unique and inspiring stories that men of all ages will immediately relate to. Contributors include: Bill McCartney, Larry Crabb, Tim Kimmel, Billy Graham, Tony Evans, and R. C. Sproul, to name a few.
(trade paper)   ISBN 0914984810 $12.95

God's Vitamin "C" for the Christmas Spirit
Kathy Collard Miller & D. Larry Miller

Subtitled: "Tug-at-the-Heart" Traditions and Inspirations to Warm the Heart. This keepsake includes a variety of heart-tugging thoughts, stories, poetry, recipes, songs, and crafts.
(hardcover)   ISBN 0914984853 $14.95

God's Vitamin "C" for the Hurting Spirit
Kathy Collard Miller & D. Larry Miller

The latest in the best-selling God's Vitamin "C" for the Spirit series, this collection of real-life stories expresses the breadth and depth of God's love for us in our times of need. Rejuvenating and inspiring thoughts from some of the most-loved Christian writers such as Max Lucado, Cynthia Heald, Charles Swindoll, and Barbara Johnson. Topics include: Death, Divorce/Separation, Financial Loss, and Physical Illness.
(trade paper)   ISBN 0914984691 $12.95

Halloween And Satanism
Phil Phillips and Joan Hake Robie

This book traces the origins of Halloween and gives the true meaning behind this celebration of "fun and games." Jack-O-Lanterns, Cats, Bats, and Ghosts are much more than costumes and window decorations. In this book you will discover that involvement in any form of the occult will bring you more than "good fortune." It will lead you deeper and deeper into the Satanic realm, which ultimately leads to death.
(trade paper)   ISBN 091498411X $9.95

A Woman's Guide To Spiritual Power
Nancy L. Dorner

Subtitled: Through Scriptural Prayer. Do your prayers seem to go "against a brick wall?" Does God sometimes seem far away or non-existent? If your answer is "Yes," you are not alone. Prayer must be the cornerstone of your relationship to God. "This book is a powerful tool for anyone who is serious about prayer and discipleship."—Florence Littauer
(trade paper)   ISBN 0914984470 $9.95

PURCHASING INFORMATION:

Books are available from your favorite bookstore, either from current stock or special order. To assist bookstore in locating your selection be sure to give title, author, and ISBN #. If unable to purchase from the bookstore you may order direct from STARBURST PUBLISHERS by mail, phone, fax, or through our secure website at www.starburstpublishers.com.

When ordering enclose full payment plus $3.00 for shipping and handling ($4.00 if Canada or Overseas). Payment in US Funds only. Please allow two to three weeks minimum (longer overseas) for delivery.

Make checks payable to and mail to:

STARBURST PUBLISHERS
P.O. Box 4123
Lancaster, PA 17604

Credit card orders may also be placed by calling 1-800-441-1456 (credit card orders only), Mon-Fri, 8:30 a.m.–5:30 p.m. Eastern Standard Time. Prices subject to change without notice. Catalog available for a 9 x 12 self-addressed envelope with 4 first-class stamps.